FOOD LOVERS' S

FOOD LOVERS'
GUIDE TO
CONNECTICUT

The Best Restaurants, Markets
& Local Culinary Offerings

4th Edition

Patricia Brooks

Guilford, Connecticut

Copyright © 2013 by Morris Book Publishing, LLC

Project editor: Lynn Zelem
Layout artist: Mary Ballachino
Text design: Sheryl Kober
Illustrations by Jill Butler with additional art by Carleen Moira Powell and MaryAnn Dubé
Maps: Rusty Nelson © Morris Book Publishing, LLC

Library of Congress Cataloging-in-Publication Data is available on file.

ISSN 1546-6728
ISBN 978-0-7627-8642-8

Printed in the United States of America
10 9 8 7 6 5 4 3 2 1

All the information in this guidebook is subject to change. We recommend that you call ahead to obtain current information before traveling.

Contents

Preface, xii

Introduction, 1

How to Use This Book, 3

Restaurant Price Key, 9

Fairfield County & Southwest Connecticut, 11

Made or Grown Here, 14

Specialty Stores & Markets, 29

Farmers' Markets, 41

Farm Stands, 45

Food Happenings, 51

Nibbles, 56

Learn to Cook, 69

Learn about Wine & Beer, 72

Landmark Eateries, 73

Brewpubs & Craft Breweries, 104

Wine Trail, 109

Northwest Connecticut, 113

Made or Grown Here, 117

Specialty Stores & Markets, 124

Farmers' Markets, 133

Farm Stands, 136

Food Happenings, 145

Nibbles, 147

Learn to Cook, 152

Learn about Wine, 154

Landmark Eateries, 154

Brewpubs & Craft Breweries, 165

Wine Trail, 166

Hartford Area & North-Central Connecticut, 173

    Made or Grown Here, 176

    Specialty Stores & Markets, 181

    Farmers' Markets, 190

    Farm Stands, 197

    Food Happenings, 213

    Nibbles, 218

    Learn about Wine, 227

    Landmark Eateries, 227

    Brewpubs & Craft Breweries, 240

    Wine Trail, 245

New Haven & Southeast Coastal Connecticut, 247

    Made or Grown Here, 251

    Specialty Stores & Markets, 264

    Farmers' Markets, 274

    Farm Stands, 280

    Food Happenings, 286

Nibbles, 293

Learn to Cook, 302

Learn about Wine, 302

Landmark Eateries, 303

Brewpubs & Craft Breweries, 325

Wine Trail, 329

Northeast Connecticut, 335

Made or Grown Here, 339

Specialty Stores & Markets, 352

Farmers' Markets, 353

Farm Stands, 357

Food Happenings, 365

Nibbles, 367

Learn to Cook, 371

Learn about Wine, 371

Landmark Eateries, 372

Brewpubs & Craft Breweries, 379

Wine Trail, 380

Recipes, 385

Appetizers, 388

Soups, 390

Salads, 393

Main Dishes, 397

Sides, 405

Desserts, 410

Appendices

Appendix A: Specialty Foods & Produce, 418

Appendix B: Food Happenings, 432

Appendix C: Wine Happenings, 435

Indexes

Connecticut Eateries Index, 438

General Index, 447

About the Author

As a young adult, Patricia Brooks spent time in Japan, Hong Kong, and the Philippines, which piqued her interest in ethnic food. Since then, she has traveled all over the world on food quests—from Mandalay to Madrid, Assisi to Ankara, Salisbury to Sydney, Dijon to Davao. She has been researching and writing about food since her first cookbook, *The Presidents' Cookbook* (with Poppy Cannon), appeared in print in 1968. She went on to write two other cookbooks; books on New England restaurants; travel books (that included restaurants and food) on Spain, Portugal, Britain, New York, and New England; and reams of articles on food and travel for national publications, including *Bon Appétit, Food & Wine, Travel + Leisure, and Travel Holiday*. In reporting on cuisines, wines, and dining, she has followed her nose and palate to ferret out the best and most unusual restaurants in many diverse milieus. Since 1977, she has been the *New York Times* Connecticut restaurant reviewer, reporting over time on more than 2,500 restaurants around the state. Among her 25 books are *Best Restaurants of New England, Country Inns of New England,* and *Connecticut's Best Dining and Wining*.

This book is dedicated to Alexander Maeyama Brooks, who someday may also be a writer.

Acknowledgments

In researching this new edition, it was evident from the get-go that people in the food business are among the most generous on Earth—or at least the earth in Connecticut. Most people I talked to were willing and often eager to share sources and ideas and offer helpful suggestions. Major thanks go to my son, Christopher Brooks, a fellow author and food-and-beer writer, who was extremely helpful by sharing his sources and ideas, to say nothing of his ever-wise editing of my finished manuscript. He was an invaluable contributor to this book. Thanks also to my good friend Georgia Bushman, whose timely suggestions and "late breaking news" about restaurant openings and closings averted some close calls in a culinary environment that changes often.

Also high on the list of helpers, whose contributions went "beyond the call," are the following food colleagues: Margaret Chatey, proprietor of Westford Hill Distillers in Ashford, whose generosity in recommending other producers and suppliers made my job easier and more exciting; Christopher Prosperi, chef-owner of Metro Bis restaurant in Simsbury, who kindly shared his wide knowledge of and dedication to the best local food sources; Ina Bomze of Fabled Foods bread company in Deep River, a source of information about so many food shops and restaurants; James O'Shea, proprietor of West Street Grill in Litchfield, who volunteered with gusto some of his favorite sources; Margaret Sapir of Wave Hill Bread & Cafe, a gracious and helpful source about farmers' markets and fellow suppliers in her end of the state; Ira Smith, proprietor of Kent Wine & Spirits, another generous source; and Andre Kreft of Savor Fine Foods, who shared names of fellow producers and food people in his neighborhood. And what can be said about Lee White, food writer and editor, that hasn't already been said? Her willingness to share information with friends easily makes her the First Lady of Connecticut Foodery.

My thanks also to Amy Lyons, my editor, who "rode herd" on the manuscript through the editorial and production process with good humor, and to all the GPP staffers, artists, and production people who helped make this new edition possible.

A special thanks as well to Rick Macsuga, a marketing representative with the Connecticut Department of Agriculture, for his help in my research of farmers' markets and family farms around the state.

Thanks as well to the following individuals and establishments for graciously sharing their recipes, many of which were adapted for home cooks. These individuals and companies are not responsible for any inadvertent errors or omissions:

Riad Aamar, Oliva

Ina Bomze, Fabled Foods

Margaret Chatey, Westford Hill Distillers

Claire Criscuolo, Claire's Corner Copia

Tina Fearnley, the Purple Pear by Tina

Toby Fossland, the Hopkins Inn

Jean-Louis Gerin, Restaurant Jean-Louis

Linda Giuca, Alforno Trattoria

Susan Goodman, Susan Goodman Catering

Kathleen Jonah Lenane, Bear Pond Farm

Sally Maraventano, Cucina Casalinga

Marina Marchese, Red Bee Honey

Mary O'Reilly, Chaiwalla

Kristin Orr, Fort Hills Farms

James O'Shea, West Street Grill

Carole Peck, Carol Peck's Good News Cafe

Debra Ponzek, Aux Délices

Chris Prosperi, Metro Bis

Maria Bruscino Sanchez, Sweet Maria's

Mary Schaffer, Napa & Co.

Adrienne Sussman, Adrienne

Bill Taibe, Le Farm and the Whelk

Preface

This is the fourth edition of *Food Lovers' Guide to Connecticut*. Why another edition, you may ask? Because food facts, like food itself, can have a short shelf life. In the case of books about food, this is especially true. Food stores open and close, farmers' markets change, restaurants close or change, and new restaurants open. In short, there's always something new on the food front.

Since the last edition of this book was published, the food scene in Connecticut has undergone radical changes. The locavore movement has spread like a forest fire. The farm-to-table philosophy has energized restaurants old and new and influenced individuals to demand only the freshest ingredients for the meals they prepare at home. The vegetarian and vegan phenomenon has spread to former carnivores, and even meat lovers have learned to love the occasional all-vegetable entrees in Indian, Chinese, Japanese, and other ethnic restaurants. These developments necessitated many new entries to the fourth edition of *Food Lovers' Guide to Connnecticut,* as well as many new sidebars, including sidebars called "Talking Turkey," which cite local sources for fresh turkeys.

You may note that this new fourth edition is half again larger than earlier editions. This is partly because so many new restaurants have been included. A trend in recent years has been for many established restaurants to add a less pricey bistro or cafe, which offers diners two options: *haute* and *bas* dining at higher and lower prices. It has also been a trend for many popular restaurants to expand and open offshoots in other locales, often in neighboring towns.

Please also note that recipes, which formerly were spread throughout the book, are now located in a special section near the end of the book.

The many beverage changes that have taken place in our state are also reflected in this edition. The rise of new, ambitious craft breweries, a concept slow to move from the West Coast to Connecticut, is now rampant throughout our state. And wineries, in an adolescent state just a few years ago, are now thriving; new ones, especially those licensed farm wineries (so designated because they are limited in grape-cultivated acreage), have mushroomed dramatically.

My observations in this fourth edition are based on both personal and professional experience. As the longtime Connecticut restaurant reviewer for the *New York Times*, I sample, analyze, and report on food regularly—and always anonymously. This experience has led to delightful discoveries as the restaurant scene has grown in sophistication and diversity. I have observed the arrival of notable French chefs and the expanding number of expert homegrown ones. I have witnessed and enjoyed the growth and range of farmers' markets and the increasing variety of crops that Connecticut family farms now produce. Wine development has been a late-growth industry here. It has been fascinating to observe the burgeoning of the Connecticut Wine Trail—especially among younger imbibers—which encourages people to traverse the state, visiting, sampling, and experimenting at various vineyards, which now exist in every region. I have also watched the growth of simple farm wineries, an even more recent phenomenon. Microbreweries, or craft breweries as they are now called, have been slower to appear, but they, too, are a fast-developing industry and also fun to observe.

Through the years, I have spent much time roaming the globe as a travel and food writer and guidebook author. My explorer's spirit has led me to remote locales to sample gastronomic exotica, such as *balut* in the Philippines, bears' claws and swallow's nest soup in China, and crunchy lime-infused grasshoppers and *huitlacoche* in Mexico. It was probably this spirit of adventure that led me to seek offbeat sources of seafood, cheese, specialty food stores, and bakeries within Connecticut, all catering to an ever-more knowledgeable clientele.

Some readers of earlier editions have told me that they keep their book handy in their glove compartments, so when they are visiting other towns in the state, they can refer to it as a quick resource. Other readers say they use the book as a guide for weekend excursions. I hope they—and you—will do the same with this new, fourth edition. The food scene in Connecticut has never been as lively, as diverse, and as much fun as it currently is. Enjoy, enjoy, it gets better and better.

Introduction

Connecticut's location between the monoliths of New York and Massachusetts sometimes causes it to be overlooked. Small it may be, but our state fairly bursts with gastronomic treasures, agricultural resources, ethnic diversity, and enterprising spirit. Connecticut Yankees have historically been great entrepreneurs and suppliers and purveyors of food—selling nutmeg from the West Indies, for example, which gave us the lasting nickname of "Nutmeggers." (A less kindly version has it that sharp-eyed "drummers" or traveling salesmen mixed wooden "nutmegs" in with the real ones they sold.) The food revolution that has been sweeping across America for the past few decades has taken hold with tenacity and exuberance in our state, making city after city, town after town, beehives of food production. Scores of new restaurants have opened and now thrive here. Even towns that in the past were somewhat culinarily deprived—such as Darien, Fairfield, and New Canaan—are bursting with new restaurants and food activities. Gourmet food stores, bakeries, cheese shops, and ethnic-food markets are now almost commonplace, part of our state's topography. Recent years have brought numerous new wineries, once a rarity in our state. They are a welcome stop on the food-and-beverage landscape, as are the many new craft breweries, another recent phenomenon.

Some of the resources in this new, fourth edition of *Food Lovers' Guide to Connecticut* may be familiar; many others may not. It is a pleasure to introduce new ones to you. Even though I have been crisscrossing the state in a quest for new food sources for almost 40 years, I continue to marvel at the new food enterprises, specialty food stores, and restaurants that continue to pop up, in the optimistic "can-do" spirit of Yankee ingenuity.

While I hope to bring new information to you, there is another purpose as well: to acquaint you with good fresh foods within easy reach so that you may revel, as I do, in the many natural resources of our state—the native clams, oysters, scallops, bluefish, and other fresh seafood; the abundance of produce grown here and its easy availability, such as at farm stands selling fresh fruits and vegetables; local festivals featuring homemade food specialties; and local teachers expert in helping you learn to make specialties of all kinds. Especially noteworthy is the return and explosion of old-fashioned farmers' markets, encouraged by the state's Department of Agriculture. These markets convene throughout the growing season, with their farm-to-table fresh produce and other farm products, including honey, cheese, fresh eggs, maple syrup, fruit jams, preserves, and pies. While we think of the US as a major industrial society, we in Connecticut at the local "people" level are able each summer and autumn to revisit our country's roots, to relish the direct contact between the growers and consumers of wonderful, farm-fresh, natural foods. The farm-to-table locavore movement resonates strongly throughout our state and is most noticeable and tangible in our farms and new restaurants. Long may it grow!

This book is organized into five chapters, beginning with the Fairfield County area at the southwest edge of the state and radiating upward to Litchfield County in the northwest. The third chapter is about Hartford and the north-central area around it; the fourth chapter covers New Haven and the southeast coast. Finally, the fifth and last chapter ends in the northeast, the least populated portion of the state. Each chapter includes a map of the area, enabling you to plan day trips for visiting and exploring.

Within each chapter, you will find the following sections:

Made or Grown Here

The large number of food producers in Connecticut may surprise you. Some are huge enterprises, such as Munson's Chocolates; others are mere "cottage industries" of food products—individual producers who have come up with a superior salsa, cheesecake, maple syrup, or handmade chocolate. Some of these producers sell their specialties to wholesalers and/or retailers (for these I have cited several sources in the area where you may buy them), whereas many others sell directly to the consumer via e-mail, a website, a catalog, or farmers' markets. I have included prize-winning dessert makers, bakers, chocolatiers, and cheese makers, among many other entrepreneurs.

Specialty Stores & Markets

This section of each chapter features a wide variety of specialty food stores, which range from ethnic-food vendors to gourmet delicatessens and fish markets. Included are stores selling cheese and chocolates, bangers and bouillabaisse, olive oils and oregano, teas and tamales—virtually every imaginable good thing to eat that can be packaged, marketed, and sold. Many of these shops are unheralded treasures, known only to locals—until now. Generally, I excluded chain stores, but you will find a list of several unusual ones in appendix A.

Farmers' Markets

At last count 127 certified farmers' markets operate throughout Connecticut, many of them in the smaller towns. "Certified" means they are approved by the Connecticut Department of Agriculture as selling only Connecticut-grown produce, and thus labeled "CTGrown." The "CTGrown" label generally signifies everything is grown or produced on a single farm. There are other worthy farmers' markets, such as those in Westport and Weston, that are abundant, diverse, and rewarding, but vendors there sell a few items grown elsewhere, both on other Connecticut farms and some produced outside the state, rather then all just from their own farms. In late 2012 there were a total of 172 farmers' markets in the state (including six or seven winter markets in a few towns).

Farmers' markets offer shoppers a chance to buy seasonal, field-fresh fruits and vegetables directly from growers. You won't find bananas, mangoes, or grapefruit here—only locally grown or home-produced products, including eggs, honey, fresh produce, preserves, baked goods, meats, cheeses, maple products, fresh and dried flowers, ornamental gourds, Indian corn, and cockscomb.

Most farmers' markets operate from late spring through October, but for specific days of the week and times, check the individual chapters of this book. Days and hours can be iffy, sometimes changing at the last minute, so the Department of Agriculture website (ct.gov/doag) is the most up-to-date source. Another source is Cityseed, a market group operating in New Haven (cityseed.org). A mere handful of farmers' markets—not the open-air ones—function during winter months indoors; they are duly noted.

Be aware that it is cash only at most farmers' markets and farm stands, but occasionally a vendor will accept a check with proper ID.

Farm Stands

There are hundreds of small farms in Connecticut, and many have roadside stands or open-sided sheds where, in season, they sell their crops, freshly picked from the field. Some stands are literally that; others are ensconced in barns or outbuildings or are substantial structures in and of themselves. Many sell, in addition to their produce, fresh eggs; honey; maple syrup; apple cider; home-baked pies, breads, and pastries; homemade preserves; and pickles. To sell their baked goods to the public, the farmers must have certified commercial kitchens. Although most of the farm stands listed in this book keep regular seasonal hours, it is always prudent to call ahead.

Some farmers offer pick-your-own schedules, as various crops ripen—most often berries, apples, pears, peaches, tomatoes, and pumpkins. Usually, each individual farm schedule is announced on the farm's voice mail, so call ahead. If you take advantage of such pick-your-own (or PYO) opportunities, be sure to carry with you sunscreen and water and wear old clothes, a hat, and comfortable shoes.

Food Happenings

Each year's calendar brings a surprising number of annual food events to Connecticut: festivals, fairs, and fund-raisers in which food occupies center stage. This section in each chapter tells you about happenings throughout the year and where they take place, whether it is the Norwalk Seaport Association Oyster Festival in Norwalk or the Dionysos Greek Festival in New Britain. If I missed any big ones that you know of, please clue me in.

Many towns and cities now have a designated Restaurant Week, in which a number of really good local restaurants participate and offer special menus, usually at ridiculously low prices, often prix fixe, to encourage you to come and get acquainted—and, hopefully, revisit. At connecticutrestaurantweek.com you will find nearly 30 links for Restaurant Weeks throughout Connecticut, including dates and the restaurants scheduled to participate. Unfortunately, such special weeks are not uniform, differing in dates from town to town and from restaurant to restaurant. Therefore it is essential to check the website for when and where.

Nibbles

This section in each chapter consists of places where you can grab a quick bite. These are spots that are usually inexpensive and notable for snacks. Food shops known for specific items or a particular special dish may also be listed in this section.

Learn to Cook

Cooking courses in Connecticut range from recreational classes and demonstrations to hands-on workshops. You will find everything from the basics of cooking to instruction in esoteric ethnic cuisines. A few cooking instructors even offer guided tours abroad.

Learn about Wine

Under this heading in various chapters, you will find information about wine tastings and sources helpful to novice and serious oenophiles alike.

Landmark Eateries

Connecticut now has an abundance of restaurants of every imaginable type—more than 12,000 of them, according to the Connecticut Restaurant Association. While this book is not a restaurant guide per se, I have included in each chapter some restaurants known for certain cuisines, specialties (such as the Spanish tapas at Barcelona and Ibiza), or a notable ambience (Golden Lamb Buttery in Brooklyn comes to mind). Considering the number and variety of restaurants in the state, our selection represents a relatively small helping of gastronomic gems. What our restaurant forkfuls have in common, in addition to memorable food, is character, personality, uniqueness—call it what you will—that adds to the pleasure of being there.

Brewpubs & Craft Breweries

With the rise of craft breweries nationwide since the early 1980s, we have come to value fresh-tasting craft beers and ales with real flavor and complexity. For awhile Connecticut lagged behind some other states in the number of its craft breweries, but now every region of the state boasts brewpubs and craft breweries; they are duly listed in this section of the appropriate chapters.

Wine Trail

Connecticut's wine industry has been a growth stock (pun intended) in recent years and is especially notable in the northwest, southeast, and northeast regions of the state. Established wineries are included in this section, along with information about their tasting facilities and special events. Note that appendix C lists additional events held at various wineries in the state throughout the year.

A popular travel adventure is the self-conducted wine tour that winds throughout the entire state, with wineries well marked along a designated wine trail. Be sure to collect a wine "passport" at the first winery you visit and have it stamped at each winery on your route. If you turn it in later, you are eligible for a drawing for valued prizes. Prizes are well worthwhile; in the past one prize was a free trip for two to Spain.

Recipes

New to this fourth edition is a separate section at the end of the book called "Recipes," which offers recipes for appetizers, soups, salads, main dishes, side dishes, and desserts harvested from people who revel in food and who love to cook it and share it, such as chefs, restaurateurs, farm growers, vintners, producers, and specialty-shop owners.

Restaurant Price Key

The prices listed in this guidebook were confirmed at press time. We recommend, however, that you call establishments to obtain current information before traveling. Dollar signs are provided only for restaurants that offer full meals and some sort of seating (or operate out of a truck). All restaurant prices are based on the following general guidelines for an appetizer, entree, and dessert for one person (using the most common prices) before drinks, tax, and tip:

$ inexpensive; most entrees under $20

$$ moderate; most entrees $20 to $25

$$$ expensive; most entrees over $25

Fairfield County & Southwest Connecticut

Aside from Bridgeport, which is the state's largest city, the south-western region consists mostly of small towns under the umbrella of Fairfield County. This county, one of the nation's richest, is often nicknamed "a New York City bedroom" because so many of the county towns are within an easy train commute of Manhattan, and many workers in the city do indeed live in the county. While densely populated, the area is still, surprisingly, a terrain of woods, rivers, ponds, and wildlife preserves. Its Long Island Sound coastline has been dubbed the "Gold Coast" because of the many CEOs, moguls, hedge-fund managers, and celebrities who live in expensive homes and McMansions on and near its shores, from Greenwich all the way up to Westport, Southport, and as far east as Stratford. Bedroom to New York it may be, but Fairfield County increasingly has a vibrant

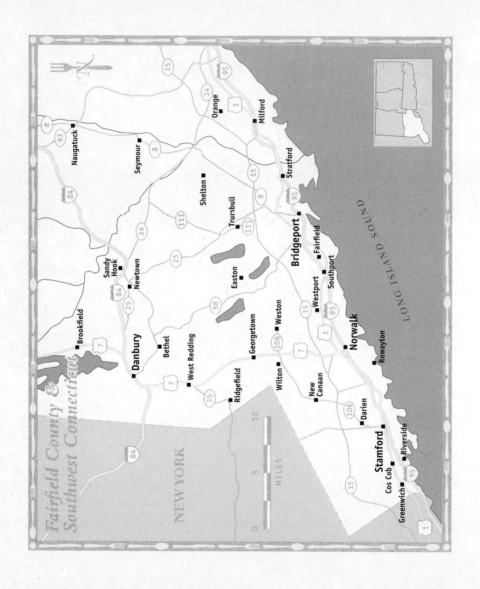

Fairfield County & Southwest Connecticut

life of its own, as many national corporations and businesses have made their headquarters here, allowing their employees to work closer to home. Various ethnic groups have also migrated here as workers and burgeoning entrepreneurs.

This combination of affluence and diversity has changed the dining landscape, attracting established New York City restaurateurs and chefs. Some have opened their own restaurants; others have grabbed the reins (or range) at historic village inns and have brought new levels of culinary expertise and sparkle to the local dining scene. As a result, the number of authentic French restaurants, bistros, and cafes in this southwestern region exceeds that in any other part of the state. Gastronomic tastes have evolved from simple to sophisticated, with almost every imaginable type of ethnic restaurant now available. Indian, Japanese, Thai, Spanish, Chinese, Portuguese, Mexican, Peruvian, Colombian, Venezuelan, Central and South American, Greek, Lebanese, Turkish, Persian, and, of course, the ubiquitous Italian are all here now. Towns formerly with scarcely a single decent restaurant—my own New Canaan (population now 19,738) comes to mind—now have literally dozens, which range from good to excellent, even in a few cases extraordinary. Deluxe restaurants are on a par with those in major cities all over the US. Comparisons are odious, of course, but in terms of diverse (and certainly pricey) dining, Fairfield County probably leads the state. Parallelling this welcome boom in restaurant diversity is the continuing growth of food-supply and specialty shops, food enterprises, ethnic markets, green markets, elegant take-out services, catering businesses, and other gustatory innovations. Southwest Connecticut is no longer a pale imitation of Manhattan, but a bona fide and exciting source of fine food in and of itself. This Gold Coast now wears a new, freshly burnished patina.

Made or Grown Here

Beldotti Bakeries, 605 Newfield Ave., Stamford; (203) 348-9029. This thriving bakery in a modest strip mall sells delicious cakes, tarts, cookies, breakfast pastries, and numerous types of crusty breads year-round, as well as kosher baked goods. The walnut-raisin bread is really special, as is the sourdough; both have a fresh-baked, warm-from-the-oven aura. Beldotti also does a thriving business at the New Canaan farmers' market in season.

Billy's Bakery, 1885 Black Rock Turnpike, Fairfield; (203) 337-5349; billysbakery.com. Owner Bill Hollis runs this amazing hubbub of a place, producing 15 to 20 types of breads (not all the same day), many of them artisanal—sourdough, cranberry walnut, French baguettes, challah, and country among them—along with sweet rolls, croissants, scones, coffee cakes, cookies, biscotti, a dozen different tarts, and cakes. Billy's boils and bakes a dozen different types of bagels and makes 10 different cream cheese spreads, from mild veggie to hot and spicy. Billy's also dishes up sandwiches, soups, and entrees to go. And for Rover, house-made biscuits at a pittance that will really make him go "woof."

Briar Patch Enterprises, 322 New Haven Ave., Milford; (203) 876-8923. Nancy Follini and Joseph Gilbert have dug clams since 1982. That's when they began their wholesale business, harvesting the juiciest, tastiest littleneck clams and bluepoint oysters from Long Island Sound, as well as sea scallops from farther out. Local and area restaurants and fish markets gobble up almost their entire "crop," but there's usually something savory available over the counter.

Bridgewater Chocolate, 559 Federal Rd., Brookfield; (800) 888-8742 or (203) 775-2286; bridgewaterchocolate.com. Since moving from Bridgewater to Brookfield in 1999, Swedish-born chocolatier Erik Landegren's homey enterprise has doubled in size. And for good reason, as the company, which produces American-style handmade chocolates from pure, premium ingredients, has won many awards from the Connecticut Specialty Foods Association for best confection, best overall food product, and best packaging. The line includes chocolates, toffees, truffles, mints, caramels, turtles, chocolate-dipped fruits, and chocolate bark, all handsomely packaged, as well

as a new line of sugar-free truffles and chocolate bars. You'll find them all at the factory; at Bridgewater's store, 12 Lasalle Rd., West Hartford (860-570-0707); at gourmet shops (including the **Pantry,** p. 132, in Washington Depot, and **Carole Peck's Good News Cafe,** p. 155, in Woodbury); and also via the company's website and catalog.

Deborah Ann's Sweet Shoppe, 381 Main St., Ridgefield; (203) 438-0065. Chocolates produced by two New York lawyers? But yes, owners Deborah Ann and Mike Grissmer sought a change of scene and jobs that would make people happy. What's happier than chocolates? This all-white, tin-ceilinged shop, with its intoxicating aromas, reminds me of the movie *Chocolat.* They make their huge variety of chocolates in Brookfield, but this shop in Ridgefield is where you'll find them for sale. There are 14 seats inside and 10 tables outside for nibbling and sipping house-made hot chocolate, tea, coffee, and lemonade, while watching the hand-molding done in the shop. Or just sample some of the truffles, turtles, buttercrunch, caramels, and other sweet delights. You can even design your own chocolate bars here. Besides the 70-plus varieties the Grissmers make, they also tempt the inner kid in us with big glass jars of hard candies. These include 52 flavors of Jelly Bellies and 17 colors of M&Ms. This sweets-minded couple also makes ice cream here: 24 rich, creamy flavors (rotated from among 40), from a formula provided by the now-defunct Mr. Shane's.

Dr. Mike's, 158 Greenwood Ave., Bethel; (203) 792-4388. Don't let appearances fool you. Inside this modest-looking ice-cream parlor, tucked into the rear of an old frame house, lurks some of the tastiest ice cream in Connecticut. Since 1975, Robert Allison has been churning out as many as 50 flavors, with a butterfat content of 16 percent. At any time there are eight flavors—four regulars (vanilla, rich chocolate, strawberry, and chocolate lace and cream) and four daily specials. In warm months 30 different flavors rotate during a given week. Most popular are rich chocolate and chocolate lace and cream, which use 22 to 24 percent cocoa butter and Bensdorf chocolate. There are several tables and a handful of places to sit on the porch. The parking lot holds 60 cars, which gives you an idea of Dr. Mike's popularity. A second Dr. Mike's (444 Main St., Monroe; 203-452-0499) is equally small, also with ample parking. And who, you might ask, is Dr. Mike? Dr. Michael Burnham was the original Dr. Mike. His daughter, Mary, started the business years ago and later sold it.

Ferris Acres Creamery, 144 Sugar St. (Rte. 302), Newtown; (203) 426-8803; ferrisacrescreamery.com. Sixty-five cows (mostly Holsteins) graze on an 80-acre farm the Ferris family has owned since 1864 and which Charles; his wife, Shirley; and their two sons operate. In 2004 Shirley opened this ice-cream shop/creamery on the property, churning milk from these dairy cows into delicious creamy ice cream. In a repertoire of 40 flavors (with 30 available daily), several are Shirley's own inventions, such as Cowtrax (vanilla

WE ALL SCREAM FOR ICE CREAM— ESPECIALLY WHEN IT'S GELATO

Daniella's Gelateria, 315 Greenwich Ave., Greenwich; (203) 992-1030. Pricey it is, as most gelaterias tend to be in relation to plain old ice cream shops, but Daniella's gelato is worth it to true aficionados. Made in small batches, about 1.5 gallons per run, there are just 10 or so flavors made daily, from a repertoire that includes tiramisu, banana, tartufo, nocciola, pistachio, strawberry, and other fruit flavors. In the rear of a very tiny shop, Simona Silvestri makes her gelato on an Italian machine, using many ingredients imported from the home country. Other sweets for sale in the narrow space are cookies, tartlets, and various patisserie treats.

Gelatissimo, 26 Forest St., New Canaan; (203) 966-5000; gelatissimo artisangelato.com. With its ice-cream-colored interior (key-lime walls, mango counters, and lemon cabinets), this place, owned by Andrea and Nuccia Mazzonetto, is so clean and crisp, it almost sparkles.

with peanut butter swirls, caramel, and tiny chocolate chunks); Elvis's Dream (vanilla base, peanut butter, banana, hunks of dark chocolate); and Bada Bing (chocolate almond, Bing cherries, and big chocolate chunks). New are Bad Habit (dark chocolate), Grasshopper (mint with crushed Oreos), and Salty Cow (vanilla with caramel swirls and chocolate-covered pretzels). Milk shakes, soft ice cream, frozen yogurt, and ice-cream cakes and pies are also available. Shirley says modestly, "Part of the appeal is the farm setting. You can

Gelatissimo opened its doors in late 2005 and is the place for rich Italian gelato: 60 flavors, 22 available at one time, made fresh daily. As at most gelaterias, the prices here are often double that of regular ice cream. Gelato cakes are also available. The tiny shop is usually packed. It has four little tables, where you may eat your gelato, as well as several wooden benches outside for warmer-weather slurping. Chocolate hazelnut, nutty pistachio, and cappuccino are my favorites—so far. Cash only.

Volta Gelateria Creperia, 30 Spring St., Stamford; (203) 883-8841; volta.us. Next door to Bar Rosso (p. 57), Volta, which opened in 2011, is just as lively a happening. While the small space scoops out 21 gelato flavors (though not all are available at one time), it also serves savory and sweet crepes, salads, sandwiches, and waffles. There's a fresh juice bar, and breakfast is served on weekends. But the big "to do" is over the delicious gelatos. Bubble gum, canolo Siciliano, cappuccino, amaretto, and avocado are just some of the offbeat flavors.

watch the cows close-up as you sit at a picnic table eating your ice cream." The creamery is open early Apr through mid-Nov.

Hauser Chocolatier, 137 Greenwood Ave., Bethel; (203) 794-1861; hauserchocolates.com. Ruedi Hauser Sr. was making chocolates as a teenager in his native Switzerland, long before he immigrated to the US. In 1983 Ruedi and his wife, Lucille, started producing their handmade chocolate truffles in Bethel. The line now includes 24 to 30 different types of chocolates, chocolate dessert sauces, chocolate-covered nuts and coffee beans, and sugar-free chocolate and cocoa. A favorite is Tom and Sally's Cow Pies (chocolate patties with nuts inside). The Hausers also create beautifully boxed assortments for corporate gifts, weddings, and special occasions, such as Valentine's Day. Hauser chocolates are sold at retail outlets throughout the US as well as via their website and catalog. Although the main factory has moved to Rhode Island, the fudge and solid chocolates are still made in Bethel, right behind the Greenwood Avenue shop, with its vintage, pressed-tin ceiling.

Il Bacio Ice Cream, 30 Germantown Rd., Danbury; (203) 794-1184. You'd never believe (until you experience it) that such incredibly good, richly seductive ice cream could emerge from this sliver of a shop, wedged between a laundromat and a martial arts studio in a small strip mall. Tony and Gina Nacimento make *from scratch* 400 different flavors (in rotation, with about 30 at a time) in the rear of the shop and have been doing so since 1988. Among the delights, mostly made from fresh ingredients, are pomegranate, an ultrachocolate Cardiac Arrest, vanilla pudding, peach, and scores of others. Cash only.

Knipschildt Chocolatier, 12 South Main St., Norwalk; (203) 838-3131; knipschildt.com. Danish-born Fritz Knipschildt is a chef-turned-chocolatier, who has been making chocolates for 14 years. His chocolate truffles were rated among the world's top three by *Gourmet* magazine. His chocolates come in 24 flavors—with female names, such as Madeline, Hannah, and Helena—all made with Valrhona and Michel Cluizel French chocolate, some South American beans, and a high amount of cocoa butter; they are 100 percent natural, free of additives and preservatives. He has also developed a new line with what he calls "Scandinavian flavors." The company sells these unusual chocolates (many have spicy as well as predictably sweet components) to upmarket stores, such as Dean & DeLuca and Williams-Sonoma. Knipschildt pastries (like his chocolate decadence cake) are sold to such restaurants as the **Spotted Horse Tavern** (p. 96) in Westport. A cozy cafe, **Chocopologie Cafe** (p. 64), is attached to the workshop and there's another brand-new **Chocopologie Cafe** in Stamford at 211 Main St. (203-999-2462).

La Sorpresa, 61 Cedar St., Norwalk; (203) 838-9809. This modest little shop-bakery reveals the ethnic diversity of Connecticut's southwestern region, which has recently attracted many immigrants from Latin America. Colombian-owned, the shop (whose exterior resembles a Spanish-style house with a red-tile roof) features freshly made sweet rolls, apple turnovers, crisp "pig's ears" pastries, breads, and rolls. A favorite is *arepesa chocolo,* a loose-textured corn cake, which, when warmed slightly, makes a tasty morning snack. A minuscule, no-frills restaurant is part of La Sorpresa, with a separate entrance and basic Colombian food at Depression-era prices.

The Little Chocolate Company, 99 Mill St., Greenwich; (203) 531-6190; thelittlechocolatecompany.com. While this bandbox of a chocolate shop is on the Byram River, at the western edge of Greenwich, the shop's interior might as well be inside Belgium. Here Belgian types of chocolates reign supreme. That may be because the shop's owner, Martine Coscia, is Belgian-born. She makes Belgian-style truffles and pralines, using Belgian Callebaut chocolate, flavoring the pralines with ginger, caramel, marzipan, Tahitian vanilla, hot pepper, or cherry and the truffles with pistachio, hazelnut, or cocoa. She also casts chocolate bars, dark, milk, or white chocolate, in such flavors as raspberry, espresso bean, or chili pepper. Verifying the shop's Belgian pedigree, there are even Tintin comic books for sale. While waiting for your candy order to be filled, you might sip a cup of rich, hot, Belgian-blend chocolate—or perhaps white chocolate or Mexican style with cinnamon and cayenne pepper. Other drink options are coffee, tea, smoothies, and milk shakes. Closed Sun and Mon.

Michele's Pies, 666 Main Ave., Norwalk; (203) 354-7144; michelespies.com. The pies have it at Michele's. Michele Albano shows a touch of rustic Vermont in her pie-baking shop, with finely lacquered pine tables, stools of cut logs, and hand-carved wood panels that highlight moose, deer, and a bear devouring pies. Pies are what Michele's is all about—sometimes 20 varieties a day, all from fresh ingredients. The fresh-fruit pies are especially abundant in summer. There's the ever-popular chocolate-pecan-bourbon pie, as well as tiramisu, key lime, and lemon-lime-blackberry pie. Name your favorite; Michele probably bakes it. She also makes chicken potpies, shepherd's pies, and six kinds of quiches. A second **Michele's Pies** is at 188 Post Rd. East, Westport (203-349-5312). Closed Sun and Mon.

Newman's Own, 246 Post Rd. East, Westport; (203) 222-0136; newmansown.com. The late actor Paul Newman still appears on the label of his many delicious food products. When he and author A. E. Hotchner started Newman's Own in 1982 as something of a lark (the website says "Fine foods since February" in Newman's wry style), it took off instantly with an initial high-quality salad dressing that featured Paul's smiling face. The company grew phenomenally, and the natural-foods line now includes tomato-and-roasted-garlic pasta sauce, three flavors of Old-Style Picture Show Microwave Popcorn, steak sauce, fruit salsas, lemonades, limeades, and red-wine-and-vinegar salad dressing. New in the Newman's Own line are diet lemonade, Sweet Enough Cereal, wines, and complete skillet meals. The company motto, "Shameless Exploitation in Pursuit of the Common Good," says it all: Profits (after taxes), more than $350 million thus far, go to a variety of charities. Newman's Own products, available in stores across the US as well as via the company website, now number more than 100 and are recognizable by their clever labels, showing Paul in a variety of hats and outfits that symbolize each product.

Nothin' But Premium Foods, (203) 803-5485; nothinbutfoods .com. Owner Jerri Graham is nut happy, and her snack bars are full of nuts. She wholesales five bar types: Chocolate Coconut Almond, Cherry Cranberry Almond, Cinnamon Currant Pecan, Ginger Lemon Cashew, and Peanut Butter Banana Chocolate, selling them in packs of 12. Crunchy, flavorful, and nutritious, they are for sale at **Aux Délices** (pp. 29, 69), **Cocoa Michelle** (p. 59), **Oscar's Delicatessen** (p. 33), and several farmers' markets (including Westport's). The extra large crunchy bars contain organic oats, nuts, seeds, dried fruits, organic cane sugar, olive oil, and honey. They are fabulous (and I'm not usually a granola bar freak). She also sells oatmeal bars, muffins, many oatmeal cookie types and granola.

R + D Chocolates, 37 Saugatuck Ave., Westport; rdchocolate.com. In rental space in Westport, Rachel and David Gordon make some delicious chocolates that they sell at the Westport and Old Greenwich Farmers' Markets and other markets in the Fairfield County area. At last count they had six unusual flavors: five ganaches (pineapple mint, Raus coffee, mint, dark chocolate, and salemme pepper) and *fleur de sel* caramel, which melts gently on the tongue.

Red Bee Honey, 77 Lyon Plains Rd., Weston; (203) 226-4535; redbee.com. Beekeeper Marina Marchese's business is really buzzing. Her local, raw, and single-origin honeys come seasonally in 15 different varietals, available by jar, bottle, case, pail, and gift set, as well as by honeycomb, sold by phone and website, retail and wholesale. She also retails varietals from other producers in season, such as clover, wildflower, buckwheat, alfalfa, goldenrod, poplar, raspberry, blueberry, and orange blossom. Red Bee is available in restaurants, such as **Le Farm** (p. 102), the **Whelk** (p. 103), **Winvian** (p. 163), the Del Mar Artisan, and **Aux Délices** (pp. 29, 69). Red Bee Honey also offers honey tastings (for a fee) by appointment. See Marina's recipe for **Honey Figs with Goat Cheese and Pecans** on p. 417.

Rich Farm, 691 Oxford Rd. (Rte. 67), Oxford; (203) 881-1040; richfarmicecream.com. If you see a long line winding up to a wood-sided shop amid the rolling hills around Oxford, you'll know you're at the right place for some really special premises-made ice cream. Rich Farm, a dairy farm for five generations, prides itself on its small-batch product. David and Dawn Rich have been making ice cream since 1994. The flavors, some 30 of them, are tremendous, ranging from the usual chocolate, vanilla, and strawberry to Cookie Monster, Peaches and Cream, Razzmanian Devil (raspberry syrup blended with chocolate chips), Mocha Almond Fudge, and German Chocolate Cake. There are cones aplenty, as well as sundaes, malted milks, and milk shakes, and more than 12 different toppings. Limited hours off season, closed Jan and part of Febr. Cash only.

Sticky-Nuts, (203) 858-9800, Ridgefield; sticky-nuts.com. This small enterprise of Zachary Butlein's consists of four different packets of gluten-free, all-natural, nut, trail-mix combinations, perfect for hiking or camping munchies or any healthful snack need. The packets—Choco Spice, Asian Fusion, Fig, and most popular Morning Grapefruit—can be purchased by e-mail, on the website, or at area farmers' markets in season.

Walnut Beach Creamery, 17 Broadway, Milford; (203) 878-7738; walnutbeachcreamery.com. Considering that everything at this popular ice-cream maker is made from scratch, even the sauces (hot here, as are the littleneck clams, steamed mussels, poached salmon, grilled shrimp, and pan-fried catfish. Check out one of the owners' other ventures, Ten Twenty Post (p. 98).

Harbor Lights, 82 Seaview Ave., Norwalk; (203) 866-3364; harbor-lightsrestaurant-ct.com; $$. Finding a good seafood restaurant that's actually on the water isn't as easy as you might think, considering Connecticut's long shoreline. But here, *voilà!* On a glass-enclosed deck (windows open in warm weather) overlooking Norwalk harbor, you can dine on the freshest seafood, imaginatively prepared, often with a Greek twist. Lobster and shrimp risotto, lobster Santorini, shrimp and scallops Mykonos, Mediterranean sea bass, swordfish Alexander, red snapper, and fork-tender octopus charbroiled are among the many deep-sea treats. Also owned by the same Greek Gavrielidis family is Estia, a brand-new Greek restaurant at 88 Washington St., South Norwalk; (203) 956-0101; estiagreekrestaurant.com.

fudge and peanut butter are favorites), it's no wonder there are long lines waiting to buy cones or cups of the rich, delicious ice cream. The flavors change daily—there are usually two dozen on any given day—and some are really unusual. Examples include Cheesecake and Trail Mix, Nutty Yankee (cranberries, coconut, and almonds), Walnut Beach Mud (Belgian chocolate and espresso brownies), Black Knight (black raspberry and white chocolate), Goat Cheese and Roasted

Cherries, Lavender and Figs, and Cheers (Chardonnay, camomile, and apricots—wow!). Cash only.

Wave Hill Bread & Cafe, 30 High St., Norwalk; (203) 529-3441; wavehillbreads.com. Named for the garden in Riverdale where baker-proprietors Mitch Rapoport and Margaret Sapir were married, their small artisanal bakery has been a virtual tsunami of rapid expansion since its 2005 opening. The bakery now turns out 300 to 1,200 loaves a day in small batches. Among the types they make: demi-baguettes, three-grain olive, roasted red pepper ciabatta, challah, and honey whole wheat, as well as croissants and muffins, sold at 50 area stores (such as Walter Stewart's Market in New Canaan) and in season at 16 farmers' markets a week. For information about the cafe, see **Wave Hill Bread & Cafe** on p. 68.

White Oaks Farm & Table, 161 Cross Hwy., Westport; (203) 716-1577; whiteoakfarmandtable.com. This producer of gourmet and specialty foods makes small artisanal batches of all-natural spreads, sauces, vinaigrettes, condiments, and gluten-free salad dressings and marinades. Among some of the gems—which are sold on the company website and in such stores as **Billy's Bakery** (p. 14), **Spic and Span Market** (p. 33), the **Pantry** (p. 132), and Walter Stewart's Market—are such food spreads as strawberry rhubarb and wild blueberry and basil, and sauces, such as apple jalapeño, Cajun peach, and Carolina honey. All-natural condiments include honey-mustard crunch, cranberry honey mustard crunch, and chunky country-style ketchup. A gluten-free line of salad dressings and condiments features sun-dried vinaigrette, balsamic vinaigrette, Gorgonzola pear, French Provençal, and artichoke Parmesan.

Specialty Stores & Markets

Aux Délices, 1075 East Putnam Ave., Riverside; (203) 698-1066; auxdelicesfoods.com. When Debra Ponzek, a former executive chef at Montrachet in New York City, and her husband-partner, Gregory Addonizio, opened this stylish gourmet shop in late 1995, they raised the bar for local takeout and catering, turning basic home entertaining into a gourmet experience. Debra's Provençal-influenced menu changes weekly. There are usually 10 to 12 entrees, more than a dozen side dishes, and at least 12 desserts from which to choose. Entrees might be peach-and-shallot-stuffed pork loin, pesto mushroom lasagna, or crab cakes with roasted yellow-pepper sauce. Desserts might be vanilla crème brûlée, strawberry shortcake parfait, tarts or lemon-coconut cake. A few burnished copper-topped tables in the tiny shop are handy for noshing on soups, sandwiches, salads, and coffee while waiting for your order. The shop also sells directly and via mail order a number of yummies, such as aged balsamic vinegars, chocolate truffles, Aux Délices spiced nuts, biscotti, biscuits, almond macaroons, crispy crepes, and butter cookies.

Gift baskets and homemade cakes and tarts are available for overnight home delivery. Other Aux Délices shops are located at 3 West Elm St., Greenwich (203-622-6644); 25 Goodwives Shopping Center, Darien (203-662-1136); in the Hyatt Hotel, 1700 East Putnam Ave., Stamford (203-344-1933); and at 1035 Post Rd. East, Westport (203-557-9600), which also sports a bistro. See Debra's recipe for **Debra Ponzek's Madeleines** on p. 411.

The Baltyk Deli, Stratford Center, 2505 Main St., Stratford; (203) 386-9400. Speaking Polish doesn't hurt when you visit this authentic outpost of Warsaw, but it isn't necessary. Owner Maria Tomaszewski sells all kinds of Polish and Eastern European foods: 12 or more types of kielbasa, sauerkraut, horseradish, three kinds of beets, four or more mustards, and Polish rye bread, fresh baked and delivered from the Brooklyn Bakery in Waterbury.

Darien Cheese & Fine Foods, Goodwives Shopping Center, 25 Old Kings Hwy. North, Darien; (203) 655-4344; dariencheese.com. Neat, compact, and immaculate, Ken and Tori Skovron's alluring shop is so full of tempting edibles that I want to scoop up everything in sight. There are dozens of types of olives in fastidious crocks and a heaping, expanded charcuterie selection, but it's cheese that rules supreme here. Ken has almost 40 years of cheese experience, and it shows. Anything you've wanted to know about cheese, he can tell you—how to cut it, at what temperature to keep it, how to store it, and what kind to buy for every occasion. He has at least 200 cheeses at any given time (including whole wheels), both imported (from all over the world, sometimes from tiny mountain villages where the annual output is minuscule) and domestic (including Connecticut's own). Of special note to cheese heads: Cheeses are cut to order, and the Skovrons age many of their wheels onsite. Shelves along one wall contain dessert sauces, rarefied chocolate truffles, jams, biscuits, and teas. In the rear are bins of coffee and accessories, such as cheese knives and trays, salad bowls, baskets, and other handcrafts. Closed Sun and Mon.

Fairfield Cheese Company, 2090 Post Rd., Fairfield; (203) 292-8194; fairfieldcheese.com. This attractive store isn't just about cheese, though there is plenty of it to admire, sample, and buy, about 100 cheeses in all. Artisanal, farmstead, European, and from all over the US, the selection is mind-boggling. This store is also about cheese utensils, cheeseboards, books, and charcuterie—a wide selection, salted, cured, and smoked. Olives, condiments, sweets, spreads, crackers are all here, too. Closed Sun.

Fairfield Meat Emporium, 949 King's Hwy. East, Fairfield; (203) 696-2322; hungarianmeatmarket.com. While this Hungarian market features meat and is famous for its house-made cold cuts, it has much, much more to show and sell, like all kinds of Hungarian goodies, from stuffed cabbage and chicken paprikash to Hungarian Trappist and Kashkaval cheeses, stews, soups, and strudels. All the

Deli Delights

Firehouse Deli, 22 Reef Rd., Fairfield; (203) 255-5527; firehousedeli fairfield.com; $. How many delis do you know of that are ensconced in an old firehouse? For Firehouse Deli that's just the beginning. This deli is known for its hefty, creative sandwiches, 15 of which are featured on the blackboard daily, such as Arthur Avenue (salami, capicola, ham, provolone, lettuce, and tomato on a hoagie roll) and the Redgate (grilled chicken, bacon, Monterey Jack, avocado, and basil mayo on a hard roll). The deli sells beer and wine as well. For breakfast it serves such treats as Gracie toast (French toast with bacon or sausage) and Bare Naked Granola. Take away or munch away in a greenhouse-like sunroom in the rear or at a picnic table in front in warm weather.

Gold's Delicatessen, Compo Shopping Center, 421 Post Rd. East, Westport; (203) 227-0101; goldsdelicatessen.com; $. This large Jewish deli has been a local institution since it opened its doors in 1958. Julius Gold sold it in 2003, but it's *still* popular for its many kosher foods and as an informal place for lunch (which can be a zoo of hyperactivity), seating 72 and offering more than 30 types of sandwiches daily. Among the deli gems for takeout are chopped liver, roast beef, brisket, various cheeses, smoked fish (kippered salmon, Nova salmon, belly lox, sable, sturgeon), pickled herring, turkey roasted daily, salads

cooked foods are made on the premises. That includes hot dogs, head cheese, and Hungarian and other sausages.

(whitefish, egg, chicken, and tuna), house-made soups, and super breads (some from Fabled Foods, p. 255, in Deep River).

Oscar's· Delicatessen, 159 Main St., Westport; (203) 227-3705; oscarsdelicatessen.com; $. In a long narrow shop, Oscar's manages to squeeze in all kinds of deli delights, display cases of eat-in and take-out snack foods, assorted deli meats, cold cuts, gravlax, other seafood, cheeses, and large display cases of various ice-cold teas and soft drinks. In the rear are tables and two rows of banquettes facing one another for snacking; out front are tables sheltered by an awning.

Spic and Span Market, 329 Pequot Ave., Southport; (203) 259-1689; spicandspanmarket.com; $. Gregory and Lori Peck run the market. The name Spic and Span sounds more like a cleanser than the upscale market and deli it is. But though its knotty pine walls and pressed tin ceiling suggest a country store, it carries a diverse line of eclectic foods, such as gourmet casseroles, the Pecks' own baked cured hams, 10 salads, 27 sandwiches, and other deli items. There are 16 different whole bean coffee varieties; an array of bottled hot sauces and marinades; a butcher counter featuring cut-to-order Angus steaks, boneless pork chops, and other prime meats; and take-out foods, such as capon in brandy sauce, beef Stroganoff, and eggplant Parmesan. That's just for starters. Closed Sun.

Fairway, 699 Canal St., Stamford; (203) 388-9815; fairwaymarket .com. Foodies alert! Anyone familiar with the Fairway stores in New York City and state will be jubilant to find that one has made its way to Connecticut. This one, located in a humongous former warehouse, with some 85,000 square feet of space, off I-95, exit 7, is easy to find. Fairway offers good value, moderate prices, and variety you wouldn't believe. Yes, it's a giant supermarket, and this book doesn't usually include supermarkets, but—and this is a big but—the volume and value make this store a must visit. One aisle has 60 varieties of olives; another entire aisle is devoted to imported pastas; yet another to olive oils. The store has 600 artisanal cheeses and 100 types of premises-roasted coffees. You'll find a huge bakery section, organic and kosher foods, and even a medical supply area. There's also a cafe on the premises (see **Fairway Cafe,** p. 60).

Fratelli Market, 17 Cedar Heights Rd., Stamford; (203) 322-1632; fratellimarketct.com. *Basta pasta!* At Fratelli's there's all kinds of pasta, more than 30 types of ravioli alone. This unusual Italian market sells pastas and diverse sauces, made in Brooklyn. While pasta is the star here, Fratelli also sells 50 different sandwiches and panini, various antipasti, some aged cheeses, fresh-made mozzarella, lunch platters, gluten-free products, and enough variety for a take-out or eat-in lunch at one of six tables on the premises.

Kaas & Co., 83 Washington St., South Norwalk; (203) 838-6161; kaasnco.com. Jan Schenkels's tidy shop has specialized in foods and decorative items (Dutch tiles, plates, jars, tea towels) from the Netherlands and Indonesia since 1990. No wonder it's known as "A Taste of Holland." Homesick Netherlanders come from as far as Pennsylvania and New Jersey for the Dutch cookies, jams, Droste cocoa, Pickwick teas, de Ruijter chocolates, Indonesian spices, honeycakes, *speculaasbrokken,* marzipan cakes, candies, and 85 types of Dutch licorice, as well as mixes and crackers. In the deli cases are Dutch cheeses—low-fat, regular, and aged Gouda, Leyden, Old Amsterdam, baby Edam, aged farmer cheese, raw-milk cheese, Friese Nagel, cumin cheese, and Rookvlees—as well as herring and mackerel. Kaas & Co. even sells *mettwurst,* a smoked sausage shipped from a Dutch butcher in Michigan. Closed Sun.

New Wave Seafood, 81 Camp St., Stamford; (203) 461-7720; newwaveseafood.com. New Wave offers astonishingly fresh fish, many caught in local waters. The company began as a seafood wholesaler in 1985, selling to restaurants, clubs, and hospitals. It now sells retail as well: the freshest of salmon, sushi-quality tuna, sole, swordfish, Chilean sea bass, grouper, halibut, and many other sea denizens, such as oysters, mussels, several types of clams, shrimp, and bay and sea scallops. There's also packaged smoked fish for sale: trout, bluefish, salmon, mackerel, white fish, and marinated anchovies.

No. 109 Cheese & Wine, 109 Danbury Rd., Ridgefield; (203) 438-5757; 109cheeseandwine.com. The cheeses in this attractive high-end shop, with its stonework wall and avocado color scheme, are so compelling that it's easy to overlook the other goodies, like many unusual charcuterie items, Russian osetra caviar, and a freezer full of such edibles as duck confit, Serrano hams, Prosciutto de Parma, and gravlox. A raft of frozen hors d'oeuvres from **Bernard's** (p. 75), an elegant restaurant in town, is available on an exclusive basis. Among three dozen or more cheeses are Rainbeau Ridge's Mont Vivant goat cheese, cave-aged Fiscalini cheddar (from California), the Spanish Casa del Bosque Manchego Anejo, Cashel Blue, and Abbaye de Belloc. Charcuterie items include *chorizo secco, saucisson* Basque, Fermin lomo, and wild boar *cacciatorini*. Closed Mon.

The Olive Market, 19 Main St., Georgetown; (203) 544-8134; theolivemarketct.com; $$. Deli cases bulge with as many as 100 tempting cheeses, mostly from France, Italy, and Spain; 10 large vats hold olives from France, Italy, Spain, and Greece. Shelves are lined with imported goodies, including more than 20 types of olive oil. Breads, muffins, and biscotti are made daily on the premises. This well-stocked store also serves breakfast, light lunch (soup, pizza, panini, and *chivito,* a Uruguayan steak sandwich), and brunch (Fri through Sun), plus prix-fixe tapas dinners 3 nights a week. The market now has the O Lounge, part of the store, which functions as a cafe and wine bar. Closed Mon.

Olivette, 1084 Post Rd., Darien; (203) 621-0643; olivettect.com. With the motto, "The art of olive oil and balsamic," on the window, this new shop telegraphs its contents *tout de suite*. There are around

24 different olive oils on display from countries famous for their olives. Closed Sun.

Oriental Food Market, 109 New Canaan Ave., Norwalk; (203) 847-0070. This all-inclusive, if cluttered and a mite untidy, source for Asian foods is especially strong on Chinese, Japanese, and Philippine products—fresh (bok choy, snowpeas, sweet pickles, tofu, Japanese pumpkins) and frozen (dim sum dumplings, Filipino *pampango lumpia,* Chinese sweet sausage). Shelves are crammed with soy sauces (including tangy soy *calamansi* from the Philippines), rice vinegars, various oils, roasted sesame seeds, kimchee mix, pickled vegetables, teas, mung beans, dried mushrooms, and sugar palm, with many available in large sizes (like 20-pound sacks of rice). Nonfood supplies include electric rice cookers and Chinese tableware. Cash only.

Penzey's Spices, 197 Westport Ave., Norwalk; (203) 849-9085; penzeys.com. Going inside this well-kept store on the Post Road is like entering spice heaven. There are over 250 spices to choose among, including 13 varieties of chili peppers, nine blends of curry powders, and eight types of cinnamon, to say nothing of such exotica as annatto (used in Carribbean, Mexican, and Latin American cooking) and *charnushka* (smoky seeds topping Jewish rye bread). A knowledgeable staff will help you choose among various paprikas (such as smoky Spanish and Hungarian sweet *kulonleges*), peppers, cardamoms (like the intense green favored in India or the subtler white used in Scandinavian baking), and spices blended for various

TRADING UP

All but one of the six Trader Joe's (traderjoes.com) in Connecticut are in the southwest part of the state. (The exception is in West Hartford.) Trader Joe's isn't a typical chain—if it were, you wouldn't find it in this book. Devotees travel across the state to load up on the many unusual items at these unusual stores, whose prices are often well below those of the ordinary food market chains. TJ's, as its fans call it, specializes in organic, vegetarian, kosher, fat-free, sugar-free, gluten-free, salt-free, and all kinds of sybaritic foods, some of which you can't find elsewhere. Great buys are imported cheeses, crackers and breads, pita breads, nuts and dried fruits, dried pastas, jams and preserves, salsas and sauces, pesto, chocolates, candies, and cookie assortments. Natural cereals, fresh soy milk and other soy products, organic fruits and vegetables, olive oils and specialty vinegars, smoked salmon, organic fresh chickens, wasabi peas, soy nuts, and other snack items are among scores of products sold here, many with the Trader Joe's label. Vitamins, herbal soaps, and shampoos are also available. The frozen cakes and pies are exceptional; even the nonfrozen baked goods are tasty. Every week new, irresistible products arrive to tempt us devout patrons at the following locations:

Darien: 436 Post Rd., (203) 656-1414

Westport: 400 Post Rd. East, (203) 226-8966

Fairfield: 2258 Black Rock Turnpike, (203) 330-8301

Danbury: 113 Mill Plain Rd., (203) 739-0098

Orange: 560 Boston Post Rd., (203) 795-5505

West Hartford: 1489 New Britain Ave., (806) 561-4771

types of dishes (seafood, salads, chili, Asian recipes). Roaming among the rustic shelves made from packing cases is a savory experience any cook will relish.

Simpson & Vail, 3 Quarry Rd., Brookfield; (203) 775-0240 or (800) 282-TEAS; svtea.com. One of the oldest tea companies in the US (second oldest to be precise), this family-run business began in 1929 and has been in Jim Harron's family since 1978. He and his wife, Joan, offer more than 300 teas, from China, Japan, India, Sri Lanka, Taiwan, Indonesia, Vietnam, Nigeria, and Bolivia. They include black, green, white, blended, organic, decaf-finated, herbal, flavored, aromatic, and even yoga teas. There are regular tastings most Sat. (Check the website for details.) In this tranquil locale you will also find dark-roasted, Swiss-water, decaf, organic, free-trade, and shade-grown coffees, as well as Mexican chocolate, Italian pastas, mixes, salsas, jellies, jams, and Devon creams. Look at the selection of tea accessories, too: pots, tea cozies, strainers, porcelain cups, and stoneware mugs. You might sample your tea, with your own picnic, in the gazebo. Closed Sun.

SoNo Marketplace, 314 Wilson Ave., South Norwalk; (203) 838-0719; sonomarketplace.com. Some 12,000 square feet of space in a former factory is now devoted to 50 food, craft, and art vendors. The brainchild of Joe Grasso of Grasso Construction and John Palino, a restaurateur, the area expands even more in warm weather with space outside for an additional 20 displays and vendors.

Steve's Market, 69 Main St., Norwalk; (203) 853-4020. Steve's modest, compact store is Greek to me—a great source of many things Hellenic: Kefalotyri and Manouri cheeses, *taramasalata,* frozen spanakopita and baklava, large pita breads, Greek cookies, whole squid—and that's just the alpha of it. Shelves are lined with jars of Kalamata olives and capers, rose and quince jams, sesame snacks, bulgur wheat, rice, biscuits, and all kinds of other tasty items. Closed Sun.

Sweet Pierre's Boutique du Chocolat, 3 Danbury Rd., Ridgefield; (203) 431-9022; sweetpierre.com. Since 2005, Nancy Saxe, co-owner with her husband, James, has been selling all kinds of chocolates in this beautiful confection of a shop. Gift boxes of premier Belgian brands, such as Neuhaus and Godiva, and Connecticut's own **Bridgewater Chocolate** (p. 15) and **Knipschildt Chocolatier** (p. 20), Asher's truffles, and other luscious chocolates. While chocolates are the main story, they aren't the only one at Sweet Pierre's. There are Heritage Hill and Lark shortbreads; fruit chews; five types of licorice; cylinders of Funkychunky popcorn, pretzels, and peanut crunch; and gift baskets galore. A second **Sweet Pierre's** is at 5 River Rd., Wilton (203-563-0000). Hours differ slightly in both stores, so it is best to call ahead.

Zumbach's Gourmet Coffee, 77 Pine St., New Canaan; (203) 966-2704. Near the railroad tracks is a teeny shop with just three tables and several more outside. There Zumbach's dispenses morning coffee to scores of regulars. But Doug Zumbach's main business is bulk: some 50 different types of coffee from 20 countries, with about 250 pounds of beans being roasted in-house every single day. Zumbach's also wholesales to restaurants, caterers, country clubs, and corporations. Cash only.

Farmers' Markets

Locations, dates, and times may change, so for the most up-to-date information about certified farmers' markets, call the Connecticut Department of Agriculture at (860) 713-2503, visit its website at state.ct.us/doag, or e-mail ctdeptag@po.state.ct.us. (**Note:** Some farmers' markets are not listed by the state agriculture department because they, for various reasons, do not totally conform to the ruling that such markets must carry *only* Connecticut-grown produce and products.)

Bethel Farmers' Market, Town of Bethel Municipal Center, 67 Stoney Hill Rd. (Rte. 6), Bethel. Thurs from 9 a.m. to 1 p.m., mid-June through Oct.

Bridgeport Farmers' Market, United Congregational Church, 877 Park Ave., Bridgeport. Thurs from 2 to 6 p.m.

Danbury Farmers' Market, Main Street at Kennedy Park, Danbury. Fri from 10 a.m. to 4 p.m., early July through Oct.

Darien Farmers' Market, municipal park lot off Mechanic Street behind Rte. 1 fire station, Darien. Wed from 11 a.m. to 4 p.m., early May through mid-Dec.

Easton Farmers' Market, next to EMS building, Sport Hill Road, Easton. Sat from 9 a.m. to noon, mid-May through mid-Oct.

Fairfield–Greenfield Hills Farmers' Market, Greenfield Hills, 1950 Bronson Rd., Fairfield. Sat from 12:30 to 4 p.m., early June through late Oct.

Georgetown Farmers' Market, 4 Old Mill Rd., Georgetown. Sun from 10 a.m. to 2 p.m., mid-June through Oct.

Greenwich Farmers' Market, commuter parking lot, exit 3 off I-95, Arch Street across from Boys Club, Greenwich. Sat from 9:30 a.m. to 1 p.m., mid-May through mid-Nov.

Milford Downtown Farmers' Market, 58 River St., corner of Darina Place and River Street, Milford. Sat from 9 a.m. to 1 p.m., mid-June through early Oct.

Milford-Village of Devon Farmers' Market, 120 Bridgeport Ave. (Rte. 1), Devon Village, Milford. Sun from 10 a.m. to 2 p.m., early July through Oct.

Milford Woodmont Farmers' Market, Robert Treat Farm, 1339 New Haven Ave., Milford. Wed from 3:30 p.m. to 6:30 p.m., early July through Sept.

Monroe Farmers' Market, Monroe Town Green, 7 Fan Rd., Monroe. Fri from 3 to 6 p.m., late June through Oct.

Naugatuck Farmers' Market, on the Green, Church Street, Naugatuck. Wed from 10 a.m. to 2 p.m. and Sun from 9:30 a.m. to 1 p.m., early July through Oct.

New Canaan Farmers' Market, Old Center School parking lot, South Avenue and Maple Street, New Canaan. Sat from 10 a.m. to 2 p.m., early May through late Nov.

Newtown–Fairfield Hills Farmers' Market, Wasserman Way, Fairfield Hills campus, Newtown. Tues from 2 to 6 p.m., mid-June through Oct.

Norwalk Health Department Farmers' Market, 137 East Ave., Norwalk Health Department, Norwalk. Wed from 11 a.m. to 3 p.m., early July through early Nov.

Norwalk-Rainbow Plaza Farmers' Market, 205 Main St., Norwalk. Wed from 11 a.m. to 3 p.m., early June through Oct.

Norwalk-Ryan Park Farmers' Market, 1 Raymond St., Norwalk. Thurs from 10 a.m. to 1 p.m., late June through late Sept.

Old Greenwich Farmers' Market, 38 West End Ave., Old Greenwich. Wed from 3 p.m. to 6 p.m., early June through mid-Nov.

Rowayton Farmers' Market, Pinckney Park, Rowayton. Fri from noon to 5 p.m., June through Oct.

Sandy Hook Organic Farmers' Market, Fairfield Hills campus-Newtown, Newtown. Tues from 2 to 6 p.m., late June through second week of Oct.

Seymour Farmers' Market, municipal parking lot, Main and Broad Streets, Seymour. Tues from noon to 6 p.m., late May through Nov.

Shelton Farmers' Market, corner of Cornell and Canal Streets, Shelton. Sat from 9 a.m. to 1 p.m., mid-June through mid-Nov.

Stamford Farmers' Market, West Park Place, Columbus Park. Mon and Thurs from 10 a.m. to 3 p.m., early July through Nov.

Stamford-High Ridge Farmers' Market, High Ridge Shopping Center, Stamford. Wed and Sun from 10 a.m. to 4 p.m., July through Oct.

Stratford Farmers' Market, Deluca Field, Main Street, Stratford. Mon from 2 to 6 p.m., late June through Oct.

Trumbull Farmers' Market, Long Hill Green, North Main Street, Trumbull. Thurs from 3 to 6 p.m., early June through Oct.

Weston Farmers' Market, Rte. 57 at High Acre Road, Weston. Sat from 9 a.m. to noon, mid-June through Sept.

Westport Farmers' Market, municipal parking lot, 26 Imperial Ave., Westport. Thurs from 10 a.m. to 2 p.m., early June through Nov. **Winter market: Gilbertie's Herb Gardens,** 7 Sylvan Ln., Westport. Sat from 10 a.m. to 2 p.m., early Dec through mid-Mar.

Farm Stands

Beardsley's Cider Mill & Orchard, 278 Leavenworth Rd. (Rte. 110), Shelton; (203) 926-1098; beardsleyscidermill.com. Dan is the third-generation Beardsley managing this 100-acre farm, and the apple of his eye is . . . apples. He has more than 30 varieties of them in 5,000 trees spread over 27 acres, some planted in 1918 and still producing old-fashioned types, such as Baldwin, Wagner, Golden Russet, and Spitzenberg, and newer ones, such as Gold Blush, all good for eating or baking. On weekends from mid-Sept to Columbus Day, you can pick your own; and from mid-Sept through Christmas Eve you can stop by to watch small batches of fresh apples being pressed into cider in Dan's cider mill. There is a store onsite that sells peaches, pears, plums, and quince, as well as local maple syrup, fruit butters, jams, jellies, cider vinegar, cider doughnuts, farm-baked cookies and donuts, and more than a dozen kinds of pies, including the popular crumb-topped apple pie. The honey is made by the same bees that help pollinate Beardsley apple trees, proving that what goes around comes around. Call ahead for pick-your-own hours and availability.

Blue Jay Orchards, 125 Plumtrees Rd., Bethel; (203) 748-0119; bluejayorchardsct.com. The Pattersons invite you to pick your own apples from the 30 varieties on their 120-acre farm. Most popular is the Macoun; second most popular is the Mutsu (the big yellow Japanese hybrid sometimes called Crispin). There are McIntosh, Gala, Cortland, Granny Smith, Empire, Fuji, and Winesap, too. Be sure to browse the farm's store and gift shop for apple pies, cider doughnuts, fresh hot apple cider (Aug through Oct), pastries from the farm bakery, as well as maple syrup, honey, jams, jellies, peaches, pears, and pumpkins. There are hayrides to the pumpkin patch in Sept and

Oct. The Pattersons also have a luncheonette and offer a Sample Tasting Corner for trying the various types of apples.

Gilbertie's Herb Farm and Gardens, 7 Sylvan Ln., Westport; (203) 227-4175; gilbertiesherbs.com. Gilbertie's is known not just for its many annuals and perennials, gift shop, gardening appliances, and pond supplies, but also as the biggest herb plant grower on the entire East Coast. It serves the casual amateur gardener and the serious botanist alike. Besides being the supersource for all kinds of herbs and other plants, Gilbertie's features demonstrations, lectures, and workshops and in the fall offers hayrides and sells pumpkins and Christmas trees.

Holbrook Farm, 45 Turkey Plain Rd. (Rte. 53 South), Bethel; (203) 792-0561; holbrookfarm.net. On their 20-acre farm, John and Lynn Holbrook raise organic vegetables. In their farm shop they sell eggs from their 200 chickens, as well as garlic, carrots, various lettuces, mustard greens, kale, sugar snap peas, Swiss chard, and other vegetables. The shop also stocks the Holbrooks' own peanut butter, fruit pies, bread, and scones, along with products from other Connecticut farms, such as maple syrup, raw milk, gourmet oils, and vinegars. Call ahead to learn what has just been harvested. There are cooking classes, too; the website will tell you what and when.

Jones Family Farms, 606 Walnut Tree Hill Rd., Shelton; (203) 929-8425; jonesfamilyfarms.com. Philip Jones began farming here in 1848, and six generations later the Joneses are still working the land. Terry and Jean Jones and their son, Jamie, manage 400 working acres in these rolling hills. Christmas trees have been a cash crop since 1947, but the farm also cultivates strawberries, blueberries, squashes, gourds, and 50 varieties of pumpkins. Hop aboard the Berry Ferry wagon to one of two locations—Strawberry Valley or Pumpkinseed Hill—for pick-your-own pleasures, from June through Oct, depending on crop conditions (call ahead for days and times). Visitors will also find a winery and tasting room (**Jones Winery,** p. 109) on the property.

Plasko's Farm, 670 Daniels Farm Rd., Trumbull; (203) 268-2716; plaskosfarm.com. In addition to the many different vegetables John Plasko's 30-acre farm produces, he has 6 acres of orchards (apples, pears, peaches, and plums). A family farm since 1920, Plasko's is also now known for its variety of fresh baked goods. Plasko's certified kitchen turns out 12 different soups (including gazpacho), two types of pesto (basil, sweet red pepper), seven different types of pies, 15 organic breads (including asiago, black olive, multigrain), and all kinds of tea breads, muffins, scones, cookies, and popular, award-winning apple cider doughnuts. Besides selling in 10 farmers' markets in season, Plasko's wholesales its baked goods to grocery stores, such as Walter Stewart's in New Canaan. The farm has an annual and popular corn maze in late summer and early autumn.

Shortt's Farm & Garden Center, 52-A Riverside Rd., Sandy Hook; (203) 426-9283; shorttsfarmandgarden.com. On a mere 4 acres, Jim and Sue Shortt produce a variety of USDA-certified organic vegetables and fruits. For sale at their farm store (and various farmers' markets) during the growing season are beets, Brussels sprouts, cauliflower, broccoli, beans, hot and mild peppers, six types of eggplants, summer and winter squashes, bok choy, cucumbers for eating and pickling, six types of lettuces, heirloom and hybrid tomatoes, and many other veggies, as well as cantaloupes, watermelons, basil and other herbs, fresh eggs, honey, and jams. The store is open May through Oct.

Silverman's Farm, 451 Sport Hill Rd., Easton; (203) 261-3306; silvermansfarm.com. You want apples? Peaches? Plums? They are all here in abundance (14 peach varieties, more than 20 apple types). You may pick your own from July through Oct—call or check the website for hours. In addition, Irv Silverman's "animal farm" has goats, sheep, deer, pigs, emus, buffalo, llamas, exotic birds, and a petting zoo. The farm market offers fresh produce (including 20 kinds of squash), flowers, 18 different farm-made pies, preserved spiced fruits, jams, and even salsas. From Aug through Oct there are tables for picnics on the grounds and, on fall weekends, tractor rides through the orchards to the pumpkin patch. Silverman's is open year-round.

Stone Gardens Farm, 83 Sawmill City Rd., Shelton; (203) 929-2003; stonegardensfarm.com. Since 1998, Fred and Stacia Monahan have been raising and selling all kinds of seasonal vegetables, flowers, plants, and Thanksgiving turkeys. You can also buy shares of beef from the Monahans. Their farm stand is open from May through Thanksgiving.

Treat Farm, 361 Old Tavern Rd., Orange; (203) 799-2453; treatfarm.com. Owner Jeff Wilson grows and sells field-fresh sweet corn, tomatoes, pumpkins, squashes, peppers, and eggplants, plus various other veggies, all grown on his 98 acres. His stand is open from mid-July through Oct and in Dec for Christmas trees.

Warrup's Farm, 11 John Read Rd., West Redding; (203) 938-9403; warrupsfarm.com. Named for a local Indian, Warrup's has been in the Hill family since the 1700s. The proprietor now is Bill Hill, who works 15 of his 300 acres, growing organic lettuces, tomatoes, garlic, potatoes, other vegetables, and herbs. He sells them all at his roadside stand, along with fresh flowers and maple syrup. You may also pick your own vegetables and flowers starting in mid-Aug. Warrup's farm stand is open from mid-Aug through Oct. During maple syrup season (the first 3 weekends in Mar), visitors to the sugarhouse can watch the entire syrup-making process, but be sure to call ahead for hours. Warrup's also sells at the Weston farmers' market each Sat in season.

Food Happenings

January

Taste of Ridgefield, Ridgefield Community Center, 316 Main St., Ridgefield; (203) 438-4585. Sponsored by the Rotary Club, this annual fund-raiser (since 1999) is usually held in late Jan or early Feb (typically the Sun before Super Bowl Sunday, but check ahead to be sure). This is a chance to critique specialties of between 25 and 30 Ridgefield eateries and be a do-gooder at the same time; 100 percent of the proceeds, usually some $30,000, goes to 32 local philanthropies. More than a "taste," the admission ticket permits unlimited samplings of appetizers, entrees, wine, and beer. Live jazz is performed in two sessions; each session is limited to 300 attendees due to fire-code restrictions. You may buy tickets in advance (with a small reduction in price) at the Community Center or at the Ridgefield Chamber of Commerce on Bailey Avenue.

February

Annual Taste of Stamford, Stamford Plaza Hotel & Conference Center, 2701 Summer St., Stamford; (203) 359-4761; stamfordcham ber.com. In a 3-hour period, from 5:30 to 8:30 p.m., on a single night in mid- or late Feb (call ahead for the date), for a set price, you might wolf down the wares of some 30 area restaurants, bakeries, caterers, and others in the food industry, as well as samplings from various vineyards, beer importers, and specialty-coffee distributors. You'll be chewing and sipping for a worthy cause: The proceeds go to the Stamford Chamber of Commerce for program development efforts, including Kids Our Future Trust Fund.

May

Fairfield County Eats! Stamford Marriott, 2 Stamford Forum, Stamford; ctbites.com. An annual fund-raiser (since 1989), this corporate-sponsored event is held in early May. Some 50 area restaurants, wineries, breweries, bakeries, caterers, and specialty-food shops and vendors participate. A single entrance fee enables you to sample a cornucopia of delicious food. Proceeds benefit the Food Bank of Lower Fairfield County.

June

Congregational Church Strawberry Festival, Monroe Town Green, 32 Church Rd. (Rte. 111), Monroe; (203) 268-9327; mcc-ucc .org. Held on a Sat and Sun in mid-June, this happy event has over 75 juried exhibitors, a crafts and fine-art show, live entertainment, games for the kiddies, all kinds of strawberry goodies (shortcake, pies, jams), and other baked goods.

Secrets of Great PBS Chefs, Norwalk; (800) 287-2788; special events@CPTV.org; cptv.org. This high-powered, 3-hour evening in late June lets you rub elbows and lift forks with famous chefs who have appeared on PBS television. The chefs, who have included Rick Bayless, Joanne Weir, and Michael Colameco, provide a live demonstration and dinner at a set price. Held annually since 2001, this event is sponsored by and benefits the Public Broadcasting System.

August

Annual Milford Oyster Festival, Fowler Field & Town Green, Milford; (203) 878-5363; milfordoysterfestival.org. If it is the third Sat in Aug, you must be in Milford, on the Green or along the harbor. This festival, which began in 1974, is billed as the largest 1-day event in New England. Between 50,000 and 60,000 people attend. Some 75 nonprofit organizations staff booths in the huge food court and elsewhere, where you can buy anything your palate desires from burgers and hot dogs to, yes, oysters, which come raw, fried, or stewed. Headline entertainers, canoe races, art and crafts exhibits (with over 200 vendors), schooner cruises, and a Classic Car & Motorcycle Hop are all part of the fun. There is a pre-festival series of events the Friday before the festival. You might check it out as well. Festival hours are from 10 a.m. to 6 p.m. Over 50 nonprofits benefit from this amazing event.

September

Annual Norwalk Seaport Association Oyster Festival, Veterans Memorial Park, Seaview Avenue, Norwalk; (203) 838-9444;

seaport.org. Reserve the weekend after Labor Day: This "biggie" started small in 1978 and now draws as many as 60,000 visitors over a 3-day period, usually held the second weekend of Sept. Oysters are definitely in the swim, with oyster boats in the harbor, an "oyster pavilion" with displays commemorating the decades of oystering in Norwalk, an oyster-shucking contest, and the "Oyster Slurp-Off," in which you can demonstrate your oyster-downing prowess. Oysters star in the International Food Court too, with 20 food booths selling them as well as clams, soft-shell crabs, lobster, shrimp, fish, calamari, jambalaya, pizza, Belgian waffles, and a host of international favorites. There are rides, games, a Pirates Coast Adventure for kids, and a Paul Bunyan contest and more. Proceeds go to community groups, social services, and scholarship programs. Marching bands, harbor cruises, tours of a World War II PT boat and others, entertainers on three stages, and arts-and-crafts exhibits keep the crowds entertained.

The Trumbull Arts Festival, Trumbull Town Hall Green, 5866 Main St., Trumbull; (203) 452-5065; trumbull-ct.gov. In mid-Sept Trumbull goes arts crazy, with art, crafts, good food, and lots of activities for the youngsters. Free admission.

New Canaan Family Lobsterfest, held on the grounds of the New Canaan Historical Society, 13 Oenoke Ridge (Rte. 124), New Canaan; (203) 856-9646; andykerchoff@hotmail.com. This annual Rotary Club–sponsored 2-day festival is held near the end of Sept under a big tent. The lobster dinner includes a 1.5-pound lobster, corn on the cob, rolls, coffee or a soft drink, fruit, and homemade baked goods. For the kids there are hot dogs and fun activities; chicken is available as an option. Proceeds benefit local and international communities.

Nutmegger Cheese & Wine Festival, Jones Family Farms, 606 Walnut Hill Rd., Shelton; (203) 929-8425; jones familyfarms.com. This rollicking event, held the next-to-last Sun of Sept, from noon to 4 p.m., is a fund-raiser for Connecticut's farmlands and to raise money for childhood nutrition. To buy tickets and learn more, contact the Working Lands Alliance at (203) 988-3270 or visit workinglandsalliance.org. The afternoon features cheese, wine, artisan breads, vineyard tours, live music, hayrides, a corn maze, cheese-making talks, and much more.

October

Greenwich Food + Wine Festival, Roger Sherman Baldwin Park, Greenwich; (203) 588-1363; greenwichfoodandwine.com. Since 2010, this annual food event supreme is usually held the first Thurs, Fri, and Sat of Oct. The venue is a gigantic tent in the park (the so-styled Culinary Village), on 6.3 acres, where all kinds of spectacular food events are scheduled. The price tag is steep, but 100 percent of the profits benefit the Hole in the Wall Gang Camp. More than 90 food and beverage vendors participate. The kick-off event is the Ultimate Wine Evening dinner. Then there are tastings, sommelier demonstrations, celebrity chefs, book signings—and the bands play on, big-name bands all.

March of Dimes Signature Chefs Auction, Italian Center, 1620 Newfield Ave., Stamford. This annual event usually is held in mid-Oct at this locale, but the locale *might* change, so it is best to call (203) 692-5884 at the March of Dimes for date, venue, and details. To support this fund-raiser for the March of Dimes, some of the area's best restaurants and chefs are on hand, along with 150 to 200 of Fairfield County's top corporate, civic, and medical leaders. There are samples and tastings of chefs' signature dishes, as well as more than 40 items in live and silent auctions.

Nibbles

Arcadia Cafe, 20 Arcadia Rd., Old Greenwich; (203) 637-8766; $. In a high-ceilinged (with ceiling fans) former post office, you can enjoy breakfast, an elevenses, lunch, afternoon snack, or early informal supper. The fresh-baked muffins (as many as 11 flavors) are grand, but—wait—there are bagels, scones, *pain au chocolat,* a quiche of the day, smoked salmon plate, charcuterie platter, *croque monsieur,* and *croque madame.*

AD, 1035 Post Rd. East, Westport, (203) 557-9600; auxdelicesfoods .com; $$. This new bistro, which serves delicious light foods and nibble-ables, is part of **Aux Délices** (pp. 29, 69), Debra Ponzek's deluxe catering and gourmet food shop. As you'd expect, if you know the meticulous work at Ponzek's other specialty food shops, the new bistro and shop are superb.

Bar Rosso, 30 Spring St., Stamford; (203) 388-8640; barrossoct.com; $$. Located in downtown Stamford, Bar Rosso is ideally situated to attract lots of after-office business—which it does. Weeknights the place really rocks, at the bar and outside (in warm weather) alike. Treats include crispy honey calamari, spiced beef carpaccio, and arugula salad. Entrees are tasty too, especially the seared rare tuna, *chitarra* and shrimp, and marinated lamb shoulder chop. And for dessert, if basil gelato is still on the menu, it's to die for, a taste sensation unlike any other.

Bodega Taco Bar, 1700 Post Rd., Fairfield; (203) 292-9590; bodegatacobar.com; $. This noisy, vibrant, nonstop taco bar in a bustling strip mall yields a surprisingly winsome array of good food at rock-bottom prices. While many Mexican comfort foods are aplenty, there are a few more international touches as well, as in portobello mushrooms stuffed with truffle cheese, panko-crusted mahimahi, and hoisin-glazed pork belly arepas. The first tipoff is the house-made chips with three salsas. If Argentino (charbroiled hanger steak) or *cochinata pibil* (suckling pig resembling vinegar-treated pulled pork) are on the menu, go for them. A second Bodega

Taco Bar is now open at 980 Post Rd., Darien; (203)655-8500; same menu, same ownership.

Bon Appetit Cafe, 5 River Rd., Wilton; (203) 563-9002; $. This petite cafe is proof that good things often come in small packages. In a storefront, no-fuss setting, some lovely, authentic French bistro food is dished up at modest prices for lunch and dinner. The soups are great, as are such treats as *escargots à la bourguignonne,* smoked salmon salad, sea scallops honey balsamic, and duck leg confit. For dessert, don't miss the tarte tatin, chocolate mousse, crème brûlée, or croissant pudding. Yum.

Burger Bar & Bistro, 58 North Main St., South Norwalk; (203) 853-2037; burgerbarandbistro.com; $. This is a great pre- or post-movie stop if you're at the Sono movie complex. The funky little place offers wonderful burgers with a choice of 18 toppings. Try the Ultimate (with sweet onions, Gorgonzola, pancetta, and aged balsamic) or Tijuana (with chorizo, green chili, and fried egg), among many options. Other zesty items: artichoke dip, Cuban spring rolls, and meat loaf. This is no ordinary burger-and-fries spot (the chef-owner is an experienced gourmet cook), though the prices are modest, with special low prices for the kiddies.

The Chelsea, 12 Unquowa Place, Fairfield; (203) 254-8200; thechelseaff.com; $. A gastro pub, as in gastronomic pub, this bustling new place combines good food with a casual, pub-like ambience.

What could be better in this age of informality? Total seating is for 62, including an extension called "The Greenhouse" with lime green plastic chairs and a summery ambience. The food is delightfully casual. Look for such gems as calamari, gnocchi, oyster buns, and Vietnamese banh mi. Serving lunch and dinner daily.

Cocoa Michelle, 54 Railroad Place, Westport; (203) 221-0020; cocoamichelle.com; $. This cafe-cum-chocolate shop sparkles. In fact the candies, imported from Vancouver, are displayed in cases resembling jewelry store treasures. A coffee bar at the entrance offers almost a dozen different coffee concoctions plus Harney teas, as well as sandwiches and salads. There are a few tables, and in an inner area are two comfy loveseats near the chocolate display cases. Be sure to sample the salted caramels and chocolate-dipped orange slices, popular favorites.

The Drawing Room, 5 Suburban Ave., Cos Cob; (203) 661-3406; thedrawingroom.cc; $. Here it's tea for two—and then some. Simply but stylishly decorated, the limited space is comfortable whether you stop by morning or afternoon for a cuppa (tea, coffee, or hot chocolate) or have a full formal prix-fixe, three-tiered afternoon tea (complete with finger sandwiches and luscious desserts) and browse in the smart-looking boutique in the rear. Fifteen loose teas are house blends, richly aromatic, and include Hot Mama (raspberry leaf, camomile, rose hip, peppermint, hibiscus and ginger) and all the usual suspects—green, black, herb, and the like. Tea sandwiches and sweets taste freshly made. The house-made scones, especially the

Prize Pizza Parlors

While New Haven is considered the pizza capital of the state, if not the entire country, don't sell other Connecticut towns short. Many have noteworthy pizza. These are some of my favorites.

Fat Cat Pie Company, 9–11 Wall St., Norwalk; (203) 523-0389; $$. This large, noisy, and cacophonous glorified pizza parlor is a fun place to go before or after the movies. (It's just a short 2-block walk from the Garden Cinema.) The pies are thin crusted with some great toppings; for the grown-ups the wine and beer lists are exemplary (the proprietors own two wine shops, so no wonder). Good salads and breads, artisanal cheeses and desserts—what more do you need in a snack or light meal?

Stanziato's Wood Fired Pizza, 35 Lake Ave. Extension, Danbury; (203) 885-1057; stanziatos.com; $. Chef-Owner Matthew Stanczak is justifiably proud of his wood-fired oven, stoked with New England hardwoods (maple, oak, hickory, and occasionally cherry), which contribute to the smoky echoes in his thin-crusted, chewy, and flavorful pies. His red pies (based on a house-made tomato sauce) include sausage, pepperoni, meatballs, and crimini mushrooms. His white pies

cranberry orange, are the best I've nibbled in years and are available for takeout. Closed Sun.

Fairway Cafe, 699 Canal St., Stamford; (203) 388-9815; fairwaymarket.com; $. Ensconced in the vast Fairway supermarket is this offer clams, fresh basil, mozzarella, a touch of balsamic, bacon, garlic, cheese, oregano, and red pepper flakes. Also available are soups and salads, mostly based on locally grown ingredients. But the star attractions are those pies. Closed Sun.

Tarry Lodge Enoteca Pizzeria, 30 Charles St., Westport; (203) 571-1038; tarrylodge.com; $$. Mario Batali has landed his gastronomic spaceship in Westport. This lively restaurant has two L-shaped bars for dining as well as imbibing, but I go to Tarry Lodge mostly for its sensational thin-crusted pizzas with their remarkably creative toppings. You can sit at the bar and watch the pizzaiolo whirl the dough and thrust it with his wooden peel into the wood-burning Mugnaini oven. Favorites are meatballs with jalapeños and fontina cheese, *guanciale* with black truffles and egg, goat cheese with pistachio-and-truffle honey, and potatoes with Brussels sprouts and pancetta. The pasta dishes are also winners and similarly offbeat, such as pumpkin fiore and garganelli with funghi trifolati. Reservations advised unless it's for takeout.

80-seat cafe. The food and choices are pretty good; the seating is a bit offhand and extemporaneous. You walk around with a tray, as in a cafeteria, selecting from a hot and cold bar with 20 interesting options, pay, and then find a place to roost and eat.

Miss Thelma's Restaurant, 140 Fairfield Ave., Bridgeport; (203) 337-9957; missthelmas.com; $. At this modest place the operative word is *soul,* old-fashioned Southern comfort food. You might try pork chops smothered in gravy, barbecued pork ribs, crispy fried chicken, fried catfish, sweet potato pie, and, on occasion, oxtail stew or chicken and dumplings. Nothing is fancy here, not the plastic cutlery or the Styrofoam plates, but the soul food is real, plentiful, and modestly priced. The weekend breakfast buffet, which lasts until noon, is a wonder unto itself. Closed Mon.

Oaxaca Kitchen, 376 Post Rd. East, Westport; (203) 557-4848; oaxacakitchen.com; $$. Prasad Chirnomuola, who owns four Indian restaurants (**Thali Regional Cuisine of India,** p. 323, in New Canaan, Ridgefield, and New Haven and **Thali Too** in New Haven), has branched out to another continent with this Mexican venture. Actually Mexican and Indian cooking share an interest in well-seasoned, often red-hot foods, so the transition from one cuisine to the other is not as outrageous as it may seem at first. You'll catch this if you try the fiery *pato a las brasas, mole rojo,* the garlicky guacamole *pepino,* or *bistec ala parrilla.* If the weather is nice, you may want to lunch outside; the interior is rather dark. Prasad's other **Oaxaca Kitchen** is in New Haven, at 228 College St. (203-859-5774).

Olé Molé, 1030 High Ridge Rd., Stamford; (203) 461-9962; $. You need to see the limited space to believe it could be converted into a visually appealing dining area. Primarily a take-out place, there are a mere four tables for two along one wall. Paper plates, cups, and plastic tableware do not hamper the enjoyment of the chunky guacamole, blue-corn calamari, blue-cornmeal-covered chicken wings, and other favorites. Salsas and moles are the stars, especially mole negro, slowly simmered with dried fruits, nuts, dried chiles, tomatoes, onions, cilantro, and various spices. Three olés for this tiny Mexican gem.

Rawley's, 1886 Post Rd., Fairfield; (203) 259-9023; $. People are as *dog*matic about hot dogs as about pizzas, and opinions do differ. One of my votes goes to this weathered shack for three reasons: 1) the way they cook their pork-and-beef wieners, starting them in a fryer, finishing them on the grill; 2) the toasted bun, which adds texture to the grilled dog (nothing turns me off faster than a flaccid, soft bun); 3) the "works"—bacon, mustard, sauerkraut, and raw onions—blanketed over the frank. You may have to wait 5 or 10 minutes for your order and then eat at one of the few counter stools. Rawley's also serves tuna melts, cheeseburgers, and other sandwiches to eat in or take out. But it's the doggone franks that are Best in Show. I'll bark to that.

Rosie, 27 Elm St., New Canaan; (203) 966-8998; rosienewcanaan .com; $. To its many fans, Rosie's is a daily habit, the cozy place where you can curl up on a huge cushion in a window seat for a

GUILTY PLEASURES

To folks with a sweet tooth, cakes, cookies, and candies are like a narcotic. And chocolates most of all. There's no such thing as a thin slice or one cookie or a single chocolate. I plead guilty. So for those who share my addiction, read on.

Chocopologie Cafe, 12 South Main St., South Norwalk; (203) 854-4754; knipschildt.com; $$. With its floor-to-ceiling windows fronting the street, this is an intimate little spot for an after-movie snack, a light lunch, or supper. It is also the display, production center, and sales room for Knipschildt chocolates, part of the space where the demonically good chocolates are made. If you eat on a stool, you can watch—as you nibble a quiche or devastating pastry—the candy-making process through a glass wall. The cafe's hot chocolate, in gigantic cups, is among the world's best: rich, dark, intense. It also comes spiked with chipotle, ginger, cloves, and cinnamon. But what else would you expect at a first-rate chocolate factory? There are now two additional Chocopologie Cafes: one in Stamford at 211 Main St. (203-333-2462), and one in New Haven at 47 High St. (203-786-5000).

Isabelle et Vincent, 1903 Post Rd., Fairfield; (203) 292-8022; isabelleetvincent.com; $$. This French pastry shop is patisserie perfection, so good you'll want to buy at least one of every tart, éclair, cake, truffle, marron glacé, macaroon, and croissant in sight. But get there early in the morning, as many goodies are often gone by late afternoon. Vincent Koenig is a seventh-generation pastry chef from France. It shows in each gastronomic masterpiece, from his miniature quiches and petits fours to his croissants, Paris-brest, Arabica, and several dozen types of bite-size pralines. His wife, Isabelle, runs the shop, where it is possible to lunch (at one of three tables for two) on a Vincent-baked baguette and perhaps a napoleon or other butter-rich pastry emerging from Vincent's kitchen. How sweet it is, all of it.

Versailles Bistro and Patisserie, 3395 Greenwich Ave., Greenwich; (203) 661-6634; versaillesgreenwich.com; $$. No, not a regal French palace, this Versailles is a patisserie-cum-cafe, where Maurice Versailles has for decades been specializing in delectable cakes, tarts, and breads. The Versailles repertoire, which is clearly worthy of being served in any palace, includes French pastry classics. You will find tarts such as opera, casino, madeleine, clairefontaine, strawberry Montmartre, and Pont Neuf, and individual desserts, such as Paris-Brest, St. Honoré, and assorted fruit tarts. A small cafe in the rear is popular for breakfast and lunch, with salads, quiches, fish dishes, chicken Riesling, and all those delectable pastries. You can eat in or take away.

simple breakfast of muffins or croissants or a big one of *huevos rancheros* or blueberry pancakes. Rosie Nammack, co-owner of this homey spot, and her staff produce all kinds of take-out or eat-in goodies: five rotating house-made soups (including curried lentil, chicken tortilla, and corn chowder), chicken enchiladas, shepherd's pie, and a variety of jumbo sandwiches. Closed Mon.

The Silvermine Market, 1032 Silvermine Rd., New Canaan; (203) 966-4050; silverminemarket.com; $$. On a quiet country road, across from the Silvermine Guild Arts Center, this deli and glorified grocery offers neighbors and passersby delicious hot soups, generous sandwiches, and several salads daily. There are a few tables on the cozy premises for noshing.

The SoNo Baking Company & Cafe, 101 Water St., South Norwalk; (203) 847-7666; sonobaking.com; $. Expert baker John Barricelli, who worked at Elm and for Martha Stewart, now commands a company that occupies a 3,600-square-foot former warehouse. Since 2005, he has been making great use of the space by whipping up gorgeous cakes, pies, pastries, and 11 types of artisan breads daily. In such space there's also room for a little cafe, which offers all kinds of tasty morsels—soups, sandwiches, and panini. Favorites of mine are the hearty, wholesome *canjiquinha* Brazilian cornmeal soup, Cuban sandwich with pork loin, and virtually all the pastries and tarts. Barricelli has recently expanded: the **SoNo**

Baking Company Cafe is now also ensconced at **A & J's Farm Market,** 1680 Post Rd. East, Westport (203-955-1111).

The Stand Cafe and Juice Bar, 31 Wall St., Norwalk; (203) 956-5670; $. Juiced! That's what you'll get at this unique place that emphasizes freshly made juices and fruit smoothies from more than 2 dozen ingredients. There're also vegan and vegetarian dishes, wraps, sandwiches, salads, and sweets to go, or eat at one of five tables inside. Organic, wholesome, and unusual are key words here. Closed Sun.

Super Duper Weenie, 306 Black Rock Turnpike, Fairfield; (203) 344-3647; superduperweenie.com; $. This hot dog haven's big claims to fame are the condiments and the side dishes made from scratch. These include sauerkraut and sweet relish (served with the New Englander hot dog, along with bacon, mustard, and onion), meat chili and hot relish (embracing the Californian, with American cheese and onion), and the New Yorker (which includes mustard, sauerkraut, and hot relish). Gary Zemola, who created Super Duper Weenie, first selling the dogs from a truck, also makes the popular Zemola's coleslaw, with horseradish and celery seed accents. The smoky doggies themselves blend beef and pork. Various burgers, grilled chicken, and tuna sandwiches are also available and the french fries are super

Taco Loco Restaurant, 3170 Fairfield Ave., Bridgeport; (203) 335-8228; tacoloco.com; $. For a quick bite or a full meal, this tidy

little place on the Fairfield line makes its own Mexican specialties with a few surprises, such as crab cakes chipotle, cumin-accented spinach enchiladas, and paella. Outdoor terrace seating in a residential neighborhood adds to the experience, as do the low prices for reliable, homey fare.

Valencia Luncheria, 162 Main St., Norwalk; (203) 846-8009; $. Michael Young's luncheonette, which he calls a "Venezuelan beach cafe," has moved a block down Main Street from its former hole-in-the-wall, no-frills location. The new, airier, and roomier site seats 60 inside, 13 at the bar (an innovation) and 32 on the outdoor patio. Valencia is no ordinary luncheonette. It offers Latin American specialties in generous portions at rock-bottom prices. Its many delights include arepas with a choice of fillings (black beans with white cheese is one of the best), ceviche, empanadas, chicken *escabeche,* sweet plantains, Valencian flan, and cinnamon rice pudding. There are 20 different juices and *batidos* (fresh fruit blended with milk). The paper and plastic have vanished: Valencia is now a regular restaurant. Even so, it remains a true discovery. Entrepeneur Young has two other new restaurants, both Mexican, both reasonable: Bodega Taco Bar, 980 Post Rd., Darien (203-655-8500) and Bodega Taco Bar, 1700 Post Rd., Fairfield (203-292-9590).

Wave Hill Bread & Cafe, 30 High St., Norwalk; (203) 529-3441; wavehillbreads.com; $. This small cafe is a spin-off from the excellent **Wave Hill Bakery** on the same premises. Proprietors and fellow bakers Mitch Rapoport and Margaret Sapir serve soup and sandwiches at tables for 16 inside and 16 outside. Closed Mon.

Whistle Stop Muffin Company, 20 Portland Ave., Ridgefield; (203) 544-8139; $. This is the creation of Lolly Dunworth Turner. Her little cafe, ensconced cosily in the Branchville railroad station since 1982, turns out scores of mouthwatering fresh-baked muffins, scones, cakes, pies, and cookies, baked right at the station, served warm to commuters and Rte. 7 passersby. Lolly also distributes her delicious wares at farmers' markets in the area. Her newest offering, which flies out of the cafe, is gluten-free chocolate truffle pie. Almost as popular are the vegan cookies.

Learn to Cook

Aux Délices, 23 Acosta St., Stamford; (203) 326-4540; auxdelices foods.com. In an all-modern 5,000-square-foot kitchen with stainless-steel tables, Chef-Owner Debra Ponzek conducts cooking classes for adults, children, and corporate groups, featuring classic French techniques, Provençal flavors, and innovative twists. Classes can also be arranged in one's home. Gift certificates for classes are available. Schedules of lessons are posted in each of Ponzek's four Aux Délices shops.

Cucina Casalinga, 171 Drum Hill Rd., Wilton; (203) 762-0768; cucinacasalinga.com. Since 1981, Sally Maraventano has conducted cooking classes in her home, which includes a Tuscan wood-burning pizza oven in her kitchen. Sally's emphasis is on Italian regional cooking, especially Sicily, the home of her grandfather. Each class, which is sometimes conducted by a guest chef, stands alone, with a theme covering a complete meal, which the class enjoys afterward. Recent themes: A Taste of Venice and Comfort Foods. There are also classes for children 10 to 16 years old, corporations, and private parties. Additionally, Sally leads annual culinary tours to Italy, where classes are taught by notable Italian chefs. A recent addition to the Maraventano repertoire is the 4-day Kids Cook Italian Summer Camp, with 10 to 12 participants. The name of her cooking school means "homestyle cooking" in Italian—which is what Sally likes to emphasize. See Sally's recipe for **Asparagi alla Parmigiana** on p. 405.

Jean Jones Cooking Classes, Jones Family Farms, 606 Walnut Tree Hill Rd., Shelton; (203) 929-8425; jonesfamilyfarms.com. Experienced nutritionist and dietician Jean Jones is serious about healthy foods. Her hands-on classes emphasize healthy eating. They are held in her well-equipped Harvest Kitchen, a kitchen facility scooped out of a large barn, across the yard from the tasting room on the Jones's 400-acre property. Themed classes bear such names as New England Lobster Picnic, Santa Fe Sunset Supper, and Kids in the Kitchen. Class size is limited to 15 and usually runs 3 hours.

Ronnie Fein School of Creative Cooking, 32 Heming Way, Stamford; (203) 322-7114; ronniefein.com. Since the 1970s, food writer Ronnie Fein has been teaching individually designed, one-on-one cooking workshops in her home, which last 3 hours and are limited to no more than four students. Usually five recipes are developed in the hands-on, single-day sessions. Part of her kitchen is devoted to kosher cooking, which she also teaches, often with recipes from her book, *Hip Kosher*.

Susan Goodman Catering, 327 Old Norwalk Rd., New Canaan; (203) 972-3793; susangoodman.com. A professional caterer, Susan Goodman teaches cooking classes on various aspects of cuisine at the Lapham Community Center, 663 South Ave., New Canaan; (203) 594-3620. For classes and sched-ule, call the center. The center also features, from time to time, single-session classes by chefs from some of the area restaurants. Call the center for specifics. See Susan's recipe for **Crispy Lobster Potato Roll** on p. 389.

Two Steps Downtown Grille, 5 Ives St., Danbury; (203) 794-0032; ciaocateringtwosteps.com. Seasonal cooking classes, held in Two Steps Downtown Grille, are conducted by owner Tom Devine. There are six sessions per season in each of which four dishes are prepared. Participants may partake of any or all sessions, with a price reduction for the series. Each session includes tasting all the prepared dishes, recipes, and wine. Classes are serious, even though there's lots of conversation and wine imbibing, which only proves that you can have fun while learning.

Learn about Wine & Beer

Mountview Plaza Wines and Liquors, 727 Rubber Ave., Naugatuck; (203) 729-5445; mountviewwines.biz. Saverio D'Archangelo, proprietor, knows all about beer—and has a beer inventory of 600 to 700 brands to prove it. He stocks the best and rarest brews in Connecticut. New arrivals include Cricket Hill, Laughing Dog, Dogfish Head, Ballast Point, Abita, Cisco, O'Hara (Irish stout), and Shmaltz. Also in stock: Sarasola (Basque cider) and various meads and ciders. Of course there are wines and liquors as well, but the big deal here is beer.

Napa & Co., Stamford Marriott, 75 Broad St., Stamford; (203) 353-3319; napaandcompany.com. Mary Schaffer, knowledgeable sommelier and co-owner of this trend-setting restaurant, conducts wine classes every spring and fall. Past subjects include Wine 101, learning the basics and how to navigate a wine list; Napa vs. the World; Champagne; STOMP!; and Wine Spectator Picks, in which you taste six wines rated over 90 points. Each class is separately booked, with different fees for each session.

Amerigo Restaurant, 456 Main Ave., Norwalk; (203) 840-1444; amerigopizza.com; $$. As you may have guessed, I like sleepers. Amerigo is such a one, a mom-and-pop restaurant that is BYOB and serves Italian food that truly tastes homemade. Robert Nelson is the chef, and his wife, Trish, is both the maître d' and a server. The place is tiny, in an unprepossessing strip mall, seating a mere 32. The big neon sign outside says Pizza, but Amerigo has other dishes to offer, such as succulent gnocchi, artichoke ravioli and shrimp, wild mushroom purse (wonderful!), chicken Santa Fe, wild mushroom ravioli, and several tasty desserts. There's nothing fancy here, but the food is good and the place is cozy. Closed Sun.

Artisan, 275 Old Post Rd., Southport; (203) 307-4222; artisan southport.com;. $$$. If you're looking for stylish dining, think Artisan, a handsome dining room in the newish (2012) Delamar Southport Hotel. Gigantic, Georgia O'Keeffe–style painted magnolias occupy an entire wall, with the rest of the dining area what I would call sophisticated rustic. The locavore food, updated New England, is just as creative. Although the menu changes seasonally, I liked especially the Artisan beef pot roast, local sea bass, duck breast *a la plancha,* and wild-mushroom-and-farro risotto. For dessert, look for the golden crisp fruit fritters, citrus crème brûlée, and assorted ice creams. There's outdoor dining in clement weather.

Baang Cafe & Bar, 1191 East Putnam Ave., Riverside; (203) 637-2114; decarorestaurantgroup.com; $$$. The first to introduce Asian fusion cooking to Connecticut, this unusual restaurant opened in 1995 with (yes) a bang! Its eclectic decor (by New York architect-designer David Rockwell) vibrates with colors and unusual shapes, yet it plays second banana to the food, which is so fresh,

it crackles, from the open kitchen directly to the table. East really does meet West here, as Western cooking techniques combine with Asian ingredients. Among my favorites is the incredible sizzling calamari salad with ever-so-lightly breaded squid, a hint of hot chile oil, and frisée and baby lettuces in a lime-miso vinaigrette. Almost as memorable are pan-fried pepper oysters, grilled Shanghai beef, and gossamer-like crispy spinach deep-fried in soy oil. In peak hours the decibel level is high, but the fresh, creative food is worth enduring the cacophony.

Basso Cafe, 124 New Canaan Ave., Norwalk; (203) 354-6566; bassobistrocafe.com; $$. Chef-Owner Renato Donzelli has the best of two culinary worlds: He was born in an Italian family and grew up in Venezuela. At his teeny-tiny restaurant he offers a happy blend of Mediterranean-cum-Italian dishes hyped with Latin American ingredients and concepts. Tuscan grilled chicken and warm goat cheese–mushroom tarts complement beef empanadas on Renato's creative menu. Artful plate presentations and an informal atmosphere combine with BYOB. (There's a liquor store just half a block away and a corkage charge at the cafe.) Closed Mon.

Bernard's, 20 West Ln., Ridgefield; (203) 438-8282; bernardsridge field.com; $$$. This white clapboard house was showing its age when Bernard and Sarah Bouissou arrived in 2000. They refurbished the building and raised the restaurant's culinary level spectacularly. It is now lovely, from the outside plantings to the four airy, impeccably maintained dining rooms—a no-brainer choice for special-occasion dining. But Bernard's kitchen skills (from years at Le Cirque in New York, where Sarah was a chef, too) are so creative they make even a regular meal special—abetted often by a soothing pianist, who seems to have total recall of every pop tune of the past 60 years—and then some. Bernard's contemporary French repertoire includes a galette of snails with wild mushrooms, roasted monkfish osso bucco wrapped in rosemary pancetta, and a signature foie gras trio. The lengthy wine list has been carefully selected, with many well-priced vintages as well as rarer ones. **Sarah's Wine Bar,** upstairs, is a relaxed bistro with simpler food (and lower prices). Both are closed Mon.

Bistro Latino, 1392 East Putnam Ave., Old Greenwich; (203) 698-9033; bistrolatinogreenwich .com; $$. Formerly Greenwich Tavern, this newly renamed restaurant has also switched its identity from olde New England cooking to south-of-the-border Latin flavors. Colombian-born owner-chef Rafael Palomino knows South American–Spanish cooking. He demonstrates it in creative renderings of such specialties as *gambas al ajillo* (shrimp in garlic sauce), *boquerones* (marinated white anchovy filets), *tortilla española* (Spanish potato omelet) and many other dishes. Señor Palomino also owns **Pacifico** (p. 320) located at 220 College St., New Haven (203-772-4002) and two restaurants in Port Chester, New York.

Blue Lemon, 15 Myrtle Ave., Westport; (203) 226-2647; bluelemonrestaurant.com; $$. Expert but understated, this charming low-key restaurant is hidden in plain sight—just off the Post Road and a block from the Westport Country Playhouse, a great choice for lunch or dinner before a performance. The menu is eclectic American-cum-global. I love the small plates, such as yellowfin tuna tartare, steamed mussels, and salmon carpaccio. Large plates might include confit of duck risotto, *arroz ala Vasca* (Basque seafood stew), seared King salmon over ginger spinach, or braised 6-hour lamb shank. Then there might be apple tarte tatin or ginger crème brûlée. The menu changes often and is always creative. One more bonus: The noise level is low, making conversation easy.

Bobby Q's Barbeque & Grill, 42 Main St., Westport; (203) 454-7800; bobbyqsrestaurant.com; $$. Get your earplugs and join the fun. This faux–rustic, double-deck place rocks, often with live music, always with conversation. The baby back ribs, brisket Reuben, and barbecue sauces are all terrific. Regulars rave about the smoky wings with six sauces to choose among, also the corn bread and pit beans. Best to reserve ahead on weekends. It's a favorite spot for large parties and groups.

Boulevard 18, 62 Main St., New Canaan; (203) 594-9900; boulevard18.com; $$. Ignore the number 18—more an image than an actual address. David Raymer, co-owner and chef, chose it to be a French bookend to his group's Italian restaurant **Strada 18** (pp. 18, 97) in South Norwalk. Boulevard 18 is located in the old Veterans Hall, a colonnaded building on Main Street, facing Town Hall. Inside, a full-wall blowup of a Paris street map, circa 1812, is a pretty good clue that French is the language of the kitchen here. The menu is so delightfully Gallic that it's difficult to choose. There are enough delicious small plates to make a meal, without even sampling the equally tasty entrees, like roasted salmon or duck magret. Small plates include cloud-like *gougère* (Gruyère-flavored choux pastries), torchon of foie gras, deep-fried Roquefort-stuffed olives, bacon and leek tart, and four different types of sausages. If the weather is warm, outside seating faces the street, and it's fun to watch the passing parade of shoppers.

Boxcar Cantina, 44 Old Field Point Rd., Greenwich; (203) 661-4774; boxcarcantina.com; $. Lively as all get out, Boxcar Cantina is more than a neighborhood hangout. On weekends it seems like the entire county is here. When this mainstay of the Greenwich restaurant scene opened in 1994, it was the first of its kind in Connecticut, its kind being northern New Mexican cooking. It was also the first to become certified green—green as in using organic chicken, Niman Ranch meats with no added hormones or antibiotics,

NOTHIN' COULD BE FINER THAN BREAKFAST IN A DINER

Here are some good ones.

City Limits Diner, 135 Harvard Ave., Stamford; (203) 348-7000; citylimitsdiner.com; $. With its art deco decor, oversize booths, and quadruple-lifesize coffee-cup-and-doughnut display, City Limits has a retro look, even though it dates only from 2002 and offers a modern American menu. There are a few old-timey dishes, like Southern fried chicken, but many others have an Asian touch: steamed bass with fresh ginger and scallions in a wine-soy sauce and crispy crab wontons, for example. An in-house bakery does a variety of sweet rolls, muffins, doughnuts, pies, cakes, and tortes, as well as excellent breads. Reasonable prices make City Limits a fun place to drop by, especially for breakfast but also for lunch, snacks, or dinner. The beer list is exceptional for a diner, with many microbrew selections from all over North America and Europe.

and locavore-friendly farm-fresh eggs and local ingredients. All that aside, the food tastes really good. Nancy Allen Roper, owner and chef, blends three cultures in her cooking: Indian, Mexican, and

The New Canaan Diner, 18 Forest St., New Canaan; (203) 594-7595; prdfamily.com; $. Step back into the 1950s at this newish but retro diner, with its marble countertop, shiny chrome trim, and vintage music, and enjoy humongous breakfast choices, as well as foot-long hot dogs, grinders, baked meat loaf, pasta dishes, and many Greek and Italian favorites dished up by owners Olga and Theodore Giapoutzis and their staff. Then there are all the floats, sodas, shakes, malts, and even egg cream. Channeling Elvis; where are you? The family owns two other diners in neighboring towns: the Post Road Diner, 312 Connecticut Ave., Norwalk (203-866-9777), and the Darien Diner, 171 Post Rd., Darien (203-655-3181).

White's Diner, 280 Boston Ave., Bridgeport; (203) 366-7486; $. Open since 1935, this old-timer is the real deal, owned and run by the same couple—Greg and Linda Cerminara—for 37 years. Featuring a cholesterol-be-darned menu of breakfast goodies, White's offers more than a dozen omelets, as well as hearty lunch choices, homemade soups, goulash, and scores of sandwich combos, with almost everything assembled from scratch. The puddings, especially the rice pudding, are local faves. A cross section of Bridgeport life parades daily through this long-standing local landmark, with its expansive counter, booths, and vintage photos of old Bridgeport. Cash only.

Anglo. She also uses butter instead of lard in her tamales. Special treats: red chile onion rings, Indian posole soup, grilled chicken enchiladas, organic salmon burritos, and flan gargantuan.

Brasitas, 954 East Main St., Stamford; (203) 323-3176; brasitas.com; $$. Brasitas is the sleeper every adventurous diner dreams of. In cozy, convivial, folkloric surroundings, a creative Latin chef combines the natural bounty of South America and the Caribbean (maize, plantain, yucca, mango, and the like) with sophisticated European techniques, coming up with Latin fusion and gems like grilled pork chop in guava-ginger barbecue sauce and sautéed chicken breast in a tequila-honey-lemon-cilantro sauce. Inventive sauces bring new vitality to many Latin American standbys, and the plate presentations are knockouts. A second **Brasitas** is in Norwalk at 430 Main Ave. (203-354-7329). The menu and prices are the same, but I prefer the ambience and creativity of the Stamford original.

Cafe Lola, 57 Unquowa Rd., Fairfield; (203) 292-8014; cafelolarestaurant.com; $$. Henri and Ivana Donneaux seem to have a winning combination. He supervises the menu (despite a day job at **L'Escale,** p. 94, in Greenwich) in this small, appealing two-room cafe, ornamented with gilded mirrors, unusual chandeliers, and individualistic artwork, and she does the welcoming. The classic Gallic bistro food is disarming, dishes like ratatouille and goat cheese, Mediterranean fish soup, *moules marinières, saumon scallopine,* and roasted duck breast. Desserts are all made in-house and are gems, such as *pot de crème au chocolat, perdu aux abricots, crêpes suzette,* and *tarte au pommes Provençal.* Closed Mon.

Chef Luis Restaurant, 129 Elm St., New Canaan; (203) 972-5847; chefluis.net; $$–$$$. In 2012 Chef Luis Lopez doubled

his dining room space and devoted fans quickly filled it. His combination of Italian-plus-Mediterranean dishes reflects his culinary credentials, working in kitchens in France, Greece, and Latin America. As a tribute to some of his famous patrons, he has named several dishes after them. Thus you might order Harry and Jill's atun a la Louisiana (seared tuna, named for Harry Connick and his wife), Lupica's pasta (spaghetti swirled with jumbo shrimp, lobster, garlic, fresh pear tomatoes, and bread crumbs, named for sports columnist Mike Lupica) or Cashman's pasta (tube-like bucatini, white wine, olive oil, imported pecorino cheese, pancetta, and onions, a nod to Brian Cashman, general manager of the New York Yankees).

Coromandel Cuisine of India, 25 Old King's Hwy. North, Darien; (203) 662-1213; coromandelcuisine.com; $$. In recent years Indian restaurants have sprouted all over the state, but Coromandel, in my opinion, outdistances most in its creative variety of south and north Indian dishes. Mirrors, murals, and colored lights create a festive ambience in limited space, while a quieter second room with a bar is only slightly more muted. The best value is the prix-fixe buffet lunch—seven or eight hot dishes, breads, chutneys, salad, and several desserts. As if that isn't plenty, piping-hot naan bread and fresh-baked, mildly spiced tandoori chicken are delivered tableside by a waiter, as part of the prix-fixe buffet largesse. The a la carte dinner menu isn't pricey either, with such pleasures as lamb chops, sizzling hot and well-seasoned Indian-style; *lasi gobi* (spicy fried cauliflower); and a delightful original appetizer, *shamm savera:* tiny spinach cups filled with farm cheese in a tangy honey-edged tomato sauce. Whether you like your Indian food mild, moderate, or incendiary, Jose and Meena Pullopilly and staff are happy to oblige. A second **Coromandel** is at 68 Broad St., Stamford (203-964-1010). This location is larger, roomier, and well decked out in Indian accoutrements. A second floor is available for parties. The regular menu is similar to the original Coromandel's, and the warm welcome from Matthew Poovathanical and staff is equally friendly. A third **Coromandel** is at 185 Boston Post Rd., Orange (203-795-9055). At **Coromandel Bistro,** 86 Washington St., South Norwalk (203-852-1213), the clientele is younger and more hip, as expected in South Norwalk. The newest **Coromandel** is at 17 Pease Ave., Southport (203-259-1213).

Dressing Room, 27 Powers Ct., Westport; (203) 226-1114; dressingroomrestaurant.com; $$–$$$. This extremely attractive space next to the Westport Country Playhouse first drew the attention of the late actor Paul Newman and experienced chef Michel Nishan. With Newman's encouragement, Chef Nishan fulfilled his dream of "a homegrown restaurant" that combines the freshest ingredients with creative cooking. Voila! Dressing Room was born. It thrives now in a faux-rustic setting, with a roaring fire in the stone fireplace (in chilly weather) and high-ceilinged, post-and-beam construction in the main dining room. Chef Nishan's dedication to farm-to-table fresh-grown, natural ingredients, mostly locally grown, is manifest in such dishes as tempura mushroom-stuffed squash blossoms, shaved fennel and peach slaw, pan-roasted trout, and homey desserts, such as chocolate bread pudding and sticky toffee pudding. Closed Mon and at lunchtime Tues.

Elm, 73 Elm St., New Canaan; (203) 920-4994; elmrestaurant.com; $$$. Chef-Owner Brian Lewis, who once partnered with Richard Gere at Gere's inn across the state line in Bedford, New York, now has his own restaurant in New Canaan—for dinner only and Sunday brunch. The decor is deceptively simple, with a starkly modern dining room and a separate barroom with a long pewter bar and cosy semicircular booths. The food, exuberantly creative and highly original, swings, from starters, such as "roots, shoots, fruits and leaves" salad, Hudson foie gras, and crunchy big-eye tuna, to entrees, such as Georges Bank sea scallops, Muscovy duck, and lobster spaghetti *alla chitarra,* and such desserts as chocolate bread pudding and chocolate *pot de crème.* Expect to pay a premium—but the food is often memorable.

Eos Greek Cuisine, 490 Summer St., Stamford; (203) 569-6250; eosgreekcuisine.com; $$. Upscale authentic Greek restaurants are hard to find in Connecticut. Eos is one and it's a pure delight, from the bas-relief of a wave along one white wall to the menu of Greek

TERRIFIC TUSCAN TRIO

Hardly a week goes by that an Italian restaurant doesn't open up somewhere in the state. These are three of my northern Italian favorites in Fairfield County.

Cava Wine Bar and Restaurant, 2 Forest St., New Canaan; (203) 966-6946; cavawinebar.com; $$. In a well-lighted version of a wine cellar, complete with rough-textured stone walls, two brothers, Vicente and Kleber Siquenza, from Equador, and their chef sister, Nube Rivera, produce some gastronomic masterpieces. The brothers are wine experts; the sister creates such scrumptious dishes as tortellini stuffed with roasted butternut squash, risotto with duck confit and diced green Granny Smith apples, squash blossoms stuffed with ricotta, grilled Montauk calamari, and grilled crab cakes, all beautifully presented. Cava's gnocchi is pure ambrosia, as is the lemon tart for dessert. The extensive wine list emphasizes regional vintages from Tuscany, Piedmont, and the Veneto. While dinner can be noisy, lunch is usually a quiet affair, good for conversation along with delicious pastas and salads. In warm weather, there's outdoor dining in front. Scena Wine Bar & Restaurant, under the same ownership, is at 1077 Post Rd., Darien (203-662-3226); $$. It too is Italian and very good, but I give the edge to Cava. The owners have another place in Fairfield: 55° Wine Bar and Restaurant, 55 Miller St., Fairfield (203-256-0099; 55winebar.com; $$$).

Cesco's Trattoria, Goodwives Shopping Center, 25 Old Kings Hwy., Darien; (203) 202-9985; cescostrattoria.com; $$–$$$. In quietly elegant surroundings—one wall lined with small mirrors, another with family photographs—this Italian restaurant mostly travels via the menu through the Veneto and northern Italy, where Chef-Owner Aldo Chiamulera is from. Pastas are big here, with spaghetti alle vongole (best clams I've had in years) and *trofi con pesto* among the most memorable. But Chef Aldo is equally skilled with dishes like pan-seared branzino and veal *osso buco.* He serves a tray of four special salts to add if you so choose. Closed Mon.

Da Pietro, 36 Riverside Ave., Westport; (203) 454-1213; dapietros .com; $$–$$$. "Isn't It Romantic?" That song pops into my mind every time I enter Da Pietro's cozy 22-seat French–Northern Italian restaurant. The friendly ambience is contagious, and the food, under the auspices of Chef-Owner Pietro Scotti, can be addictive, whether it's the mussels Posillipo, *ris de veau braisés,* or *canard aux Baies* (duck in a wild cherry and Calvados sauce). Check out the excellent prix-fixe dinner: three courses and coffee offered Mon through Thurs. Closed Sun.

specialties. The only drawback: It's noisy, noisy, noisy. The goodies range from delicious *mezedes,* or starters, such as *imam bayaldi* (baby eggplant), to a gooey custardy dessert called *galaktoboureko*. I could make a meal of appetizers alone, such as spanakopita (phyllo spinach pie), *loukaniko* (grilled pork sausage), *keftedes* (Greek meatballs), and *saganaki* (grilled cheese flambéed). But then I'd miss the grilled salmon, moussaka, and char-grilled baby lamb chops.

Gabriele's Italian Steakhouse, 35 Church St., Greenwich; (203) 622-4223; gabrielesofgreenwich.com; $$$. You want power dining? You want to see how the 1 percent dine out and entertain? You'll find it at this handsome steak house, named for its owner, Danny Gabriele. The setting is dark, the tables are well spaced, and the staff is helpful and genial. The meat is marvelous—porterhouse, Wagyu flatiron, aged prime beef, and many other prime cuts—and so are the accoutrements, such as sides of creamed spinach, mascarpone mashed potatoes, mini *burrata,* mac and cheese. Portions are generous—and so are the prices. You'll quickly see why this is such a hedge-fund favorite. Everything is top quality. Open for dinner only.

Il Palio, 5 Corporate Dr., Shelton; (203) 944-0770; ilpalioct .com; $$. Il Palio's two expensively outfitted dining rooms, with fireplaces, exposed wood ceilings, and polished wood floors, are handsome backdrops for some expert, mostly Tuscan, cooking, now the handiwork of Margherita Aloi, formerly of Aloi in New Canaan. She knows what she is doing in such pasta dishes as *lasagna alla Bolognese antica, linguine con vongole, ravioli di melanzone* (eggplant, roasted pepper, and mozzarella-stuffed ravioli in fresh tomato fondu), and *fettuccine con scampi*. Other memorable dishes are the *osso buco, risotto del giorno,* and luscious desserts, such as *riso dolce* (pistachio-studded rice pudding), vanilla crème brûlée, and tiramisu. The menu changes seasonally. Closed Sun and for lunch Sat.

Lao Sze Chuan, 1585 Boston Post Rd. (US 1), Milford; (203) 783-0558; $$. Chinese restaurants are ubiquitous in Connecticut; good ones—not so much. That's why it's a pleasure to come upon this Sichuan gem hiding in plain sight on the Post Road. As is often the case in some of the better, more authentic Chinese restaurants, decor is secondary to the food. ("Beware the gilded dragons!" is my motto.) The regional Sichuan cooking is bona fide, visible in such dishes as braised pork shank, sautéed lamb with cumin and onion, braised spicy tofu and pork, and lobster Sichuan. More conventional but tasty are the sweet potato pancakes, Nanjing-style steamed salted duck, and prawns in oyster sauce with mushrooms and bok choy. If you're feeling adventurous, give the braised pigs' ears a try or even the more outré ox tongue and tripe. For most of us the fiery Sichuan cooking—in a dish like wild-pepper chicken—is adventurous enough. Beer and wine are available too.

Little Thai Kitchen, 4 West Ave., Darien; (203) 662-0038; little thaikitchen.com; $$. Small in size, huge in hot, spicy Thai flavors, this taste of Thailand in Darien is welcome to all lovers of Siamese food. Dishes like the clear hot soups, *larb* (ground beef dusted in toasted rice powder) salad, *plar goong* salad, *sambal* chicken, and various curries are spot-on. Brave the noise and concentrate on the delicious food. A quieter version of the same restaurant is in Greenwich at 21 St. Roch Ave. (203-622-2972). The same owners also have **Little Buddha** located at 2270 Summer St., Stamford (203-356-9166). It features Thai, Chinese, and Asian fusion cooking in an even smaller space, just opposite the Ridgeway Shopping Plaza.

Lolita Cucina and Tequila Bar, 230 Mill St., Greenwich; (203) 813-3555; lolitamexican.com; $$. It's party time and that means a lively, festive dinner at Lolita's. Even the decor, with the crimson glass chandeliers, say "party." Groups of 30- and 40-somethings seem to agree, as the place jumps with loud conversation and even louder music. Despite the cacophony, the food is very good. Note especially the crispy masa oysters, spinach-and-cheese quesadillas, ancho-chile chicken, shrimp ajillo, and garlic-lime chicken. There's a full bar, but the stars are the 50 different tequila cocktails and sangria by the glass or pitcher. While the many tasty small plates are a definite option, entrees are great too. Dinner only. Reservations are taken only for six or more.

Match, 98 Washington St., South Norwalk; (203) 852-1088; match sono.com; $$. In warm weather the entire front wall of Match opens to the street, with the first row of tables putting you within touching distance of the crowds passing along the sidewalk. No matter what the season, co-owners Matthew Storch and Scott Beck take a hands-on approach to ensure that the food is first-rate. Pastas, wood-fired chicken, seared tuna, and luscious desserts are all memorable. Befitting the South Norwalk locale, the atmosphere at Match is casual, but the food is always thoughtfully prepared. On weekends this area is a vibrant scene, and that liveliness can be contagious. Storch and other partners have opened a second restaurant in Fairfield called **The Chelsea** (p. 58).

Matsuri, 390 Post Rd., Darien; (203) 655-4999; $$. Amiable, efficient service is a hallmark of this high-speed Japanese restaurant. Its star performers are sushi and sashimi, which are so fresh they fairly sparkle. There are other dishes, both traditional Japanese and Asian fusion ones, including Vietnamese spring rolls, Indian pancake, and pan-seared Chilean sea bass. The *nigiri, maki,* and rolls are so fresh and appealing, they make me want to visit Matsuri on a regular basis for my sushi fix.

Morello Bistro, 253 Greenwich Ave., Greenwich; (203) 661-3443; morellobistro.com; $$–$$$. Probably my favorite restaurant space in all Connecticut, the interior, designed by Rafael Guastavino Jr. in the early 20th century, is heavenly, with its all-tiled interior and rounded arches, high ceilings, and two levels. Alas, the golden amber tiling invented by Señor Guastavino, a Catalan architect, has been painted over or stained to a dark brown, thus erasing much of the magic from this landmark space. Nevertheless, the northern Italian food is very good indeed. *Fonduta di formaggi, hamachi crudo, tagliatelle verde,* spinach ravioli, rack of lamb, and a slew of luscious desserts are just a few of the delights on a seasonally changing menu.

Napa & Co., Stamford Marriott, 75 Broad St., Stamford; (203) 353-3319; napaandcompany.com; $$$. While located at the edge of the Marriott, Napa & Co. is not connected to the hotel. The space is relatively compact and can be noisy, but the natural, modern American food is worth it. A new chef, Leonardo Marino, brings his own special flair to a place long on flair already. I love all the extra touches, like the small plate dishes (such as foraged-mushroom risotto or duck and foie gras meatballs) for tiny appetites, the thoughtful choices in the excellent cheese plate with a variety of American and European cheeses, and an intriguing selection of fresh-brewed teas (not bags). Co-owner Mary Schaffer is a knowledgeable sommelier; her 350-bottle wine selection is impeccable. Specific wines are suggested for each entree, such as a Huia Gewürztraminer from New Zealand paired with wild black sea bass (with artichoke-porcini marmalade and polenta). See Chef Leonardo Marino's recipe for **Slow Baked Halibut, Stuffed Artichokes, Barigoule Broth, and Truffle Butter** on p. 401.

Ondine, 69 Pembroke Rd. (Rte. 37), Danbury; (203) 746-4900; ondinerestaurant.com; $$. Like a real trouper, Chef-Owner Dieter Thiel continues to make Ondine *the* local place to go for first-rate French food in French country inn surroundings, at very reasonable prices. It is possible to order a la carte, but Ondine's prix-fixe menu is an even better bargain: five courses (soup, salad, a choice from among 10 appetizers, 10 entrees, and 10 desserts) and coffee or tea—all at a price some restaurants charge for two courses alone. Such dishes as *confit de canard, billi-bi,* black seabass with artichoke heart ravioli, sea scallops poached in white wine, hazelnut soufflé, and tarte tatin complement tables dressed with fresh flowers, candles, and Staffordshire china and comfortable, padded plush chairs. In its handsomely appointed, two-tiered dining room, Ondine offers *haute* dining at *bas* prices. It's enough to make you hum "La Marseillaise." Dinner only, but open for dinner all afternoon Sun. Closed Mon and Tues.

Pontos Taverna, 7 Isaac St., Norwalk; (203) 354-7024; pontostaverna.com; $. *Hospitable* is the key word in this simple storefront decorated with a few Greek artifacts. Owned by Nikolaos Kiriakidis, it is run by him, his seven siblings, his father, and his mother. The atmosphere is as warm, welcoming, and homey as the food, which has an authentic flair, with big portions and small prices. Dolmas, wonderfully tender lamb chops, souvlaki, *saganaki,* gyros, and other authentic Greek dishes are all available, as well as moderately priced Greek wines. All that and it's just half a block from the Garden, the local art movie theater.

Rebeccas, 265 Glenville Rd., Greenwich; (203) 532-9270; rkateliers .com; $$$. Reza Khorshidi and Rebecca Kirhoffer, a husband-and-wife culinary team, have made Rebeccas elegant without being rarefied, mastering the art of turning less into more. In a cool and minimalist decor, each dish speaks of the finest ingredients. Every detail is exquisite and nuanced, from, say, salmon gravlox with wild rice blinis or asparagus soup with lobster to grilled Dover sole in lemon sauce or *kanpachi* sashimi with wasabi dressing, followed perhaps by pear tarte tatin or a selection of artisanal cheeses. Service is as seamless as the entire meal and the well-chosen wine list. Closed Sun and Mon.

The Restaurant at Rowayton Seafood, Rowayton Avenue, Rowayton; (203) 866-4488; rowaytonseafood.com; $$. In tight quarters facing the boats moored at Cavanaugh's Marina, this no-frills restaurant turns out some mighty fresh seafood. No wonder! It is owned by the adjacent fresh-seafood store of the same name. The raw bar features local bluepoint oysters and others from Maine and British Columbia. You might also spear the deep-fried Ipswich clams and oysters, steamed or broiled lobsters, or grilled or pan-roasted fish. The lobster rolls, copiously packed with fresh chunks of tender lobster, celery, and onions lashed together with mayonnaise, are popular at lunch. In warm weather the deck overlooking Five Mile River is the place to be, but deck seating is first-come, first-served, no reservations.

Roger Sherman Inn, 195 Oenoke Ridge, New Canaan; (203) 966-4541; rogershermaninn.com; $$$. This landmark inn looks old-fashioned and traditional, but the food, modern American (with a French accent), makes it an "inn" place to be. In any of five intimate dining rooms, you can enjoy such dishes a s lobster ravioli, pan-seared Arctic char, wild mushroom fricassee, sweetbreads with lemon and capers, wild striped bass, and desserts like warm apple-cheddar bread pudding, Grand Marnier soufflé, or pear upside-down cake. Professional service and a decibel level conducive to conversation are further elements in what is a splendid dining experience. While the main dining room has a cheerful mien, with a wall of windows, historic paintings along two walls, and well-spaced tables, I'm partial to the smaller room down a few steps with Tiffany windows and a fireplace lined with Dutch tiles. In summer the place to dine is the old-fashioned porch, where if you're lucky, you can view the moon. Closed Mon and at lunchtime Sat.

Sails American Grill, 148 Rowayton Ave., Rowayton; (203) 853-7245; sailsamericangrill.com; $$. Sails replaced River Cat Grill, one of my favorite casual restaurants, and I like this new one just as well, especially in winter when its wood fire is blazing away. Sails offers modern American food that is fresh, light, and creative. Consider truffle mac and cheese or house-made gnocchi or Maine clam bellies to start, then as an entree roasted Amish chicken breast, or black sesame-crusted tuna or perhaps a grilled shrimp salad. If you

WATER VIEWS—
A FAIRFIELD COUNTY RARITY

Surprisingly, despite its Long Island Sound shoreline, Fairfield County has relatively few scenic, upscale waterfront restaurants. L'Escale at the Delamar Hotel is a lovely exception at 500 Steamboat Rd., Greenwich (203-661-4600; lescalerestaurant.com; $$$). Its dining terrace, with its own raw bar, overlooks Indian Harbor and is nose to nose with many yachts. The stylish indoor dining room is so pretty and relatively quiet—with hand-crafted metal candelabra, fireplace, area rugs over handmade tile floors, and backlighted cabinets—an exterior view isn't really necessary, in spite of a wall of windows. The food has always been memorable, but Frederic Kieffer, a chef of distinction, has recently joined the staff as executive chef. The food, whether you dine inside or out, more than matches the ambience, and Chef Kieffer adds his fondness for provençale cooking, with dishes such as saffron mussels soup, golden gazpacho, pan-seared foie gras, *fromage de Chevre et artichauts crus,* roasted jumbo prawns, L'Escale bouillabaisse, baby squid *a la plancha*, and grilled lamb chop. Such desserts as quince and apple tart, semisweet chocolate tart, and black-and-white soufflé are as memorable as L'Escale's serenity. No wonder couples, foursomes, corporate diners, and those who prefer conversation to deafening "buzz" flock here.

have room for dessert, salty turtle or warm chocolate ooze cake are yummy options. Popular for lunch and dinner, Sails is the kind of casual, neighborhood place I'd like to have around the corner. Only Rowayton is so lucky. There's live music Sat evenings after 10 p.m. when the bar and compact dining room really rock. In warm weather you might eat outside in the small fenced-in patio facing the road. Closed Mon.

Sal e Pepe, 97 South Main St., Newtown; (203) 426-0805; sale peperestaurant.com; $$. From the outside, this tidy place looks like just another Italian restaurant in a small strip mall. Inside, it is a model of neatness and decorum, good service, and surprisingly nice food. I think you'll like the goat cheese fritters, steamed Manila clams, pear and beet salad, roasted pistachio-encrusted salmon, and pork chop al Gorgonzola. The desserts are tasty too, especially the Nutella mousse pie with Oreo cookie crust.

The Schoolhouse at Cannondale, 34 Cannon Rd., Wilton; (203) 834-9816; theschoolhouseatcannondale.com. I can't think of a better way of going back to school than to visit this charming cafe in an old restored one-room country schoolhouse. With banquettes facing each other on two sides of the simple schoolroom, you can concentrate on a very good farm-to-table menu. The food is carefully prepared and creative, and the servers couldn't be more gracious and helpful. If any of these dishes are on the menu, do not hesitate, they are all worthy: corn and littleneck chowder, pork three ways, seared Long Island duck breast, or fillet of beef. Sunday brunch is especially satisfying here, a really relaxed affair. The brunch eats are good too: housemade vanilla granola (with pecans, yogurt, and berries), crisp-edged French-roasted brioche (with berries and maple syrup), and smoked salmon Benedict. Closed Mon and Tues.

Splash, 260 Compo Rd. South, Westport; (203) 454-7798; decaro restaurantgroup.com; $$$. Splash, located at town-owned Longshore Country Club, has the same ownership as **Baang Cafe & Bar** (p. 74) in Riverside. Splash's Pacific Rim menu is different and the dining room, with its stylized 3-D "wave" wall mural, has an even higher decibel level. In warm weather it's best to arrive early enough to sit on the deck (no reservations taken for the deck) with a water's-edge view of Long Island Sound. Otherwise you'll need a megaphone to be heard by your tablemates. The deck is open until late fall, with heaters at the ready to reduce the chill. The food is very good indeed—creative and original, especially dishes like crackling calamari salad, green salad with goat cheese dumplings, five-spiced grilled chicken, and maple-glazed organic salmon. Sunday brunch is wildly popular with locals.

Spotted Horse Tavern, 26 Church Ln., Westport; (203) 557-9393; spottedhorsect.com; $$. I love the homey, casual tavernesque decor of this new restaurant, which was built on a spot once occupied by an 1808 historic local landmark. The house was a teardown, but the suggestion of a vintage tavern remains. Inside, blow-up photos of horse heads are appealing—if you are into horses. You can also sit outside in warm weather. More interesting to me is the short menu which features some terrific dishes, like Crispy Point Judith calamari, Gray Goose cobb salad (taste and textural contrasts), and Sichuan shrimp and calamari (sweet and spicy). The steamed Maine mussels were the best I've had in years—fat, sassy, and full of salty flavor. I'd also go with the grilled pork chop, marinated in Dr Pepper soda of all things, as tender and flavorful as pork can be. Most desserts are from **Chocopologie Cafe** (p. 64) in South Norwalk, and thus guaranteed to be luscious. The horseshoe-shaped bar in a separate room is a lively scene as well.

Strada 18, 18 Washington St., South Norwalk; (203) 853-4546; strada18.com; $$. In a long storefront made attractive by an exposed brick wall, simple decor, and good lighting, this lively restaurant is guided by David Raymer, co-owner and creative chef. His deft touch produces such pleasures as orecchiette with sausage, roasted chicken *diavolo,* lamb shank, house-made mozzarella, and desserts, such as strawberry-rhubarb crumble, flourless chocolate cake, and a remarkable black-pepper biscotti. His sorbets (especially the white peach) and gelatos (even his experimental one made with Guinness) are inspired. David and his partners have recently opened **Boulevard 18** (p. 77) in New Canaan.

Ten Twenty Post, 1020 Post Rd., Darien; (203) 655-1020; ten twentypost.com; $$. Some places are just plain fun. That describes Ten Twenty Post to a double T. Its *fin de siècle* decor, bouncy brasserie atomosphere, and homey menu are suited to snacks or a full meal—with so many tempting items you could choose a dozen or more in an eye blink. Since this place is owned by the same group that owns **Elm Street Oyster House** (p. 26) in Greenwich, it is no coincidence that Ten Twenty Post has lots of well-prepared seafood. I'm partial to the baked and pan-fried oysters, fried belly clams, the *moules* dishes, and grilled Atlantic salmon. Don't shortchange such land choices as duck confit, braised short ribs, or bistro steak. There is something tasty for everybody—almost guaranteed.

Terrain Garden Cafe, 561 Post Rd. East, Westport; (203) 226-2750; shopterrain.com/westport-restaurant; $$–$$$. For restaurant dining, the closest thing to eating in a garden may well be lunching or dining at the Garden Cafe in Terrain, an upscale gardening supply center. In warm weather the brick-lined patio is the place of choice, where big beach umbrellas shield you from the sun and you are surrounded by a small waterfall and potted plants (all for sale). Inside, large palms and ferns add to a garden environment that is augmented by the farm-to-table menu that changes weekly. The food, generally, is fabulously fresh and tasty, notably the veal sweet-breads, gnocchi with beach mushrooms, and pork belly sticky bun. There are a few cutesy touches, like bell glass canning jars used for water and clay pots used as repositories for warm rolls. Never mind. The food is good and the background props—plants and gardening paraphernalia—are fabulous. Closed for dinner Sun and Mon. Best to check ahead.

Thomas Henkelmann at Homestead Inn, 420 Field Point Rd., Greenwich; (203) 869-7500; thomashenkelmann.com; $$$. Several years ago it might have been difficult to say "who's on first" as deluxe restaurants go. But then Chef Thomas Henkelmann and his wife, Theresa, bought the highly regarded Homestead Inn in Greenwich (even then a mecca for fine dining) and added his name (and prestige) to the mix. The rambling 1799 house and barn with Victorian additions is a stellar dining establishment, where everything is fine-tuned, from the valet parking and cordial, highly polished service to the gracious surroundings and superb French cuisine. There are two main dining rooms, the larger with fireplace, wood posts, and exposed wood-beamed ceilings (great in winter), the other intimate and snug. A third dining area is a glass-enclosed porch, ideal in summer, with views of the lawn and formal gardens. Staffers are attentive without hovering. The same attention is paid to the food, as you will discover in dishes like trio of Hudson Valley duck foie gras, cannelloni of Maryland crabmeat, tenderloin of veal wrapped in prosciutto, Dover sole with artichoke chips and truffled mashed potatoes, loin of venison with bow-tie pasta gratin, and sautéed foie gras. An exceptional wine list matches the seasonal menu. You might even spend the night in one of the inn's 18 handsomely furnished guest rooms. It is no coincidence that a place this special is affiliated with the esteemed Relais & Châteaux group. Closed Sun and Mon.

Tinto Bar Tapas, 10 Wall St., Norwalk; (203) 866-8800; meigasrestaurant.com; $$. Ethnic restaurants come and go, but this bewitching one, on the ground floor of a restored trolley barn, has long been a reliable source of delicious Spanish food. Regulars may know that Tinto was formerly Meigas. But a major renovation, a new name, and a new menu concept are proof that a Meigas by any other name is still a refreshingly agreeable Spanish restaurant. The whole place has been enlarged, with the second, more private dining room now open and part of one large dining area. The decor is new and jazzy, with emphasis on a huge bar with 20 bar stools and high tables seating 25. All in all, Tinto seats around 150 people. Tapas is more than part of the name, it's the major game. There are at least 35 tapas or small plates on the menu—such as *escabeche de atún, ensalada de jamón, piquillo rellenos*—plus only a few entrees. Owner Carlos Hernandez has a second restaurant called **Solun Bar & Tapas** at 245 Amity Rd., Woodbridge (203-298-9741).

Tuscany, 1084 Madison Ave., Bridgeport; (203) 331-9884; iliketuscany.com; $$. This bustling, convivial storefront restaurant is full of surprises. First, in addition to the starters listed on the short menu, seven appetizers are brought to your table on a large tray so you may choose. Then a second tray of nine uncooked, house-made pasta samples is presented, as your waiter describes the dishes with which they will be served. The unusual visual presentation

Row Row Row Your Boat— or Watch Others Rowing

Westport has its share of Saugatuck River views. Here are two of my favorites.

River House Tavern, 299 Riverside Ave., Westport; (203) 226-5532; riverhousewestport.com; $$$. There's nothing fancy about this riverside retreat. It's bright, airy, and decidedly not tavern-esque. Inside, big windows let you watch the scullers rowing past on the Saugatuck River. On the airy deck, bordered with summer flowers and shaded by umbrellas, you feel even closer to the water. Some of the tavern culinary pleasures are the River House chowder, chilled tomato-jalapeño soup, seared diver scallops, fried Ipswich clams, and desserts, such as warm blueberry peach crumb pie and pineapple upside down cake. Reservations recommended.

The Boathouse at Saugatuck, 521 Riverside Ave., Westport; (203) 227-3399; saugatuckrowing.com; $$. If you expect to find standard alpha-male type food in a boathouse restaurant, look again. The food is far more interesting and creative than that. You might eat on the open deck overlooking the dock and marina on the Saugatuck River or inside watching the river action from a wall of five big windows in a quasi-rustic room, with beautiful oak-teak floors whose wood is like that on a boat deck. Whichever place you choose, you might be munching on roasted oysters, sautéed mussels, grilled market-fresh fish, chilled Montauk lobster salad, or any number of intriguing pasta dishes. Located in the private Saugatuck Rowing Club, the restaurant, thankfully, is open to the public. Closed Sun and Mon. Reservations advised on weekends.

The Talented Mr. Taibe

Connecticut has been a magnet for some terrific chefs in recent years and one of the best is certainly Bill Taibe. He first came to my attention when he owned the late Relish in South Norwalk. He then starred at Napa & Co., and now he has not just one but two restaurants of his own, both in Westport. See Bill's recipe for Crab Fondue on p. 388.

Le Farm, 256 Post Rd. East, Westport; (203) 557-3701; lefarmwest port.com; $$. This restaurant came first, a real locavore place, with farm-fresh almost everything. With the freshest natural ingredients, Bill shows his considerable creativity, in such dishes as hamachi crudo, griddled Hudson Valley foie gras, tagliatelle white Bolognese, and ricotta gnocchi with braised pork and mushrooms. The menu changes almost nightly, so you might miss Bill's skate-wing "day boat," lightly cooked and surrounded by fried capers,

is only topped by the high quality of the food itself. The specials menu changes daily. Risotto with asparagus and shrimp, and grilled polenta with wild mushrooms and melted Gorgonzola are just two of many delightful dishes you may encounter. Closed Mon.

ZaZa, 122 Broad St., Stamford; (203) 348-2300; zazagastrobar .com; $. The name ZaZa suggests fun and excitement, and this ZaZa, trumpet mushrooms, and a heavenly celery-root puree, or the chef's ricotta gnocchi, as ethereal as snow flakes, served with braised pork with mushrooms in a subtle tomato gravy. Closed Sun and Mon. Reservations are essential as Le Farm is tiny.

The Whelk, 575 Riverside Ave., Westport; (203) 557-0902; thewhelk westport.com; $$. This dinner-only location opened in 2012. Situated just above the Saugatuck River (but without a direct view of it), the Whelk has the feel of a seaside seafood shack, but more stylish, with large harbor lights mounted above the long bar and a banquette of slatted picnic chairs and shabby-chic benches, though it is much more substantial than that. The food is inspired, from a luscious peeky-toed crab fondue to brown butter shad roe (in season), griddled octopus, roasted Copps Island oysters and whole blackback flounder in lobster butter with caviar. Even the shucked local oysters are special—four different types: Chatham petites, rock nook, northern cross, and Wellfleet. Check out the interesting wine list as well. Closed Sun and Mon.

a gastro pub, doesn't disappoint. The best place to eat in warm weather is the open terrace in the rear (shielded from a public parking lot by an evergreen hedge). It is convivial without being deafening. I love the wide variety of small plates. Order a bunch for a meal in itself. Creamy lobster polenta, baby lamb chops, spicy calamari, risotto, grilled asparagus, gnocchi pesto, Atlantic roasted salmon, Margherita and California pizzas—the small plates are so varied and tasty that I don't have to choose among a limited number of favorites. And with a couple of companions sharing, I can have them all. The entrees are good too—roasted salmon, *linguine Mediterraneo bianco,* and Mediterranean branzino for instance—and don't forget the desserts, such as the flourless chocolate cake.

Brewpubs & Craft Breweries

The Brewhouse, 13 Marshall St., Norwalk; (203) 853-9110; sono brewhouse.com. This large facility was once a first-rate brewery, and the tanks and brewing equipment still haunt the premises. But now the Brewhouse is simply a restaurant, serving regular pub-grub food and lots of different craft brew products, from California, Massachusetts, Missouri, Vermont, and Maine. Known for its exuberant and humongous Sunday brunch, it is so popular it has two seatings, at 11 a.m. and 1 p.m. Happy Hour is Mon through Fri, from 5 to 7 p.m.

Cavalry Brewing, 115 Hurley Rd., Building 9A, Oxford; (203) 262-6075; cavalrybrewing.com. Mike McCreary, formerly executive officer with the Second Armoured Cavalry Regiment in Iraq (in 2003), is now, since 2010, this small brewery's owner-brewer. He learned his brewing skills at the source: breweries in northern England. He imports such British ingredients as Maris Otter malt and Fuggles hops and adjusts local water to a gypsum level like that of Burton-on-Trent, source of Bass Ale. The results, in this industrial park facility, are four flavorful ales: Dog Soldier Golden Ale (mildly sweet), Marauder India Pale Ale (hints of apricot and peach), Nomad Stout (a roasty flavor), and Hatch Plug Ale (an amber, hinting of nutty, toasted malt). Tours are available by appointment, though the brewing plant is compact, making tours necessarily brief. Free samples are available and half-gallon growlers are for sale.

Half Full Brewery, 43 Homestead Ave., Stamford; (203) 309-2821; halffullbrewery.com. This is yet another of Connecticut's new breweries (as of Nov 2012); its primary product is Bright Ale. Golden in color, with a floral hop aroma and crisp, clean palate, Bright Ale is targeted to imported beer drinkers. "It's not one of those beers that is super bitter or intimidating, that blows people away," says Conor Horrigan, founder of the brewery, "but it's got an amazing nose on it and great flavor." Among Half Full's other products are a dry stout and a couple of India Pale Ales. For tastes and half-gallon growler purchases, the brewery is open for tours most Sat and occasional Fri afternoons.

Monster B's Bar & Grille, 489 Glenbrook Rd., Stamford; (203) 355-1032; monsterbs.com; $. Beer for what ales you? Try this congenial bar-cum-pub. While neither a brewpub nor a brewery, Monster B's is worthy of your attention (and worth including in this section) for it's 30 beers and ales on tap. It's an awesome assortment—more than 150 bottled beers from craft breweries in many states and countries around the globe. (Belgian choices number more than 20 brands.) If imbibing doesn't keep you busy, there are darts and pool.

There's pub grub too, of course, with assorted burgers, sandwiches, salads, a few entrees, a locally famous chili, and even a kiddie menu. And in warm weather you can—and should—do your imbibing on the outdoor deck.

New England Brewing Company, 7 Selden St., Woodbridge; (203) 387-2222; newenglandbrewing.com. Rob Leonard, a well-respected brewmaster in the trade, runs the show at this microbrewery, which opened in 2001. The year-round products are a widely praised Atlantic Amber, Sea Hag IPA, and Elm City Lager. Other specialty brews are made from time to time throughout the year.

SBC Downtown Restaurant Brewery, 131 Summer St., Stamford; (203) 327-2337; sbcrestaurants.com; $$. This offshoot of **Southport Brewing Company** (see below) opened its cavernous faux-industrial quarters in 2001. The stacks of barley-malt sacks and gleaming fermenters near the entrance suggest that SBC takes beer seriously. Co-owners William and Mark da Silva (brewer) and Dave Ruligliano (executive chef) had 5 years of success at Southport Brewing Company before expanding here. Slightly sweet, somewhat spicy Stamford Red is one of the more complex-tasting house beers. Request sample tastes of others (27 in all, with about 8 available at any given time), such as Rippowam Lager, One Way IPA, and Bull's Head English Pale Ale. Chef Ruligliano presides over the menus at Southport's and all the SBC kitchens, with tasty hanger steak, crunchy "brew fries," and assorted pizzas as reliable menu items. Thursday is Karaoke Night, and Sunday evening is "family time" (with a magician). There are now three additional **SBC locations,** with similar brews, menus, hours, and entertainment: 850 West Main St., Branford (203-481-2739); 33 New Haven Ave., Milford (203-874-2337); and 1950 Dixwell Ave., Hamden (203-288-4677).

Southport Brewing Co., 2600 Post Rd., Southport; (203) 256-BEER; sbcrestaurants.com; $$. A loyal clientele has been enjoying the brews and food here since it opened in 1997. Once past the copper-clad beer tanks by the entrance, you are in a large restaurant-cum-brewery where a wide range of estery, ethereal ales are made. Your best bet is a sampler assortment. Fifteen beers on tap range from the refreshing Bones Light to nearly opaque, espresso-like Black Rock Stout and Fairfield Red, an award-winning deep amber. Seasonals include Old Blue Eyes blueberry ale, Mill Hill Pilsner, and SouthToberfest. Southport's strengths are in the three P's: pints, pizzas, and porterhouse steaks. The kitchen was voted best brewery-restaurant in the state in several recent surveys. Early-evening and late-night happy hours on weekdays keep this convivial place humming, with schedule and hours the same as at all the SBC locations (see **SBC Downtown Restaurant Brewery,** above).

Tigin Irish Pub, 175 Bedford St., Stamford; (203) 353-8444; tigin irishpub.com; $. Tigin is the real deal, an authentic Irish pub, not a brewery, not a brewpub. Its interior was actually brought over from the old country. Cozy rooms and alcoves, gas fireplaces, a dartboard, even a traditional Irish snug, where women can drink facing, but sheltered from, the bar, are all part of Tigin's charm. Eight Irish brews on tap, nine more in bottles, plus eight Irish whiskeys and Fado Irish Coffee are all here. A hearty Irish breakfast is available from 11:30 a.m. all day, as well as a more varied menu than the usual pub grub. Tuesday night there's a pub quiz at 8 p.m. On the first Thursday of the month, the Irish Band entertains live. Soccer maniacs aren't the only fans of this old-fashioned snuggery pubbery.

Two Roads Brewing Company, 1700 Stratford Ave., Stratford; (203) 355-2010; tworoadsbrewing.com. With Phil Markowski as partner and brewmaster, this brand-new brewery would seem to have it made. As head brewer at **New England Brewing Company** (pp. 106, 328) back in 1989, when it was still in Norwalk, Phil created the wonderfully refreshing Atlantic Amber, which went on to win many awards. After a long stint at Southampton Publick House, where he won an additional 20 or so medals for his beers, Phil returned to his roots in Connecticut. At Two Roads Brewing, he is in charge of a 100-barrel brewhouse, where he makes Road to Ruin, a double IPA., a dry-hopped Pilsner called Ole Factory, a Belgian-style *saison,* and sundry seasonals. Overlooking the entire operation is a spacious mezzanine-level taproom, where most of Two Roads' suds may be sampled.

Wine Trail

The Connecticut Wine Trail shows where the state's wineries are located, the best roads to reach them, and important information about each area (hours for tastings, tours, picnicking, nearby points of interest). In Fairfield County and southwest Connecticut, DiGrazia, Jones, and McLaughlin are the wineries included on the trail. Visit ctwine.com to print out a map.

DiGrazia Vineyards, 131 Tower Rd., Brookfield; (203) 775-1616; digrazia.com. Paul and Barbara DiGrazia founded their winery in 1978 with four types of wine. They sell over 15 different wines, based on homegrown French vinifera hybrid grapes, plus inventive combinations of fruit and flavors, and have garnered gold, silver, and bronze medals for their efforts. Their strong suits, in my view, are their dessert wines, such as Winterberry (grape, black currant, and raspberry), Autumn Spice (white grapes, pumpkin, and spice), and two popular new combinations: Wild Blue (blueberry and brandy) and Paragran (pear and pomegranate). The tasting room and gift shop are inside a low-slung contemporary building festooned with fresh garden flowers. There's a picnic area on the arbored patio. Tours are daily from May through Dec and Sat and Sun from Jan through Apr. Group tours can be arranged with advance notice.

Jones Winery, 266 Israel Hill Rd., Shelton; (203) 929-8425; jones familyfarms.com. Having studied viniculture at Cornell University, Jamie Jones, the sixth generation of Jones in the family farm, and his wife, Christiana, worked for more than 5 years to turn about 5 acres of the family's 400-acre farm into a viable winery. Jamie's grapes now yield some smooth wines. They include Heritage Barn

$$–$$$. A marriage of French and Japanese, Nuage (as in New Age) offers the best of two culinary traditions, with seafood the specialty in this serene place. Nuage's decor is as subtle as its food, the latter being exemplified by such lovely dishes as black cod with miso; monkfish pâté with sesame miso, caviar, and scallion; and rock shrimp tempura with a creamy-spicy sauce. Appetizers are so outstanding I usually make a meal of them, ordering two instead of an entree. Prices at Nuage can be rarefied, but so is the dining experience.

Tengda Asian Bistro, Goodwives Shopping Center, 25 Old Kings Hwy. North, Darien; (203) 656-1688; asianbistrogroup.com; $$. The word *tengda* means prosperity, which seems to suit this large, almost cavernous space. There's a good sushi bar in the rear, with 28 types of sushi and 14 special rolls. I'm just as partial to the various pan-Asian dishes on the menu, notably Thai crab cake, crispy calamari salad, spicy mango chicken, Tengda curried seafood hot pot, and Szechuan crispy peppercorn chicken. There are three other Tengdas in Connecticut, but in my view the Darien one is tops. The others: The original Tengda, 1330 Post Rd. East, Westport (203-255-6115); the second Tengda (more a combo of Asian and European), 21 Field Point Rd., Greenwich (203-625-5338); and a third, Tengda Asian Bistro and Hibachi, 1676 Boston Post Rd., Milford (203-877-8888).

Red, a dry European-style Ripton Red, and Woodlands White (a bestseller), with a sweet crispness. For all-out wine-plus-fruit flavor, Jamie then adds (as appropriate) apples, pears, black currants, strawberries, blueberries, and/or raspberries in Dawn's First Blush, Harvest Time, Strawberry Splendor, Blueberry Bliss, and Raspberry Rhapsody. Call for the days and hours that the vineyard is open. There is a homey, rustic tasting room, which Christiana manages, in an old barn, alongside a small shop selling wine-related gift items. Among many events at the farm and vineyard are a Nutmegger Cheese and Wine Festival in late Sept and a farmers' market every Fri. in season. Check the website for other events and farm suppers.

McLaughlin Vineyards, 14 Albert's Hill Rd., Sandy Hook; (203) 426-1533; mclaughlinvineyards.com. Bruce McLaughlin is the president and winemaker at the 15-acre vineyard that is part of a beautiful 160-acre farm property his family bought in the 1940s. This Housatonic River Valley estate produces 60 percent of the fruit for their Chardonnay, Merlot, Cabernet Sauvignon, and Riesling and contracts for the rest. Blue Coyote, a blend of Vidal and Aurora, is the vineyard's most popular wine. Also pleasing is Snow Goose, a blend of whites. In Feb and Mar you can watch maple syrup being made in the sugarhouse, ride a tractor, cross-country ski, and hike the trails. In summer you might order in advance a catered picnic basket and lunch alfresco on the grounds. From the end of May through Oct, there are jazz and bluegrass concerts (call for details). New England food products—jams, salad dressings, McLaughlin's own maple syrup, local honey, and wines—are for sale in the country store, an adjunct of the tasting room, which is open during the Sun music series. Gift certificates are available. Closed Mon and Tues from Feb through June 1. Winery tours are by appointment only.

Northwest Connecticut

This corner of Connecticut includes Litchfield County, long known as a weekend escape hatch for the rich and famous—the likes of Meryl Streep, Kevin Bacon, other actors, fashionistas, and politicos like Henry Kissinger—who come not to be seen but to avoid being seen. It is no wonder that people in pressure-cooker jobs gravitate here. It is a beautiful land of undulating hills; placid lakes, such as Waramaug (which is surrounded by several delightful country inns); and the meandering Housatonic and Farmington Rivers. Trout streams and wooded nature preserves, such as the White Memorial Foundation & Conservation Center, with its 35 miles of hiking and cross-country ski trails just outside Litchfield, round out the picture of this halcyon terrain.

Litchfield the town is a treasure of another kind, with a much-admired Village Green and wide carriageways lined with imposing 18th-century clapboard houses. Don't be deceived: The village may

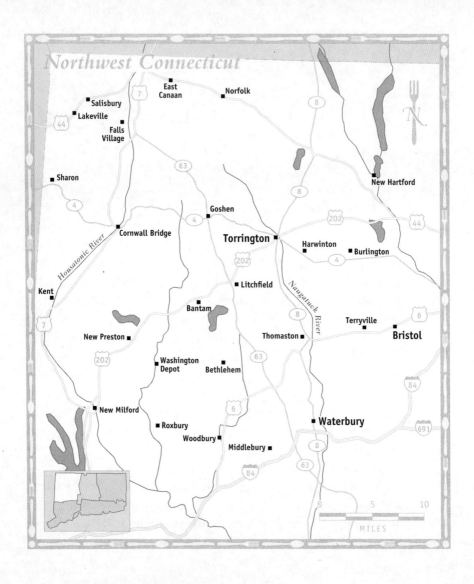

Northwest Connecticut

Salisbury
Lakeville
Falls Village
East Canaan
Norfolk
Sharon
New Hartford
Goshen
Cornwall Bridge
Torrington
Harwinton
Burlington
Kent
Litchfield
Bantam
Terryville
New Preston
Thomaston
Bristol
Washington Depot
Bethlehem
New Milford
Roxbury
Woodbury
Middlebury
Waterbury

Housatonic River
Naugatuck River

MILES
5
10

N

look drowsy, but it has one of the area's most sophisticated restaurants and a European gourmet food shop with home-baked German and Dutch breads and pastries. As in so much of this area, pastoral beauty is cosseted with urban comforts.

This is a landscape studded with secluded country estates and postcard-pretty villages, such as Salisbury, Lakeville, and Sharon, with steepled churches, scenic greens, and historic town halls. The sleepy town of Woodbury is an antiquer's idea of heaven with many antiques shops tucked into vintage houses along the town's mile-long thoroughfare. The street also boasts several fine restaurants and one of the state's most complete natural food markets. Kent's main street is bordered by art galleries; craft shops and boutiques with clothing, ethnic jewelry, and artifacts; a bakery; a chocolatier; and other specialty food stores and cafes as you might expect in such a bustling art center. No wonder New Yorkers flock there on summer weekends.

The region is also a patchwork quilt of farmlands, with some local farms still worked by descendants of the families that started them in the 1700s. Generations have raised cattle, sheep, and pigs; planted maple trees for sugar; and cultivated fruits and vegetables. Many still sell their produce at old-fashioned roadside farm stands, often operating on the honor system. The woods and backroads offer wide-angle vistas of hillsides dappled with old orchards and new vineyards. A surprising number of independent food entrepreneurs—butchers, bakers, candlestick makers, and producers of smoked meats and game, cakes and candy, ice cream, chocolates, cheese—have their homes and workshops here, in villages and hamlets tucked among wildflower meadows, woods, and fields. You will find them in these pages.

This tranquil area appeals to many people as much for what it lacks as for what it has: no superhighways, casinos, blinking neons, huge resort hotels, ubiquitous advertising signs, an excess of strip malls, fast-fooderies, chain hotels, or theme parks. These omissions are seen as positives by those who live or weekend here. Such residents are a motley crew: high-powered New York executives; novelists; musicians; actors; nature lovers; sportsmen who fish, canoe, and go tubing on the Housatonic; balloonists soaring high above Mohawk Mountain; hikers of the Appalachian Trail or the summit of Mount Tom near Bantam or Bear Mountain (Connecticut's highest peak), just outside Salisbury. Whether sportsmen or stage stars, artists, artisans, diplomats, or CEOs, they all have chosen this north-by-northwest area for its restful pleasures. One of these pleasures is good food, which everyone's taste buds can appreciate.

The Naugatuck River is a natural border between Litchfield and Hartford counties that leaves Waterbury and Bristol, both east of the river, in a kind of no-man's-land, so I have arbitrarily included both of them here.

Bantam Bread Company, 853 Bantam Rd. (Rte. 202), Bantam; (860) 567-2737; bantombread.com. In the rear lower level of an old clapboard house is a little bakery where Niles Golvon (with helpers) makes and sells his fresh-from-the-oven breads. The aromas are so intoxicating I can rarely leave without liberating a loaf of Kalamata-olive sourdough. Other compelling choices include sunny flax sourdough, semolina, baker's white, caraway rye, French white, wheat-free whole spelt, and holiday fruit and nut. There are five kinds of pound cake, ricotta cheesecake, and five cookie varieties as well. Certain breads are baked only on specific days of the week, like Irish soda bread on Thurs, sourdough raisin bread Thurs and Sat, and challah on Fri. Niles's tarts—like the latticed berry and fresh peach—are equally seductive, with wonderfully crisp and flaky crusts. In limited display space, jams, vinaigrettes, maple syrup, **Bridgewater Chocolate** (p. 15) chocolates, and imported pastas are also sold. Closed Mon and Tues.

Collinsville Baking Company, 8 Wicket St., Pine Meadow; (860) 238-7691; collinsvillebaking.com. When you visit this neat, tidy shop, which is situated in a colorless industrial park, and see the rows and rows of breads stacked on racks, you'll never believe that man can't live by bread alone. There are so many breads here— ciabattas, rye, country French, whole wheat, semolina, six-grain, baguettes, bagels, bialys—you name it, they bake it. They also bake scones, oversize cookies, eight or more types of biscotti, tarts, torts, almond horns, cream puffs, and other pastries. Then, for a change of pace, they serve soups, made from scratch (black bean, carrot ginger bisque, and lentil, among others), and spreads and dips, which they serve at a handful of tables and overstuffed chairs. Closed Mon and Tues.

Fascia's Chocolates, 2066 Thomaston Ave.; Industrial Commons Park, Waterbury; (203) 753-0515 or (877) 807-1717; fasciaschoco lates.com. Loyal fans swear by the hand-dipped, homemade chocolates that John Fascia; his wife, Helen; and their family have been making since 1964, when John worked as a toolmaker and made chocolates in his spare time. Fascia's produces over 50 types of chocolates and numerous combinations: boxed chocolates, gift baskets, molded holiday specialties (Santas, Easter bunnies, and so forth), assorted chocolate truffles, cream centers, caramels, toffees, buttercrunch, and chocolate pretzels. Corporate gifts are a big part of the business. Fascia's ships all over the US, but if you're in the neighborhood, you might drop by the factory showroom. Popular favorites are the pecan turtles, gourmet truffles, and chocolates with double-dip cordial cherries. Among 23 retail outlets, Elizabeth Richards Gifts, 951 Chase Pkwy, Waterbury (203-754-4438), has the full product line.

The Gracious Gourmet, PO Box 218, Bridgewater, 08807; (860) 350-1214; thegraciousgourmet.com. Here are the goodies produced by this busy entrepeneur: two chutneys (dried fruit and mango pineapple), eight spreads (among them, fig almond, balsamic four onion, tropical fruit, passion fruit mango, rosemary pear, and spiced sour cherry), eight tapenades (among them, dilled carrot tomato, artichoke Parmesan, fennel blood orange, chile red pepper, black olive, and portobello mushroom), and four pestos (such as garden tomato and lemon artichoke chile). They are all available on the website and in some area stores.

La Palette Bakery Cafe Gallery, 49 DeForest St., Watertown; (860) 945-3336; lapalettebakery.com. No mixes are used in the scrumptious baked goods produced in this small bakery cafe. The Gallic influence is strong in the flaky croissants; the firm, moist scones; the crusty baguette; the round loaves of foccacia; and the single-servings of quiches. The glass display cases reveal tarts, cakes, pies, chocolate-enveloped éclairs, luscious cream puffs, assorted cookies, and four flavors of biscotti. The principal baker is Carlos Perez (a co-owner with his mother, Debra). Carlos learned his considerable skills at the French Culinary Institute (now the International Culinary Center). Also made in-house are the Belgian-style chocolates: pralines, espresso bark, and milk and dark chocolates. See **La Palette Bakery Cafe Gallery** on p. 149 for information about the cafe. Closed Mon.

Lombardi's Bakery, 177 East Main St., Torrington; (860) 489-4766. This homegrown bakery has been a local fixture since 1978, turning out cookies by the platter and the piece, as well as fruitcakes, éclairs, napoleons, tiramisus, and all kinds of pastries, including Hungarian *kolache*. My favorites are the heavenly, cloud-like almond macaroons. Breads are another Lombardi specialty, even fresh pizza dough. Closed Mon. Cash or checks only.

Matthews 1812 House, 250 Kent Rd. (Rte. 7), Cornwall Bridge; (860) 672-0149 or (800) 662-1812; matthews1812house.com. What began in 1979 in the kitchen of Deanna Matthews's 1812 farmhouse with a few brandied apricots and fruit-nut cakes is now a flourishing line of cakes, candies, cookies, and dessert sauces and toppings, sold via the website and catalog (165,000 printed each year) and in a compact shop on the factory grounds. Fresh, all-natural ingredients are used, and everything is hand baked. New products are added regularly, like the lemon-rum-sunshine cake and shortbreads with currants, orange, and a "sparkle" of sugar. My favorites are the marzipan cake and shortbreads. A good way to get acquainted with the line is the 1812 Cake Sampler of four loaf cakes (country spice, chocolate-raspberry liqueur, chocolate rum, and lemon-rum sunshine) or the Cookies Deluxe tin (53 cookies, 8 different types).

Nodine's Smokehouse, 39 North St. (Rte. 63), Goshen; (860) 491-4009; nodinesmokehouse.com. You name it, Nodine's (pronounced no dine) probably smokes it: sausages (venison, chorizo, kielbasa, beef, maple, chicken with sun-dried tomatoes or with green peppercorns), whole game (Cornish game hen, pheasant, turkey, goose, duck, chicken), fish (bluefish, mackerel, trout, salmon), meats (pork and beef), and various Cajun-spiced items (andouille sausage, tasso ham, Bayou bacon), as well as New England cured ham, available in spiral cut and boneless. Then there are the smoked cheeses (cheddar, provolone, Gruyère, Swiss, Pepper Jack). In business since 1969, Johanne and Ronald Nodine and their son, Calvin, sell to shops and restaurants throughout Connecticut and New York City. A modest shop, inside an old dairy barn on the 10-acre property, is crammed with smoked goods, New England–made crackers, jams, and jellies. People stop by for fresh-made soup, sandwiches with as many trimmings as a delicatessen, and giant homemade cookies (delicious!). The beef barbecue on a sesame-seeded bun is really smoky and flavorful. Smoking was originally done in the barn, but now it's done in Torrington. Factory tours can be arranged by calling (860) 489-3213. For ordering, the entire product line is listed on the website and in a mail-order catalog. Some items are also available at retail outlets, such as **O'Rourke's Diner** (p. 221) in Middletown and **Bishop's Orchards Farm Market and Winery** (p. 280) in Guilford.

Savor Fine Foods, 30 Echo Lake Rd., Waterbury; (860) 274-9000; savorfinefoods.com. Andre Kreft has been making unusual cookies and biscuits, sweet and savory, since 2010. He sells them wholesale, on his website, at farmers' markets, and in select cafes and shops, such as **Terrain Garden Cafe** (p. 98) in Westport, **Darien Cheese & Fine Foods** (p. 30) in Darien, and the **Smithy** (p. 133) in New Preston. He makes some 36,000 a week, which he sells in 8-ounce bags. Among Andre's gems: coconut ginger, Krakatoa (chocolate, cardomom, orange, and black pepper), lavender, black olive (from Moroccan olives), olive and orange, roasted leek, nicasia (rosemary, lemon, and smoked sea salt), seasonal smoked red onion and smoked yellow onion. Two new ones are Naugatuck (made with birch extract, maple syrup, and candied cranberries) and Doris Day (organic, made with fennel, candied ginger, and orange). His best-seller is Firefly, a hot pepper cookie. Orders are shipped via UPS and have a 6-week shelf life.

Sweet Maria's, 159 Manor Ave., Waterbury; (203) 755-3804 or (888) 755-4099; sweet-marias.com. As a teenager, Maria Bruscino Sanchez worked in a neighborhood bakery. After college, she moon-lighted from her advertising job—literally—to bake cakes at night. Since 1990, she has been fulfilling a childhood dream, whipping up delicious cakes and cookies in her own well-named bakery, whose motto is "More than just another pretty cake." Her huge repertoire includes layer, loaf, tea, carrot, amaretto apple, birthday, and wed-ding cakes; cheesecakes; apricot, strawberry, and pineapple mousse cakes; and special creations, such as Maria's Booze Crooze (yellow cake with rum, coconut, and pineapple). Fan favorites are Fluffernut-ters, magic cookie bars, peanut butter balls, anginetti (lemon-drop cookies) and biscotti in six flavors. A new cake, Maria's favorite, is the toasted almond cake. Custom cakes can be special ordered.

Maria's also sells, via her website and mail order, loaf and Bundt cakes, 15 different cookie types (including the award-winning pignoli and chocolate almond),  and her five cookbooks. The bakery has a petite cafe with five tables for on-the-spot nibbling. Closed Mon. See Maria's recipe for **Sweet Maria's Chunkey Monkey Cake** on p. 415.

Sweet Sunshine Gourmet Conveniences, 457 Bantam Rd., Litchfield; (860) 567-3529; sweetsunshine.com. In 1998, in honor of their Louisiana-born father, Paul and Van Sarris developed a line of chili sauces, which they call Sweet Sunshine, described as "flavor before fire." There are now six all-natural Sweet Sunshine sauces, labeled upward by heat level as sweet, warm, roasted shallot and garlic, Jamaican jerk, hot, and atomic. Sold to restaurants and online, the various sauces have won numerous awards in a number of food shows.

Waldingfield Farm, Washington Depot; (860) 868-7270; waldingfieldfarm.com. As the leading grower of organic heirloom tomatoes in the state, Patrick Horan, one of the owners, thought it was probably natural to take the next step: bottling sauces from the farm's "seconds," which are first in flavor, but slightly blemished in looks. The tomatoes are processed and bottled in New Haven. There are now three products: Heirloom Tomato Sauce, the Farmer's Marinara, and the Farmer's Bloody Mary mix. They are sold at various farmers' markets and independent groceries.

Winding Drive Jams & Jellies, 744 Main St. South, Middle Quarter Unit 95, Woodbury; (203) 263-6961; windingdrive.com. Fran Adams and Ron Pinto, a dynamic husband-wife team, founded this specialty business in 2008 and have been going full speed ahead ever since. In 2012 they won several awards at the annual Connecticut Specialty Food Association show, including one for their roasted garlic and onion jam. They sell their artisan jams, jellies, and marmalades—made from locally grown, preservatives-free fruit—to such stores as **Bantam Bread Company** (p. 117), **Whistle Stop Muffin Company** (p. 69), **Holmberg Orchards** (p. 282), **Nodine's Smokehouse** (p. 120), **Carole Peck's Good News Cafe** (p. 155), and **Wave Hill Bread & Cafe** (pp. 28, 68).

Specialty Stores & Markets

Artisan Food Store, 760 Main St. South, Southbury; (203) 262-9390; artisanmade-ne.com. This artisan-friendly shop, owned by Tom and Sally Camm, has been open since 2003. There are 112 artisan cheeses, from Maine to Virginia (including Connecticut, of course); handcrafted chocolates; all kinds of jams, jellies, sauces, condiments, sourdough breads, coffees, and teas; and many all-natural products. Closed Mon.

Avventura, 72 America St., Waterbury; (203) 574-1274; avventura deli.com. This started as a run-of-the-mill neighborhood grocery, but Rosario Minnocci bought it in 1990 and turned it into a first-rate delicatessen and in-house pastry shop.

Rosario and his wife, Lucy, now have an expanded salad bar and a pastry chef who daily turns out delicious cookies, cannoli, ricotta zeppoli, éclairs, *sfogliatelle,* and some 18 different pastry treats. The deli pro- 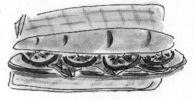 duces sandwiches, wraps, panini, hot and cold grinders, and a host of to-go items like corned beef and cabbage, stuffed shells Florentine, *soffrito,* numerous eggplant-based dishes, and even a few Mexican specialties. The salad bar offers house-made items too. Also house-made are breads stuffed with mozzarella and pepperoni or broccoli rabe or spinach. Closed Sun.

The Dutch Epicure Shop, 491 Bantam Rd. (Rte. 202), Litchfield; (860) 567-5586; dutchepicure.com. German-born pastry chef Wolfgang Joas and his Dutch wife, Betsy, immigrated to the US in 1967 and took over a simple Dutch bakery. With their daughter, Wilma, they have made it a gallimaufry of Dutch and German treats, all baked by Wilma or Wolfgang: cakes; 25 types of cookies; breads; seasonal specialties, such as New Year's Eve Berliner; Easter eggs filled with house-made truffles; Christmas stollen and Dutch chocolate letters; and German-style pretzels. Wilma also makes chocolate mice and chocolate-covered marzipan. This well-stocked shop disperses eight different kinds of Gouda, Dutch hard goat cheese, other Dutch and European cheeses, sausages and meats (supplied by a

German butcher in New Jersey), jams, jellies, Dutch licorice, condiments, *stroopwafels, speculaas* spice cookies, *pannekoeken* mixes, Indonesian sambals, spices, seasonings, ingredients for *rijsttafel,* and Indian mixes and curries. A freezer bulges with house-made soups, casseroles, chicken potpies, quiches, and *spaetzle.* Among nonfood items are Delftware, German soaps, and 4711 cologne. Closed Mon and Tues. If you can't make it to Litchfield, you can place an order on the website.

Flour Garden Bakery, 107 Main St. North, Woodbury; (203) 263-7355. In 2000 owners Linda Gajevski and Bob Gotta began making vegan cookies for Wesleyan University. They have since graduated to all kinds of French and Viennese treats, all made from scratch with butter, not lard. There are breads too—pumpernickel, multigrain, and lots more—but they play second fiddle to dazzling displays of Linzer tortes, biscotti, almond macaroons, Danish (cherry or cheese), and croissants, plus cookies galore (sugar, shortbread, palmiers) and colorfully decorated layer cakes (whipped cream, butter cream, chocolate, coconut, mocha, and carrot). There are also tarts, such as English lemon, raspberry crumb, frangipane, and Alsatian plum, and variations offered for vegan, sugar-free, and gluten-free diets. There are rich, flaky pie crusts, too, cradles for strawberry-rhubarb and seasonal fillings, mostly made from fruits grown locally. Allow 3 business days for special orders.

Harney & Sons Fine Teas, 1 Railroad Plaza, Millerton, New York (on Rte. 44); (518) 789-2121 (shop) or (800) 832-8463 (factory, for a catalog); harney.com. The Harneys have been selling tea since 1983. They outgrew their space in Salisbury and are now just across the state line in Millerton, New York, 2 miles from Lakeville, in an 1879 smokehouse. Even though Harney & Sons is now out of state, it has such strong Connecticut ties and identity that it *must* be included here. In addition to wholesale, mail-order, and Internet business, with teas shipped all over the world, this handsome shop/tasting room, with its wide pine floorboards, retails Harney teas and tea samplers, as well as tea-related items, such as teapots, cozies, tea strainers, and Harney's book about tea. Sample several of the 200-plus varieties of tea in smart black canisters with gold labels that line the shelves and cabinets. Among the selections are black, green, white (including a delicate Winter White Earl Grey), organic, herbal, decaffeinated, floral, holiday, sachet, and art teas. Also for sale are English scone mixes, shortbreads, honey, and crispy Brittany crepes, among many upscale products. You don't have to be a tea lover to enjoy a visit to Harney's, which now has a small restaurant that serves lunch as well as afternoon tea. Tours of the factory require an appointment.

Hunt Hill Farm Trust, 44 Upland Rd., New Milford; (860) 355-0300 or (800) 353-SILO; hunthillfarmtrust.org. The largest section of this interesting store, which is part of Ruth and the late Skitch Henderson's Silo Farm, is devoted to high-end culinary tools, pots, pans, casserole dishes, cookware, glassware, utensils, linens, and other accoutrements. There is a section in which nonperishable Connecticut-made food products are sold, such as honey, maple syrup, jams, raspberry-wasabi dipping mustard, olives, condiments, gift baskets, and the farm's own Silo Salt. Despite its remote location, the store and its notable cooking school, the **Silo Cooking School at Hunt Hill Farm** (p. 153), have been going strong since 1972. Store items can also be purchased on the Hunt Hill Farm website. Hours change with the seasons, so it is best to call ahead.

The Kent Coffee & Chocolate Company, 8 Main St., Kent; (860) 927-1445 or (800) 927-4465; kentcoffeeandchocolate.com. More than the life-size, overstuffed, black gorilla positioned near the entrance, the heady aromas of chocolate and coffee have lured passersby to this shop/cafe since Sandra Champlain opened it in 1991. We can't think of a bet-ter place to stop for a cup of coffee, tea, or cocoa, while visiting the area's many art galleries. Many of Kent's chocolates are house-made—like the chocolate bark and the chocolates in 16 different flavors. Most popular are the hand-dipped truffles, pecan turtles, and chocolate-dipped pretzels. Kent's thick, old-fashioned fudge comes in six seductive flavors, including chocolate peanut butter, penuche, mudslide fudge, and Heath bar fudge. There are also organic and raw chocolate products. Coffee is a big deal here, too, with Arabica beans imported from Sumatra, Kenya, Colombia, Costa Rica, Guatamala, and elsewhere, roasted in small batches for maximum flavor and aroma. Available by mail order and on the website are over 50 coffee blends; 100 teas; 21 chocolate assortments; fudge; and several nicely packaged gift items, such as maple syrup miniatures, King Ludwig's Bavarian nuts, and four types of tea jams. Join the gorilla and sit and sip, or, in summer, carry your iced coffee or frozen cappuccino outdoors to the Board of Directors bench and watch the passing scene.

La Molisana Italian Sausage, 350 Congress Ave., Waterbury; (203) 574-1272; lamolisanasausage.com. When Tullio and Assunta Lupo opened their small store in 1998, they named it after Italy's Moliese region. Their mainstay then—and now—is sausage. They offer a range of Italian sausages, including an unusual dry sausage, *soppressata, coppa,* and garlic pork sausage. The Lupos sell other house-made foods as well—marinated mushrooms and eggplants, meatballs, provolone-stuffed peppers, house-seasoned olives, and two types of panini. Also for sale are various Italian cheeses, anchovies, pastas, cookies, coffee, and other Italian goods, as well as, occasionally, rabbit. Closed Sun.

The Litchfield Candy Company, 245 West St., Litchfield; (860) 567-1500; litchfield-candy.com. Who would ever believe that this little red building could be so full of surprises? But that's the wonder of this small, packed-full-of-candy shop. There's probably every kind of candy ever made—except Hershey bars. Do you remember Bazooka Joe gum, fruit chews, malted milk balls, Mary Janes, Charleston Chews, Jelly Bellies, gummy bears, Sourheads, candy cigarettes and necklaces, and licorice from your childhood? They're all here! Gift baskets spill over with hard candies and chocolates. There are 30 types of licorice—from the Netherlands, Finland, Sweden, even Australia—also gift boxes of marzipan, chocolates from Belgium and elsewhere, truffles, turtles, toffees, and pralines. Elmer Odell opened the shop in 2004 and obviously enjoys every inch of it, as do I.

The Monastic Art Shop, at the Abbey of Regina Laudis, 273 Flanders Rd., Bethlehem; (203) 266-7727; abbeyofreginalaudis.com. This small shop is on the grounds of a cloistered convent, which is scenically snuggled into the hills. It boasts many products made by the Benedictine community. Sister Noella Marcellino learned cheese making by a French expert. Now the abbey community uses the milk of Dutch belted cows to produce boutique, French-style cheeses and a sharp English-type cheddar, all of which are first-rate. Also in the shop are honey, herbs, vinegar, and hot mustards, along with such noncomestible products as woven and knitted scarves, stoles, and sweaters (all made from abbey sheep wool); cards; books; religious art objects; and compact discs of abbey chants. Closed Wed.

New Morning Natural and Organic Foods, 129 Main St. North, Woodbury; (203) 263-4868; newmorn.com. Shoppers partial to organic and natural foods may be awestruck, as I was on my first visit, by the magnitude of this family-owned supermarket. The store recently moved and now has 7,500 square feet of display space. I can't think of anything that's missing. John Pittari Jr., who founded the business almost 40 years ago, has fresh fruits and vegetables, chicken, fish, cereals, breads, virtually every kind of packaged natural-food product along with herbs and spices, teas, soy and organic milk and cheeses, and packaged frozen meals (vegetarian and organic) all here. There are bins with beans and lentils (including black turtle beans, adzuki, and black-eyed cowpeas), dried fruits, nuts (including five different types of cashews), seeds (flax, brown sesame, and Hungarian pumpkin among them), a large organic produce section, rice, couscous, hulled barley, quinoa, whole wheat, and organic coffees, even farm-fresh eggs. Help yourself to fresh soup from three huge cauldrons in a small soup corner. A deli case displays take-out salads, salmon cakes, and other entrees, and there is a catering department as well. Vegetarian, vegan, natural, and organic choices are many. You can order your Thanksgiving turkey days in advance and other game too, with notice. This store is definitely worth a visit. Call for available game and to place orders.

Nine Main Bakery & Deli, 9 Main St., New Preston; (860) 868-1879. Just off New Preston's town center, Nine Main is a welcome addition to this part of the Litchfield Hills landscape. The inspiration of owner Liz Johnson, the tidy shop, with its mere five tables, is so immaculate it glistens. Salads, sandwiches, and two soups are available daily. Cookies, scones, and muffins are oven-fresh from the kitchen. The muffins come in 27 flavors—lemon raspberry, blueberry, banana, peanut butter, and butterscotch pecan among them. Cakes made to order are also available. There is a small selection of Connecticut-made preserves, chutneys, and salsas for sale, as well as artwork by local artists.

The Pantry, 5 Titus Rd., Washington Depot; (860) 868-0258; $$. Since it opened in 1977, the Pantry has been a meeting place for locals, who congregate for lunch, coffee, snacks, and specialty food shopping. Michael and Nancy Ackerman bought the business in 1986 and have maintained amazing consistency in this delightful gourmet food shop and cafe. The seating for 35 is surrounded by racks and shelves chockablock with packaged delicacies; herbs; spices; various olive oils; mustards; jams; and goodies, such as chocolates from **Bridgewater Chocolate** (p. 15), chocolate lace, marzipan, and truffles; as well as European pottery; baskets; Le Creuset pots; and other high-end culinary supplies. A refrigerated display case features English, French, and regional artisanal US cheeses. People come from miles away to enjoy the baked ham and other made-to-order sandwiches, fresh-baked breads, muffins, and mouthwatering pastries, all prepared on the premises. The Pantry also does catering and has a snappy take-out business, with salads, entrees, and sandwiches to go. Closed Sun and Mon.

The Smithy, 10 Main St., New Preston; (860) 868-9003; the smithystore.com. In the center of New Preston, in a vintage, neatly restored blacksmith shop, Howard Rosenfeld sells food products made within a radius of 70 miles of his store. This means ice cream from the Big Dipper in Prospect, fresh veggies from the **Stone Wall Dairy Farm** (p. 143) in Cornwall Bridge, and a myriad of other food items grown locally and regionally. Closed Tues.

Farmers' Markets

For up-to-the-minute information about dates and times, call the Connecticut Department of Agriculture at (860) 713-2503, visit its website at state.ct.us/doag, or e-mail ctdeptag@po.state.ct.us.

Bantam Farmers' Market, Bantam Borough Hall, Rte. 202, Bantam. Sat from 8:30 a.m. to noon, May through Oct.

Bristol Farmers' Market, 99 Farmington Ave., Bristol; (860) 583-5700. Wed from 3 to 6 p.m. and Sat from 10 a.m. to 1 p.m., early July through Oct.

Burlington Farmers' Market, 268 Spielman Hwy., Burlington. Fri from 3 to 6 p.m., early July through Oct.

Cornwall Farmers' Market, Wish House lawn, West Cornwall. Sat from 9 a.m. to 12:30 p.m., June through Oct.

Kent Farmers' Market, Kent Green, Kent. Sat from 9 a.m. to noon, mid-May through Oct.

Litchfield Hills Farm-Fresh Farmers' Market, Center School parking lot, 125 West St., Litchfield; litchfieldhillsfarmfresh-ct.org. Sat from 10 a.m. to 1 p.m., June through mid-Oct. Winter market: Litchfield Community Center, 421 Bantam Rd., Litchfield. Sat from 10 a.m. to 1 p.m., Nov through May.

Middlebury Farmers' Market, Middlebury Senior Center, 1172 Whittemore Rd., Middlebury. Tues from 10:30 a.m. to noon, end of June through Oct.

Morris Farmers' Market, Morris Senior Center, Morris. Wed from 10:30 a.m. to noon, July through Oct.

New Hartford Farmers' Market, Pine Meadow Green, Rte. 44 and Church Street, New Hartford. Fri from 4 to 7 p.m., end of May through early Oct.

New Milford Farmers' Market, Town Green, 1 Main St., New Milford. Sat from 9 a.m. to noon, mid-May through mid-Nov.

Norfolk Farmers' Market, in front of Town Hall, 19 Maple Ave. Norfolk. Sat from 10 a.m. to 1 p.m., mid-May through mid-Oct.

Riverton Farmers' Market, Riverton Center (Rte. 20), Riverton. Sun from 11 a.m. to 2 p.m., late June through late Sept.

Southbury Farmers' Market, Southbury Town Hall, 501 Main St. South, Southbury. Thurs from 2 to 6 p.m., mid-June through mid-Oct.

Thomaston Farmers' Market, Seth Thomas Park, 100 South Main St., Thomaston. Thurs from 2:30 to 6 p.m., early July through Oct.

Torrington Farmers' Market, Torrington Library parking lot, corner of South Main and New Litchfield Streets, Torrington; (860) 485-0815. Tues from 3 to 6 p.m. and Sat from 10 a.m. to 1 p.m., early June through Oct.

Waterbury on the Green Farmers' Market, downtown Green, West Main Street, Waterbury. Thurs from 10 a.m. to 2 p.m. early July through Oct.

Waterbury-Mall Farmers' Market II, west parking lot, Brass City Mall, Waterbury. Thurs 2 to 5 p.m., mid-July through Sept.

Waterbury–South End Farmers' Market, Washington Park House, Sylvan Avenue, Waterbury. Tues from 2 to 5 p.m., early July through Oct.

Watertown Farmers' Market, Watertown Library parking lot, 470 Main St., Watertown. Sat from 9 a.m. to 1 p.m., mid-July through Sept.

Winsted Farmers' Market, East End Park, Winsted. Fri from 4 to 7 p.m., early July through mid-Sept.

Woodbury Farmers' Market, Hollow Park, 43 Hollow Rd., Woodbury. Wed from 3 to 6 p.m., from mid-July through Sept.

Farm Stands

Averill Farm, 250 Calhoun St., Washington; (860) 868-2777; averillfarm.com. The Averill family has farmed these 260 hilltop acres since 1746, with some holdings obtained from Chief Waramaug. The house dates back to 1830, the barn to the early 1800s. Sam and Susan Averill took over the farm in 1990, and now their son, Tyson, the family's 10th generation, is helping out. In their 27-acre orchard the Averills grow many apple varieties and 12 types of pears, most available for picking your own. The Averill farm stand also stocks honey, fresh apple cider, apple cider doughnuts, maple syrup, pumpkins, Vermont cheeses, and cut flowers. The stand is open mid-Aug to Thanksgiving. After Thanksgiving, Christmas trees, cider, and some fruits are available at the homestead.

Eagle Wood Farm and Retail Store, 325 New Hartford Rd., Barkhamsted; (860) 379-5978; eaglewoodgourmetfood.com. **Animals** are the "crops" for sale at this unusual farm retail store (not a stand). David Finn, a cabinetmaker in his spare time, raises various breeds of pigs, goats, and cows to produce hormone-free (but not certified organic) meats (including kielbasa, hot dogs, and knockwurst), fed on a vegetarian diet, ready-made for the barbecue grill. Special orders, such as suckling pig, should be placed at least 2 weeks in advance. David also does a steady online business.

Ellsworth Hill Orchard & Berry Farm, 461 Cornwall Bridge Rd. (Rte. 4), Sharon; (860) 364-0025; ellsworthfarm.com. When Michael Bozzi and his family bought this 70-acre farm in 2000, it had 3,000 plum and apple trees (18 varieties, including HoneyCrisp, Gala, Macoun, Northern Spy, Cortland, Empire, Macintosh, Granny Smith, Ida Red, and Golden Delicious), and the Bozzis added blueberries, strawberries, raspberries, cherries, peaches, plums, and Asian pears, an autumn specialty. They also planted Australian pumpkins one year and came up with a pink one that made headlines nationally. June through Nov is pick-your-own time for berries, apples, peaches, pears, cherries, pumpkins, and gourds. In the big farm retail store near the road, you can buy Bozzi's apple cider, unpasteurized and free of preservatiuves; home-baked cider doughnuts; three kinds of fruit pies, muffins, and pastries, as well as all the fresh fruit in season. The Bozzis welcome visitors to roam their fields, explore the 6-acre corn maze (which is keyed to a sheet of crossword-style puzzle clues), and enjoy the woods and views of buildings that date back to the 1700s. Hayrides in Sept are another popular attraction. Open daily June through Nov. Cash only.

Freund's Farm Market and Bakery, Rte. 44, East Canaan; (860) 824-0650; freundsfarmmarket.com. In a huge, barn-red building next to a large greenhouse, Theresa and Matthew Freund sell fruit, vegetables, maple syrup, honey, and cut flowers from the family farm, which includes a 240-cow dairy complex. In a full kitchen on the second floor, Theresa and helpers bake whole-grain breads and baguettes, pies, cakes, cookies, and doughnuts. Pies are a specialty, some two dozen types (even sugar free), and Theresa's bite-size holiday cookies can be ordered in 3-pound assortments on 12-inch dome platters. Also for sale are Theresa's own jellies, salsas, Cabot and McCam cheeses, and Guida ice cream. Freund's catering orders are especially heavy during the Christmas holiday season. "This all started," Matthew says, "back when my mother sold her corn under a maple tree by the side of the road." Closed Jan through Mar.

Lamothe's Sugar House, 89 Stone Rd., Burlington; (860) 675-5043; lamothesugarhouse.com. On 350 leased acres, this working farm has grown from seven taps for maple sugar in 1971 to its current 4,400, making Lamothe's the largest producer in the state. From mid-February through March on Sat and Sun visitors can watch the maple sugar–making process. The country store sells maple sugar products year-round, from soup to nuts, or rather from maple syrup to maple sugar–coated nuts, as well as gift baskets and other gifts and Connecticut-made products. The syrup itself comes in three stages of grade A: light amber, medium amber, and dark amber. Maple products include maple candy, maple cream, maple-walnut caramels, maple sugar, even maple vinegar, barbecue sauce, honey, and jams. Lamothe's wholesales and mail orders its products, too, which can be ordered via their website. As if they aren't busy enough, Robert and Jean Lamothe also raise a dozen or so pigs a year, which should be ordered ahead—half-size or whole hog.

Maple Bank Farm, 57 Church St. (Rte. 317), Roxbury; (860) 354-7038; maplebankfarm.com. This venerable property has been in the Hurlbut family since 1730, when John Hurlbut was granted 6 acres by the king of England. Cows, sheep, and pigs were the first main-stays, but over time, the family added fruit and vegetable crops. Cathy Hurlbut and her husband, Howie Bronson, have been living in the "new" 1830 farmhouse since 1980. The foundation of John Hurlbut's original house lies visible within 100 feet of the current farm stand. Depending on the season, the stand overflows with apples, heirloom tomatoes, potatoes, carrots, garlic, fresh herbs, jams, apple cider, maple syrup, pies, pastries, and breads, as well as other farm products, annuals, perennials, and garden supplies. You can pick your own blueberries in July and August. You can also buy yarn, produced from the farm's sheep. Open March through mid-Dec. Closed Mon.

Maple View Farm, 276 Locust Rd., Harwinton; (860) 485-0815; mapleviewfarmct.com. Mark and Carole Gauger grow a variety of small organic fruits and vegetables, including kale, kohlrabi, peppers, and tomatoes, which they sell at farmers' markets in Torrington, Collinsville, and elsewhere. The farm has been certified organic since 1991. The small farm stand is now located in their garage and operates on the honor system. Select your organic tomatoes, cucumbers, peppers, onions, potatoes, and blueberries and put your payment in the small cash box.

March Farm, 160 Munger Ln., Bethlehem; (203) 266-7721; marchfarms.com. The Marchukaitis family has been farming here since 1915. Tom March, with a shortened surname, is the current patriarch in charge. Harvest season begins in May with salad greens, basil, and greenhouse tomatoes, then continues with blueberries in July, sweet corn and peaches in Aug, and 16 apple varieties, including Ginger Gold, Honey Crisp, Mutsu, Macoun, and Paula Red, in Sept. All (plus pumpkins) are available as pick your own, or, if you prefer, stop by the centrally located farm store (open daily from Apr to just before Christmas), where you will also find honey, jams, jellies, apple products (jelly, salsa, butter, and Dutch apple jam), the cider mill's syrup, and mulled cider. And from March on, Sue March's commercial kitchen turns out pies (including peach praline and strawberry-rhubarb), cookies, and cider doughnuts. A corn maze, after the late summer harvest, remains open until the first snowfall. There is also a hayloft playscape and a pondside animal yard.

Roberts Orchard, 125 Hill St., Bristol; (860) 582-5314; e.ferrier@att.net. An apple a day keeps the doctor away, but if you want more than that, Roberts is happy to oblige—with Macoun, Mcintosh, Cortland, Honey Crisp, Jonagold, Mutsu, and Red Delicious. The Apple House farm store is ensconced in a big red barn, along with the bakery and cider making and storage facility. There you can buy fresh cider (a wall tap enables you to draw your own into a jug), apple butter, apple cakes, mini cider doughnuts (freshly made on Sat and Sun), and apple crumb pies (a specialty), along with fresh apple, cranberry apple, pecan, mince, and pumpkin pies, hot-out-of-the-oven pumpkin bread, honeywheat bread, a variety of homemade muffins, and Roberts's own homemade jams and jellies (made from peaches, raspberries, and other fruit grown on the 70-acre farm). In addition, there are hayrides and a Pumpkin House (open weekends, with a narrated story and life-size characters). Open after Labor Day through Thanksgiving. Custom pie orders, especially for Thanksgiving, should be placed several days in advance.

Rustling Wind Creamery, 148 Canaan Mountain Rd., Falls Village; (860) 824-7084; rustlingwind.com. In a minuscule shop attached to the cheese-making facilities of this 233-acre farm, Joan Lamothe sells—on the honor system—all kinds of home-grown and homemade products. These range from honey, jellies, jams, pickles, relishes, salsas, and maple syrup, to goat's-milk fudge and goat's-milk soap (both from the farm's 30-some goats), to sweaters, scarves, and mittens (from the wool of the farm's resident sheep). Also in the shop are various cow and goat cheeses (which Joan also sells online). The cheeses are available during summer at farmers' markets in Norfolk and Cornwall. Open daily year-round.

Starberry Farm, 81 Kielwasser Rd., Washington Depot; (860) 868-2863; starberry@snet.net. For more than 30 years, Sally and Bob Futh have been leading a fruitful (ahem) existence on their 25-acre farm, growing 18 types of apples and 28 types of peaches, apricots, cherries, and plums. They invite you to pick your own, from cherry time in July through Nov or pick up some of their homemade pies, jams, and jellies. Stop by from June to Thanksgiving (even later if the weather cooperates, but call ahead).

Stone Wall Dairy Farm, 332 Kent Rd. South (Rte. 7), Cornwall Bridge; (860) 672-0261; stonewalldairyfarm.com. Chris Hopkins, aided by leased land from the town of Cornwall, only began raising cows for milk in 2004. Today 20 contented Jerseys, munching on the 120-acre farmland, supply their rich, creamy, raw, unpasturized milk to contented customers and merchants all around the western part of the state. In a section of the big red barn, Chris also sells beef and eggs from his organically raised chickens. Vegetables are raised on the property too, by Jonathan Kirschner, and sold, also on the honor system, at a stand—along with honey, beef, and pork bacon—at the front of the farm. Open year-round; tours arranged by request.

Sullivan Farm, 140 Park Ln. (Rte. 202), New Milford; (860) 354-0047; sullivanfarmnm.org. You want homegrown? You want natural? Think Sullivan's Farm, with its seasonal vegetables, berries, honey, maple syrup, peanuts, jams, jellies, chocolate, maple fudge, and even pickles. Just 3 miles north of New Milford's center, Sullivan's is a 126-acre property, which now belongs to the New Milford Youth Agency; the "farmers" are mostly high school students. There's the Great Brook Sugar House, which has been making syrup the old-fashioned way since 1983. In February or March you might take a tour conducted by a costumed guide, who walks you through 3 centuries of maple syrup making. (You'll spot the sugarhouse by the steam floating skyward from its cupola.) Check the website for dates and hours. The farm stand is open daily in season.

Tonn's Orchard, 270 Preston Rd., Terryville; (860) 675-3707 or (860) 585-1372. Herbert Tonn and his family take their produce to several farmers' markets during the week, splitting time on weekends from Aug through Oct between their 8-acre peach and apple farm and orchard and their in-town fruit stand. You can pick your own on weekends, starting with peaches in July, moving on to 15 apple varieties (including Paula Red and McIntosh) as they ripen from August through October. Meanwhile, Tonn's fruit stand at 418 Milford St., Burlington, sells fresh sweet corn, tomatoes, blueberries, raspberries, and cucumbers daily, from July through October.

Windy Hill Farm, 18 Hillhouse Rd., Goshen; (860) 491-3021. Doug Allen has been cultivating vegetables on his 400-acre farm since 1978, while also maintaining 25 to 30 Herefords that he sells wholesale on the hoof and as feeder cattle. Sweet corn, tomatoes, potatoes, cucumbers, pumpkins, and other veggies are available freshly picked throughout the growing season, from mid-July through mid-October, as well as Doug's own maple syrup and fresh eggs. Call ahead for specific crops.

March

Maple Sugaring Demonstrations, Flanders Nature Center, Flanders Road, Woodbury; (203) 263-3711; flandersnaturecenter.org. Demonstrations at the sugarhouse are usually the first 3 Saturdays in Mar, from 1 to 4 p.m. (followed by a grand finale with pancakes, maple syrup, and fixings), but check the website to be sure.

September

Goshen Fair, Goshen Fairgrounds, 116 Old Middle St. (Rte. 63), Goshen; (860) 491-3655; goshenfair.org. The well-established Goshen Fair, held on Labor Day weekend, has various exhibits of the many farm animals on display. In addition you'll find all the fixin's of an old-time county fair, with live music, a parade, a skillet toss, rides, games of chance, an obstacle course, lots of home-baked food, pie-eating contests, and other competitions, such as steer, rabbit, and poultry judging. Free for children 12 and younger.

Pig Roast at Miranda Vineyard, 42 Ives Rd., Goshen; (860) 491-9906; mirandavineyard.com. This annual pig roast, held in mid-Sept, celebrates the Connecticut Farm-to-Chef program, with great food, live bluegrass music, and other events. The admission fee supports the farm program.

Harvest Celebration, Hopkins Vineyard, 25 Hopkins Rd., Warren; (860) 868-7954; hopkinsvineyard.com. In mid-Sept they whoop it up at Hopkins Vineyard's free-admission harvest fest, with live music; complimentary wine tastings, cheeses, and a wine glass; plus an early-bird discount on cases of wine.

Harvest Festival, Haight-Brown Vineyard, 29 Chestnut Hill, Litchfield; (860) 567-4045; haightvineyards.com. Music, grape-stomping contests, hayrides, wine tastings, a pig roast, and other festivities occur at this fall fete, usually held over 2 days, the third weekend of Sept. Call ahead for the dates and times.

October

Harvest Festival at Miranda Vineyard, 42 Ives Rd., Goshen; (860) 491-9906; mirandavineyard.com. Held in mid-Oct, this annual wine festival offers tastings of local vendors' wares, music, grape stomping, local artists' artworks on exhibit, and a bunch of activities. Admission is free. Call ahead for specific date and times.

December

Gingerbread House Festival, St. George's Episcopal Church, Tucker Hill Road at Rte. 188, Middlebury; (203) 758-2165. This bazaar and fair, run by church volunteers, has been going strong since 1972. A casserole and salad luncheon is served on opening Sat (usually the first one in Dec), and more than 50 gingerbread displays of miniature houses, trees, animals, and people are sold the following Sat, at the end of the weeklong fair. For sale throughout are homemade ginger cookies and such inedibles as handmade knitted scarves, hats, and gloves; wooden decorations; and tree ornaments. All proceeds go to St. George's Episcopal Church. Call for hours.

Nibbles

Chaiwalla, 1 Main St., Salisbury; (860) 435-9758; chaiwalla@snet .net; $. Inside a little clapboard house set back from the road in the center of town, this charming tearoom has been an oasis for breakfast, tiffin, lunch, and leisurely afternoon tea 5 days a week (only Fri, Sat, and Sun in winter) since 1989. Freshly made salads, quiches, and sandwiches are standard offerings, as are the delicious house-made tarts, pies, and cakes, such as whiskey cake, carrot cake, and strawberry-rhubarb cobbler. Oh, do I love this place! You can count on loose-brewed tea here, as owner Mary O'Brien is, like me, a real tea enthusiast. That zeal carries over to a retail and mail-order business, selling fine and rare teas, which she collects from China, Japan, India, Morocco, and elsewhere in the tea-growing world. Among her selections are Sherpa, the Himalayan climbers' tea; five types of Darjeeling; Nilgiri; Terai; China Keemun; several Assams; fine green Kashmir Kawab from North India; and rare white tea. According to Mary, the name Chaiwalla means "tea bearer" in Hindi and Sanskrit. Closed Mon and Tues. See Mary's recipe for **Chaiwalla's Strawberry-Rhubarb Cobbler** on p. 410.

Country Bistro, 10 Academy St., Salisbury; (860) 435-9420; the countrybistro.com; $. With a friendly style, tasty wholesome food, and down-to-earth prices, Country Bistro, operated by mother-daughter team Jacqueline Heriteau and Holly Hunter Stonehill, has a loyal following. It offers an assembly of delicious soups, herb-roasted flank steak on a ciabatta roll, and many other choice lunch platters. The rustic one-room eatery is packed most mornings, when hearty breakfast fare is served, and the brisk business continues all day with nine different sandwiches, lunch platters, and popular take-out supper entrees, such as meatloaf with garlic-mashed potatoes, shepherd's pie, chicken potpie, and layered polenta-beef casserole.

Gilson Cafe/Cinema, 354 Main St., Winsted; (860) 379-5108 or (860) 379-6069; gilson cafecinema.com; $. Movies and munchies are what you'll find at this novel cafe, which isn't adjacent to a movie theater, it is *in* the theater. Small tables are side by side so you can watch the big screen even as you eat. The five-page menu is studded with sandwiches; soups, such as New England clam chowder; cobb and other salads; and pasta dishes, such as cheese tortellini with marinara sauce, all reasonably priced. Waitresses circulate discreetly through the theater while the movie is in progress, filling orders for hot chocolate, cappuccino, carrot cake, Reese's peanut butter pie, tuxedo mousse cake, and even hot-buttered popcorn. There is also a full bar.

The John Bale Book Company Cafe, 158 Grand St., Waterbury; (203) 591-1801; johnbalebooks.com; $. Mother may have admonished you not to read while you're eating. But don't tell that to folks at this two-story antiquarian bookstore. There's a small cafe on the ground floor, where you'll find soups, salads, stews, and sandwiches made-to-order. The bookstore also serves breakfast (muffins, fruit cups, oatmeal, egg sandwiches). There's usually background music, sometimes even a live pianist and on Sat open mike.

La Palette Bakery Cafe Gallery, 49 DeForest St., Watertown; (860) 945-3336; lapalettebakery.com; $. The cafe part of this fabulous French bakery consists of two tables and numerous chairs where you can nibble on specialty sandwiches, such as a Monet (roasted turkey breast, cranberry mayo, house-made stuffing, and cheese), a Da Vinci (like a *croque monsieur,* French-style grilled ham and cheese) or a Van Gogh (chicken, Emmentaler cheese, caramelized onions), sample a fresh-baked fruit tart or a devastating cream puff and sip a cup of coffee. While nibbling, you can enjoy viewing the art on the walls, the work of area artists. Closed Mon.

The Museum Cafe at Mattutuck Museum Arts & History Center, 144 West Main St., Waterbury; (203) 753-2452; mattatuck museum.org; $. For a snack or break from museuming, order a hot panini sandwich, fresh tossed salad, or dessert (or all of the above), then enjoy it/them between museum viewings.

Padre's Mexican Cuisine, 362 Main St., Winsted; (860) 738-3061; $. Adjacent to the **Gilson Cafe** (above), this little hole-in-the-wall, with an L-shaped bar, six stools, and a couple of tables, turns out some tasty Mexican food, such as quesadillas, empanadas (filled with beef, chicken, or veggies), and tamales. Everything but the churros are made on the premises. The bar also makes excellent margaritas. Closed Sun through Tues.

Panini Cafe, 7 Old Barn Rd., Kent; (860) 927-5083; $. James Fox's Panini offers takeout, but also has a few tables where you can play checkers while chomping on a Bronx sandwich (a version of a Reuben with sardines, turkey, cheddar, and avocado), a Rattle-snake (turkey, bacon, andouille sausage, cheddar, and cilantro), Ba-Da-Bing (salami, pepperoni, artichoke hearts, provolone, ham, onion, and green peppers), or one of a dozen other toasted panini sandwiches. You might also savor a soup—there are 30 to 35 on the roster, including gumbos—salad, or gelato, such as hazelnut or mint chocolate chip. There is seasonal outdoor seating as well. Closed Tues.

Passiflora Tea Room, Cafe and Herbal Shoppe, 526 Main St., New Hartford; 860-379-8327; passiflorateas.com; $. This has done double duty since it opened in 2003. One room in the historic 1850 brick house is a tearoom; the other is an herbal apothecary, with herbal and nutritional items for sale. It's the tearoom that is my magnet, with its 160 types of herbal and traditional teas, breakfast, lunch, smoothies, and yummy sweets. Many of the items are organic, with some ingredients even grown in owner Karen Tyson's garden.

Sun from 2 to 4 p.m. there's Gather with Friends, music by local musicians, tea, and dessert. Closed Mon and Tues.

Rathskeller Restaurant and Bar, 88 Main St. South, Southbury; (203) 264-0186; rathskellerct.com; $. Look for *gemütlich* coziness rather than high-speed bar atmosphere at this funky place, even though the bar, with its brass elbow rail, occupies a sizeable part of the room. While there are six or so draft beers available, it's the restaurant and friendly staff that attract family types. House-made soups, burgers, a dozen or more sandwich choices, buffalo wings, Carolina pulled pork on Kaiser rolls, pumpkin ravioli in sage sauce, and a dozen or more intriguing entrees are among the inducements that make the fare different from the usual pub grub. There's even a children's menu. Among the treats: a house-made zesty chili with jalapeño and corn bread, pork chop on the bone with Gorgonzola and hot cherry peppers, and desserts, such as key lime tart with raspberry sauce and chocolate Grand Teton mousse cake. Almost everything is also available for takeout. And note the odd salt-and-pepper shakers on each table: Locals often ask to be seated on the basis of where their favorite set is. Closed Sun.

Wood Creek Bar and Grill, 3 Station Place, Norfolk; (860) 542-1200; woodcreekbarandgrill.com; $$. Look for one of the most prepossessing edifices in Norfolk, the 101-year-old Royal Arcanum Building. Inside it you'll find this cozy, inviting bar and grill, serving well-prepared comfort food, such as buffalo wings, three-cheese pizza, grilled chicken and shrimp, and burgers. The accoutrements could be formidable—globe-shaped sconces, dark-stained pine banquettes, and window casements—but somehow the cheery, family-friendly ambience and menu surmount that. Closed Mon.

Learn to Cook

Carole Peck, Cooking Classes and Provence Culinary Tours, 694 Main St., Woodbury; (203) 266-4663; good-news-cafe .com. Carole Peck of **Carole Peck's Good News Cafe** (p. 155) fame was a pioneer in cooking with natural local ingredients. She teaches classes in the spring and fall at the Viking Center (formerly Delia's Culinary Forum) in Wallingford. Check her website for dates and details. Carole also leads 1-week culinary tours to Provence, France, staying at her home there. She offers two tours in May–June and two more in Sept–Oct. These are private tours by special arrangement. See her website for specifics.

Cooking with Adrienne, 218 Kent Rd. (Rte. 7), New Milford; (860) 354-6001; adriennerestaurant.com. Chef Adrienne Sussman, who began cooking at Commander's Palace in New Orleans, teaches cooking one Sat a month at **Adrienne** (p. 154), her New Milford restaurant. Classes often follow a theme, season, or holiday (such as Summer Soups, Stocks and Sauces, and Harvest Dinner) and last 3 hours. The course price includes wine.

The Silo Cooking School at Hunt Hill Farm, 44 Upland Rd., New Milford; (860) 355-0300 or (800) 353-SILO; hunthillfarmtrust .org. Ruth and Skitch Henderson began this comprehensive cooking school in 1972 on their farm in the rolling hills outside New Milford. They offered the first recreational cooking classes in the state. Classes, conducted by famous chefs, cookbook authors, restaurateurs, and noted nutritionists, cover a wide range of gastronomic interests, skills, and age groups. The website provides detailed descriptions of upcoming classes, and you may register online. Courses usually consist of a single class of about 3 hours, and there are even custom-designed classes for kids. Carole Peck of the **Carole Peck's Good News Cafe** (p. 155), Chris Prosperi of **Metro Bis** (p. 202), Rachael Ray, Martha Stewart, and Jacques Pepin are a few of many chefs who have taught at the Silo.

Sweet Maria's, 159 Manor Ave., Waterbury; (203) 755-3804; sweet-marias.com. In the off-season at Sweet Maria's Bakery, proprietor and baker supreme Maria Bruscino Sanchez conducts basic cake-decorating, cookie-baking, and seasonal-dessert classes at the bakery, usually during Sept and Oct and Feb through Mar. Check the website for the schedule. Classes are limited to 12.

Learn about Wine

Kent Wine & Spirit, 24 North Main St., Kent; (860) 927-3033; kentwine.com. In this large, utilitarian store, proprietor Ira Smith stocks vintages from all the wine-producing areas of the globe. France, Germany, Italy, and California are especially well represented. There are also numerous specialty beers and ales (note its fine range of Belgian ales alone) and as many as 85 types of single-malt scotches. Mr. Smith conducts regular wine tastings every Sat and is usually on hand other times to field questions about various wines, including rarities that he stocks. As he jokingly says, he "provides free advice at all prices." He also provides free delivery service. Check the website for special tastings and events.

Landmark Eateries

Adrienne, 218 Kent Rd. (Rte. 7), New Milford; (860) 354-6001; adriennerestaurant.com; $$. In 1996 Chef Adrienne Sussman opened her restaurant in an 18th-century frame house. The building complements the carefully prepared New American food that she serves, much of which is based on fresh, local ingredients. During summer, there is outdoor seating on the expansive lawn. In winter the three small dining rooms with wood-manteled fireplaces are especially inviting. Depending on the month, Adrienne's menu, which changes seasonally, may list Maine lobster cakes on a roasted corn sauce, grilled line-caught Rhode Island tuna, or beggar's purse full of wild mushrooms. Save room for such desserts as mango and pastry cream, warm flourless chocolate cake, tangy lemon tart with a gingersnap crust, or house-made ice cream. Sunday brunch is especially festive here. Otherwise, Adrienne is open for dinner Tues through Sat. See Chef Adrienne Sussman's recipe for **Adrienne's Lobster and Filet Mignon Wrapped in Phyllo** on p. 397.

Carole Peck's Good News Cafe, 694 Main St. (Rte. 6), Woodbury; (203) 266-4663; good-news-ecafe.com; $$. There's so much to like about this sunny, informal place, which seats 170, from its roomy booths and original art on the walls to its tasteful choice of recorded classical music. That's for starters. The real subject is the food. Chef-Owner Carole Peck, abetted by her partner Bernard Jarrier, was a groundbreaker in using local ingredients, long before the word *locavore* came into the foodie vocabulary. Her creativity has come up with scores of winners, such as quesadilla of shrimp cilantro and goat cheese and wild boar schnitzel. Then there are her desserts, such as mile-high coconut cake and pumpkin cheesecake with dates. Closed Tues. See Carole's recipe for **Puree of Chestnut Soup** on p. 390.

Community Table, 223 Litchfield Turnpike (Rte. 202), Washington; (860) 868-9354; communitytablect.com; $$–$$$. CT, as this relatively new, contemporary-looking restaurant is known, has caused a mild earthquake in this part of Connecticut for its locavore habits. The menu is changed completely every 2 or 3 days, depending on market availability. This means remarkably fresh-tasting food, as though plucked minutes before from the garden. What has caused the stir, besides the freshness, is the chef, Joel Viehland, a voyager from the famous Noma in Copenhagen, where he was internationally known for his marriage of complex flavors and pursuit of the freshest ingredients. Dining is in two rooms, totaling 40 seats, with a communal table in one room. Among the dishes you might find are seared Stonington scallops, harpooned swordfish, herb-crusted lamb loin, buffalo rib eye, and desserts, such as blackberry tarragon soufflé or a luscious *pot de crème*. There is no bar, no liquors, but some wines from Connecticut and New York State. Open for dinner only, Thurs through Mon, and for Sunday brunch. No reservations and on weekends there's almost always a wait. Closed Mar.

G.W. Tavern, 20 Bee Brook Rd., Washington Depot; (860) 868-6633; gwtavern.com; $$. This 1850 house on the Shepaug River has morphed into a restaurant for all seasons. In summer you can sit under the trees on the flagstone patio; in other seasons it's indoors in a post-and-beam setting before a roaring fire in the floor-to-ceiling flagstone fireplace. A portrait of G. W., aka George Washington, hangs above the fire, honoring the tavern's namesake for the time he once passed through Washington Depot. The American menu

Pizza Paradise in Litchfield County

New Haven may be the pizza capital of North America, but these two pizzerias in Litchfield County offer somee pretty heavenly pizza of their own.

Bohemian Pizza, 342 Bantam Rd., Litchfield; (860) 567-3980; $. The name seems like an oxymoron but is intended to suggest an offbeat pizza style (to match the funky offbeat decor). It comes down to building your own pie. The basic pie is 18 inches across, with one of three base layers (red, pesto, or white ricotta). From there you can construct your own toppings: There are 23 options at $1 or $2 each, including anchovies, spinach, basil, sun-dried tomatoes, Nodine's andouille sausage, goat cheese, and chopped clams. A complete menu features pastas, salads, spring rolls, and quesadillas, but pizzas are the indisputable stars. There's also a short wine list, a bunch of specialty drinks, and some 2 dozen imported and microbrew beers.

Doc's Trattoria & Brick Oven Pizza, 9 Maple St., Kent; (860) 927-3810; docstrattoria.com; $$. In three dining rooms and a terrace, Doc's proprietors, Roberto and Paulette Pizzo, serve crunchy, flavorful, thin-crusted pizza with a dozen or so different toppings (takeout's available too). Genovese, casino, margherita, and caprini are just a few of the choices. Doc's also offers dishes such as *vitello Marsala, pollo francese* and lots of pastas, such as penne Vessuviana and rigatoni alla Bolognese. Desserts might be cannoli, biscotti, and chocolate torte. But the pizzas are the *raison d'être* for a visit.

honors him even more with such old-time specialties as chicken pot-pie; macaroni and cheese; George Washington meatloaf; crispy fried oysters; crocks of chili; locally raised duck, quail, and venison; and, oh yes, cherry pie. There's even a salad called The General (romaine, anchovies, garlic croutons, and lemon-mustard vinaigrette).

The Hopkins Inn, 22 Hopkins Rd., New Preston; (860) 868-7295; thehopkinsinn.com; $$. A touch of the Tyrol on a hillside overlooking Lake Waramaug—that is just the beginning of the Hopkins Inn story. Under the ownership of Beth and Franz Schober, the inn has been going strong since 1977 (with a winter break for the restaurant each year, Jan through Mar). Chef Franz, with Beth's son, Toby Fossland, brings his classical Austrian culinary training to modern versions of *wiener schnitzel, backhendl* (free-range chicken and lingonberries), and *rahmschnitzel* (veal in white wine mushroom sauce), among many hearty dishes. Beth runs the inn, with its 11 guest rooms and two apartments, in a comfortable, restored 1847 frame house. There are two alpine-style dining rooms, one with a fireplace, both with Austrian *gemütlich* to spare. In summertime you may dine under a giant horse-chestnut tree on the flagstone terrace overlooking the lake. There are many extravalue touches, such as the small loaf of warm, crusty bread served with appetizers—one reason the inn has such a loyal clientele. Desserts are traditional: peach Melba, Grand Marnier soufflé glacé, Toblerone sundae, and pear Hélène. The

Schobers also bottle their popular Hopkins Inn House Salad Dressing and Hopkins Inn Caesar Salad Dressing, which they sell at the inn and at markets throughout western Connecticut. They also sell their spinach dressing, but just at the inn. Closed Mon. See Chef Toby Fossland's recipe for **Mango Shrimp Salad** on p. 394.

John's Cafe, 693 Main St. South, Woodbury; (203) 263-0188; johnscafe.com; $$. Open since the mid-1990s, John's is an attractive bistro-like cafe with an open, lively manner. The modern American food (with a Mediterranean accent), always good, is better than ever under the stewardship of Chef-Owner Bill Okesson III. There are standout dishes, such as house-smoked salmon, sautéed white gulf shrimp, house-made potato gnocchi with smoked chicken, sautéed pork Milanese, and pan-roasted duck breast. Desserts are memorable too, like the maple cheesecake with toasted pecan crust, blueberry bread pudding, profiteroles, and key lime pie. There is a bargain prix-fixe menu every day, in addition to the regular menu. Even though John's Cafe has a fine wine list, Sun and Mon are BYOB days, with no corkage charge—a friendly gesture to oenophiles who might wish to bring their own special favorites. The menu changes with the seasons, and there is a wine special of the week, pegged to menu choices.

The Mayflower Inn, Rte. 47, Washington Depot; (860) 868-9466; mayflowerinn.com; $$$. Despite the early American name, this is a highly sophisticated inn, totally rebuilt in 1992, on the site of a former private school. It is furnished in English-country-house style, with fireplaces, a library, and comfortable lounges. Although the chefs seem to frequently change, the kitchen consistently turns out first-rate American and continental specialties. On a menu that changes seasonally, there are certain givens: house-made pastas, breads, and pastries; organic herbs from the inn's gardens; house-smoked salmon; and game sausage. The extensive wine cellar has won a *Wine Spectator* Award of Excellence. Dining in any of the three dining rooms is a special experience—with tables set with Limoges china, fine crystal, and silver. In warm weather you may eat on the terrace overlooking the well-kept grounds and gardens. The Mayflower is a member of the prestigious Relais & Châteaux—no surprise.

Oliva, 18 East Shore Rd. and Rte. 45, New Preston; (860) 868-1787; olivacafe.com; $$. Oliva began as a minuscule cafe on the ground floor of an eccentric 1860 frame house in the town center. Success has caused this delightful place to expand from a mere 32 seats to 75, and Oliva now occupies the two upper floors as well and in clement weather spreads out onto the open-sided terrace. In whatever space he is allotted, Chef-Owner Riad Aamar accomplishes miracles.

He formerly cooked at **Doc's Trattoria & Brick Oven Pizza** (p. 157) and still serves superb pizzas with a variety of toppings, as well as excellent Mediterranean and Italian dishes. That's part of the Oliva story. The Oscars, in my view, go to Riad's North African specialties, like Moroccan eggplant, a tantalizing starter with mint, mixed Moroccan spices, pecans, and lemon; baked Moroccan lamb *kefta;* and grilled stuffed calamari with mixed nuts, prunes, spices, and lemon. Just thinking of Chef Aamar's spice-scented entrees makes me hungry for his grilled Moroccan chicken with caramelized pear, prunes, mushrooms, and almonds and his lemon-stuffed borsellini with pecans, garlic, basil, and fresh tomato cream sauce. Seductive aromas and combinations give this restaurant real distinction. As the guidebooks might say, for the adventurous palate Oliva is definitely worth a detour. Closed Mon and Tues; reservations a must. See Chef Riad Aamar's recipe for **Baked Layered Moroccan Eggplant and Beef Ragu** on p. 398.

Pastorale Bistro & Bar, 223 Main St., Lakeville; (860) 435-1011; pastoralebistro.com; $$. During my first dinner at this cheerful bistro, which is ensconced in a clapboard 18th-century house (where Noah Webster supposedly once spent a summer), I thought there was a twang of familiarity about the fine food. It turned out to be the work of Burgundy-born Frederic Faveau, who years ago put the Birches Inn on Lake Waramaug on the culinary map. Frederic and his wife, Karen Hamilton, who manages Pastorale, have made this undertaking a charming oasis in a somewhat arid dining-out landscape. The bistro, on both floors, looks like a modern version of an old-fashioned tavern. I like the snugness of the Red Room downstairs with its oversize fireplace, but upstairs has its charms, too. The food is anything but old, with a short French/New American menu and dishes such as roasted red beet tarte tatin, *escargot gratiné,* French onion soup, chicken *paillard, cassoulet, bouillabaisse,* seared jumbo scallops, grilled organic Scottish black pearl salmon, and *boeuf bourguignonne.* Good bread and superb desserts, such as vanilla lemongrass *pot de crème,* warm pear cake, and apple and almond tarte, are a few of the touches that make Pastorale such a delightful place. Dinner only Tues through Sat, plus a very special Sunday brunch that begins at noon. So eat, sip, and be merry—easy to do in such amiable surroundings.

West Street Grill, West Street, Litchfield; (860) 567-3885; west streetgrill.net; $$$. Some of the area's finest cooking can be found in the stylish L-shaped dining room here that is hung with mirrors and vibrant paintings by local artists. Irish-born James O'Shea was an innovator in combining fresh ingredients in creative ways. Many of Connecticut's freshest farm-grown products—sweet corn, heirloom tomatoes, and basil—as well as eggs from free-range chickens and artisanal cheeses make their way to his tables. Fairly new on the menu is a delicious shepherd's pie. Current chef, Jim Cosgriff, carries on the O'Shea tradition for high standards and consistency, an O'Shea passion (which may explain his success). There are many pleasing details here; note the sprightly Royal Doulton service plates, *fleur de sel* on each table, and bread baked fresh each morning. Part of the appeal—aside from the consistently good food—is the warm welcome provided by James and his partner, Charles Kafferman. Also fun is checking out fellow diners, often celebs like Philip Roth and Henry Kissinger, many with weekend homes nearby. Typically, such "names" can be found at table 21 and the other tables in the row down the center of the restaurant (considered prime seating to those who care about such distinctions). A new year-round addition is Bistro Night every Thurs and Sun, when a special menu and lower prices almost have locals dancing in the aisles. See James's recipe for **Vegan Kale Salad** on p. 395.

Winvian, 155 Alain White Rd., Morris; (860) 567-9600; winvian .com; $$$. Named for the original owners of this vast 113-acre property, Winthrop Smith and his wife, Vivian ("Win" plus "Vian" = Winvian), this pricey Relais & Châteaux resort spa also has dining for both guests and nonguests. The main dining gallery and smaller private dining rooms, some cozy with fires in cooler weather, are what I would call regally countryish, handsomely furnished and maintained. The separate bar, with a fireplace and a few tables for dining, is a delight. The mostly organic food is ambitious, but it is the setting that twinkles brightest. Reservations strongly urged.

Wood's Pit BBQ & Mexican Cafe, 123 Bantam Lake Rd. (Rte. 209), Bantam; (860) 567-9869; woodspitbbq.com; $. Don't let the Tex-Mex specialties fool you: Like most authentic barbecue joints,

Woodie Haas's rustic-looking place is as plain as toast, but it serves some of the best barbecue in Connecticut. Top choices are ribs, ribs, and more ribs (I am not, uh, ribbing you). Most popular are the platters of pork ribs—lean, meaty, dry rubbed, and full of the rich, deep-down flavor derived from slow-pit cooking and green (not dry) hickory, oak, and apple woods. All platters come with jalapeño cornbread and two sides, the best being ranch-baked beans. The Rib Tickler is another winner: lean St. Louis–style pork ribs, richly smoked. Other meat triumphs are the melt-in-your-mouth tender sliced beef brisket and pulled pork (pork shoulder smoked for 18 hours, then shredded and seasoned with spices and sauces). Onion rings—too-thick-for-me pinwheels in a shroud of batter—are served in a novel way, on a wooden spindle. The house barbecue sauce—a blend of ketchup, vinegar, brown sugar, and a secret cache of spices—is lip-smackingly zesty, not overly sweet. Happy hour, Tues through Sat from 2 p.m. to 5 p.m., brings reduced prices on drinks starters and sandwiches. There's also takeout. Closed Mon.

The Woodward House, 4 The Green, Bethlehem; (203) 266-6902; thewoodwardhouse.com; $$$. Little Bethlehem finally has the restaurant it deserves. Located in an old 1740 clapboard house on the northwest corner of the Green, this is a delightful place for a first-rate dinner. Chef-owner Jerry Reveron and his wife, Adele, have turned four small dining rooms into visual gems, with their brightly painted walls hung with vibrant modern paintings. Good looks are just part of the story. The modern American food is elegant and meticulously served. While the menu changes seasonally, look for such treats as Cajun lobster bisque with lobster chunks and andouille sausage, cod *en croute,* grass-fed beef tenderloin with foie gras, and, for dessert, a house-made sorbet or warm blueberry compote. The holiday season is as festive as a restaurant in a town named Bethlehem should be, with each dining room decorated in a different gala motif. Closed Mon through Wed.

Brewpubs & Craft Breweries

Backstage, 84 Main St., Torrington; (860) 489-8900; backstageeatdrinklive.com; $. Located next to the Warner Theatre, this popular bar has the slogan "Eat, Drink, Live." Though not a brewpub, Backstage features 80 different craft beers, with 24 spigots on tap at a time, and 70 available by bottle. It's also a fun place for comfort food, such as burgers and sandwiches with names like Green Thumb, Moe's Picnic, and Bear Claw. Desserts are a specialty too. It's a popular place for brunch on weekends.

White Horse Pub, 258 New Milford Turnpike, Marbledale; (860) 868-1496; whitehorsecountrypub.com; $. John and Lisa Harris had a vision: To turn the run-down, 35-year-old Marlborough Pub into a lively gathering place "serving good honest food at affordable prices"—and in just a short time, they've done it. With a roaring fire indoors in cool weather and a sunny deck and patio for summer dining, the Harrises have it made. Some of the dishes are real pub grub, English style, as befits an Anglo-style pub: steak house shepherd's pie, fish-and-chips, and bangers-and-mash. There are also American dishes, such as chicken potpie, country ribs and barbeque chicken, and rum-and-coke baby back ribs. There's even a children's menu.

Wine Trail

Since the last edition of this book, the wineries in northwest Connnecticut have increased from 3 to 10, though several are quite small and are called farm wineries. Most of the wineries listed below are on the Connecticut Wine Trail; visit ctwine.com for a map and more information.

Connecticut Valley Winery, 1480 Litchfield Turnpike, New Hartford; (860) 489-9463; ctvalleywinery.com. Owners Anthony and Judith Ferraro produce reds, such as Black Tie Cabernet Franc, Chianti, Olé Sangria, and Ruby Light, and whites, such as Chardonel (a white hybrid), white sparkling Spumonte Muscato, Dolce Vita, and Orange Vidal. Their estate-bottled wines are Deep Purple, Dolce Vita, and Midnight. Ferraro specialties are Black Bear (a red dessert wine), Just Peachy, and Raspberry Delight. They have won 25 medals, including 2 international gold medals for their Black Bear. Tastings are year-round on Sat and Sun and Thurs through Sun during the wine trail season (May through Nov). Check the winery's online newsletter for notice of special events, meetings, and special wine dinners.

Haight-Brown Vineyard, 29 Chestnut Hill Rd., Litchfield; (800) 577-9463; haightvineyards.com. You'll know you have arrived at this winery when you see the huge wooden tun at the entrance. At the sprawling building in the center are the works, where the grapes are converted and aged. In the spacious upstairs tasting room/show-room of the main building, you may sample the end products—14 different wines. Self-guided tours are simple, following the Vineyard Walk. Haight-Brown hosts several annual events, beginning with the Barrel New Vintage Tasting the first two weekends of Apr. The tasting room is open daily in season, from Memorial Day through Nov, but call ahead. The winery is open by appointment for the rest of the year.

Hopkins Vineyard, 25 Hopkins Rd., New Preston; (860) 868-7954; hopkinsvineyard.com. High above Lake Waramaug and across the road from the Hopkins Inn (no connection) is the farmland settled by Elijah Hopkins in 1787. Over the years his descendants have grown tobacco and grain crops and have raised sheep, racehorses, and dairy cattle, with Bill and Judith Hopkins settling on grapes—and wines—in 1979. A huge 19th-century barn has been converted into a winery, with a tasting bar and showroom, called Hayloft Wine Bar (in the old hayloft). Bill and Judith's daughter, Hilary, is now the winery president.

Among their 13 wine types are Chardonnay, Cabernet Franc, Vidal Blanc, and several semisweet and sweet wines (including the popular ice wine); some have won awards in national and international competitions. Their 2011 Westwind semisweet white won first place in a 2012 *Connecticut* magazine tasting test. Hopkins is open for tastings and self-conducted tours most of the year—call ahead for specific hours.

Jerram Winery, 535 Town Hill Rd. (Rte. 219), New Hartford; (860) 379-8749; jerramwinery.com. Jerram occupies a 4-acre spread in the aptly named Town Hill district of a small town that was settled in the early 1700s. To develop the winery, owner James Jerram drew on his agriculture studies at Rutgers University, operations management at Rensselaer Polytechnic, and years in the food and beverage industry. He began his winery in 1998 with grape varieties that included Chardonnay, Seyval Blanc, and Vignoles. He now offers 10 wines, including Gentle Shepherd, S'il Vous Plaît, Aurora Vespers, Marechal Foch, and White Frost. Tastings are offered Thurs through Sun, May through Dec; Sat and Sun, Jan and Apr; and by appointment only Feb and Mar. The tasting room doubles as an art gallery and often as a backdrop for catered events, such as weddings and special parties.

Land of Nod Winery, 99 Lower Rd., East Canaan; (860) 824-5225; landofnodwinery.com. The land has been in the Adams family since 1780. Now, on 155 scattered acres, the wine specialties here include Cabernet Franc and four dessert wines: raspberry, blueberry-raspberry, peach, and chocolate-raspberry medley. Tastings are Fri through Sun Apr through Nov.

Miranda Vineyard, 42 Ives Rd., Goshen; (860) 491-9906; miranda vineyard.com. Manny Miranda learned winemaking from his father and grandfather in Portugal. Manny and his wife, Maria, began planting grapes in 2001 and opened their farm winery in 2007. They now produce nine main wines on their 30-acre property: Woodridge White (a blend of Chardonnay and Seyval Blanc grapes), Woodridge Red, Rosé, Goshen Farmhouse, Chardonnay, Merlot, Seyval Blanc, and Vino Fino. The winery is open year-round (with restricted hours in winter) and offers tastings and tours by appointment. Each month the winery features an art exhibit by different area artists.

Northwinds Vineyard, 471 Lake Winnemaug Rd., Watertown; (203) 233-3941. There are 3,600 vines on 5 acres, land that was once farmland yielding corn and hay. Nowadays Northwinds, using an organic approach, produces estate-grown wines: four whites (Traminette, Zephyr, Vidal Blanc, and Rosé), and two reds (Boreas and St. Croix). In the fall there are also Rieslings and dessert wines. Tastings are held Sat from June to just before Thanksgiving. The farm is also open the Sat before Christmas for wine sales.

Sunset Meadows Vineyards, 599 Old Middle St. (Rte. 63), Goshen; (860) 201-4654; sunsetmeadowvineyards.com. This small farm winery, which won a gold for one of its wines at a 2012 international wine competition, is open year-round, with the tasting room open Sun, Mon, Thurs, Fri, and Sat. There is often live jazz and other music on weekends. The winery also hosts private parties and corporate functions. At tastings, cheese, pâtés, crackers, and cold meats are usually available with the wine.

Walker Road Vineyards, 17 Walker Rd., Woodbury; (203) 263-0768; walkerroadvineyards.com. Jim Frey has been making wine since 2007 on his 8-acre farm, which is classified as a farm winery. To qualify as such one must grow onsite a significant portion of the grapes (roughly 25 percent) used in wine production. Walker Road produces two wines: Gertrude's Garden, a white table wine made from a blend of Seyval Blanc and Sauvignon Blanc, and a red table wine, made from purchased grapes and fermented St. Croix grapes. Frey's production is small, but he sells to **Community Table** (p. 156) in New Preston and a few other restaurants in the area. Tastings are held the first weekend of each month.

White Silo Farm and Winery, 32 Rte. 37 East, Sherman; (860) 355-0271; whitesilowinery.com. In 1986 Eric Gorman bought a portion of a dairy farm, Upland Pastures, and in 2010 he and his family planted grapes on 1 acre of the property. They now grow white Cayuga and red Frontenac grapes, and their specialty is small batch fruit and grape wine production. The wines include sparkling Red Raspberry, a dry Rhubarb, Black Currant, Upland Pastures White and Red, White Silo Sangria (one of their bestsellers), and four semi-sweet wines. All wines are produced and bottled on the premises.

Tastings occur Apr through Dec, Fri through Sun, and major holidays at a 25-foot bar in the tasting room (which is in a large red barn) or in the terrace gardens outside. For the tasting you can order in advance a cheese plate or gourmet picnic lunch box. Also for sale at the farm are gourmet farm products, including quince, black currant, and rhubarb mustards. Check the website for the farm's many special events.

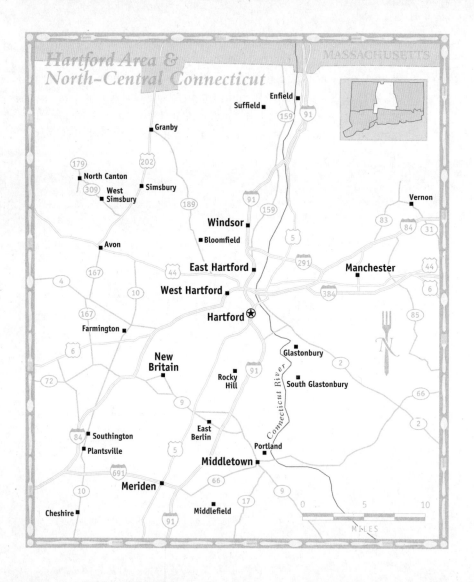

Hartford Area &
North-Central Connecticut

MASSACHUSETTS

Enfield
Suffield
159   91

Granby

179
202

North Canton
309   West   Simsbury
Simsbury
189

Avon
167
4
10
167

Farmington

Bloomfield

Windsor
159
5
291

East Hartford
West Hartford

Hartford ✪

New
Britain
72
6
9

Rocky
Hill
91

Connecticut River

Vernon
83   84   31

Manchester
44
384
6
85

Glastonbury
2

South Glastonbury
66
2

N

East
Berlin
84   Southington
Plantsville
5

691

Middletown

Portland

Meriden
66

10
17   9
91

0   5   10

Cheshire
Middlefield

MILES

Hartford Area & North-Central Connecticut

Hartford, as the state capital, is a centripetal force that has brought to its center all kinds of artistic, cultural, political, ethnic, and culinary forces. These include a steady stream of new restaurants, ethnic grocery stores and bakeries, specialty food shops, and an influx of people from diverse ethnic backgrounds (including Vietnamese, Afghans, and Jamaicans) to enjoy them. Mark Twain, who lived in the city for 20 years, called Hartford "the best built and handsomest town I have ever seen." He would have marveled at the variety and spiciness of the city at present.

During the first half of the twentieth century, Hartford's major culinary happenings, fiestas, and shopping took place along Franklin Avenue, the Italian neighborhood consisting of restaurants, bakeries, Italian delis, food importers, and mom-and-pop food shops, some of which are still in their original locales. One of our favorite Hartford food events is the seasonal downtown farmers' market held within the gates of the splendid Old State House, the oldest state house in the country, designed by Charles Bulfinch in the Georgian style in 1796.

Hartford spills over into leafy, suburban West Hartford, which has become an enticement of its own for foodies, with new restaurants, cafes, coffeehouses, and all kinds of specialty food shops. Three of the state's largest international ethnic grocery markets are within its town limits.

Radiating out from Hartford in all directions are some of the state's oldest towns, such as Windsor and Suffield to the north and preserved-in-amber Old Wethersfield to the south, with all its stately 18th-century houses locked in time. On the east side of the Connecticut River is Glastonbury, which is both sophisticated and rural at the same time, and whose well-groomed vintage houses are home to many Hartford movers and shakers. The town is tucked among orchards and farms that have been around for centuries and remain among the most productive in the state. Northeast is Manchester, with one of the most notable Italian restaurants in a state that has an abundance of excellent ones.

What makes the entire terrain around Hartford so appealing is that it is still agricultural, dappled with historic little towns that are surrounded by wooded hillsides, cultivated fields, and valleys. The fertile banks of the Connecticut River, which squiggles south from Massachusetts through the middle of the region, have been productive farmlands for generations, and the number of small family-run farms (defined as up to 500 acres) in this area continues to lead the state. These family enterprises produce gargantuan salad bowls of fresh vegetables and fruits, most of which they sell at their own farm stands and at farmers' markets all around the area. Many farmers invite you to pick your own berries, apples, and other crops in season.

An especially beautiful town is Farmington, one of Hartford's upscale suburbs, with many handsome houses, the intriguing Hill-Stead Museum, smart restaurants and food shops, and a prime location along the tumultuous Farmington River.

Northeast of Hartford is neatly manicured, sedately rural Simsbury, another self-sufficient, attractive suburb. There you will find several good restaurants and food outlets. Southwest of Hartford is New Britain, an enclave so full of Polish groceries, meat markets, and restaurants, with signs written in Polish, that you may think you have landed in Warsaw.

South of Hartford is Middletown, once a mill town, but which now caters to its Wesleyan University clientele, with a vegetarian restaurant, a funky old diner, and assorted ethnic eateries—a big change from its distant past. The surrounding countryside blossoms in spring with flowering orchards. One of the biggest, at Middlefield, has the largest indoor farm market in the state.

Made or Grown Here

Avery's Beverages, 520 Corbin Ave., New Britain; (860) 224-0830; averysoda.com. Talk about toddling down Memory Lane. Avery's is one of the last four independent producers of soda pop (an old-fashioned term for a soft drink) in the state, operating since 1904. While this small company makes cola, ginger ale, and a version of 7-Up, it is best known for its fruit drinks, such as pineapple, kiwi, blue raspberry, and watermelon, and in its "totally gross sodas" line that includes Dog Drool, Toxic Slime, and Bug Barf. Avery's also schedules a lot of children's parties, during which the kids learn how soda pop is made and get a chance to make their own concoctions. Closed Sun and Mon.

Bear Pond Farm, 89 Lake Shore Trail, Glastonbury; (860) 657-3830; bearpondfarm.com. Wherever he travels, entrepeneur-producer Craig Colvin always takes along his most valuable possessions: his recipes for pestos and tomato sauce. Thus in his move from Washington Depot to Glastonbury he was good-to-go, producing his pestos and sauce at his new locale. His pestos are premium basil, vibrant cilantro, fresh lemony, tomato basil, vegan spicy thai, and jalapeño artichoke, plus a new one, pepperoni pesto, and an all-natural sun-dried tomato sauce. Bear Pond is a certified organic greenhouse grower, and its nut-free products are sold at Whole Foods, and independent stores throughout the US. See Bear Pond's recipe for **Cilantro Couscous Salad** on p. 393.

The Bridge, 598 Washington St., Middletown; (860) 346-3663; bridgetofu.com. This small manufacturing plant produces tofu. Every step, from soybeans soaked in water to soy curds pressed into tofu cakes, is done onsite. According to Stephen Lapenta, owner and president, the company makes 6,000 pounds of tofu a week, processed through stainless steel vessels that bear a resemblance, ever so vaguely, to a beer-brewing system. The Bridge is mostly wholesale, but interested visitors are welcome to see the process and sample the results. The Bridge also makes tofu-related products: tofu salad, seitan (made from wheat flour), and *amasake,* a nonalcoholic rice-based drink.

Chimirri's Italian Pastry Shoppe, 1075 Silas Deane Hwy., Wethersfield Shopping Center, Wethersfield; (860) 529-2527; chimirrispastry.com. While the multitiered wedding cakes and the giant fruit cakes that serve more than 100 guests take center stage in the window of this classic Italian bakery, it's the cookies, cannoli (filled to order to preserve the shell's crispness), éclairs, brownies, bear claws, fruit pies, and cheesecakes that are the foundation of Lorena Chimirri's business. Sweets are not the only goodies here. The bakery, which was started in 1970 by Lorena's parents, makes Sicilian-style pizzas (available by the slice) and breads stuffed with sausage and pepperoni. Also for sale on weekdays are bakery-made hot sandwiches—sausage, eggplant, meatball—and grinders stuffed with ham, turkey, or chicken cutlets.

Giff's Original, PO Box 1212, Cheshire, 06410; (203) 699-8605; giffsoriginal.com. For the tang of New England in your cooking, there's nothing quite like the cranberry pepper relish and cranberry ginger chutney made by Marie "Giff" Hirschfeld. Marie began concocting relishes and salsas in her kitchen and now sells eight all-natural, no-fat, no-preservatives, low-salt, gluten-free products at specialty food stores around the state, including **Lyman Orchards** (p. 206) in Middlefield and all the Highland Park Markets. In the line as well are mango spice salsa, which won an award and was voted number one (twice) by the Connecticut Specialty Foods Association; and the brand-new pomegranate onion relish and tomato lemon chutney. Her new hot and spicy cooking sauce is another award winner as best cooking sauce. Marie also sells through her website, shipping via parcel post or UPS.

Mortensen's Ice Cream Shoppe, 27 Shunpike Rd, Cromwell; (860) 632-1094. There are two ways to get Mortensen's creamy, handmade ice cream: at this ice-cream-only shop, which opened in 1999, or at the shop-cum-restaurant at 3145 Berlin Turnpike, Newington (860-666-8219), open since 1977. Both locations offer a plethora of flavors—from a total cast of 125—sometimes as many as 50 at one time. Some of the faves are toasted almond fudge, Vermont maple walnut, and Amaretto cherry chip.

Nip 'N Tang, PO Box 370416, West Hartford, 06101; (860) 231-9420. In the late 1980s Joan Snyder combined horseradish with

fruits, and the results eventually became Nip 'N Tang, sweet-hot com-
bos that enhance meats, poultry, and many other dishes. Ms. Snyder's
products are versatile as dips, spreads, marinades, salad dressings,
glazes for meats and poultry, and as toppings for yogurt or ice cream.
Nip 'N Tang, subtitled "fruited horseradish delight," products are
packaged in attractive 12.5-ounce squat jars in five different compelling flavors: apricot (the first), blueberry, pineapple, cranberry
orange, and pomegranate plum. They can be found in markets and
specialty shops around Connecticut and across the US.

Noack's Meat Products, Inc., 1112 East Main St., South Meriden; (203) 235-7384; noacks.com. On display are traditional German foods: sausages, hams, and other smoked pork products, most
of which are made from naturally raised, antibiotic-free pigs. All of
these are reportedly nitrate free, and processed in a USDA-inspected
plant in south-central Connecticut. Included among the sausages
are pork bratwurst, *hildesheimer, weisswurst,* knockwurst, kielbasa,
and cold cuts, such as liverwurst, *krakauer, presskopf,* and *gelbwurst.*
Noack's also sells such imported goods as European breads and
baked goods, and spices used in cooking. Hours vary, best to call
ahead. Closed Sun and Mon.

Thompson Brands, 80 South Vine St., Meriden; (203) 235-2541;
thompsonbrands.com. Possibly the oldest candymaker in Connecticut, dating back to the 19th century, the Thompson Candy Company
changed its name to Thompson Brands, as it now encompasses three
distinct divisions: Thompson Candy, Thompson Organics, and Adora

Calcium. The first makes all the molded milk and dark chocolate seasonal treats—Santas, Easter bunnies, snowmen, eggs, ducks, and other novelties—long associated with the Thompson name. Thompson Organics is a line of chocolates, bars, and chunk chocolate for baking, made from organic cocoa beans from Central America. Adora Calcium, new and trendy, is a way to have your chocolate and eat it, too: healthful chocolate rich in calcium and vitamin D. You can buy all Thompson chocolates in the small shop attached to the factory or in stores throughout Connecticut and the US. Adora Calcium chocolates are available at Shaw's, Stop & Shop, Target, and other chains.

Tschudin Chocolates & Confections, 100 Riverview Center, corner of Main and Court Streets, Middletown; (860) 759-2222; tschocolates.com. In addition to handmade chocolates—bonbons, truffles, hand-cut ganaches, brittles, caramels, barks, bars, and one-of-a-kind pieces—Rob Lucheme, Tschudin's owner, uses herbs, spices, fresh fruits, and even habaneros to flavor the chocolates. Tschudin also makes and sells made-to-order tarts; exotic cakes, such as a white chocolate pignoli mousse cake; and aromatic breads. In warm weather be sure to try a moussicle, served on a stick, of course. Youngsters love to go through the kids entrance to see the production area. There are 2-hour tours and tastings (for a fee), but you'll need to reserve ahead.

Tulmeadow Farm Ice Cream Stand, 255 Farms Village Rd. (Rte. 309), West Simsbury; (860) 658-1430; tulmeadowfarmstore.com. Two outside windows make it convenient for the crowds that line up for the rich, creamy (16 percent butterfat) ice cream produced at this old farm. You can go inside if you like, as the ice-cream stand is attached to the **Tulmeadow Farm Store** (p. 210). The ice-cream repertory consists of 50-some flavors, available in cones, pints, and quarts, though not all flavors are available at one time. A perennial favorite is Red Razz Chocolate Chip, and more exotic flavors include pumpkin, Indian pudding, vanilla peanut butter cup, and ginger. There are benches and wagons outside where you can sit and savor your ice cream. Whole Foods and some independent grocers in the area sell Tulmeadow's ice cream by the quart.

Specialty Stores & Markets

A Dong Supermarket, 160 Shield St., West Hartford; (860) 953-8903. In a space as big as an airport hangar—32,000 square feet of it—Phuong and Khiem Tran, a Vietnamese couple, have fulfilled an Asian immigrant's wildest food dream: a market with every conceivable type of comfort food from home, and then some. At first glance, A Dong looks like any big American supermarket, but then peer at the products: fresh, canned, baked, dried, pickled, and frozen foods from Vietnam, Laos, Cambodia, Thailand, China, the Philippines, Korea, and Japan, all impeccably organized and displayed.

Fresh-roasted, lacquer-colored, crispy whole ducks and suckling pigs hang from hooks. A bakery section has *banh mi* sandwiches and bean cakes. There are fresh produce and frozen foods sections, a wide selection of Chinese and other teas, and even a department full of oriental china, pots, cooking utensils, and imported gift items. If you are an Asian food aficionado, A Dong's is a one-stop, must-shop center for sure.

Connecticut Creative Store, 25 Stonington St., Hartford; (860) 297-0112. In spacious quarters, as part of the Hartford Botanical Gardens in Colt Park, this Department of Agriculture–connected store is a showcase for made-in-Connecticut merchandise—handcrafts, garden products, clothing, and food. One entire room displays food items: jams, condiments, sauces, spices, oils, mixes, and other edibles. It's a nifty way to see in one place the wide range of food enterprises (more than 30, sometimes close to 50) within our state—and to buy some, too. The store is open Wed through Sat. It is at its best and most fully stocked around Christmas; it tends to look understocked and rather forlorn at some other times.

The Crown Market, 2471 Albany Ave., West Hartford; (860) 236-1965; thecrownmarket.com. Picture a New York–style Jewish delicatessen enlarged to supermarket size and you'll have an idea of what Crown is like, stocked with every imaginable type of kosher food, including a wide assortment of baked goods, poultry, and meats. There are many nonkosher foods as well, mainly natural and organic. Closed Sat.

D & D Market, 276 Franklin Ave., Hartford; (860) 296-3261; danddmarket.com. This interesting market, which opened in 1932, has more than kept up with modern times. It stocks the usual fruits and vegetables, all kinds of pasta, jars of grape leaves, and eight different balsamic vinegars. The deli section boasts an entire case full of olives—cured 12 different ways—octopus salad, anchovies in oil, marinated artichokes, and salted capers. But what really sends its many fans into high fives are the dozen different Italian sausages, all store made; among them are extra hot, sweet and hot, veal, chicken, broccoli rabe, and pesto. There are also dried sausages, such as *ariccia porchetta, calabrese,* and *sporessata;* whole prosciutto hocks; and chicken breasts stuffed with sautéed spinach, mushrooms, and bread crumbs. Closed Sun.

Daybreak Coffee Roasters, 2377 Main St., Glastonbury; (860) 657-4466 or (800) 882-5282; daybreakcoffee.com. Carmelo Bongiorno and his sister, Linda Kenneman, have a shop that offers more than just a terrific cuppa. At any one time, they sell 40 different types of fresh, high-quality roasted coffee beans from around the world (regular, decaf, Organic Fair Trade, flavored), which they roast before your eyes. While sipping a latte, espresso, cappuccino, or one of the special roasts, either in the shop or outdoors in warm weather, you may chew on a fresh Daybreak-baked scone, muffin, turnover, or cookie. The shop also offers breakfast and lunch items; see **Daybreak Coffee Roasters** on p. 219. It's a good source for gifts, too, with about 30 gift or custom-packed baskets from which to choose and all kinds of food items, many made by other Connecticut gourmet food producers.

DiBacco Food Imports, 553 Franklin Ave., Hartford; (860) 296-7365. Like so many of the Italian stores along Franklin Avenue, DiBacco, after decades in business, has extremely loyal customers, who come for the wide array of imported Italian foods—an incredible variety of dried pastas, olive oils, cheeses, coffees, and packaged, canned, and dried goods. Then there are Mario and Angela DiBacco's fresh-baked Italian breads and pizzas, store-made Italian sausages (which are also sold to other retailers), soups, and grinders made daily for lunch takeout or to eat at one of the four tables on the premises. Closed Sun.

Divine Treasures Belgian Chocolates, Parkade Plaza, 460 Middle Turnpike West, Manchester; (860) 643-2552; divinetreasures chocolates.com. Candyland dreams can easily come true in this delightful little 6-year-old shop, wedged into a shopping mall space between a Chinese restaurant and a tobacco shop. (Talk about extremes!) Among the divine treasures in three large, glass-fronted display cases are more than 50 different dark Belgian chocolate–covered bonbons, made in the kitchen in the back of the shop. Most are made with natural organic sweeteners, like brown rice syrup, and all are dairy-free, vegan-friendly chocolates, a rarity. Among the gems are truffles, pralines, and chocolate bark with various combinations of ingredients: raisins, toasted almonds, peanuts, dried Maine blueberries, orange peels, hazelnuts, cranberries, bananas, walnuts, pistachios, macadamias, and Grand Marnier. An unusual trio is ginger, cayenne pepper, and cinnamon, or a quartet of roasted cardamom, cinnamon, nutmeg, and chocolate ganache.

Everybody's Market, 1021 South Main St., Cheshire; (203) 272-2266; everybodysmarket.com. While this efficient market's slogan, "Where You're Somebody," is kind of crazy (aren't we all somebody somewhere?), nothing else is dubious about this superlarge (about 35,000 square feet) supermarket, whose variety of good foods, organic and otherwise, is awesome. Its origins go back to the 1930s, but the market is 21st-century up-to-date, with every edible an eager foodie might desire. The market's forte is its diverse perishables: fresh produce, meats, pastries, deli items—even gourmet box lunches. There's a great variety of cheeses, a fresh-flower-and-plant area, even a coffee bar with three tables where you can sip and nibble pastries or sandwiches while you shop. The European-style bakery offers cookies, tarts, tortes, cakes, pies, and artisanal breads. The market also does catering.

Gulf Shrimp Seafood Company, 240 Atwater St., Plantsville; (860) 628-8399; gulfshrimpco.com. Forget the idea of gulf shrimp.

Chad Simoneaux, proprietor, was honoring his home state of Louisiana when he set up his wholesale seafood business in 1991, but the reams of seafood he buys fresh 5 days a week in Boston have nothing to do with the Gulf of Mexico. In an enormous, 18,000-square-foot plant, Chad and his wife, Camille, have fish and shellfish so fresh that the many restaurants and retailers they sell to (like **Metro Bis,** p. 202, in Simsbury and the **Hopkins Inn,** p. 158, in New Preston) swear by their wares. No wonder, as they make wholesale deliveries within 12 hours of the catch, 6 days a week. In late Apr and May, they get Connecticut River shad and shad roe, and from mid-May through Sept, they stock fresh soft-shell crabs. Retail orders get overnight delivery via FedEx. Chad and Camille also have retail space in their plant, where they sell fresh seafood directly to the public, Mon through Sat.

Among the more popular critters are blue prawns, live lobsters, farmed Hawaiian *kampachi,* and fully prepared fresh-frozen items, including stuffed shrimp, clams casino, seafood chowders, soups, fried whole-belly clams, and seafood egg rolls. Closed Sun.

Modern Pastry Shop, 422 Franklin Ave., Hartford; (860) 296-7628; modernpastryshop.com. This old-fashioned, otherworldy Italian pastry shop specializes in over 30 different Italian and French pastries, cakes, and cookies; wedding cakes are a specialty. Among those available are some devilishly rich cakes, such as Italian rum

An International Bazaar on Farmington Avenue

On 1 block of Farmington Avenue in West Hartford, near the Hartford line, two ethnic food markets cater to an international clientele and are chock-full of imported foods that appeal to adventurous home cooks.

Cosmos International, 770 Farmington Ave., West Hartford; (860) 232-6600. A veritable supermarket of mostly Indian and Pakistani foodstuffs, Cosmos sells huge sacks of rice, dried fruits, nuts, spices, jars of hot sauces, pickles, chutneys, pappadum mixes, chappati flour, a variety of teas, curry pastes, butter ghees, cooking oils, and spicy mixes. There is a fresh produce section with Indian eggplants, okras, and fiery chiles, and even a deli case with Indian specialties prepared by a Cosmos chef—lamb *vindaloo,* chicken *tika masala, masala dosas, pakoras*—ready for takeout. There are foods from Egypt, Greece, Israel, and elsewhere in the Middle East as well.

Delicacy Market, 774 Farmington Ave., West Hartford; (860) 236-7100; delicacymarket.com. Two doors down from Cosmos, Delicacy Market is crammed with eastern European favorites. They include Estonian, German, Russian, and Polish sausages; cold cuts and 29 salamis from all over; 46 types of smoked fish; Lithuanian and Latvian breads; 17 imported cheeses, including Swedish; grains, lentils, and beans; Ukrainian and Russian hard candies; Russian teas; dried fruits, nuts, and seeds; salted and pickled vegetables; store-made pierogies, blintzes, and raviolis; and yogurts and butters from Israel, Latvia, and Poland. There are also fresh fruits and vegetables, hot soups, and meals for takeout, such as potato pancakes and stuffed cabbage.

cake, lemon mousse, cream-puff cake, and tiramisu. As you linger over your choices by the well-worn counter, you might make like a regular and order a cuppa coffee. Closed Mon.

Mozzicato De Pasquale Bakery & Pastry Shop, 329 Franklin Ave., Hartford; (860) 296-0426; mozzicatobakery.com. Gino and Gisella Mozzicato purchased De Pasquale's bread shop, a Hartford fixture since 1908, in 1975, and they combined it with their pastry shop, which they had opened 2 years before. The spacious, immaculate quarters became the best of two worlds: marvelous breads (Italian, Tuscan, rye), rolls and heaven-sent cakes (rum cake, tiramisu, torta al cappuccino, lemon and raspberry mousse, hazelnut, napoleon, almond tortes, Italian cherry nut, Easter, Christmas, special occasion), and more than 20 types of delectable cookies (pignoli, amaretti, canali, rococo, taralli, crescents). Elaborate wedding cakes are a bakery staple, too, as are pastries like cannoli, profiteroles, cheesecakes, and marzipan. Mozzicato also makes thick-crusted pizzas daily, as well as Italian-style gelatos in 12 luscious flavors. In warm weather lemon granita is added to the lineup, as tartly refreshing as any you'd find on the streets of Napoli. Next door, through a separate entrance, is the **Mozzicato Caffè,** a large room seating 40 at booths and tables, where you can enjoy an espresso, cappuccino, or latte with a Mozzicato pastry or pizza and perhaps a cordial (there's a full bar). Historic Franklin Avenue has undergone many changes in recent times, but Mozzicato De Pasquale continues to thrive, a favorite of Italians and new arrivals alike.

Nature's Grocer, 81 East St., Vernon; (860) 870-0020; natures grocervernon.com. This health foods shop does double duty. Not only are some surprising things packed into its five compact aisles, but Nature's Grocer is also **Nature's Cafe,** with eight tables, serving waffles, pancakes, French toast, and omelets in the morning and soups and salads at lunch. Most of the food is prepared in-house, and many items are gluten and wheat free. Many of the products sold on the shelves are also free of wheat or gluten—bagels, muffins, breads, rolls, and Glutino pretzels. There are even more organic products—lentils, grains, cereals—and one aisle bursts with ethnic foods from around the world.

Omar Coffee Company, 41 Commerce Ct., Newington; (860) 667-8889 or (800) 394-OMAR; omarcoffeecompany.com. Since 1937, the John Costas family has been importing 80-plus kinds of green coffee beans from all over the world and slow roasting them to sell retail and wholesale to outlets in Connecticut and across New England. This spacious store, attached to the factory, is like a club lounge with comfy chairs and bar stools. It makes a great rest stop for a cup of one of the daily specials, along with biscotti for dipping. There are also coffee gift baskets and bulk coffee for sale. Omar funds a scholarship program at the University of Connecticut, so buying any of four Husky Blend coffees aids the program.

Rein's Delicatessen, 435 Hartford Turnpike (Rte. 30), Vernon; (860) 875-1344; reinsdeli.com. Just off I-84, at exit 65, Rein's Deli, in an unexceptional, low-slung building, seems rather unassuming to be a pilgrimage site. But for generations of expatriated New Yorkers and others who crave New York Jewish deli food, Rein's has been satisfying their culinary lusts since 1972. Nova, lox, borscht, matzo balls, kreplach, chopped herring, pastrami, roast and corned beef, bagels, cheese blintzes, potato pancakes, name it, you'll find it at Rein's. You'll also find tasty soups, some 40 sandwiches, and house-made desserts, such as marble halvah and orange-poppy-seed pound cake. Rein's is also a full-fledged restaurant (called "the way-off Broadway lounge"), serving breakfast, lunch, and dinner.

The Wild Raspberry, 34 Shunpike Rd., Cromwell; (860) 635-5037 or (866) 945-7277; thewildraspberry.com. The owner of this delightful shop, which opened in 2004, is Fariha Hasanova who bought it in 2011. She is proud of her cheeses, as many as 67 most of the time, and about 100 around Christmas. They are from most cheese-producing countries, as well as Connecticut's own **Cato Corner Farm** (p. 341). The shop also has many gourmet and specialty foods, gift baskets, cheeses of the month, and unique cookie bouquets, made of fresh-baked cookies.

Farmers' Markets

For up-to-the-minute information about dates and times, call the Connecticut Department of Agriculture at (860) 713-2503, visit its website at state.ct.us/doag, or e-mail ctdeptag@po.state.ct.us.

Avon Farmers' Market, Enforce Place (Rte. 10 and Rte. 44), Avon. Fri from noon to 3 p.m., from mid-July through Sept.

Avon Meat House Farmers' Market, 395 West Main St., Avon. Tues from 3:30 to 6 p.m., from late June through Sept.

Berlin Farmers' Market, Veterans Memorial Park, Massirio Drive and Farmington Avenue, Kensington. Sat from 9 a.m. to 1 p.m., from the end of June through the first week of Nov.

Bethany Farmers' Market, old airport property (Rte. 63), Bethany. Sat from 9 a.m. to 1 p.m., end of June through early Oct.

Bloomfield Farmers' Market, Bloomfield Town Hall, 800 Bloomfield Ave., Bloomfield. Sat from 9 a.m. to noon, early June through mid-Oct.

Collinsville Farmers' Market, 4 Market St., Canton; collinsville-farmersmarket.org. Sun from 10 a.m. to 1 p.m., mid-June through mid-Oct.

Cromwell Farmers' Market, 52 Missionbary Rd., Covenant village of Cromwell. Wed from 2 to 5 p.m., early June through Sept.

Durham Farmers' Market, town green (Rte. 17), Durham. **Thurs from 3 to 6, early May through early Sept.**

East Granby Farmers' Market, 3 Turkey Hill Rd., East Granby. **Wed from 3:30 to 6:30 p.m., mid-June through Sept.**

East Hartford Farmers' Market, Raymond Memorial Library, 840 Main St., East Hartford. **Fri from 8:30 a.m. to 1 p.m., early July through Oct.**

East Windsor Farmers' Market, Revays Gardens, 840 Main St., East Windsor. **Fri from 9 a.m. to 1 p.m., early July through Oct.**

Ellington Farmers' Market, Arbor Park, Town Center, 35 Main St. (Rte. 286), Ellington. **Sat from 9 a.m. to noon, early May through Oct.**

Enfield Farmers' Market, Town Green (Rte. 5), Town Hall, Enfield. **Wed from 3 to 6 p.m., early July through mid-Oct.**

Farmington Hill–Stead Museum Farmers' Market, 35 Mountain Rd., exit 39 off I-84, Farmington. **Sun from 11 a.m. to 2 p.m., early July through mid-Oct.**

Glastonbury-Melzen's Farmers' Market, Love Park, Glastonbury. **Two Sat per month, 10 a.m. to 1 p.m., June through mid-Oct.**

Granby Connecticut Valley Farmers' Market, 18 Hartford Ave., Granby. Sat from 10 a.m. to 2 p.m., from early June through Oct.

Hampton Farmers' Market, 436 Hartford Turnpike (Rte. 6), Chapels Greenhouse, Hampton. Fri from 3 to 6 p.m., June through late Dec.

Hartford–Billings Forge Farmers' Market, grassy courtyard on Billings Forge campus, north of Firebox restaurant, 539 Broad St., Hartford. Thurs from 11 a.m. to 2 p.m., early June through Oct. **Winter indoor market:** The Studio at Billings Forge, 563 Broad St. Thurs from 3:30 to 6 p.m., Nov through May.

Hartford Capitol Avenue Farmers' Market, First Presbyterian Church of Hartford, 136 Capitol Ave., next to Bushnell, Hartford. Mon from 10 a.m. to 1 p.m., early July through Oct.

Hartford-Homestead Farmers' Market, Chrysalis Center, 255 Homestead Ave., Hartford. Wed from 3 to 6 p.m., from late June through late Oct.

Hartford North End Farmers' Market, 2299 South St., Hartford. Wed from 10 a.m. to 1 p.m., end of June through Oct.

Hartford Old State House Farmers' Market, Old State House, 800 Main St. entrance, Hartford. Tues, Wed, and Fri from 10 a.m. to 2 p.m., June through Oct. Oldest open-air market in Connecticut.

Hartford Park Street Farmers' Market, Walgreen's parking lot, corner of Park and Washington Streets, Hartford. Mon from 9:30 a.m. to 1 p.m., July through Oct.

Hartford Regional Market, 101 Reserve Rd., exit 27 off I-91, Hartford. Daily from 5 a.m. to noon, year-round; the largest food-distribution terminal between New York and Boston.

Hartford West End Farmers' Market, United Methodist Church parking lot, 571 Farmington Ave., Hartford. Tues and Fri from 4 to 7 p.m. from early June through August, but 3:30 to 6 p.m. in Sept and Oct.

Manchester-CCC Farmers' Market, 35 Oakland St., Manchester. Thurs from 3 to 6 p.m., July through Oct.

Manchester Community College Farmers' Market, MCC Bicentennial Band Shell, Manchester. Wed from 1:30 to 5:30 p.m., early June through Oct.

Manchester Farmers' Market, town parking lot, corner of Main and Forest Streets, Manchester. Sat from 8 a.m. to 12:30 p.m., early July through Oct.

Marlborough Farmers' Market, 45 North Main St., Marlborough. Sun from 11 a.m. to 3 p.m., mid-June through Nov.

Meriden Farmers' Market, The Hub, intersection of State and East Main Streets, across from Amtrak Station, Meriden. **Sat from 8 a.m. to noon, early July through Oct.**

Middletown Farmers' Market, South Green, Old Church Street, Middletown. **Tues and Thurs from 8 a.m. to 1 p.m., July through Oct.**

Middletown II Farmers' Market North End, It's Only Natural Market parking lot, Middletown. **Fri from 10 a.m. to 2 p.m., mid-July through Oct.**

Middletown Wesleyan indoor market, outside USDAN town center, Middletown. **Every other Wed from 11 a.m. to 2 p.m., Nov through March.**

New Britain Farmers' Market, St. Ann's Church, 109 North St., New Britain. **Mon from 2 to 4 p.m., late July through Oct.**

New Britain/Urban Oaks Farmers' Market, 225 Oak St., New Britain. **Fri from 3 to 6 p.m. and Sat from 10 a.m. to 1 p.m., year-round.**

Newington Farmers' Market, rear of Market Square, behind 100 Market Sq., Newington. **Thurs from 3 to 6 p.m. and Sat from 9 a.m. to 1 p.m., mid-June through Oct.**

Plainville Farmers' Market, Rte. 10, Plainville High School, Plainville. **Sun from 9 a.m. to 5 p.m., July through Sept.**

Rocky Hill Farmers' Market, Town Hall, Center Street, Rocky Hill. Thurs from 4 to 6 p.m., late June through first week of Oct.

Simsbury—Community Farm Farmers' Market, 73 Wolcott Rd., Simsbury. Sat from 10 a.m. to 2 p.m., early June through mid-Nov.

Simsbury Farmers' Market, Simsmore Square Green, 540 Hopmeadow St. (Rte. 10 and Rte. 202), Simsbury. Thurs from 3:30 to 6 p.m., late June through first week of Oct.

Southington-Plantsville Farmers' Market, Town Green, 997–1003 South Main St., Plantsville. Fri from 3 to 6 p.m., early July through Oct.

South Windsor Farmers' Market, 771 Main St. at Pleasant Valley Road, South Windsor. Sun from 10 a.m. to 2 p.m., early July through mid-Oct.

Suffield Farmers' Market, Town Green (Rte. 75), Kent Memorial Library and Bridge Street, Suffield. Sat from 9 a.m. to noon, mid-June through Oct.

West Hartford Farmers' Market, LaSalle Road public parking lot, intersection of Arapahoe and LaSalle Roads, West Hartford. Tues and Sat from 9 a.m. to 1 p.m. and Thurs from 11 a.m. to 3 p.m., first week of May through mid-Dec.

West Hartford Whole Foods Farmers' Market, Whole Foods parking lot, across from Blueback Square, 50 Raymond Rd., West Hartford. Mon from 3 to 6 p.m., early June through Oct.

West Suffield Farmers' Market, Ebb's Corner Plaza, West Suffield. Sun from 11 a.m. to 3 p.m., early May through Oct.

Wethersfield Farmers' Market, Keeney Memorial Cultural Center, 200 Main St., Wethersfield. Thurs from 3 to 6 p.m., June through Oct. **Winter market:** Trinity Episcopal Church, 300 Main St., Wethersfield. Thurs from 4 to 7 p.m., Nov through Jan.

Wilson/Windsor Farmers' Market, Connecticut Service for the Blind, 184 Windsor Ave., Windsor. Tues from 3 to 6 p.m., late July through Oct.

Windsor Farmers' Market, downtown, corner of Maple Avenue and Broad Street, Windsor. Thurs from 3:30 to 6:30 p.m., late June through Oct.

Farm Stands

Arisco Farms, 1583 Marion Rd., Cheshire; (203) 271-0549; ariscofarms.com. At Alex and Beverly Arisco's 70-acre farm, you are welcome to pick your own tomatoes and peppers. They have a big variety of peppers: goat horn, jalapeño, cherry hot, and long hot. Also for sale at their farm store are sweet corn, eggplants, squashes, and other veggies, plus tea breads, frozen pies, and Giff's relishes and marinades. The Ariscos have farmed here since the late 1950s. You will find them at their farm store every day from mid-July through Thanksgiving, but it's best to call ahead to be sure of hours.

Belltown Hill Orchards, Farm Market and Bakery, 483 Matson Hill Rd., South Glastonbury; (860) 633-2789; belltownhillorchards .com. Donald Jr. and Mike are the third generation of the Preli family that has farmed in Glastonbury's rolling hills since 1910. They follow the CORE Values approach—ecologically balanced growing practices and Connecticut State Pest Management techniques for ecologically based agriculture. You are welcome to pick your own berries, pears, peaches, sweet and tart cherries, apples (24 varieties), pumpkins, and tomatoes. There are also 12 varieties of red, green, and blue grapes (ready in mid-Aug). Fruit pies, whoopee and cream pies, sugar-free pies, fruit squares and crisps, apple cider doughnuts, and caramel and fudge apples vie for attention with jams, jellies, and other canned products in Grandma's Pantry.

Botticello Farms, 209 Hillstown Rd., Manchester (on the border of Glastonbury and East Hartford); (860) 649-2462; botticellofarms .net. With more than 50,000 square feet of greenhouse space, planting on this 350-acre farm begins in Dec. This is the only operating farm left in Manchester. At the farm stand, veggies make the world go round, the likes of squash (zucchini, summer, acorn, butternut, buttercup, and Hubbard), nine peppers (among them cubanelles, habaneros, jalapeños, Thai hots, Hungarian hots, and Italian sweets), onions, cucumbers, seven tomato types, eggplants, corn, pickles, sugar pumpkins, jack-o'-lanterns, gourds, potatoes (Green Mountain, Yukon Gold, Chefs, and red), and Indian corn. Also for sale are seasonal fruits from other local farms and orchards: strawberries, raspberries, blueberries, peaches, nectarines, many kinds of apples and plums, and several pear varieties. The pick-your-own vegetable season runs from Apr to Dec.

Clark Farms at Bushy Hill Orchard & Cider Mill, 29 Bushy Hill Rd., Granby; (860) 653-4022; bushyhill.com. Nora and Harold Law bought Bushy Hill in 1976 and now have 15,000 trees on 75 acres. The apple trees are all limited to 6-foot heights, and the peaches are on trellises up to 7-feet high, making it easy for pick-your-own efforts, which also extend to 2 acres of raspberries and an acre of blueberries. There are 18 apple varieties grown that include Ginger Gold, Jonamac, Sansa, Autumn Sunshine, and of course McIntosh. To pollinate apple blooms, Nora and Hal have 32 beehives, but bears persist in snatching their honey! Their bakery turns out doughnuts; cookies; Amaretto muffins; apple, blueberry, and pumpkin pies; even puff pastry Bavarian strudel—and their famous cider doughnuts. Also on the grounds: a goat herd (for petting and to make goat soap), a cider mill, and ice cream parlor that sells quarts of ice cream from the **Tulmeadow Farm Ice Cream Stand** (p. 181). And there are horseback rides and tractor rides and on weekends tractor wagon tours of the orchards.

Deercrest Farm, 3499 Hebron Ave., Glastonbury; (860) 633-4407; deercrestfarm.net. The Bronzi brothers, Huchinson and Jonathan, and their wives turn out a cornucopia of fresh fruit and vegetables at their 100-acre farm each year. Their farm stand reflects that abundance in all manner of produce, from 26 kinds of apples, eight types of pears, apricots (which Jonathan calls "fussy and delicate"), 10 types of nectarines, eight types of peaches, four of plums, nine types of blueberries, plus beans, peas, five types of hot of peppers, potatoes, eggplants, broccoli, cauliflower, oh, yes, and 10 types of squash, including turban. Farmers on this land have been known since 1900 as "the peach growers." The Bronzis' father bought the property in 1965 and continued the tradition. The stand, which also sells fresh apple cider pressed in the mill next to the stand, is open from May through Dec.

Dondero Orchard Farm Stand & Bakery, 529 Woodland St., South Glastonbury; (860) 659-0294; donderoorchards.com. The Dondero family began farming in 1911. Succeeding generations are still going strong, growing 15 types of apples and three types of pears, including Bartlett, plus such miscellaneous fruits and vegetables as strawberries, rhubarbs, freestone peaches, lettuce, peas, asparagus, and, appearing later in the growing season, nectarines, corn, blackberries, raspberries, cabbage, turnips, onions, winter squashes, and pumpkins. The bakery part of the business is responsible for homemade fruit pies, tea breads, strawberry shortcakes, apple dumplings, cookies, caramel apples, jams, pickles, and jumbo eggs. The greenhouse displays over 1,000 hanging plants. And for man's best friend, there are even Fat Paw Homemade Dog Biscuits. Open June through Dec, the farm stand and bakery close just before Christmas Eve and reopen when the first crops ripen.

Drazen Orchards, 51 Wallingford Rd., Cheshire; (203) 272-7985; drazenorchards.com. The Drazens have been farming their 30-acre spread since 1951. The current crops, all grown by son Gordon Drazen, with the help of his son and daughter, consist of 18 varieties of apples (including McIntosh, Empire, Liberty, Jonagold, Gingergold, Gala, Mutsu, and Cortland), eight types of peaches (both yellow and white), nectarines, and two types of pears, all of which are available for picking from mid-Aug through Oct. Note that the apples are dwarf varieties for easy picking. Not in the mood to pick your own? No problem. The Drazen farm stand carries all those fruits, along with sweet corn, tomatoes, cider, honey, gourmet relishes, donuts, deep-dish pies, and fresh flowers. Open from the second week in Aug until Thanksgiving.

Easy Pickin's Orchard, 46 Bailey Rd. (Rte. 191), Enfield; (860) 763-3276; easypickinsorchard.com. Brian Kelliher's family has been

Hippest Hartford-Area Bistro

Metro Bis, 7B Simsburytown Shops, 928 Hopmeadow St., Simsbury; (860) 651-1908; metrobis.com; $$–$$$, boasts the charm and insouciance of a French bistro, with banquettes, antique hutch, a wall of mirrors, and front doors from a Paris metro. This personable cafe, really an innovative *American* bistro, serves contemporary food with some Asian spins at affordable prices. Chef Chris Prosperi, who owns the bistro with his wife, Courtney, is an enthusiastic booster of Connecticut products, which enhance his creative cuisine. He occasionally cooks at local farmers' markets.

You might find on the menu Thai, Korean, Middle Eastern, and Italian touches. There might be crispy Thai spring rolls; metro Maine lobster and mascarpone ravioli; house-smoked salmon; grilled tandoori marinated leg of lamb; chili-seared, farm-raised catfish; grilled marinated veal chop; or rainbow trout—just a few of many memorable choices from a menu that changes often.

There is usually a four-course tasting menu with selected wines for a nominal price offered at dinner. And how could I forget the desserts, such as key lime tart and maple white chocolate bread pudding? Be sure to pick up one of Chris's own bottled salad dressings as you leave. There are three: caesar, tomato ginger, and balsamic vinaigrette, all deliciously tangy. Metro Bis also hosts cookbook authors and special wine dinners once a month. Closed Sun. See Chris's recipe for Metro Bis's Brussels Sprouts, Bacon, and Honey on p. 409.

farming their 50 acres since 1951. This family affair includes help from Brian's brother and two sisters and their families, who live nearby. The pick-your-own harvest includes vegetables, such as tomatoes, peppers, eggplants, Spanish onions, leeks, beans, cabbage, cauliflower, and beets; herbs, such as basil, cilantro, dill, and parsley; and fruit, such as apples (225 apple trees, 19 varieties, including Macoun, Gala, Jonagold, Kinsei, Rubinette, and Sayaka), Japanese and prune plums, Asian pears, yellow and white peaches, raspberries, blueberries, and pumpkins. The Kellihers offer free wagon rides every Sun after Labor Day; on the 3rd Sun in Oct, there is an annual gourd hunt. Open late June through Oct.

Flamig Farm, 7 Shingle Mill Rd., West Simsbury; (860) 658-5070; flamigfarm.com. Twenty-four miles from Waterbury and founded in 1907, Flamig is an educational resource farm, but you can also buy farm-fresh eggs here. Children love the petting zoo, summer camp, and haunted hayrides. Open daily from Apr through mid-Nov.

Gigi's Native Produce, 48 Shaker Rd., Enfield; (860) 881-8297; gigisnativeproduce.com. Gina (Gigi), Ron, and daughter, Olivia, Veser sell a whole alphabet of fresh produce at their awning-shaded roadside cart, all grown on their 25-acre farm. You'll find strawberries, sweet corn, Silver Queen corn, tomatoes, peppers, squashes, pole beans, cucumbers, native potatoes (Red Bliss and Yukon Gold), and melons in season. There are also herbs, homemade pies, honey sticks in 12 flavors, native butter, homemade dog cookies, and fresh flowers. The sign says: NATIVE HONEY IS AVAILABLE IN JARS AND IN BEARS! Open June through Sept.

Gotta's Farm and Cider Mill, 661 Glastonbury Turnpike (Rte. 17 south), Portland; (860) 342-1844; gottasfarm.com. It is pick-your-own time when the apples ripen at Richard Gotta's farm, from Sept onward. There is fresh-pressed cider, too. But be sure to visit the farm stand for the sweet corn, tomatoes, peppers, squashes, and melons, which ripen at various times. There is also a bakery with pies, breads, and cookies. Check it out from June through Oct. The farm has two locations. The second is at 1339 Portland/Colbalt Rd., **Portland,** with the same variety of produce.

Hickory Hill Orchards, 351 South Meriden Rd., Cheshire; (203) 272-3824; hickoryhillorchards.com. Lynn and Fred Kudish have been busy at their farm for more than 20 years, keeping up with the sales of their own and other local produce. Their pick-your-own fruits, available after mid-Aug, include 14 types of apples (among them McIntosh, Macoun, Red and Golden Delicious, Ida Red, Rome, Fuji, Mutsu, Winesap, and Cortland). They sell flowers from local nurseries through Dec. There are also hayrides, picnics, and weekend events. The farm store is open mid-Aug through Nov; pick-your-own time runs the same months.

High Hill Orchard, 170 Fleming Rd., Meriden; (203) 294-0276; highhillorchard.info. Wayne Young, the manager of High Hill Orchard, runs a busy farm, selling his tomatoes, onions, peppers, beans, eggplants, pumpkins, peaches, apples, pears, blueberries, flowers, and fresh-pressed apple and pear cider in season. Peaches, three types of pears (Bosc, Bartlett, and Howell), 9 of 12 apple varieties, and pumpkins are available for picking, through the second week of Nov. Apple varieties include Empire, Northern Spy, Macoun, Liberty, Ginger Gold, McIntosh, Spencer, Cortland, and Delicious. Open mid-July to Christmas. Closed Mon.

Karabin Farms, 894 Andrews St., Southington; (860) 620-0194; karabinfarms.com. If you seek variety in picking your own produce, visit Diane and Michael Karabin's 50-acre farm, which they have owned since 1984. They have 2,000 fruit trees and sell 14 types of apples, six types of peaches, pumpkins, and, from post-Thanksgiving through much of Dec, poinsettias and Christmas trees, which you may cut yourself if you wish. Their farm store, with knotty pine walls, also offers cheeses, their own farm-fresh eggs and maple syrup, honey, Tulmeadow ice cream in quarts, flowers (raised in four attached greenhouses), five varieties of heirloom tomatoes (Brandywine, Green Zebra, Moskvitch, Peach, and Pineapple), and country furniture. The store is open daily from early Sept through late Oct. From Aug through Dec they sell their home-baked pies. For picking your own, there are hayrides (weekends only) to the pumpkin fields and apple orchards from Labor Day to just before Halloween. Call or check the website for hours and availability.

Lyman Orchards, junction of Rte. 147 and Rte. 157, Middlefield; (800) 349-6015 or (860) 349-1798 (store); lymanorchards.com. The Lyman family, currently in its 8th generation, has been farming here as far back as 1741; its spread now covers 1,100 acres, with 300 acres of berries, apples, peaches, pears, and pumpkins. Lyman Orchards includes an 18-hole golf course and club and the state's largest indoor farm store, the **Apple Barrel Farm Market,** which is to farm stands what a Humvee is to a Geo—humongous. There, year-round, you will find the orchard's fruit, cider, cider doughnuts (and holes), other bakery goods, preserves, vinegars, salsas, applesauce, and condiments, as well as many other Connecticut-made food products. Deli items include soups, salads, specialty sandwiches, and hearty country breakfasts. The orchards are open for farm tours; pick-your-own apples, peaches, pears, blueberries, strawberries, and raspberries are available from June through Oct. Lyman's calendar is packed with events: an Easter apple hunt, summer music festival, blueberry bake off, apple-pie baking contest, a clam bake, a baseball corn maze with Yankees and Red Sox, several summer fresh-fruit festivals and a winterfest celebration; call for dates. The orchards and market are open daily year-round.

Ogre Farm/George Hall Farm, 180 Old Farms Rd., Simsbury; (860) 658-9297; georgehallfarm.com. George Hall, who comes from a long farming line, works with his son, George Jr., on a 60-acre spread that has been largely organic since 1967 and certified organic for more than 20 years. Their Ogre Farm/Hall roadside farm stand is stocked with all their homegrown produce, which they also sell at the farmers' markets in West Hartford, Naugatuck, Simsbury, and New Haven. Ogre's seasonal produce—everything picked fresh daily—includes lettuce, carrots, beets, parsley, potatoes, various tomatoes, sugar pumpkins, lots of sweet corn, spinach, eggplants, sweet potatoes, herbs, cabbages, and cauliflowers. They also sell honey from eight hives, free-range eggs (from some 250 chickens, fed on nonmedicated grain), and large pumpkins (not organic). Open from the first week of July through Halloween.

The Pickin' Patch, 276 Nod Rd., Avon; (860) 677-9552; thepickin patch.com. The name sounds whimsical, but farming is serious business to Janet and Donald Carville. Janet's grandfather was the 17th generation of Woodfords that settled this property, which once totaled 500 acres and is one of the state's 10 oldest farms (and Avon's oldest business). The Carvilles specialize in small fruits—blueberries, strawberries, raspberries, and melons—along with peas, beans, spinach, various lettuces, squashes, beets, 10 tomato varieties, peppers, Silver Queen corn, their own butter, and, in Oct, pumpkins. From their 13 greenhouses, they sell cut flowers, perennials, and potted vegetable plants. Their farm store, with their own butter and sugar sweet corn, plus all kinds of veggies and fruits, is open daily May through Oct.

Rogers Orchards–Home Farm, 336 Long Bottom Rd., Southington; (860) 229-4240 and **Rogers Orchards–Sunnymount**

HARTFORD—HOME OF THE FIRST AMERICAN COOKBOOK

A signature year for American cooking was 1796, when Amelia Simmons (about whom little is known) published a 47-page paperback, titled *American Cookery*. Until then, English cookery books were the standard, but the different climate, crops, and facilities in the US begged for a book for American cooks. In her book Amelia included foods unheard of in Europe: cranberry sauce, pumpkin and mince pies, Rye 'n' Injun (a dark bread made with molasses, yeast, and white corn), spruce beer, watermelon-rind pickles, and five recipes using cornmeal. For the next 35 years, her recipes were reprinted, often without credit. No copyright or royalties for poor Amelia, whoever she was!

Farm, Meriden-Waterbury Turnpike (Rte. 322), Southington; (203) 879-1206. rogersorchards.com. Eight generations of Rogerses have farmed here since 1807; currently John and his son, Peter, till 250 acres. Theirs is Southington's largest farm and the state's largest apple grower. Their spread includes 20 apple varieties, the most popular being McIntosh, Macoun, Cortland, and Empire. You may pick your own on weekends in Sept and Oct. Available at both Rogers farm stands are peaches, pears, nectarines, apricots, plums, vegetables, apple cider, doughnuts, honey, and apple and other fruit pies. Both stands are open daily from late July through mid-May.

Rose's Berry Farm, 295 Matson Hill Rd., South Glastonbury; (860) 633-6001 and **Rose's Berry Farm at Wickham Hill,** 1200 Hebron Ave., Glastonbury; (860) 657-3119. rosesberryfarm .com. The Rose family operation has existed since 1908; its apple trees and berry patches now cover 100 acres of rolling hills. At the South Glastonbury farm, you may pick your own apples, strawberries, blueberries, raspberries, and pumpkins. The farm store stocks farm-fresh pasteurized apple cider, six types of homemade pies, muffins, jams, and fruit vinegars. At the greenhouse you may buy blueberry plants, fresh flowers and, in season, Christmas trees. Rose's farm stand is situated a few miles north in Glastonbury on Wickham Hill, where most of the farm produce is retailed from May through Oct. There are fall school tours, pumpkin tours, and hayrides, and later Christmas trees for sale by appointment. See **Rose's Berry Farm** on p. 222 for details about Rose's Sunday breakfasts in season.

Scott's Orchard & Nursery, 1838 New London Turnpike, Glastonbury; (860) 633-8681; scottsorchardandnursery.com. Woody and JoAnn Scott welcome you to Apple Hill from mid-Mar through Dec 24. Their pick-your-own fruits include eight varieties of peaches (ripening Aug through Sept), three varieties of plums (into Oct), pears (Sept through Oct), and nine types of apple, including Cortland, Macoun, Empire, McIntosh, and Winesap (Aug through Oct). Additionally, there are horse-drawn hayrides weekends from mid-Sept through late Oct. Check the website for the pick-your-own schedule.

The Sugar Shack at Sweet Wind Farm, 339 South Rd. (Rte. 179), East Hartland; (860) 653-2038; sweetwindfarm.net. **Arlow** Case and his wife, Susan, have owned their farm for more than 40 years. At this self-service farm stand, they sell a wide range of seasonal vegetables, including cucumbers, peppers, pumpkins, summer and winter squashes, zucchini, and tomatoes, as well as produce from other farms, Giff's relishes and marinades and their own homemade maple syrup (available year-round). There are also pony rides and sugarhouse tours. The stand is open July through Sept. There is open house on maple sugaring days in Mar; call for days and hours.

Tulmeadow Farm Store, 255 Farms Village Rd. (Rte. 309), West Simsbury; (860) 658-1430; tulmeadowfarmstore.com. **The 260-acre** Tulmeadow Farm has been in the Tuller family since 1768. Don Tuller and his relatives grow greenhouse tomatoes (Cherokee Purple, Oxheart, Striped German, Mr. Stripey, and Brandywine), assorted greens, and other vegetables; sweet corn and pumpkins are their biggest crops. All are available in season in their farm store, along with fresh fruit (grown by neighbors), Lamothe's maple syrup, honey from Jones Apiaries, Griffin Farmstead goat cheese, goat milk, and cow milk yogurt, Nodine's smoked meats, farm-raised beef, fruit pies, chicken potpies, herbs, cut flowers, and perennials. The store is open daily year-round, but hours change with the seasons, so it is best to call ahead. In one of the store's two rooms, farm-made ice cream is sold from Apr through mid-Oct (see **Tulmeadow Farm Ice Cream Stand**, p. 181). While the farm doesn't raise turkeys itself, it does take orders and sell them from other farms for Thanksgiving.

Urban Oaks Organic Farm, 225 Oak St., New Britain; (860) 223-6200; blog.urbanoaks.org. If you expect a conventional farm, Urban Oaks will surprise you. It consists of four large greenhouses on 4 acres on a city street. Here, certified organic farming is done under carefully supervised climatic and atmospheric control, with strict supervision of the process. Urban Oaks is a nonprofit farm project that sells year-round, primarily to restaurants, specialty markets, and retail stores. From Aug through Oct, you may buy at the farm stand fresh specialty salad and other greens (lettuce, kale, and chard), carrots, heirloom tomatoes, herbs, peppers, zucchini, apples, pears, and produce from Urban Oaks and eight other certified organic farms in Connecticut and neighboring states (see **New Britain/Urban Oaks Farmers' Market**, p. 195). An indoor winter market is open year-round.

Woodland Farm, 575 Woodland St., South Glastonbury; (860) 430-9942; woodlandfarmllc.com. Arden and Harold Teveris have been farming here since 1963. Harold's grandfather, Albert Carini, bought the property in the late 1800s. Now the Teveris's third son, Peter, owns the 30-acre farm and tends it with his children. They produce fruit jams, prize freestone peaches, summer and

FOR BARBECUE & BLUES

Black-eyed Sally's BBQ & Blues, 350 Asylum St., Hartford; (860) 278-RIBS (7427); blackeyedsallys.com; $–$$. At Sally's the painted brick and midnight-blue, pressed-tin walls and ceiling provide a funky backdrop for some of the best barbecue in the Nutmeg State, with Cajun and Creole specialties as well. James and Dara Varano opened Sally's in 1995, with Memphis barbecue as their inspiration. They have spent a lot of time working on their rubs, spicy mixtures that they use on their slow-smoked ribs, pork butts, and beef briskets. The Varanos also like having the feel of a "down and dirty Memphis juke joint." They get that effect with colorful paintings of Muddy Waters and other blues greats and live entertainment Mon (jazz) through Sat evenings, making theirs the jumpingest blues spot around. Headline acts have included Johnny Rawls and Sonny Rhodes Blues Band. As for the slow-smoked ribs, Sally's forte, I recommend Sally's pig-out (andouille, pork ribs, and pulled pork with smoked cheddar grits and red beans). If you like your ribs more incendiary, rub on some of Sally's fiery Cajun beer barbecue sauce. Another dynamite meal might begin with Louisiana gumbo or sweet-corn-and-chicken chowder, Uncle Jaimo's spicy barbecue wings, or Cajun popcorn (nubbins of deep-fried Louisiana crawfish tails in a zesty Tennessee tartar sauce). Then move on to beef brisket, blackened catfish with sweet potato mashers, cornmeal-crusted fried Maryland oysters, or "Damned Good" chicken with honey mustard glaze. As a finale, there's bourbon pecan pie or Mississippi mud pie. Closed Sun.

late-harvest apples, red and yellow plums, pears, nectarines, and sweet and sour cherries. They are known for their blueberries, raspberries, and strawberries, and especially their peaches, which begin to produce from early July through mid-Sept. In the fall it's time for their fresh-pressed apple cider. Open daily from Aug through Dec.

Food Happenings

May

Dionysos Greek Festival, St. George Greek Orthodox Church, 301 West Main St., New Britain; (860) 229-0055. This annual 3-day event began as a fund-raiser but is now a celebration of Greek culture. It usually begins on the Fri of Memorial Day weekend and ends Sun at 8 p.m. In between you can feast on homemade Greek foods— the likes of spanakopita, gyros, shish kebab, and baklava, fresh from the kitchen at St. George Greek Orthodox Church. In addition you will find Greek jewelry and handcrafts, Greek music, dancing, and entertainment. A Dionysian happening for sure. Opa!

June

North Canton Strawberry Festival, North Canton Community United Methodist Church, 3 Case St. (corner of Rte. 179), North Canton; (860) 693-4589; gbgm-umc.org/northcantonumc. Going strong on the 3rd Sat of June (Father's Day weekend) since 1951, this free strawberry celebration includes bake and tag sales, plant and burger booths, an auction, and activities for children. The festival is most famous for its towering super-duper strawberry shortcake, made with homemade biscuits, butter, strawberries, and tons of fresh whipped cream.

The Connecticut Chefs Showcase, Hartford; (800) 287-2788. Usually held in mid-June at a floating location, this stellar annual event benefiting Connecticut Public Broadcasting has been going strong since 2003. Featuring a silent auction of fine, collectible wines; wine dinners prepared by five distinguished statewide chefs; and a mystery box, this event does indeed showcase superior foods and wines. Call for information about the next event.

Lyman Orchards Strawberry Festival, junction of Rte. 147 and Rte. 157, Middlefield; (860) 349-1798; lymanorchards.com. This jubilant fest is usually held in mid-June. There are all kinds of games for kids, live music, even Frisbee golf. And of course food, lots of it.

South Windsor Strawberry Festival & Craft Fair, Rotary Pavilion, Nevers Road Park, South Windsor; berryfest.org. There are lots of activities at this free mid-June event, sponsored by the South Windsor Republican Town Committee: the World's Best Shortcake, a Miss Strawberry pageant, amazing face art, craft items, and food galore.

Ye Olde-Fashioned Strawberry Festival, Plantsville Congregational United Church of Christ, 109 Church St., Plantsville; (860) 628-5595. Since 1993, this daylong festival (always on a Fri in mid-June) has been a celebration of the strawberry. Centerpieces are luscious strawberry shortcakes, but visitors—usually about 500 of them—also enjoy hot dogs and nostalgic music.

September

Wapping Fair, Evergreen Walk, 100 Cedar Ave., South Windsor. This festive event is held Thurs, Fri, and Sun of the first weekend of Sept. Expect carnival happenings, rides, games, magicians, a cake-eating contest, and, yes, even racing pigs and ducks.

Cheshire Fall Festival and Marketplace, Bartlem Park (Rte. 10), Cheshire; (203) 272-2345; cheshirechamber.com. An annual event since 1991, this festival is usually held the first weekend of Sept and is sponsored by the Chamber of Commerce and coordinated with the town of Cheshire. There is live entertainment, a craft fair, and booths galore, with some 80 displays by the town's civic and business organizations. A food court features between 6 and 10 booths, sponsored by local restaurants, dispensing—among other tasty treats—chowder, fried dough, sandwiches, and the famous Blackie's hot dogs. The festival is free, as are the fireworks and parking.

Celebration of Connecticut Farms, (860) 247-0202; ctfarmland.org. Usually held on the Sun after Labor Day, this moveable feast changes venue every year and roams the entire state. (For details contact Connecticut Farmland Trust, 77 Buckingham St., Hartford; 860-247-0202.) An annual outdoor fund-raising event—usually a sellout weeks ahead—benefits the Connecticut Farmland Trust, which protects the state's dwindling farmlands. The celebration is usually cochaired by a well-known individual, such as actress Meryl Streep, Connecticut radio talk show host Faith Middleton, or Chef Jacques Pepin and features 25 to 30 of the state's best chefs, who prepare dishes from Connecticut-made foods. There are cheese artisans, local vintners, ice-cream makers, and other food producers, as well as music, art, and tours. For food lovers, this event is a must.

The Annual Art of Wine and Food Dinner at the New Britain Museum of American Art, 56 Lexington St., New Britain; (860) 229-0257; nbmaa.org. This is a big-deal fund-raiser, usually held on a Tues evening the second week of Sept. Fifteen to 18 area restaurants and the same number of vineyards participate, and guests can sample everything. An honorary guest host—past hosts include chefs Jacques Pepin and Todd English—is honored and the evening includes both silent and live auctions. Call the museum for details.

Apple Harvest Festival, Town Green, Main Street, Southington; (860) 628-8036; www.southington.org. This 2-weekend festival gives locals a double whammy. It begins the last Fri, Sat, and Sun of Sept and then leapfrogs to the next weekend (the first weekend of Oct) for more fun and games. It's been going strong since 1968. The free festival kicks off with a road race, a parade, crowning of a queen, a street fair, and live music until 8 p.m., with a bed race, pie-baking contest, and dozens of apple products and other goodies for sale. There's even free shuttle service to the Green. Hours vary on different days; call or check the website for details.

Apple Harvest, Riverfront Park, Welles Street, Glastonbury; (860) 659-3587. The weekend right after Columbus Day in mid-Oct, you can depend on this free, annual 2-day harvest event at the Community Center to be apple polished, as it has been since 1974. Expect to find apple pies, puddings, cakes, and other apple-centered delicacies provided by about 200 vendors, with an emphasis on local farmers and products, along with farm trucks piled high with shiny fresh apples. The Chamber of Commerce sponsors an Apple Pie Booth. Other foods include old standbys: soups, stuffed potatoes, and ice-cream sandwiches. A noon parade from town hall is followed by carnival rides, singing groups, 150 craft booths, live music, and, of course, apples galore. There is also an apple pie bake-off and an apple pie-eating contest. In all, the event attracts some 200 volunteers in what is an ebullient community effort. Call for specific dates.

Signature Chefs Auction, Hartford Golf Club, 134 Norwood Rd., Hartford. An annual event, this evening includes at least 20 different restaurants, wineries, and craft breweries touting their wares, while guests graze and sample throughout. Silent and live auctions, which raise money for the March of Dimes, are highlights. The date varies, but it is usually the last Mon of Oct, and it is usually held at the Hartford Golf Club. But things can change, so check with the March of Dimes at (860) 815-9354 to be sure.

Nibbles

Bar On20, 1 State St., Hartford; (860) 722-5161; ontwenty.com; $$. The restaurant name may be a puzzle until you realize that Bar On20 is on the top floor of the 20-floor-high Hartford Steam Boiler Insurance Company Building, one of the tallest in Hartford. But a bar? Yes, a stunning 21st-century bar with first-rate food service, both small and large plates of pure ambrosia. The menu changes constantly, but some of the treasured dishes remain locked in memory, such as gazpacho, chicken breast stuffed with foie gras, Wagyu beef on a leek tart, and braised pork shoulder. But don't neglect the bar part of On20, with its amazing range of regular and creatively new and different drinks. The space, too, is beyond modern, with indoor heights and levels. Bar On20 is also available for private and corporate events. *Fair warning:* Since Bar On20 is located in an office building, its operating hours are atypical. Call ahead.

Capitol Lunch, 510 Main St., New Britain; (860) 229-8237; capitollunch.com; $. Top dogs can be found here, but what makes patrons stand in line to order isn't just the frankfurters (aka Cappie dogs)—it's the Famous Sauce, a thick, brown, clove-scented meat sauce lathered over the crisp-skinned dog. You can also order burgers, onion rings, and fries, but it's the sauce that's been the magnet at this tidy, modest place since 1929 when it began life as a shoeshine shop and then began selling hot dogs. The rest is local history. To-go pints of Cappie's Famous Sauce are available. Open daily, but hours vary; it's wise to call ahead.

Daybreak Coffee Roasters, 2377 Main St., Glastonbury; (800) 882-5282; daybreakcoffee.com; $. The title says only half of it. Besides roasting coffee beans from all over the world, Daybreak also serves breakfast paninis, along with bacon, eggs, ham—the whole banana. Sourdough bread paninis are also a lunch staple, filled with meats from Boar's Head. Also popular are the Hale & Hearty soups; favorites are mulligatawny and Senegalese chicken with peanuts. There is seating for 25 indoors and 16 outside in warm weather.

Harpo's Bakery, 908 Main St., South Glastonbury; (860) 657-4111; harposbakery.com; $. You might expect to see a bewigged live replica of Harpo Marx here, but *this* Harpo is Dave Slade, who gained the nickname as a kid when he had curly blond hair. That curly mane is gone now, but the bakery recipes live on. Many are a legacy of his grandparents, who owned an Italian bakery for more than 50 years. Harpo opened his store in 1992. Among his gems are crusty Italian bread, pizza, many cookies (biscotti, almond paste, butter balls, and then some), cupcakes, bagels, turnovers, and seven types of muffins. The bakery has two large tables, where you can sit and chomp on sweets or on breakfast sandwiches, burgers, chili dogs, omelets, pizzas, or other comestibles. And remember—if you cherish trivia—that "Harpo" spelled backwards is "Oprah."

Harvest Cafe and Bakery, 1390 Hopmeadow St., Simsbury; (860) 658-5000; harvestcafebakery.com; $. Who says modest prices mean unappealing surroundings? That's certainly not the case at this attractive eatery in an otherwise mundane shopping complex. Changing art displays decorate the cafe's peach and salmon walls. The food is good too. Breakfast choices highlight egg dishes, granola, oatmeal, and a porridge that includes barley/flax/ rye/oats/quinoa/wheat germ. At lunch there are seven salads, quiches, house-made soups, and sandwiches on such house-baked breads as whole wheat, jalapeño cheddar, Indian grain, or cranberry Irish soda.

Main Street Creamery & Cafe, 271 Main St., Old Wethersfield; (860) 529-0509; mainstreetcreamery.com; $. This is a great lunch stop if you are touring the historic houses of the old town. Hefty sandwiches, such as the favorite corned beef (cut to order!) or pastrami on rye; soups; and 28 flavors of Praline's ice cream are staples in this down-home place. Ice-cream pies and banana splits are perennial favorites. Open daily, mid-Mar through Oct. Cash only.

O'Rourke's Diner, 728 Main St., Middletown; (860) 346-6101; orourkesmiddletown.com; $. Since 1946, O'Rourke's has been a much-loved, if slightly grungy, Main Street mainstay and tourist attraction. People love it—or don't. In 2006 it burned down, to the dismay of its many devotees. Fund-raising by alumni of Wesleyan University helped owner Brian O'Rourke rebuild in record time. Known for its comfort food, especially breakfast items, the diner features 33 different omelets (including the aptly named six-egg Belly Buster), 10 types of eggs Benedict, banana bread French toast, and Irish Galway (poached eggs over grilled brown bread with smoked salmon, bacon, hollandaise, and home fries). For lunch, there's vegan soup, along with the usual soups, salads, and sandwiches. BYOB.

Pond House Cafe, 1555 Asylum St., Hartford; (860) 231-8823; pondhousecafe.com; $. This delightful cafe on a pond in rose-filled Elizabeth Park is one of Hartford's little secrets, especially tranquil when the roses are in bloom, sitting outside on the patio or covered porch. Inside is pleasant any season because of the great window views. Nibble on a few starters or pizza or enjoy a full meal, New American style. Favorite dishes: roasted pear salad, grilled crab cake, roasted lamb chops with cumin, harissa-marinated duck hash, grilled mahimahi, lemon linguini. BYOB. Sunday brunch is a great time to be here (try the smoked salmon Benedict!), but reservations are a must. The Pond House also caters private parties and banquets. It's a great place for special events. Closed Mon.

The State's Unique Gustatory Twofer

Cavey's Restaurant, 45 East Center St., Manchester; (860) 643-2751; caveysrestaurant.com; $$ (Italian), $$$ (French). Cavey's is really two separate and distinct restaurants (northern Italian and modern French with some Asian accents) both in the same freestanding building, under the same ownership, though with separate kitchens and different but equally well-trained waitstaffs. Open for dinner only, both restaurants are excellent. No wonder then that they have been Hartford-area favorites since the Cavagnaro family first opened them in 1933; the current chef-owner is Stephen Cavagnaro. The Italian Cavey's two ground-floor dining rooms are as airy as a Mediterranean villa. I like the warm colors, friendly ambience, and modern interpretation of northern Italian cooking. House-made pastas are really special, as in farfalle with chicken and peppers or grandmother's ravioli in brown butter or Bolognese sauce. I also savor Cavey's carpaccio, mussel, and polenta soup; Painted Hills Farm rib eye of beef with

Rose's Berry Farm, 295 Matson Hill Rd., South Glastonbury; (860) 633-7467; rosesberryfarm.com; $. A full-fledged farm, Rose's offers one concession to the Nibbles section: a delightful Sunday breakfast open to the public with full service. You might call it breakfast with a view, because you eat on the deck, overlooking apple orchards, ponds, and scenic vistas. The repast is truly brunchish: pancakes, French toast with local fresh fruit, waffles, sauce *au poivre;* veal scallopine piccata; pan-roasted cod; and fresh figs wrapped in prosciutto with Gorgonzola dolce. But really, almost everything the kitchen produces is a winner.

Elegance remains the operative word (along with priciness and jackets for men) in the French Cavey's more formal decor. Recent makeovers have made the room lighter and more informal, and, in the spirit of this more casual era, the classic seasonal French menu has been modernized with a few Asian and Middle Eastern touches. Recent gems include starters of seared foie gras with braised Swiss chard and cranberry cassis sauce, duck confit with braised red cabbage and cauliflower, and grilled calamari with Asian stir-fry in a sweet chili sauce. Excellent also are the herb-crusted loin of lamb Navarin, pan-roasted Broken Arrow Ranch antelope, and herbed monkfish medallions in a buttercup squash sauce. The wine list is a wonder as well. Both restaurants are closed Mon; the French is also closed Sun. A piano bar, adjacent to the Italian restaurant, has a full menu and a bar menu, with live music Thurs through Sat.

fresh fruit, and juices. Breakfast is offered during good weather from early June through late Oct.

Scotts Jamaican Bakery, 1344 Albany Ave., Hartford; (860) 247-3855; scottsjamaicanbakery.com; $. Small and bustling, Scotts, located at the corner of Kent, is a mecca of West Indian baked goods, with fresh-baked corn bread, cinnamon bread and rolls, plantain and coconut tarts, and a host of other Caribbean pastries. A small freezer contains Scotts' popular Jamaican beef patties, shaped like empanadas, ready to take home for a quick meal. There's beef stew too and fried croaker or whiting. Three other locations are at **3381 Main St.** (860-246-6599), **630 Blue Hills Ave.** (860-243-2609), and **801 Windsor St.** (860-246-6776).

Shady Glen, 840 East Middle Turnpike East, Manchester; (860) 649-4245; $. A mural of elves and pixies picnicking on ice cream in a shady glen is a reminder of Shady Glen's main product: some of the state's best ice cream. It is made one level below the diner in as many as 30 flavors, most with natural flavorings. Chocolate Almond Joy and chocolate peanut butter are among the favorites. Another reason folks flock to this diner: unusual cheeseburgers, with cheese that oozes over onto the grill, ending up both soft and crunchy. A second **Shady Glen** is at 360 West Middle Turnpike, Manchester (860-643-0511).

Smokin' With Chris, 59 West Center St., Southington; (860) 620-9133; smokinwithchris.com; $. If you pass the back patio of this place, the smoky aromas will lead you right inside. Owner Chris Conlon uses apple, cherry, and hickory wood to fuel his locomotive-like black smoker. The result, in this sprawling restaurant, is some delicious baby back ribs, brisket, and Conlon-named Sloppy Spare Ribs.

Stretch's Pizza, 995 Main St., Newington; (860) 667-9100; stretchspizza.info; $. Stretch's is proof that New Haven isn't the only Connecticut town with exceptional pizza. The pizza here—called New Haven style—has a thin crust with lots of flavor, and the toppings are first-rate. Stretch's also makes other very good Italian dishes—lasagna, chicken pesto and the like, as well as fresh, tasty calzones. In fact, Stretch's prides itself on fresh everything. The restaurant doesn't have a freezer, so fresh is practically guaranteed. Delivery is available too. Closed Mon.

Sun Splash Jamaican Restaurant, 692 Maple Ave., Hartford; (860) 548-3050; sunsplashjamaicanrestaurant.com; $. Anyone homesick for the sunny shores and beaches of the Caribbean will revel in some of the island's popular dishes at this highly informal place, which does a sizeable take-out business. Enjoy oxtail in a rich, zesty sauce; jerk-seasoned chicken or pork; tripe with beans; goat curry; and other island favorites. A second **Sun Splash** (428 Franklin Ave.; 860-904-9310), is more of a sit-down-and-dine place.

Sweet Harmony Cafe & Bakery, 158 Broad St., Middletown; (860) 344-9646; sweetharmonycafebakery.com; $. This harmony-ous cafe has the old-fashioned charm of a village tearoom, with oak floors and wing chairs. Even so, it turns out some delicious modern dishes, such as a variety of quiches, seven salads, 13 sandwiches, and—its signature—unusual house-made cakes. Trang Tran, the chef, is responsible for such delights as a coco-nut-frosted mango cake filled with pineapple mousse, pistachio cake with strawberry mousse, kumquat cake with passion-fruit mousse, and limonade fizz. Hours are irregular; it's best to call ahead.

Munching at the Museum(s)

Two excellent museums—one in Hartford, the other in New Britain—offer good wholesome, creative food if you want time out from your art viewing.

EATS Cafe at the Wadsworth, the Wadsworth Atheneum, 600 Main St., Hartford; (860) 278-2640; thewadsworth.org; $–$$. Catered by Healthy Source Catering, the lunches at this great museum are healthy, tasty, and provide a welcome break from viewing the great Atheneum collection. The elegant dining room has huge windows that overlook several outdoor sculptures. Closed Mon and Tues, as is the museum.

Cafe on the Park, New Britain Museum of American Art, 56 Lexington St., New Britain; (860) 229-0257; nbmaa.org; $. The cafe has a plain-Jane look but tables face big wide windows with a pleasing view of Walnut Hill Park. If it's warm enough, you can lunch on the open terrace. The menu is simple and self-service, cafeteria style, with soups, salads, sandwiches, quiche of the day, and several interesting, creative daily specials. There are usually three wines available. The menu changes seasonally, but you might encounter watermelon gazpacho, lobster roll, an artisan cheese plate, buffalo sliders, chicken salad croissant, and several tasty desserts. Jordan Caterers supplies the fresh-tasting food and also caters big splashy events at the museum.

Learn about Wine

Spiritus Wines, 220 Asylum St., Hartford; (800) 499-WINE; spiritus.com. This celebrated wine shop, which opened in 1982, has educated the wine palates of thousands. The owner, Gary Dunn, became a wine lover while living in France. He shows his discernment and taste in his wine holdings; his inventory is as select as ever. In addition to the monthly *Spirit Writings* newsletter, a website is continuously updated with wine news and notice of upcoming wine tastings. Ask about Spiritus's legendary food/wine dinners at specific restaurants in the area. Spiritus offers free delivery on orders over $100 anywhere in the state and any 12-bottle purchase gets a 10 percent discount. There's also free curbside parking, which is a bonus in downtown Hartford.

Landmark Eateries

Apricots Restaurant & Pub, 1593 Farmington Ave. (Rte. 4), Farmington; (860) 673-5405; apricotsrestaurant.com; pub $, restaurant $$. Facing the surging Farmington River, Ann Howard's Apricots is a delightful place for lunch or dinner. A converted trolley barn, the two-story building boasts a parlor and pub on the ground floor with its own full menu, casual fare, a piano bar, and a patio by the river. Upstairs there are three separate dining rooms. From the upstairs windows, you have a wonderful river view. Warm, inviting, and unpretentious are words that fit both the decor—with delicate apricots painted on the walls along with some exposed brick—and the contemporary American cooking. Ann Howard, the founder, a prize-winning baker of note, was one of the first to emphasize the freshest of ingredients. Lunch dishes like pan-blackened tilapia, a signature chicken potpie, and spinach Florentine ravioli are memorable. So are such dinner entrees as oven-baked captain's cut North Pacific cod, grilled ginger-glazed Atlantic salmon, and honey-roasted organic frenched chicken breast with baby gnocchi. The praise keeps piling up. Closed on most major holidays.

Arugula Bistro, 953 Farmington Ave., West Hartford; (860) 561-4888; arugula-bistro.com; $$. Christiane Gehami opened Arugula, a Mediterranean bistro, in 1996, and it has been going strong ever since. Not only is the creative food well prepared, but the informal setting also adds to a pleasurable dining experience. The menu changes often, but if you find seared ahi napoleon with roasted eggplant and wonton or croissant bread pudding, go for it (them). Closed Mon.

Bricco Trattoria, 124 Hebron Ave., Glastonbury; (860) 659-0220; billygrant.com; $$. This is Master Chef Billy Grant's third restaurant, the first outside the charmed circle of West Hartford. As expected by anyone familiar with his work, his Italian food is masterly—such dishes as glazed veal sweetbreads, veal saltimbocca, spaghetti

BARCELONA BECKONS

Barcelona Restaurant & Wine Bar, 971 Farmington Ave., West Hartford; (860) 218-2100; barcelonawinebar.com; $$. With six outposts in its mini-empire, Barcelona is a name to reckon with, suggesting tapas and other intriguing tidbits. Like its siblings, the Barcelona in West Hartford offers a convivial atmosphere and offbeat decor, where a youngish crowd likes to hang, nibbling light snacks and meals suited to sophisticated urban tastes. The menu highlights 30 or more tapas (little plates), so intriguing they invite lots of mixing and matching. Irresistible choices include spinach/chickpea casserole, sautéed shrimp with garlic, sherry-braised short ribs, ham and chicken croquettes, cornmeal-crusted skate wings, and lots of mussels and other seafood combos. The Spanish-accented and Mediterranean entrees, such as pan-roasted wild striped bass and Rioja-braised lamb shank, are nifty, as are the desserts and assorted Spanish cheeses. There is also a late-night menu. The wine list—with some marvelous Spanish choices, along with South American, US, and other nations—is an oenophile's dream. The other Barcelonas are Barcelona SoNo, 63–65 North Main St., South Norwalk (203-899-0088), the original, which opened in 1996; Barcelona Greenwich, 18 West Putnam Ave., Greenwich (203-983-6400), with a lively bar and late hours; Barcelona Fairfield, 4180 Black Rock Turnpike, Fairfield (203-255-0800); Barcelona Stamford, 222 Summer St., Stamford (203-348-4800); and Barcelona New Haven, Omni New Haven Hotel, 155 Temple St., New Haven (203-848-3000), the largest and most dramatic, with a bullfighter mural and a 20-person chef's table carved from a single walnut tree. Check with individual Barcelonas for schedules and hours.

carbonara, and potato gnocchi, and that's just the beginning. Everything is farm-to-table fresh and the menu changes daily. The setting is attractive too, a large high-ceilinged spot in brick and dark wood wainscoting in a small high-end mall. The two other Grant enterprises are: **Restaurant Bricco,** the flagship of the group, at 977 Farmington Ave. (860-236-1930), and **Grant's Restaurant and Bar,** West Hartford Center, 78 LaSalle Rd. (860-233-0220), both in West Hartford.

Cracovia, 60 Broad St., New Britain; (860) 223-4443; $. In a small city where Polish is the second language, this cafe, owned by Gregory Adamski, is one of four Polish restaurants and many consider it the best. At first sight, what sets Cracovia (named for Kraków, Poland's second-largest city) apart from an ordinary luncheonette is the beautifully executed mural on the wall behind the long lunch counter: a Polish knight in armor on horseback wielding a lance. Another knight graces the rear wall. Nothing else here is fancy, but it is a neat and tidy local hangout in what is predominantly a Polish neighborhood. If you want a crash course in Polish cooking, try the roast pork stuffed with plums, goulash with dumplings, cheese blintzes, pierogi, *golabki* (cabbage stuffed with ground meat and rice in a tomato sauce), or potato pancakes. You might sample one of six Polish beers to go with your meal. Cracovia also does a hearty breakfast with French toast, omelets, and egg sandwiches with ham, bacon, or Polish kielbasa sausage. *Fair warning:* Portions are enormous.

Maxi-Mum Dining Delights

Max Downtown, City Place, 185 Asylum St., Hartford; (860) 522-2530; maxdowntown.com; $$$. There are now eight Maxes in the Hartford area, each different. My favorite is still Max Downtown, the flagship. The Maxes are not a chain (no clones here) but a miniempire created by entrepreneur Richard Rosenthal, who has a flair for matching very good cross-cultural food with a contemporary "with-it" environment and friendly service. At Max Downtown I like the bold good looks, the vibrant mural on the upper wall, and the buzz and bustle of business diners. The robust menu features items such as crispy tempura lobster; basil-crusted rack of lamb; grilled veal chop stuffed with caramelized onions, mascarpone, and pancetta; Max's signature Kansas City strip steak; steak *au poivre; tournedos Rossini*; hickory-smoked "cowboy cut" beef rib chop with chili onion rings; and peanut butter honeycomb pie. For lunch, nothing tops Max's super cobb salad, an all-time favorite. An excellent, globally diverse wine list offers 2 dozen wines by the glass. Other Maxes are Max Amore (860-659-2819) and Max Fish (860-652-3474), both in Glastonbury; Max a Mia (860-677-6299) in Avon; Max's Oyster Bar (860-236-6299) and Max Burger (860-232-3300), both in West Hartford; and Max's Tavern (413-746-6299), over the line in Springfield, Massachusetts. All have different looks, decor, and menu emphasis. All are *max*-imum fun. Each Max has its own operating hours, so call ahead.

Feng Asian Bistro & Lounge, 93 Asylum St., Hartford; (860) 549-3364; fengrestaurant.com; $$. This is surely one of Hartford's most dramatic-looking restaurants, with luminous lighting, gleaming wood floors, and rough-hewn tan stone walls. And the food matches. In three rooms—main dining room, sushi bar, and lounge—you'll eat well on Asian food presented in a novel way. You can make a meal of assorted starters, like miso-glazed Chilean seabass, pan-seared yellowtail, Shimosa salmon, and wasabi tuna tempura. You may cook your own Kobe beef or let others do the work and simply enjoy the results. Whether you go pan-Asian or stay with various sushi combinations, you'll have an enjoyable evening. Other restaurants in the same group are **Feng Asian Bistro & Hibachi,** 110 Albany Turnpike, Canton (860-693-3364); **Ginza & Hibachi,** 1295 Silas Deane Hwy., Wethersfield (860-563-8811); and **Ginza & Hibachi,** 19 Wintonbury Mall, Bloomfield (860-242-8289).

Firebox, 539 Broad St., Hartford; (860) 246-1222; fireboxrestaurant.com; $$. The name, Firebox, sounds down-to-earth, but the handsome decor and elegant food at this modern American restaurant are upscale, without being wildly expensive. Popular dishes are lamb ragu, chicken saltimbocca with Serrano ham, and cast iron duck. There are two dining rooms, the front one with exposed brick arched windows and 30-foot-high vaulted ceilings, the rear one with whitewashed brick walls, Amish farm tables, and a gas fireplace set in the wall at eye level like a work of art. A hallmark of the food is that much of it, especially the produce, is locally grown. Firebox works on the principle that "the best food travels the shortest distance." The space was originally a wing of a late 19th-century brick factory called Billings Forge, near the Capitol in Frog Hollow, a run-down neighborhood. The building was bought and restored by the Melville Charitable Trust, a national philanthropic organization based in Hartford. Firebox relies on local products as much as possible and underwrites a farmers' market in the adjacent parking lot. Firebox is living proof that you can have your cake and support a worthy cause at the same time. Through its success, the trust aims to encourage other vendors and merchants to join it in helping to rehab the area. So enjoy your honey-pepper-roasted chicken, corn and shrimp risotto, Stonington flounder, and other Firebox treats, knowing that in doing so, you're making a worthwhile contribution, too. Closed Mon.

It's Only Natural, 386 Main St., Middletown; (860) 346-9210; ionrestaurant.com; $$. After winning awards as best vegetarian restaurant in the state, owner Renara Magee turned her place totally vegan. Bread is baked early in the morning every day. The dishes are so creative at this unconventional place, you don't have to be a vegetarian or vegan to enjoy them. On a menu that changes four times a year and often borrows from many cultures, you may find hummus platters, spicy Cajun tempeh cutlets, sweet potato enchiladas, and the ever-popular sweet potato fries. It's Only Natural has two dining areas and an outdoor patio. Portions are gargantuan; organic wine and beer are available.

Little Mark's Big BBQ, 226 Talcottville Rd. (Rte. 83), Vernon; (860) 872-1410; littlemarksbbq.com; $. The building that harbors this barbecue magnet may be cool blue, but what's inside can be red hot, judging by the various house-made barbeque sauces, whose recipes traveled here from West Texas, Georgia, the Carolinas, and Kansas City. Little Mark's popular baby back ribs and spare ribs hail from Texas in their lip-stinging spicy rubs. The ribs are smoked for 6 hours, the moist and tender shredded beef brisket and pulled pork twice as long. In addition to all the tasty barbeque beef and pork dishes, Little Mark's serves deep-fried Louisiana 'gator tails, chicken tenders with a Georgia mustard sauce, crispy egg rolls, Cajun burgers, blackened catfish, teriyaki chicken, and other globally inspired dishes

Little Taste of Texas, 19 Oakland Rd., South Windsor; (860) 436-1234; dannyslittletasteoftexas.com; $. Despite all the trimmings—Conestoga wagon in front and saddle, boots, spurs, and holsters inside—owner Dan Bell says the secret to good barbecue is the rub, a mix of spicy and citrus, and he has worked hard at perfecting his. He attributes his taste for barbecue to the 8 years he lived in Texas, when he learned that good barbecue means a low and slow method of smoking meats. He opened his restaurant in 1998, and it's been a steady favorite ever since. Closed Mon and Tues.

Millwright's Restaurant and Tavern, 77 West St., Simsbury; (860) 651-5500; $$. Let's have a shout out for Millwright's, a great addition to Simsbury's fine dining scene. Located in space once occupied by Hop Brook Mill, Millwright's exists on three levels, with the tavern at the lowest level, and a 10-seat communal table in the middle of the major dining room. This table offers diners an eagle eye's view of the kitchen. That's where Tyler Anderson and crew are preparing their mostly New England fare—regional American with a modern flourish. Tyler was formerly chef in residence at the Copper Beech Inn in Ivoryton and knows whereof he cooks. Among the dishes on a farm-to-table menu that changes often, you may encounter smoked salmon *rillettes,* torchon of foie gras, veal sweetbreads, roast duck, lobster bake with chorizo or agnolotti with smoked ricotta. The tavern is more casual, and so is the food. Open for dinner and Sunday brunch.

Monte Albán, 531 Farmington Ave., Hartford; (860) 523-7423; $. Monte Albán may lack the grandeur of the Zapotec ruin for which it is named, but it is memorable in its own right, known locally for its authentic Oaxacan dishes and flavors. The place is small, with golden walls, tile accents, and a pleasant terrace in front for dining in good weather. The food is decidedly not Tex-Mex, but features such dishes as *posole* soup, *mole poblano, mole pipian,* and a quartet of chicken, fish, and shrimp dishes. Enchiladas *huerteñas* is especially zesty—three enchiladas with three different salsas (rojo, mole, and verde).

Nat Hayden's Real Pit Barbeque, 226 Broad St., Windsor; (860) 298-8955; haydensrealbbq.com; $. Barbeque joints aren't a rarity in Connecticut, but there aren't many restaurants that specialize in the slow-cooked, wood-smoked meat cooking that constitutes a good barbecue. Here's one of the good 'uns. Nat Hayden was a local hero in the American Revolution; his father was one of Windsor's first settlers. I'm not sure how his name connects with barbecue because the menu here follows a Southern trail, with Memphis-style ribs (smoked for 7 hours), Carolina pulled pork (from shoulders smoked 14 hours), dry-rub Texas-type brisket (13 hours), and New Orleans gumbo and blackened catfish sandwiches. Never mind, it's the food that counts. Hayden's uses cherry, hickory, and apple woods to condition the meats, which include andouille sausage and chicken, as well as beef and pork standards. Everything is made from scratch, including sauces, rubs, sides (11 of 'em), and desserts. Closed Mon.

Peppercorn's Grill, 357 Main St., Hartford; (860) 547-1714; peppercornsgrill.com; $$–$$$. This stylish restaurant with a dramatic glass facade is near the Wadsworth Atheneum. It exists on two levels, having recently expanded into space formerly occupied by **Spiritus Wines** (p. 227) (now on Asylum Street). Peppercorn's attracts a youngish, 30-something crowd and also Italian-food mavens, who consider it among the best Italian restaurants in a city full of good ones. I especially like the carpaccio, calamari fritti, the wonderfully crisp salads, various risottos, the gnocchi of the day, and the luscious pastas (*ravioli all'arancia* is particularly winning). Even the desserts, not usually an Italian-restaurant strong suit, are superb, especially the warm chocolate Valrhona cake and chocolate bread pudding. Sal and Dino Cialfis, owners since 1989, also have another Italian restaurant, **Piccolo Arancio** at 819 Farmington Ave., Farmington (860-674-1224).

Salute, 100 Trumbull St., Hartford; (860) 899-1350; salutect.com; $–$$. Hartford being the center of our state government, it's only natural that the political movers and shakers would gravitate to a favored dining hot spot. One of the big-timers is Salute, where you'll need a scorecard to keep track of all the politicos. But you won't need to keep score on the food, which is mostly Italian and pretty darn good most of the time, whether you order flatbread pizza and potato lasagna or mac and cheese, short ribs, or spasta pesto. You can count on the pasta dishes for sure—and desserts like tiramisu and pumpkin crème brûlée. *Mangia*—and enjoy the local celebrity watch.

Shish Kebab House of Afghanistan, 36 LaSalle Rd., West Hartford Center, West Hartford; (860) 231-8400; afghancuisine.net; $. Possibly the only Afghan restaurant in the entire state, Shish Kebab has been acquainting customers with Afghan culture, at least its culinary aspects, at really reasonable prices since 1988. The restaurant has two stories and a patio, with the dining area upstairs (there's an elevator); the rooms are pleasingly decorated with Afghan artifacts. If you find Indian cuisine too spicy, Afghan food might fit you to an A (for Afghan). It uses many of the same ingredients and is well seasoned and tangy enough for most palates without being incendiary. I'm partial to several kebabs (lamb is particularly tasty), *ashak* (stuffed with chopped spinach, beef, yellow split peas, garlic, and coriander), *mantoo* (steamed dumplings with onions, ground beef, and house-made yogurt), *kabeli palow,* and desserts, such as baklava and *fernee* (rice pudding with rose water and cardamom). There is a small wine list and several Indian beers, which go well with the food. You might finish with Afghan tea, a sweet-spicy blend of black tea with cardamom and milk.

Treva, 980 Farmington Ave., West Hartford; (860) 232-0407; treva ct.com; $$. Dorjan Puka isn't the first Albanian chef to discover the joys of Italian cooking, but he may be one of the best—if Treva is any indication. He has had lots of experience in the Max's Hartford-area dining empire (see **Max Downtown,** p. 231) and now he is on his own as chef-owner of Treva. The two narrow dining rooms don't telegraph the range of cooking going on in the kitchen. (If the weather's obliging, you might prefer sitting outside on the patio.) But the results, wherever you're seated, are heavenly and readily apparent in dishes such as grilled octopus, black tagliatelle with seafood or Bolognese, duck breast with fiddlehead ferns, or almost any of the pastas. Lunch, brunch, and dinner are all on the menu, and reservations are recommended.

Trumbull Kitchen, 150 Trumbull St., Hartford; (860) 493-7417; maxrestaurantgroup.com; $$. I love the buzz at this non-Max Max, a high-energy brasserie that is the only Richard Rosenthal–owned "Max" with a different name (see **Max Downtown,** p. 231). Richard co-owns it with Chef Chris Torla. Together they have made it the place to be for the under-40 crowd. The cool look and modern decor are backdrops for dishes, such as braised lamb osso bucco, bagel-crusted salmon, Hilda's meat loaf, grilled marinated hanger steak, and seafood pad Thai, and light fare, such as tapas, stone pies (pizzas), creative salads, dim sum, and sushi. The menu is available for takeout too. The Rosenthal touch is also evident in the well-chosen wine list that navigates the planet.

Utsav Indian Cuisine, 575 Talcottville Rd. (Rte. 83 North), Vernon; (860) 871-8714; utsavcuisine.com; $. From the large window in this small Indian restaurant there is a head-on view of the strip mall in which Utsav is located. Never mind the stodgy vista, concentrate on the very good South Indian food at very modest prices. The dishes might include hot and spicy Chettinad chicken, Amma's fish curry, *badami jhinga,* and *avial,* a vegetarian specialty from Kerala. There are other pleasing north Indian dishes as well. Utsav—or "festival" in Sanskrit—is indeed a festival of good food served by a friendly staff at very moderate prices.

The Watch Factory Restaurant, 122 Elm St., Cheshire; (203) 271-1717; watchfactoryrestaurant.com; $$. No one is setting a time limit on your meal at this former watch factory. The high ceilings, spaciousness, and multiple windows—to say nothing of the very good food—are all conducive to lingering. Austrian chefs, especially ones as talented as Chef-Owner Marcus Patsch, are a rarity in Connecticut, so his expertly prepared Austrian specialties encourage leisurely savoring. Among the especially memorable dishes: *wiener schnitzel, Jager schnitzel,* potato pancakes, apple strudel, and black forest cherry roulade. Even dishes that are not rich and creamy are beautifully rendered. So take your time, sit back, and enjoy!

Brewpubs & Craft Breweries

Back East Brewing, 1296A Blue Hills Ave., Bloomfield; (860) 214-0088 or (860) 309-2821; backeastbrewing.com. According to Tony Karlowicz, one of the founders of Back East, none of Connecticut's new breweries is directly affiliated with a restaurant. And he's glad they aren't. As he says, "in a brewpub, not only does the beer have to be good," but so does the food, the service, and the atmosphere. He adds, "We didn't want to run a restaurant." And they don't. But Back East *does* run a taproom—happily. Four days a week visitors can buy half-gallon growlers and sample the brewery's entire line, which includes Golden Ale, Back East Ale, and Misty Mountain IPA. Bottling is still being done by hand, and it takes most of a day to package a 10-barrel batch.

Cambridge House Brew Pub, 357 Salmon Brook St., Granby; (860) 653-2739; www.CBHGranby.com; $. In this microbrewpub the theme is English. Ah yes, Cambridge, I get it. The bar, recently bought by Scott Riley, is indeed pub-like, with dartboards, dominos, checkers, and of course beers and ales. Check the website for the live music schedule. The beer and ales are brewed on the premises. The menu may change, but there are a dozen taps, usually five or so house brews. Always on tap are Abijah Rowe, a gold medal-winning IPA, and Copper Hill or some other Kölsch (German-style beer). Seasonal beers include Pigskin Brown (typically brewed in the football season), Moonbeam Stout (bourbon barrel-aged imperial stout), Buck (a hearty German lager), and Alt-45 (German-style ale). Like many an English pub, Cambridge House offers a bit of substance for the body as well as the spirit, with burgers, pizzas, sandwiches, pastas, and rib eye steaks. Closed Mon.

City Steam Brewery Cafe & Restaurant, 942 Main St., Hartford; (860) 525-1600; citysteambrewerycafe.com; $$. An awesome Romanesque, three-story, brownstone structure, designed by architect H. H. Richardson in the 1870s, was completely renovated in 1979 and now houses a Marriott Residence Inn and the City Steam Brewery Cafe & Restaurant. The cavernous premises also include a comedy club and a billiard hall. Brewmaster Ron Page is in charge of the handcrafted beers. Some of his popular quaffs are Colt

Light Lager (named for gun maker Samuel Colt, a Hartford native), Naughty Nurse Pale Ale (a sunset-hued bestseller), and Original City Steam (an English-type brown ale).

Eli Cannon's Tap Room, 695 Main St., Middletown; (860) 347-3547; elicannons.com; $. This popular spot is neither a brewpub nor a microbrewery. So why, you may ask, is it included here? As the purveyor of one of the most diverse, exciting, and captivating lists of worldwide brews, it belongs on any dedicated beer drinker's must-visit list. With 36 real ales that rotate on tap (to ensure freshness), among 22 to 36 spigots, domestic and imported, this is probably beer nirvana—a favorite watering hole (since 1994) for Wesleyan students and suds lovers all over Connecticut. Emphasis is on microbrews and typically might include Lagunitas, Smuttynose, Dogfish Head, Coney Island Sword Swallower (an amber pale ale), Smithwick's Irish Ale, and Avery. Proof of its seriousness, the pub displays portable blackboards listing each beer available and the date the keg was tapped (ensuring freshness). Along with cold beer, Eli Cannon's serves up a warm atmosphere and hot food, describing its offbeat menu as "Irish/English Pub/ American Trailer Park Fusion." You'll find competently made sandwiches, spicy wings, burgers, fish-and-chips, plus real meals, salads, and desserts. Claim a seat on the attractive, umbrella-shaded, flower-decked patio out back (dubbed the "beer garden of Eden") when the weather warrants being outdoors. Closed Mon.

The Half Door, 270 Sisson Ave., Hartford; (860) 232-7827; the halfdoorhfd.com; $. An Irish gastro pub, this lively spot offers good food and over 100 beers and ales from 12 countries. You'll find several Chimays, and other Belgian brews including Corsendonk brown and pale ales and De Dolle's Teve Mad Bitch. There's often live music.

Olde Burnside Brewing Company, 780 Toland St., East Hartford; (860) 528-2200; oldeburnsidebrewing.com; $$. In what was his family's old ice-house (1911), which still makes and sells ice as the great Burnside Ice Company (one of only three companies still producing block ice), Bob McClellan established his new brewery, dubbed Olde Burnside. In short order Olde Burnside's smooth, mellow flagship brew, Ten Penny Ale, was voted Hartford's Best Microbrew in a reader's poll in the *Hartford Advocate* in 2005, 2006, and 2007. Keeping it company now are two other ales, the hearty black'n'tan-style Dirty Penny Ale and Penny Weiz (hey, I get it, *penny–wise*), a golden version of a Belgian *witbier* or wheat beer (50 percent wheat, 50 percent barley) with a fruity taste. All are available on draft or in distinctive half-gallon growler bottles. Visitors are welcome with tours (by appointment) and free samples. Call ahead before visiting.

Relic Brewing Company, 95B Whiting St., Plainville; (860) 255-4252; relicbeer.com. This is the smallest brewery in the state right now, with a batch run of just 30 gallons and a lilliputian tasting area that doubles as a tool shop and storage room. Although small physically, Relic, which opened in 2012, has great ambitions, having released more than 20 different beers in its first 2 months of business. One of those is a lavender beer that proved to be both popular and potent. Other offerings include a Session IPA, Double Alt, Transatlantic IPA, Fortnight IPA, and American Lager. It sells its beers via quarts and half-gallon growlers. Mark Sigman, the owner and brewer, has indicated that Relic will eventually feature a larger taproom with a 12- to 15-foot-long bar.

Thomas Hooker Brewing Company, 16 Tobey Rd., Bloomfield; (860) 242-3111; hookerbeer.com. Named after one of Hartford's founding fathers, this newish brewery dubs its fresh-tasting products "Connecticut's beer." A beer fancier might take a Saturday tour (the small fee includes a tasting glass) to learn how the beer is made and even have a sampling of four draft beers in the tasting room. Every first and third Fri, there's also an open house with tasting. Hooker makes and packages eight beers year-round and four seasonals. These include a dry, aromatic American Pale Ale, the bitter citric Hop Meadow IPA, Irish Pale Ale, Blonde Ale, Hooker Watermelon Ale, No'Easter Lager, a smooth Hooker Lager, and an Imperial Porter. Half-gallon growlers are available for sale at the brewery.

Tullycross Tavern & Microbrewery, 1487 Pleasant Valley Rd., Manchester; (860) 644-BREW (2739); tullycrosstavern.com; $$. Formerly John Harvard's Brew House, Tullycross offers tastings of five samples of your own choosing. There are 12 brews and five taps available at any one time. Among the choices are Tullycross Tavern Ale (between light and IPA), Das Hefeweizen (a wheat beer), Tully's Irish Red (a medium-bodied malt with caramel flavor), Silk City Irish

Stout, Rain Delay Rye Pale Ale (malted rye and 100 percent Galaxy hops from Australia), and the seasonal Oktoberfest and Pumpkin (an amber ale with cinnamon, nutmeg, ginger, and allspice). From flat-bread pizza and buffalo wings to platters of burgers and fries, juicy New York strip steaks, shepherd's pie, Brewmaster Meatloaf, and pub brisket, the food is solid and tasty pub grub.

Wine Trail

Rosedale Farms and Vineyards, 25 East Weatogue St., Simsbury; (860) 651-3926 or (860) 810-4440; rosedale1920.com. With a 4-acre vineyard, classified as a small farm winery, Rosedale produces several attractive dessert wines from its own grapes. Among the whites are Simsbury Celebration, Three Sisters, and Serendipity (Riesling). Summer Bouquet is a blush (a blend of Vignoles, Seyval, Vidal, and Traminette grapes) and reds include Farmington River Red and Lou's Red. The farm also grows and sells tomatoes and grapes. In summer there's a tent for tastings and a wine bar behind the farm stand and wine dinners. The tasting room is open Sat and Sun, from the end of June through Oct.

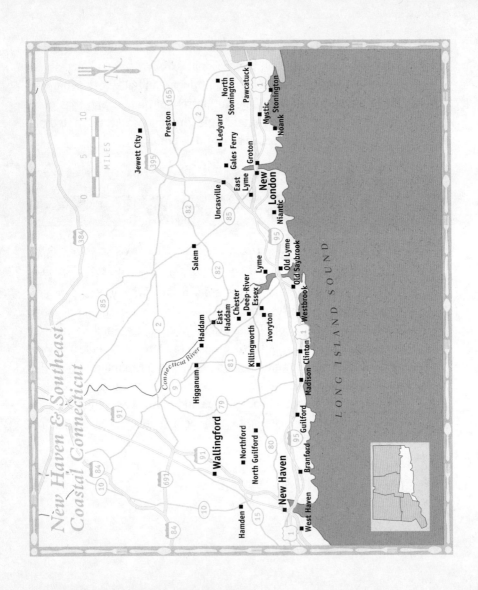

New Haven & Southeast
Coastal Connecticut

LONG ISLAND SOUND

MILES
0   5   10

N

Hamden
West Haven
New Haven
North Guilford
Northford
Wallingford
Branford
Guilford
Madison
Higganum
Haddam
East Haddam
Chester
Deep River
Essex
Ivoryton
Killingworth
Clinton
Westbrook
Old Saybrook
Old Lyme
Lyme
Salem
Niantic
East Lyme
New London
Uncasville
Gales Ferry
Groton
Ledyard
Mystic
Noank
North Stonington
Stonington
Pawcatuck
Preston
Jewett City

Connecticut River

New Haven & Southeast Coastal Connecticut

New Haven is the cultural magnet of this Long Island Sound coast-line—with Yale University, the University of New Haven, three museums, three theaters with live performances, symphonies, and art, architecture, and science lectures. The city's 16-acre Green is the site of music concerts and many arts festivals and happenings. And in recent years, New Haven has also become one of the state's most wide-ranging restaurant cities, with a gastronomic variety—reflected in its Japanese, Chinese, Malaysian, Thai, Vietnamese, Korean, Turkish, Ethiopian, Lebanese, French, and Italian restaurants—as amazing as its cultural diversity. Wooster Street, the old Italian neighborhood, has its own ambience—with tiny stores, gelato parlors, pastry shops, restaurants, and pizzerias. There are so many pizzerias—and really good ones—in Greater New Haven that

The Great Pizza War—
and the Winner is . . .

In New Haven, the self-styled pizza capital of the world, the contest between Frank Pepe Pizzeria Napoletana (157 Wooster St., New Haven; 203-865-5762; pepespizzeria.com; $) and Sally's Apizza (237 Wooster St., New Haven; 203-624-5271; $) has extended far beyond the confines of the old Italian neighborhood of Wooster Street. Fans (as in fanatics) of each are ready to fight (or eat) to the last savory bite. Pepe's is older, dating back to 1925; Sally's dates back to 1938. Both serve thin-crusted, crispy-edged, smoky-flavored pies, whose dough is fed into authentic coal-fired brick pizza ovens at the ends of long-handled wooden peels. Both pizzerias feature a New Haven creation: white clam pie, made with fresh-shucked clams, garlic, oregano, olive oil, and grated Romano-pecorino cheese. The owner of Sally's once worked at Pepe's.

it is no surprise, and no exaggeration, that the city dubs itself the pizza capital of America.

The entire southeast area of Connecticut has much to offer visitors who love good food and the good life. Just following the shore can keep you in seafaring and seafood nirvana, with stops at the picturesque seaside towns of Branford, Guilford, Madison, Clinton, and Westbrook along the way. Favorite summer habitats of vacationing New Yorkers, these towns have as their heritage

I give the edge to Pepe's; I'm smitten with its paper-thin, slightly salty, chewy crusts; fine-flavored ingredients; and the option of a dozen or more different toppings. It's fun to watch the Rhode Island littleneck clams being shucked for the white clam pizzas. Fans enjoy the pared-down basics of the pizza parlor itself, with its modest booths, plain metal trays lined with white butcher paper on which the oval pies are served, and pitchers of beer. Check out Sally's, too, as well as The Spot, owned by Pepe's, also located on Wooster Street, which in our book is Pizza Plaza, USA.

Flash! There are now Frank Pepe Pizzeria outposts in Fairfield (238 Commerce Dr.; 203-333-7333), in Danbury (59 Federal Rd.; 203-790-7373) in Manchester (221 Buckland Hills Dr.; 860-644-7333), and in Uncasville (1 Mohegan Sun Blvd.; 860-644-7333), all in the same top form as the New Haven original.

Still another New Haven pizzeria, Modern Apizza, (874 State St., New Haven; 203-776-5306; modernapizza.com), is also popular locally for its pizzas and its tasty calzones, stuffed with mozzarella, ricotta, and Parmesan, served with a marinara dipping sauce.

beaches (including the expansive Hammonasset Beach State Park), inlets, points, and coves for fishing, swimming, and boating, as well as grassy New England greens and a plethora of historic colonial houses. The 1639 Whitfield House in Guilford is believed to be the oldest stone building in New England. Guilford alone has 200 or more 17th-, 18th-, and 19th-century houses and five distinguished historic house museums. It also has a village green that is considered one of the prettiest in the entire Northeast. Of equal appeal to visitors are the various food options all along the shore: clam and lobster shacks, ice-cream parlors, delicatessens, coffeehouses, cafes, and restaurants with water views.

This section of the coast is scalloped with scenic shore villages that are popular fishing and boating centers: Niantic, Waterford, Groton, and Noank. Of special nautical interest are these three: New London, at one time a whaling center, home to one of America's greatest playwrights (Eugene O'Neill) and now to the U.S. Coast Guard Academy; Mystic, with Mystic Seaport, the reconstructed 19th-century New England whaling village (where parts of the movie *Moby Dick* were filmed); and Stonington, almost too postcard pretty to be real, with its old lighthouse and long, picturesque Water Street. Inland a few miles at Ledyard and Uncasville are Connecticut's two Indian casinos, Foxwoods and Mohegan Sun. Their prime interest to food lovers is not the gaming but the 58 eateries they boast between them, several of which are upscale establishments run by famous Boston chefs Todd English and Jasper White and New York's Bobby Flay. No more than a few miles in from this easternmost shore are orchards, fields of vegetables, and dairy and cattle farms.

Add to the litany of the area's prime attractions a clutch of delightful Connecticut River towns with three distinguished village inns among them, all noted for fine food. At East Haddam is Goodspeed Opera House, a landmark musical theater overlooking the river. Gillette Castle State Park, the former fantasy house-fortress of William Gillette (who popularized Sherlock Holmes on stage in the early 20th century), roosts high above the river; its ample grounds are a state park, which welcomes picnicking and hiking. Essex, with its photogenic marina, Connecticut River Museum, and vintage steam train that runs on 12 miles of tracks along the river, is celebrated for its strict zoning code (no neon signs) and just as much so for the fabulous Sunday brunch at its village inn. The river itself is the habitat of Connecticut's official state fish, the native shad; along the riverbanks you will see an occasional shad shack, where you can purchase this seasonal fish and its delicious roe.

Linking all the towns in the southeastern slice of the state is an awakened commitment to fine food. Superb fresh seafood is a longtime given, but in recent years there has been a flowering of new restaurants: Indian, Mexican, Thai, Vietnamese, Turkish, and the like. They have been accompanied by gourmet markets, delis, cheese shops, and bakeries that did not exist here 20-odd years ago. The discoveries awaiting you are many.

Made or Grown Here

Chabaso Bakery, 360 James St., New Haven; (203) 562-7205; chabaso.com. When Charles Negaro opened the cafe in his Atticus Bookstore in New Haven in 1981, he produced yummy pastries, bars, and cookies but tried in vain to find top-quality sandwich bread. In 1995 he started his own bakery: Chabaso (named after his three children, Charlie, Abigail, and Sophia). Chabaso turns out over two dozen different types of bread loaves, made with natural

The streets of New Haven see a variety of food trucks. And here they are. **The Big Green Truck Pizza,** (203) 752-9547; biggreentruckpizza .com. You want pizza, but you don't want to go out for it? Or you want a pizza party in your own backyard without the fuss of doing it on your own? OK, that's where the Big Green Pizza Truck comes in—right to your door, with its International Harvester K-B 5 truck, carrying a built-in wood-fired pizza oven, cappuccino machine, sink, refrigerator with the pizza dough inside, and four large wood panels that form four tables for your very own pizza party. You'll not believe what emerges from this truck: piping hot pizza, green salad dressed in balsamic vin- aigrette, gelato for dessert, and cappuccino. The truck arrives at 11 a.m., sets up, serves, and departs at 4 p.m. or arrives at 6 p.m. for din- ner service and leaves at 11 p.m. No dishes to do, no mess to clean up. This amazing truck-to-door service operates from Mar through Nov.

The Cedar Street Food Carts, at the corner of Congress Avenue and York Street. These carts are a phenomenon and one of New Haven's best-kept food secrets. As many as 22 food carts, each equipped with its own shade umbrella, are arranged on both sides of Cedar Street in a pocket-park setting, where they sell a smorgasbord of ethnic foods between noon and 2 p.m. every weekday (not quite so many on weekends). The reason for this culinary constellation? To provide a quick, easy, and inexpensive lunch to hospital personnel and vis- itors at nearby Yale New Haven Hospital. So stroll along and take your pick: Japanese, Chinese, Malaysian, Thai, Mexican, Caribbean, Indian, Pakistan, soul food, Ethiopian, Middle Eastern, hot dogs, Ital- ian ices, Korean *boolgogi,* Ethiopian *injera,* pad Thai noodles, Indian *chana Marsala,* falafel, pork burritos, and much, much more, most at

$5 or $6 a portion. Some carts are outposts of local restaurants—like Bangkok Thai and Swagat, for instance—giving a sample of what you might find at the source and a chance to participate in a spontaneous New Haven happening. On weekends the carts can be found at Long Wharf Theater, just off I-95 at exit 46.

The Cheese Truck, c/o Caseus Fromagerie & Bistro, 93 Whitney Ave.; (203) 624-3373; thecheesetruck.com. A sideline of Caseus, a local gourmet cheese shop and bistro, this specialty truck does its road runs on demand. For parties, office meetings, or whatever, the Cheese Truck is ready to go with all kinds of cheesy treats: Mac and cheese, quiches, you name it.

The Cupcake Truck, various locations; (203) 675-3965; followthat cupcake.com. What started in New Haven is now based in Westport, but Marsha and Todd Rowe's cupcake trucks travel all over, from Boston to New York. In fact, theirs was the first cupcake truck in the US. Now the cupcake fad has gone crazy. Here's how it works: The Rowes bake eight basic cupcake types each day, then pack them into a refurbished bread truck, and drive all along the coast to sell them one-on-one, like Good Humors. What's made the Rowe recipe so successful, aside from the freshness of the cupcakes, is the rich variety of the frostings, which allow people to customize their confections. There are a few exotic favorites, like Chocolate Ruin, Red Velvet Jones, Sweet Potato Pecan, Lemon Meringue, and Loco Coconut, with special occasions and holidays meriting new creations. The truck also handles special orders and corporate events, using an antique, late-19th-century truck from Holland. Best advice is to "follow that cupcake" or check the website for their schedule. They have over 3,000 Twitter loyalists following the truck.

ingredients—among them, seven kinds of *ciabatta, pugliese,* seven grain, rosemary olive, country sourdough, cranberry-pecan multigrain, raisin, three kinds sesame semolina, baguettes (wheat, seeded, and Parisian)—and scores of delicious rolls, *demis, batards, boules,* sweet rolls, sticks, and desserts. In addition to supplying Atticus, Chabaso wholesales to more than 50 stores in Connecticut, including Costco, **Trader Joe's** (p. 38), Nica's in New Haven, Cilantro in Guilford, and Stony Creek Market in Branford. The late Julia Child once said, "How can a nation be great if its bread tastes like Kleenex?" With Chabaso around, Julia might have stopped worrying. Closed Sun.

Dagmar's Desserts, 247 Main St. (across from Town Hall), Old Saybrook; (860) 661-4661; dagmarsdesserts.com. Dagmar is Dagmar Ratensperger, owner and baker of her sweets shop. Fittingly, as a native of Nuremberg, she specializes in Bavarian (and Austrian) cakes, pastries, and strudels, including such delights as *zweschgenkuchen* (fresh plum tart), *käsekuchen* (cheesecake made with the sour curd cream-like quark), *linzer tortes,* Franconian apple strudel, *Sacher torte,* and many other pastries known and unknown to her enthusiastic customers. In all she makes 37 different pastries. At Christmastime, the shop is filled with the aroma of ginger, cinnamon, almonds, and marzipan, and assorted cookies, cinnamon stars, spicy ginger cookies, stollen, and other holiday goodies are all on display. There's even a mini-bistro with 10 tables, where you can savor your goodies with a cup of steaming coffee or tea. Closed Mon.

Fabled Foods, 500 South Main St., Deep River; (860) 526-2666. Not only are the foods (i.e., breads) fabled but so is the story. This thriving artisan bakery began in 2000 in Deep River. Ina Bomze and her late husband, Austin Laber, began to wholesale their fabulous breads to upscale restaurants, markets (such as Whole Foods), and shops around Connecticut (**Gold's Delicatessan,** p. 32, in Westport, for one). Austin was an inspired self-taught baker, but with his untimely death in 2002, Ina became the spark plug of this enterprise. Supported by a talented staff of 11 bakers, she produces dozens of different breads in several main categories. They are sourdough (which includes a best-selling sourdough bread, sourdough olive and rosemary, sourdough pecan raisin, sourdough *batards* and *boules*); rustic Italian breads (*pugliese* and *ciabatta*); N.Y. rye; pumpernickel; foccacia; classic country; French; Kaiser rolls; and specialty breads (various challahs, made on Fri only, and Irish soda *boules*). Some of the favorites are semolina *batards,* Asiago *boule,* multigrain (with 12 grains), 12-grain cranberry walnut, caramelized onion rolls, and six-grain spelt (Sat only). The fresh, fragrant products are delivered by three delivery trucks all over the state. See Ina's recipe for **Ina's Cannelini Beans and Escarole** on p. 406.

4 & Twenty Blackbirds Bakeshop, 610 Village Walk, Guilford; (203) 458-6900; 420blackbirds.com. At three little marble tables, patrons sit reading the *New York Times,* while sipping a cup of coffee and nibbling a fresh-baked muffin or almond scone. That is the modus operandi at this nifty bakeshop. The pleasures also involve inhaling all the delicious baking aromas as batches of cookies, *rugalach,* cakes, tortes, tarts, pastries, or pies (no, no blackbirds) emerge from the oven, which is visible behind the counter. Fruit tarts follow the local growing season. Saturday is specialty-bread day (like focaccia), but the scrumptious cakes and cheesecakes are daily delights. Mainly known for its exquisite desserts, the shop also sells a select array of chocolates, and other high-end comestibles. Closed Sun and Mon. Wednesday is production day, but if the door is open, customers may slip in and order, even though the shop is technically closed.

Foxon Park, 103 Foxon Blvd., East Haven; (860) 467-7874; foxon park.com. This survivor is one of only four soft-drink manufacturers left in the state, down from hundreds 50 years ago. Foxon produces 18 flavors of sodas that include root beer, Gassosa, and White Birch Beer, its bestseller, according to Anthony Naclerio, president and production manager. He is the grandson of the founder, Mattaeo, who started Foxon in 1922 selling spring water. All the sodas made at Foxon follow Mattaeo's recipes, which are unique. Supermarkets are now the biggest customers for the sodas, which have recently, despite all the conglomerate chain sodas, been a growing business. Nostalgia anybody? Closed Sun.

Gelato Giuliana, 168 North Plains Industrial Rd., Wallingford; (203) 269-2200; gelatogiuliana.com. Giuliana Maravalle's gelatos have no dairy or fat; they are purely, intensely fruity, which is what makes them so delicious. In all, Giuliana's gelatos come in some 27-plus flavors, plus five yogurt-based gelatos. There are also seasonal flavors, like pumpkin and *panettone,* and four kosher-fruit gelatos. Choosing is difficult. Will it be apple cobbler or honey pecan? *Panna cotta* or s'mores? Maybe peanut butter and chocolate or key lime. Or perhaps one of the newer flavors, such as blueberry-pear William. The gelatos, along with frozen yogurt, are available at upscale shops; groceries, such as Whole Foods; and restaurants in Connecticut and elsewhere in New England.

Hallmark Drive-In, 113 Shore Rd., Old Lyme; (860) 434-1998; $. What is a better place to be on a sweltering day than an old-fashioned ice-cream stand along the shore? That's what Hallmark is, an unpretentious drive-in—a seaside shack to be candid—that has been operating for more than 100 years. Gary and Peg Legein have owned it since 2000 and now make—in 5-gallon batches at a time—25 flavors, such as strawberry and fresh peach in season, ginger (with imported ginger), grape nut, mint chip, Black Hall Mud (coffee, chocolate chips, Oreo cookies, and walnuts), banana nut, raspberry, and peanut-butter-cup crunch, all with 16 percent butterfat content. Still, in spite of the great flavor range, the most popular are vanilla, chocolate, and black raspberry. There is a restaurant indoors, where you can get breakfast, as well as grinders and fried clam rolls. But on a warm day, nothing beats sitting outside in the picnic area, licking your ice cream and gazing at the Lynde Point Lighthouse in the distance. Closed mid-Nov through mid-Mar.

Judies European Bakery and Cafe, 63 Grove St., New Haven; (203) 777-6300; judies.net; $. Judies is a twofer: a bakery making appealing breads (sold retail and wholesale all along the shore) and a cafe specializing in breakfast and lunches made from those breads. The breads include peasant and Italian baguettes, sesame breads, and panini. In addition to those regulars, every day a different specialty bread is baked, such as English oatmeal, Russian black, English cheddar, challah, herb bread, orange ricotta, brioches, four kinds of muffins, almond bear claws, and blueberry tea cakes. The cafe, open weekdays, does a lively trade in house-made soups, salads, and grilled sandwiches and paninis of all kinds. It is also a great place to stop by for coffee, cappuccino, or espresso.

Libby's Italian Pastry Shop, 139–141 Wooster St., New Haven; (203) 772-0380; $. Libby's is synonymous, in New Haven, with Italian ices. Liberato Dell Amura began making gelatos and granitas in 1922, and his family continues the tradition. In this unassuming little Wooster Street shop (near **Frank Pepe Pizzeria Napoletana,** p. 248), you will find 25 flavors of intensely delicious Italian ices. Besides the usual flavors, there are piña colada, blue raspberry, *sambuca,* amaretto, mango, and cranberry. Libby's also sells Italian pastries. Signatures are the 20 varieties of Sicilian cannoli and 10 types of biscotti. Inside the shop is a semi-enclosed area called Caffè Villa Gina, where patrons enjoy various coffees and desserts in the evening. Closed Tues.

Old Lyme Ice Cream Shoppe, 34 Lyme St., Old Lyme; (860) 434-6942; oldlymeicecream.com. Local folks swear by the creamy 16 percent butterfat content ice cream made here—with reason. There are 35 flavors in all (16 available daily on a rotating basis), plus house-made Italian ices (try the lemon or strawberry kiwi), sherbets, and yogurts. There are a few tables inside and out front where you may also enjoy take-out soups, 12 types of sandwiches (with fun names like Phat Albert, Petunia Pig, and Froghorn Leghorn), muffins, and Danish pastries. But the ice cream and ices are the big draw, along with the coffee bar, which offers Ashlawn Farm coffees, cappuccino, espresso, latte, and mocha, plus teas and hot chocolate. Closed Jan and Mon.

Palmieri Food Products, Inc., 145 Hamilton St., New Haven; (800) 845-5447; palmierifoods.com. Since 1920, the Palmieri family has been making all-natural, additive-free pasta sauces. At present they have 12 tomato-based sauces, along with horseradish and cocktail sauces, a salsa, a barbecue sauce, and a buffalo-chicken-wing dip, all distributed and sold around the state at Stop & Shop stores, XPECT Stores, Geissler Markets, and, in this area, Robert's Food Center, Madison. The spaghetti sauce remains Palmieri's most popular item. Palmieri's is also a bottling facility for many small producers, such as farmers who want to transform excess crops into bottled sauces and spreads to sell at their farm stands under private labels.

Pasta Cosi, 1018 Main St. on the Green, Branford; (203) 483-9397; billyspastacosi.com/store. Pasta Cosi, a line of five robust, flavorful Italian sauces, was developed in Billy DiLegge's funky little Italian restaurant, **Pasta Cosi** (p. 298), at this same Branford location. Sauces in the line, gluten free, low in salt, and natural, include roasted garlic, vodka, arrabbiata, puttanesca, and marinara and are sold at **Star Fish Market** (p. 273) in Guilford, all Stop & Shops, and other stores throughout the state. They are also available here at the restaurant and via the website.

Sankow's Beaver Brook Farm, 139 Beaver Brook Rd., Lyme; (860) 434-2843; beaverbrookfarm.com. Suzanne and Stanley Sankow are multitaskers. Using the wool from their Romney Border Luster and East Frisian sheep—part of a flock of 700 that roam their 175-acre farm (a viable dairy farm since 1917)—they make blankets, sweaters, caps, hats, scarves, and mittens, which are sold in the wool shop on the grounds. From the sheep and Jersey cows (all raised free of growth hormones and antibiotics), Suzanne produces some great farmstead cheeses (Summer Savory, feta, Pleasant Valley, Pleasant Son, Pleasant Cow, Nehantic Abbey, and Farmstead, among them), as well as ricotta, and thick yogurt, all available in the farm market shop on the grounds, along with USDA-inspected lamb roasts, chops, patties, and sausages (salami, pastrami, *landjäger,* and garlic fennel). Pleasant Cow, Sankow's most popular cow's-milk cheese, was chosen by *Saveur* magazine as one of the 50 best cheeses made in the US. This is one of the few dairies in the state licensed to sell raw milk. Its kitchen processes 400 Cornish Cross chickens a month.

Products made in Sankow's farm kitchen are sold in the farm market shop as well: shepherd's pie; lamb Bolognese; lamb curry stew; lamb-and-white bean chili; cheese spreads, such as horseradish ricotta and Greek *tzatziki.*

Thornton Wilder, who lived in Hamden for 29 years, once wrote, "My advice to you is not to inquire why or whither, but just enjoy your ice cream while it is on your plate."

Sankow products, including Stanley's heirloom and greenhouse tomatoes, are available at 10 farmers' markets in season: Greenwich, Old Greenwich, Westport, Farmington, Madison, Wooster Square in New Haven, West Hartford, and Bishop's Orchards markets among them. On the Sat and Sun after Thanksgiving, Sankow's holds its Annual Farm Days, when visitors may watch the sheep shearing, sample meats and cheeses, enjoy a horse-drawn hayride over the grounds, and watch spinning demonstrations. It's a fun—and free—time down at the farm.

Stonington Seafood Harvesters, 4 High St., Stonington; (860) 535-8342. This small, one-family company is famous among discerning Connecticut chefs for its sea scallops, which Captain Billy Bomster Jr. and his brothers, Joe and Mike, dredge from the Atlantic Ocean depths on their western-rigged scallop trawler, the *F/V Patty Jo*. What makes the Bomster scallops different is that they are shucked by the crew and flash-frozen in heavy, 1-pound plastic pouches within minutes of coming onboard, instead of sitting on ice in the hold for 2 weeks before the boat lands. This quick process protects the flavor, color, and firmness, leading family patriarch Bill Bomster to believe they are the "world's finest all-natural, unadulterated, scrumptious sea scallops." Judge for yourself. You can order with UPS next-day delivery to your door. The scallops come in five 1-pound pouches shipped in a foam box that preserves their cryogenic condition. At the Bomster self-service freezer on High Street, the scallops, along with fresh-frozen local seafood (cod, flounder, tuna steaks, hand-cut salmon fillets), are for sale on the honor system. You can also buy them from McQuade's Marketplace in Mystic, among many area outlets. Seasonally, from July through Nov, the Bomsters sell Key West pink shrimp, too.

Walking Wood, 104 Seymour Rd. (Rte. 67), Woodbridge; (203) 393-1029; wooziewikfors@snet.net. Woozie Wikfors began raising poultry in 1998 when a friend gave her two adolescent emus, Stella and Mnck (because "mnck, mnck" is the sound it makes). They're still laying and may for another 25 years—emus live long productive lives. She sold their huge, deep-forest-green eggs at a premium and soon found herself raising chickens as well. She now has 30 different heritage breeds, which include Cochin and Polish crested hens, and raises Pekin, Cayuga, and Welsh Harlequin ducks; Black Spanish turkeys; rare breeds of rabbits (American Blue and Havanas); and quail (Wisconsin bobwhites and Coturnix) too. All the livestock are free-range and organic, scampering over her 5.5 acres (which back on to 300 acres). Woozie calls them "my girls" and praises to the sky the merits of free-range and organic. During the season, Woozie sells her eggs at several farmers' markets. She also sells chickens, quail, and rabbits. A farm visit may be arranged by appointment.

Wentworth Homemade Ice Cream, 3697 Whitney Ave., Hamden; (203) 281-7429. Since 1988, Regina Banos's homey ice-cream parlor, in an old house with a gazebo and yard, has been going strong. Her 40 flavors of natural house-made ice creams are delicious, with 16 percent butterfat content and all-natural flavorings. The coffee ice cream begins with brewed coffee, and the peach, banana, and other fruit ice creams are all made with real fresh fruits. Flavors include butter pecan, rum raisin, Heath bar crunch, Snickers cheesecake, mint Oreo, mocha lace, maple walnut, red velvet chocolate Reeses Cup, and chocolate fudge brownie, plus, in the fall, coconut pineapple and pumpkin. There's even ice cream for dogs: K-9 crunch. Closed Sun.

Specialty Stores & Markets

Ashlawn Farm, 78 Bill Hill Rd., Lyme; (860) 434-3636; farmcoffee .com. This farm has been in the same family since 1909. Chip and Carol Dahlke have turned their century-old, 100-acre farm into a coffee roastery. Some 20 types of coffee beans, from all over the coffee-growing world, eight decafs, and more than seven flavored coffees are roasted in the old milking barn. They feature a flavor of the month, which might be French vanilla, toasted almond, cinnamon

Danish, or some other. Chip sells to upscale shops, groceries, cafes, and restaurants in this area and claims coffee doesn't get any fresher than Ashlawn's. I believe him. Closed Sunday and Monday.

Atlantic Seafood, 1400–1410 Boston Post Rd., Old Saybrook; (860) 388-4527; atlanticseafoodmarket.com. New and larger space is a backdrop for the freshest of fish and shellfish presented on immaculate trays in refrigerated display cases in this compelling market. The freezer is especially attention grabbing, packed with seafood dishes—stuffed clams, clam chowder, lobster bisque, marinated mussels, 8 to 10 different salads, house-made crab cakes, 20 sides, salads and soups, and other dishes (all made in-house). There are complete gourmet meals that might feature poached salmon, swordfish cakes, ginger tilapia, clam and sausage, or lobster pie. "Only the freshest" is owner Lisa Feinman's Atlantic Seafood motto, and you are urged to call ahead to find out what piscine wonders have just arrived from Point Judith, Rhode Island, or New Bedford, Massachusetts, the seagoing sources of all these nautical denizens of the deep. If you're planning an old-fashioned clambake, Atlantic Seafood can be the source for everything you need, except the logs and sandpit. Wild Alaskan salmon, sushi-fresh yellowfin tuna, littleneck and steamer clams, Mystic River oysters, sea scallops, mako shark, whole live lobsters, and all kinds of tasty fresh fish are available.

Bon Appetit, 2979 Whitney Ave., Hamden; (203) 248-0648; bonappetitct.com. In 1971 Roland and Andrea Blakeslee opened their gourmet food shop and have stayed ahead of the curve ever since. Today this attractive, well-organized shop is like a wish list of every high-quality delicacy you can imagine: condiments, dips and spreads, dessert sauces, deli meats and salads, pâtés, cheeses, jams, mustards, oils, olives, rices, teas, and vinegars. A large assortment of local, regional, and international cheeses is flanked by glass-covered displays of fresh croissants, bagels, Danish, pastries, cookies, and luscious cakes. Tables, cupboards, display cases, even wine barrel tops are covered with good things to eat from all over the world, including Connecticut. Closed Sunday.

Caseus Fromagerie & Bistro, 93 Whitney Ave., New Haven; (203) 624-3373; caseusnewhaven.com. Caseus is two-faced: a remarkable cheese shop and a bistro serving lunch and dinner (see **Caseus Fromagerie & Bistro on** p. 295 for bistro info). As a cheese shop, Caseus (Latin for "cheese") on its two levels unfolds a wide world of wonderful artisanal cheeses (more than 100), both domestic and imported. Owner Jan Sobocinski keeps the cheeses company with olives, honeys, unusual pickles, Vosges and Poco Dolce chocolates, Raphael jams from France, Valderrama extra-virgin olive oil from Spain, Jim's Organic Wonderbrew coffee, and other select food items. Closed Sun.

Celtica, 1008 Chapel St., New Haven; (203) 785-8034; gotirish .com. This shop, which recently moved around the corner from its former College Street address, losing its tearoom in the process, is a bazaar of Irish goods, from nubbly sweaters to delicate glass, porcelain, and food products like assorted teas, Kate Reilly's Irish Soda Bread mix, Tommy Moloney's sausages, and various biscuits and cookies.

The Cooking Company, Swing Bridge Market Place, 1610 Saybrook Rd., Haddam; (860) 345-8008. Subtitled "A Prepared Food Market," this is no small-potatoes operation. Chef-Owner Susan Bauer and assistants prepare a vast panoply of delicious foods for customers to take away, reheat, and consume at home. It is also possible to nosh on the premises at one of 24 seats both inside and, in warm weather, just outside. Fresh salads (like grilled chicken Caesar pasta, Greek, Cobb, or the super-popular Southwest), soups, prepared entrees (walnut-crusted pork loin, Greek chicken, chicken enchiladas, among a rotating list), frittatas, sandwiches (12 different ones, including grilled panini), and multilayered wraps are a few of the freshly made possibilities. There are deli items (Genoa salami, maple-smoked turkey, spicy capocollo ham) and a frozen-foods section, where soups, appetizers, and desserts are showcased. To tempt the sweet tooth, there are fruit pies, oversize cookies, brownies, and cakes. A coffee bar with Ashlawn Farm coffees is just inside the entrance, and a rear room is stocked with fancy gourmet items: olive oils, vinegars, pickled vegetables, preserves, and other comestibles. A second **Cooking Company** shop is at 187 Rte. 81, Killingworth

(860-663-3111). It has a patio and make-your-own salad bar, plus similar seating. Both shops are closed Sun.

Dr. Lankin's Specialty Foods, 220 Rte. 12, Ste. 5 #391, Groton; (888) 256-6635; awesomealmonds.com. For a primary-care physician to develop a side business selling almonds may sound slightly, um, nutty, but these almonds are for real. So is Dr. Ken Lankin, who doesn't just play one on TV. Studying almonds for a college thesis on nutrition gave him a desire to experiment with roasting and flavoring these tasty nuts, which are so rich in vitamin E. Eventually he created Awesome Almonds in three flavors: orange-vanilla, cinnamon-vanilla, and cocoa-java. According to the good doctor, the California-grown almonds are good for cholesterol, heart disease, obesity, and other health problems. You can buy the Awesomes directly from the firm's website or at Mystic Sweets & Ice Cream Shoppe in Mystic and **Lee's Oriental Market** (p. 270) in New London, among many shops in this area. The nuts have no preservatives, salt, cholesterol, or added oils and are a gluten-free, vegan, and kosher-certified product. Closed Sat and Sun.

Fromage Fine Foods and Coffees, 873 Boston Post Rd., Old Saybrook; (860) 388-5750; fromagefinefoods.com. In moving from square footage of 300 to 1,800, this delightful gourmet shop has prospered and now has more tasties than ever. Owner Christine Chesanek sells some 210 different international cheeses, intriguing house-made cheese spreads, and customized gift baskets and cheese platters. On display are containers with 18 types of olives, a charcuterie section with Italian prosciutto, pancetta, Spanish *jamon serrano,* chorizos, and 20 types of salamis, and a coffee selection with 25 varieties from all over the world. There are venison and wild boar pâtes; interesting breads from Fabled Foods, Howard's, and Judies European Bakery; puff pastry and *phyllo* dough; and fresh pastries. The inventory continues with teas, spices, condiments, olive oils, caviar, local honey and jams, and a frozen-food section with ready-to-heat duck breasts, *phyllo hors d'oeuvres* (sold by the dozen), and other items. In short, it's one-stop shopping if you're planning a party. With all the extra space, Christine has added a fine display of high-end glass- and tableware, Melamine trays, and other table accessories.

Given Fine Chocolates & Indulgences, 696 Boston Post Rd., Madison; (203) 245-4646; givenchocolates.com. It's a given that this is the place to shop for all kinds of candies, so you might as well give in (ouch!). The selection ranges from Garrison and Moonstruck chocolate truffles to Knipschildt (whom some consider the Tiffany of handmade chocolates). Given has also teamed up with Fascia's and Joyzelle's Buttercrunch of Branford, giving you an ever-greater selection of chocolates. Given's distinctive robin's-egg blue boxes make great gift containers. Create your own truffle collection,

chocolate platter, or holiday gift baskets. Indulge the kiddies in your care at the "candy wall"—lined with huge glass jars of jelly beans, other penny candies, and retro candy bars.

Hong Kong Grocery, 71 Whitney Ave., New Haven; (203) 777-8881. Cluttered aisles and crammed-together cans, bags, and jars of all kinds of Chinese foods do not deter the crowds from this diminutive, if sometimes confusing, market. A prime source of fresh Chinese produce, 25-pound sacks of rice, and scores of hard-to-find Chinese and other Asian items, it is no wonder the place is jammed most of the time.

Lee's Oriental Market, 432 Williams St., New London; (860) 443-9665. What this small market lacks in size it makes up for in variety and orderliness. A fresh-food case has, among other veggies, napa cabbage, daikon, Korean radishes, bitter melons, lemongrass, and soybean sprouts. In the freezer are soybean kernels, egg-roll wrappers, gyoza skins, fish and fish cakes, grated cassava, and shu-mai dim sum. There are shelves full of various teas, a wide range of rice (including 25-pound sacks of Thai jasmine rice and sticky rice), dried mushrooms, roasted sesame seeds in quantity, gallon tins of soy sauce, packaged soups, and assorted candies and sweets. Chinese foods dominate, but there are Japanese, Filipino, Korean, and Thai goods as well, all neatly presented in well-kept surroundings.

Liuzzi Gourmet Food Market, 322 State St., North Haven; (203) 248-4356; liuzzicheese.com. As Italian delis go, Liuzzi's is a

standout. It not only sells numerous artisanal cheeses (including Spanish *Garrotxa*), but also stocks all kinds of cold cuts, many house-made or cured, such as *sopressata* and *abruzzese;* multitudinous types of olives, marinated mushrooms and anchovies; and scores of dried goods like olive oils and Italian pastas. Many cheeses are made in-house, like the fresh and smoked mozzarella, ricotta (both large curd and whipped), *caccioricotta,* and *caciocavallo.* In addition, there are take-home entrees (ham pie, house-made meatballs, spinach lasagna) and fresh-frozen pastas. All this and a butcher counter with fresh cuts of meat. Closed Sun.

Mystic Market East, 63 Williams Ave., Mystic; (860) 572-7992. **Mystic Market West,** 375 Noank Rd. (Rte. 215), Mystic; (860) 536-1500. mysticmarket.com. These two intriguing markets specialize—in their words—in "catering * cuisine * confection." Though both markets have the same ownership—Charles Spathakis—Mystic Market East has a larger selection of baked goods, elegant cakes, cannoli, tarts, eclairs, pies, and dessert trays of miniature pastries. **Mystic Market West** specializes in fresh-baked breads, condiments, and other comestibles to satisfy most gourmet needs, such as cheeses from all over the world, gourmet dips, oils, sauces, fine coffees and teas, salads, and sandwiches. If you want someone else to do the work for your party, wedding, or another special "do," the markets' catering wing, called **Coastal Gourmet,** offers numerous specialty menus.

Romeo and Cesare's Gourmet, 771 Orange St., New Haven; (203) 776-1614; romeoceasersgourmetshop.com. Have you ever been in a shop so packed with gourmet goodies you have difficulty navigating the aisles? That's Romeo and Cesare's. Name the gourmet goody, they've probably got it. Sausages galore—whole dry-cured ones like *capocolla,* chorizo, *sweet coppa,* and *crespone,* plus fresh house-made sausage. Buffalo mozzarella, aged provolone, and *tuma persa* are just a few of the many cheeses. Then there are the nine types of imported nougat—filled with figs and nuts, candied fruit, or marzipan—as well as cakes and tarts galore. The cannoli and pignoli cookies are made on the premises. The deli section is alive and thriving, with hot sandwiches, all kinds of salads, and such entrees as chicken cacciatore, chicken Marsala, beef pizzaiola, and eggplant parmigiana.

Saeed's International Market and Cafe, 464 Ocean Ave., New London; (860) 440-3822; $. This popular Middle Eastern–Mediterranean grocery has space galore—3,500 square feet of space. Owner Patti Said carries cheeses from all over the Middle East and Europe. A deli case features meats, spinach and cheese pies, baklava, other honeyed pastries, and fresh *phyllo* dough. An olive bar displays 12 different bins of briny olives. Grains include couscous, *mograyeh* (Israeli toasted couscous), and lentils, plus all kinds of nuts, spices, and seeds. Also available: kosher and Italian organic lines; olive oils from Crete, Greece, Lebanon, Israel, Spain, and Italy, plus other oils (walnut, almond, grape seed, basil, sesame, hazelnut, and pepper); hummus; Greek yogurt; *taramasalata;* a variety of coffees and teas;

and breads and other baked goods. At any of 10 tables, you can sit and munch gyros and other hot sandwiches, or nibble a pastry or Turkish delight, along with a cup of coffee from an expanded coffee list. In warm weather you might do your snacking outside on one of two patios. Closed Sunday.

Simon's Marketplace, 17 Main St., Chester; (860) 526-8984; $. Tiny as Chester is, it has blossomed into a real foodie town. Credit this large, wonderfully inclusive market, owned by Jim and Jody Reilly, for some of the local excitement. The spacious store has 24 seats for breakfast, lunch, and snacking. Other attractions include a gourmet delicatessen case with salads and meats; Jim's Organic Free Trade coffees in bulk; and 10 flavors of Salem Valley Farms ice cream. Take-out dishes, such as shepherd's pie and stuffed eggplant, are made on the premises and change daily. Another big draw: fresh-made scones (different each day) and a number of sandwiches. Simon's also sells toys, greeting cards, and gifts.

Star Fish Market, 650 Village Walk, Guilford; (203) 458-3474; starfishmkt.com. I am not out to sea when I call this the prettiest seafood store I have ever seen, with displays so artistic you might think you are in an art gallery. The fish are displayed on plates in the refrigerated glass case, one fillet or fish per plate, sometimes with a single sprig of herb adorning it—sea-fresh, pristine, immaculate. Star Fish sources all seafood to ensure that it follows government guidelines. The entire shop is beautiful, with shelves and tables full of deluxe products: olive oils, dried pastas, sauces, seafood accoutrements. A section with frozen and smoked fish, sausage, Niman Ranch meats, chicken, and game is also inviting, as are the large and choice imported artisanal cheese selections, cured charcuterie, and bread display. Star Fish, a sterling little store in an upscale shopping complex, is a work of art, a still life of perfection. Closed Sun and Mon.

Sweet Cioccolata, 28 North Colony St. (Rte. 5), Wallingford; (203) 294-1280; sweetcioccolata.com. Since 1998 Rachel Ceste has been selling her unusual chocolates, wholesale and retail. "Create your own gift" is her motto, and the shop is full of baskets and individually wrapped chocolates (like almond bark, chocolate peanut clusters, and chocolate-covered pretzels), to be individually selected by you and popped into the basket (there are preassembled baskets too if you don't want to choose your own). House-made treats include chocolate-dipped strawberries, dried apricots and pears, chocolate-covered Oreos and shortbreads, and chocolate turtles. Very popular are caramel-dipped, chocolate-covered apples and pears. Closed Sun and Mon.

Farmers' Markets

For up-to-the-minute information about dates and hours, which can change from year to year, call the Connecticut Department of Agriculture at (860) 713-2503, visit its website at state.ct.us/doag, or e-mail ctdeptag@po.state.ct.us. All the New Haven farmers' markets listed here are projects of CitySeed (203-773-3736; cityseed .org), a local nonprofit dedicated to promoting local development, sustainable farming, and the slow-food movement. In Cityseed farmers' markets all items are from Connecticut farms, bakeries, or producers, and most are organic or pesticide free.

Branford Farmers' Market, parking lot behind Town Green, Branford. Sun from 10 a.m. to 1 p.m., mid-June through Oct.

Chester Village Farmers' Market, town center, Chester. Sun from 10 a.m. to 1 p.m., mid-June through Oct.

Clinton–Chamard Vineyards Farmers' Market, 115 Cow Hill Rd., Clinton. Sun from noon to 3 p.m., late May through Oct.

Clinton Farmers' Market, 48 Main St., Clinton. Fri from 3 to 6 p.m., end of May through Oct.

Deep River Farmers' Market, in front of Deep River Library, Main Street, Deep River. Thurs from 3 to 6 p.m., June through Oct.

East Haddam Farmers' Market, Town grange, Town Street, East Haddam. Wed from 4 to 7 p.m., mid-June through Oct.

East Haven Farmers' Market, East Haven Town Hall, 250 Main St., East Haven. Sun from 9 a.m. to 12:30 p.m., early July through first week of Oct.

East Lyme Farmers' Market, East Lyme High School parking lot, East Lyme. Sun from 10 a.m. to 1 p.m., mid-July through Oct.

Essex Farmers' Market, Main Street, behind the Griswold Inn, Essex. Fri from 3 to 6 p.m., mid-June through Sept.

Griswold/Jewett City Farmers' Market, Griswold Town Hall, 28 Main St., Jewett City. Mon from 3 to 6:30 p.m., mid-June through early Nov.

Griswold–Pachaug Village Farmers' Market, 852 Voluntown Rd. (Rte. 138), Geer's Earth and Landscape Products, Jewett City. Sat from 9 a.m. to noon, end of June through Oct.

Groton Farmers' Market, Groton Shopping Plaza, next to the post office, Rte. 1, Groton. Wed from 11 a.m. to 6 p.m., mid-July through early Nov.

Guilford Farmers' Market, 2351 Durham Rd., Guilford. Sat from 9 a.m. to noon, from late June through Oct.

Hamden–Downtown Farmers' Market, Town Center Park, next to Miller Library, 2663 Dixwell Ave., Hamden. Fri from 11 a.m. to 3 p.m., end of June through first week of Oct.

Hamden–Spring Glen Farmers' Market, Spring Glen Church, 1825 Whitney Ave., Hamden. Wed from 3 to 6 p.m., late June through Oct.

Higganum Village Market Farmers' Market, Town Green, intersection of Rte. 81 and Rte. 154, Higganum. **Fri from 3:30 to 6:30 p.m., June through Oct.**

Ivoryton Village Alliance Farmers' Market, next to Ivoryton Playhouse, Ivoryton. **Sat from 9 a.m. to 1 p.m., mid-June through late Oct.**

Ledyard Farmers' Market, Ledyard Center fairgrounds, Ledyard. **Wed from 4 to 7 p.m., early June through Sept.**

Lyme-Ashlawn Farmers' Market, 78 Bill Hill Rd. (at Ashlawn Farm), Lyme. **Sat from 9:30 a.m. to noon, June through Nov.**

Madison Farmers' Market, 261 Meeting House Rd., Madison Historic Town Green, Madison. **Fri from 3 to 6 p.m., early May through Oct.**

Madison Rest Area Farmers' Market, southbound rest area, I-95, Madison. **Thurs and Sun from 10 a.m. to 5 p.m., May through Oct.**

Mystic/Denison Farmers' Market, across from Denison/Pequotsepus Nature Center, 120 Pequotsepus Rd., Mystic. **Sun from noon to 3 p.m., early June through Oct.**

Mystic Farmers' Market, Quiambaug Fire House, 50 Old Stonington Rd., Mystic. **Tues from 2 to 6 p.m., May through late Oct.**

New Haven Cityseed Downtown Farmers' Market, Church Street on the Green at City Hall, New Haven. Wed from 11 a.m. to 3 p.m., mid-June through late Nov.

New Haven Cityseed Edgewood Park Farmers' Market, Edgewood Park, corner of West Rock and Whalley Avenues, New Haven. Sun from 10 a.m. to 2 p.m., May to mid-Dec. Winter market: Sun from 10 a.m. to 1 p.m., Jan through May.

New Haven Cityseed Wooster Square Farmers' Market, Russo Park, DePalma Court between Chapel and Wooster Streets, New Haven. Sat from 9 a.m. to 1 p.m., May through mid-Dec. Winter market: Sat from 10 a.m. to 1 p.m., from Jan through Apr.

New Haven Fair Haven Farmers' Market, Quinnipiac River Park, corner of Grand Avenue and Front Street, New Haven. Thurs from 2:30 to 6:30 p.m., mid-July through Oct.

New Haven/The Hill Farmers' Market, Connecticut Mental Health Center, corner of Park and South Streets, New Haven. Fri from 11:30 a.m. to 3:30 p.m., mid-July through Oct.

New Haven State Street Farmers' Market, grassy lot next to 1010 State St., in front of State and Mechanic Streets, New Haven. Sat from 9 a.m. to 1 p.m., Aug through late Nov.

New London-Fiddleheads Food Coop Farmers' Market, 13 Broad St., New London. Sat from 9 a.m. to 4 p.m., Oct through Apr.

New London Field of Greens Farmers' Market, Montauk Avenue, New London. Tues and Fri from 9:30 a.m. to 2 p.m., mid-June through Oct.

Niantic Farmers' Market, Methodist Street parking lot, Niantic. Thurs from 3 p.m. to 6 p.m., late May through Oct.

North Guilford–Dudley Farmers' Market, 2351 Durham Rd., North Guilford. Sat from 9 a.m. to 12:30 p.m., first week of June through Oct.

Old Saybrook Farmers' Market, Cinema Plaza, 210 Main St., Old Saybrook. Sat from 9 a.m. to 1 p.m. and Wed from 10 a.m. to 12.30 p.m., June through Oct.

Orange Farmers' Market, Orange city fairgrounds, 525 Orange Center Rd., Orange. Wed from 3:30 to 6:30 p.m., late June through Oct.

Pawcatuck Farmers' Market, Park on the River, West Broad and Main Streets, Pawcatuck. Thurs from 2 to 6 p.m., from July through Oct.

Stonington Farmers' Market, Community Center, Stonington. Sat from 9 a.m. to noon, early May through Oct.

Wallingford Gardeners' Market, Railroad Station Green (Rte. 5 and Rte. 150), Wallingford. Sat from 9 a.m. to noon, mid-July through mid-Sept. Cooking demonstrations feature local produce and gardeners' products.

West Haven Farmers' Market, West Haven Green, corner of Campbell Avenue and Main Street, West Haven. Thurs and Sat from 10 a.m. to 2 p.m., early July through Oct.

Farm Stands

Bishop's Orchards Farm Market and Winery, 1355 Boston Post Rd., Guilford; (203) 458-7425; bishopsorchards.com. This is one enormous operation with a market, bakery, and winery—like a mini-supermarket, which has grown through time from a simple roadside stand. Five generations of Bishops have farmed here since 1871. Of the farm's 320 acres, 140 are devoted to apples alone, 22 to peaches, 27 to pears, plus miscellaneous parcels for strawberries, blueberries, raspberries, and pumpkins. You may pick your own from June through Oct. Seasonal fruits are offered as they ripen: strawberries first, in mid-June; blueberries next, July through Sept; raspberries and peaches, in mid-Aug; pears and apples at the end of Aug; and apples and raspberries continuing into mid-Oct. Oh yes, pumpkins ripen in late Sept and are available for Halloween. Bishop's sells their produce, their own pies and breads, pasteurized apple cider, apple butter and other preserves with their label, herbs from their greenhouse, cut flowers, fruit baskets, and gift packs (which they will ship). The market also sells some grocery items made elsewhere. The Bishop's Orchards' own fruit wines are available in the store for sampling and purchase. In 2012 their Celebration apple wine, Bishop's Farmhouse Style Hard Cider, and Bishop's Happley ImPeared, won first, second, and third places respectively in a *Connecticut* magazine tasting. Two other seasonal **Bishop's Orchards** locations are at 1920 Middletown Ave., Northford; and 480 New England Rd., Guilford. A very efficient hotline (203-458-PICK) for PYO is a day-to-day guide to what's available, where, when, and at what prices. They are open Sept through Oct, weekends only.

Four Mile River Farm & Greenhouse, 124 Four Mile River Rd., Old Lyme; (860) 434-2378; fourmileriverfarm.com. Teaching history for years in Hamden wasn't enough for Nunzio Corsino II, so in 1985 he began to farm his 18 acres, raising Yorkshire pigs (12 at a time) in open pens; Angus, Hereford, and Charloisis cattle (a herd of 30 to 35); and free-range laying hens (100), all without chemicals, antibiotics, or growth hormones. The certified meats are cut, processed, vacuum-packed, and flash frozen. Nunzio markets directly from his farm at five farmers' markets, as well as to area restaurants (**River Tavern,** p. 321, in Chester and Flood Tide in Mystic, for instance). The Corsino farm stand (with a freezer inside one of the outbuildings) has fresh eggs, steaks of various sizes, beef patties, beef kielbasa, mulch hay, and handcrafts made by Irene, Nunzio's wife—all sold on the honor system. Pigs are sold by special order with customers requesting in advance the desired division: chops, roast, ham steaks, bacon, and the like.

Hindinger Farm, 835 Dunbar Hill Rd., Hamden; (203) 288-0700; hindingersfarm.com. From the hills here you can see across Long Island Sound, a view Ann Hindinger; her late husband, Bill; and their children, George and Liz, enjoyed for years, as did Bill's grandfather, when he bought the farm in 1893. The produce is grown using modern techniques and sold at the Hindingers' farm stand. Depending on the season, you'll find apples, peaches, pears, strawberries, and such vegetables as asparagus, rhubarb, peas, cucumbers, beans, eggplants, and especially sweet corn and tomatoes. All these are at the store, as they ripen, beginning the first of May right up to Christmas (closed Mon). In addition to this fresh bounty, the Hindingers have added jellies, jams, salsas, maple syrup, fresh flowers, apple cider, cheeses, and gifts. Each year the family holds a strawberry festival in June. Call for date and time.

Holmberg Orchards, 12 Orchard Dr. (Rte. 12), Gales Ferry; (860) 464-7305; holmbergorchards.com. Here's another big farm and orchard beckoning you to pick fruit as it ripens: 15 varieties of apples, peaches, pears, nectarines, blueberries, raspberries, and pumpkins in season. You can finish up at the big farm market building for its freshly baked pies, turnovers, muffins, applesauce and apple crisp, newly harvested vegetables, and fresh-pressed apple cider. Stop by in the fall for their bales of hay, gourds, cornstalks, winter squashes, and dried flowers. Open daily year-round, with pick-your-own fruits available from July through Oct.

In 2010 the Holmbergs started winery planting and now have Pinot Blanc, from Alsatian white grapes, and also hard ciders available for tastings and sale. Tastings are Sat and Sun from May through early Nov.

Postscript: Russell Holmberg, the fourth generation of Holmbergs to work the farm, partnered with Margaret Chatey of **Westford Hill Distillers** (p. 350) in producing pears in her eau-de-vie bottles. To some 429 Bartlett pear blossoms he attaches her fancy Italian bottles with, sometimes, as many as 25 bottles "sprouting" on a single tree. Then—voilà!—in time the pear grows within each bottle. The end result is Westford Hill's Poire Prisonnière eau-de-vie.

J. DeFrancesco & Sons, Forest Road, Northford; (203) 484-2028; defrancescofarm@att.net.com. Anthony DeFrancesco began truck farming here in 1907, gradually expanding the farm—and his family, eventually siring four sons—with his wife, Philomena. At present, their grandson, Joe; his wife, Linda; and *their* four sons run 100 acres that now include 7 acres of greenhouses for flowers. Outdoor plantings of fruit and vegetables include peas, beans, strawberries, tomatoes, eggplants, cantaloupes, watermelons, a dozen varieties of sweet corn, and pumpkins. These are sold to stores, restaurants, and at the farm stand, over which Linda reigns. The stand is in a venerable old horse-and-carriage barn and is open daily from Palm Sunday through Halloween. Call for specific days and hours in other seasons. The proceeds from admission to

Digesting Hamburger History

Louis' Lunch, 261–263 Crown St., New Haven; (203) 562-5507; louislunch.com; $. Louis is a local celebrity and here's why: New Havenites insist that the hamburger was born in their city, the creation of Louis Lassen in 1900. According to Louis's grandson, Ken, it was midday when a man dashed in to Louis's luncheonette and breathlessly ordered a quick meal he could eat on the run. Louis slapped a freshly broiled beef patty between two slices of bread, and the customer rushed away, unaware he was part of history. Louis' (pronounced "Louie") Lunch is a pocket-size landmark on the National Register of Historic Places. Moved from its original spot in 1967, the tiny redbrick building with its red-shuttered windows was reconstructed, with bricks contributed by hundreds of nostalgic devotees. Ken Lassen still uses Louis's original recipe, broiling each fresh-ground beef patty—reportedly more than 90 percent lean, ground fresh each morning—on the antique vertical cast-iron grill, serving it between toasted bread slices. Cheddar cheese spread, fresh tomato, and caramelized onion are the garnishes of choice. And whatever you do, don't ask for mustard or ketchup, which are taboo to Louis purists. Closed Sun, Mon, the second week of Jan, Good Friday through Easter Sunday, and all of Aug for "the annual spoon inventory."

the corn maze go to treat autism. You might inquire about the possibility of purchasing a share of the harvest.

Maple Lane Farm, 57 Northwest Corner Rd., Preston; (860) 889-3766, 24-hour picking hotline (860) 887-8855; maplelane.com. **This one-time cow pasture has evolved into Allyn Brown III's pristine 120-acre farm, where you can pick your own strawberries, raspberries, and blueberries all summer long, plus 12 apple varieties and peaches into fall, and you can cut your own Christmas trees, garlands, and wreaths in Dec. The trees, on 3 acres, are Canaan fir, blue spruce, and white pine. There is no farm stand *per se* here now, but picking one's own is definitely "in." And with the dwarf trees, picking is much easier and safer. During the fall pumpkin season, there are weekend hayrides. Open Apr through Christmas.**

Medlyn's Farm Market, 710 Leetes Island Rd., Branford; (203) 488-3578. **With a range of vegetables that includes eggplants, beans, peas, sweet corn, tomatoes, squashes, potatoes, peppers, and pumpkins, you're not likely to go home disappointed. The market also has melons, rhubarbs, and strawberries in their growing seasons plus free-range eggs, flowers, jams, and jellies. Open June through late Oct.**

Scott's Yankee Farmer, 436 Boston Post Rd. (Rte. 1), East Lyme; (860) 739-5209; scottsyankeefarmer.net. **Wainwright and Audrey Scott planted orchards and opened a farm stand in the 1960s. Now son Tom and his wife, Karen, have taken over the 125 acres,**

cultivating apples, strawberries, raspberries, and blueberries for picking fresh during the growing season, June through Oct. Also for sale are vegetables, cider, jams, honey, pies, homemade doughnuts, and more. There are weekend wagon rides in autumn and a corn maze operating until Halloween weekend. The farm stand is open from mid-Apr through Dec.

Smith's Acres, 4 West Main St., Niantic; (860) 691-0528; smiths acres.com. The busiest stand in several farmers' markets belongs to Joe and Teri Smith, and now their daughter, Kirsten, where buyers line up patiently to buy the Smiths' big juicy ripe tomatoes, apples, and, in the fall, various types of squashes, parsnips, and other root veggies, all CtGrown. Open from 2 weeks before Easter until Christmas Eve.

Food Happenings

March–May

Taste of the Nation New Haven, New Haven; (203) 430-6453; ce.strength.org/newhaven. This is New Haven's largest, most successful, annual fund-raising event, going strong since 1987. It benefits the Connecticut Food Bank and Christian Community Action. There are more than 50 different wines available for sampling, cooking demonstrations, a Champagne seminar, and an auction. Many of the area's finest restaurant chefs participate. The month in which the event is held and the location change, so it's imperative to call well ahead.

June

Annual Shad Bake, Essex Elementary School, Centerbrook; rotary clubofessex.com. This genial family event, held since 1973, is usually a first Sat-in-June "happening." Fresh shad, cooked on oak planks, is the big draw, along with clams and oysters—though hot dogs and chicken are on hand for nonshad eaters. All in all, almost 1,000 people leave the event full and happy. There's live music, children's rides, and family activities, with funds from the event going to Rotary Club good works.

First Congregational Church Strawberry Jazz Festival, Town Common, Madison; (203) 245-2739; fccmadison.org/ourevents. This event is held around the first of June and brings together local arts and crafters, jazz aficionados, and strawberry shortcake. Hard to go wrong with art and crafts on display and for sale, music to listen to, and good food to munch on.

Annual Strawberry Festival at Hindinger Farm, 835 Dunbar Hill Rd., Hamden; (203) 288-0700; hindingersfarm.com. This mid-June event is usually held the Sat before Father's Day. Clowns, good food, and hayrides on tractors are all part of the fun. Hindinger Farm also offers some wonderful views.

Branford Festival, Town Green, South Main St., Branford; (203) 488-5500 or (203) 488-8304; branfordfestival.com. This perennial 3-day event occurs over Father's Day weekend in June. It begins Fri evening with food, music, and entertainment. The highlight on Sat is a craft and community expo, with 180 displays. The festival ends on Sun with a road race. Call for schedule and details.

July

Lobster Festival & Arts & Crafts Show, Niantic Town Hall grounds, 108 Pennsylvania Ave., Niantic; (860) 739-2805; nianticlions.org. If it is the first weekend of July, it's time for Niantic's annual Lobster Festival, combined with a juried arts and crafts exhibition. Since 1978, this festival has been a summer highlight. The major star is always lobster, but there is also plenty of fresh clam chowder, fresh strawberries and shortcake, fried dough, curly fries, and other delicious consumables, including chicken barbecue. Expect to find craftspeople, painters, and sculptors displaying their newest wonders both for sale and pleasure. The festival is a major fund-raiser of the Lions Club.

Clinton Bluefish Festival, Clinton Andrew Memorial Town Hall, Clinton; clintonbluefishfest.com. This town has gone all out for bluefish since 1973 and is proud of its sobriquet "Bluefish Capital of the World." The 2-day festival each year (usually in mid-July) begins on Fri and picks up again Sat. There are numerous food booths, serving seafood, pulled pork, fish chowder, fried dough, and more. The popular seafood chowder cook-off is a singular event in which patrons can taste the winning entries. There's live music both days, games, entertainment, and a fishing tournament, in which dedicated anglers compete to land the biggest bluefish ever.

Market "En Plein Air," Florence Griswold Museum, 96 Lyme St., Old Lyme; (860) 434-5542; flogris.org. This is an event within an event. Historic Old Lyme celebrates the annual town-wide Midsummer Festival, usually the last Fri and Sat in July, which about 6,000 people attend (see oldlymemidsummerfestival.com for details). There is a live concert on the riverbank Fri evening, and on Sat the beautiful grounds and gardens of the Florence Griswold Museum become "En Plein Air," a French-style, open-air market. It bursts with top-quality Connecticut products—fresh produce, breads, fine cheeses, meats, specialty foods, and flowers—as well as imaginative fun projects and activities and a chance to visit the museum at a reduced admission charge.

August

New Haven Food & Wine Festival at the New Haven Open at Yale, New Haven; (855) 464-8366; newhavenopen.com. Tennis fans and foodies look forward to this annual festival, which takes place on the last Sat in Aug. There is wine tasting and signature dishes from well-known local restaurants, such as Pacifico, Bentara, Caseus,

Ibiza, Union League Cafe, and Claire's Corner Copia. This is a chance to meet celebrity chefs, cookbook teachers, and authors. A single price ticket includes a seat at the New Haven Open at Yale.

September

Haddam Neck Fair, 26 Quarry Hill Rd., Haddam Neck; haddam neckfair.com. The entire Labor Day weekend is fair time. Expect tractor pulls, skillet throws, and various other competitions throughout the long weekend. Children under 12 are free; 3-day weekend and senior passes are available. No pets are allowed.

October

Celebrate Wallingford, South Main and North Main Streets, Wallingford; (203) 284-1807; wallingfordcenterinc.com. Since it began in 1986, Celebrate Wallingford has been a popular annual event, highlighted by Taste of Wallingford, in which local restaurants offer their specialties at street-side booths. The celebration, held the first weekend of Oct, lasts 2 days, with the fun including live entertainment, arts, crafts, a food court, and activities for children. Call or check the website for the current year's dates and times.

Apple Festival & Craft Fair, Old Saybrook Middle School, Sheffield St., Old Saybrook; (860) 388-0121. Traditionally held Columbus Day weekend (or as near to it as possible), this annual 1-day

Saturday festival features apples in many tempting forms, other edibles (including homemade sauerkraut, hot dogs, and chili), and an abundance of handcrafts. The festive event is sponsored by the Old Saybrook Women's Club and benefits a scholarship and research on autism and Asperger's syndrome. It is always prudent to call ahead to confirm the date and times.

Elm City Legends, New Haven; (860) 815-9356; marchofdimes .com/connecticut. Held midweek in late Oct or early Nov, this food event is one of three major annual fund-raisers for the Connecticut March of Dimes. The other two are held in Hartford and Stamford. The New Haven event, which changes locales and dates each year, consists of a sit-down dinner, with silent and live auctions and awards. Chefs from various restaurants (along with other vendors) participate by donating such appetizing packages as cooking lessons with a master chef, a cocktail party for guests in a local restaurant, a wine dinner with experts, lunch with a local television personality, and a catered dinner for eight in your home. For details call (860) 812-0080.

Annual Apple Festival, Town Green, Rte. 85, Salem; (860) 859-1211; congregationalchurchsalem.org. Having hosted these celebrations since 1969, Salem's Congregational Church really knows the drill. Traditionally held the last Sat in Oct, this exuberant festival opens at 9 a.m., after weeks of preparation by church volunteers busy making apple pies, turnovers, crisps, Bettys, crumbs, Swedish apple puddings, applesauce cakes, and other apple goodies for the

big event. Various apple treats are available in the Old Center School building, as well as outside at such sundry stands as the Apple Fritter booth, the Apple Sundae & Hot Dog booth (in which apple sauerkraut is served with the weiners), and the Piece of the Pie booth (apple pie with or without cheddar cheese). At the crafts booths stuffed teddy-bear dolls wear an apple theme: a slick Jonathan or a Delicious femme fatale with feather boa. The Tea Room features hot apple pancakes served with tea or coffee. There is continuous music in the gazebo. The party's over when all the apple goodies have been sold, usually by around 1 p.m.

Nibbles

Atticus Bookstore Cafe, 1082 Chapel St., New Haven; (203) 776-4040; atticusbookstorecafe.com; $. This cafe in a bookstore began in 1981 with a couple of tables, a counter, and display cases at the edge of the bookstore, and now it takes up one-third of the store. There are now 18 tables for two and two large group tables, proof that readers and shoppers like a handy place for a wholesome sandwich or quick pick-me-up. Fresh-tasting soups, sandwiches, and delicious muffins, cookies, and tarts are the standards here, with the combo of a cup of soup and a huge half-sandwich one of the better deals. There are entrees too, like twice-baked mac and cheese, chicken potpie, and roasted salmon with quinoa tabouli. Breads and baked goods come from **Chabaso Bakery** (p. 251), which just happens to have the same ownership.

Bar Bouchon, 8 Scotland Ave., Madison; (203) 318-8004; $–$$. Pedigree is everything in this one-room, 20-seat cafe/restaurant. This is the handiwork of Jean-Pierre Vuillermet, the co-owner and chef of **Union League Cafe** (p. 324) in New Haven. The small bistro shines with such dishes as steak tartare, pike quenelles, pistachio sausage with lentils, fois gras burger, and *croque monsieur* and *croque madame*. You can do a lot more than just nibble here, though portions are generally small. The dinner menu features the likes of braised beef cheeks daube and cod Lyonnaise. Call ahead for reservations, which are essential.

Bartleby's Cafe, 46 West Main St., Mystic; (860) 245-0017; bartle bysmystic.com; $. This tea and coffee shop has been a real hangout since 1999—and no wonder. There are about 30 different loose teas available and coffee drinks run from Bartleby's own house coffee to latte, café au lait, espresso, cappuccino, and more. There is also a goodly selection of sandwiches, salads, soups, and sweets, such as lemon coconut cake, carrot raisin tea bread, and huge cookies. To engage you as you nibble or sip, there are newspapers, games, free Wi-Fi access, and the changing exhibits of paintings by local artists on the walls.

Brie & Bleu, 70 State St., New London; (860) 443-9463; thames river.com; $$. There's more to this cheese shop than meets the eye, tempting as the artisanal cheeses are. The shop doubles as a bistro. With a mere 13 tables, patrons sample from a short bistro menu that is mated with wines. Choices might include short ribs, seared duck breast, organic free-range chicken, cheese combos, and various bruschettas. As if cheese and bistro weren't enough to keep them busy, proprietors Charlotte Hennegan and Fred Argilagos also own Thames River Wine & Spirits next door (connected to the shop/bistro). The brick cellar of the wineshop is a trip in itself, like entering a spooky vault. (*The Cask of Amontillado,* anyone?) Closed Sun and holidays.

Cafe Flo, Florence Griswold Museum, 96 Lyme St., Old Lyme; (860) 434-5542; flogris.org; $. This cafe makes a convenient snack stop while viewing the museum's collection of American impressionst paintings. It wraps around the verandah of the Marshfields House beside the Lieutenant River. Catering is supplied by Gourmet Gallery of Stonington and includes soups; sandwiches; main courses, such as beef stew and *banh mi* (a baquette stuffed with spicy grilled pork, veggies and cilantro); and desserts, such as warm apple crisp and house-made ice cream. The menu changes three times during the cafe's open season, which is from June 1st to the end of Oct. During that time, cafe hours are the same as those of the museum.

Caseus Fromagerie & Bistro, 93 Whitney Ave., New Haven; (203) 624-3373; caseusnewhaven.com; $$. As a bistro, in limited, rather cramped space, Caseus functions just as well as in its fromagerie section, serving both French-inspired lunch and dinner, small and large plates. Everything made with cheese (like the mac and cheese and *tart du jour*) is especially delicious, and free-range organic chicken and day-boat scallops are just two of many other intriguing dishes. Closed Sun. Reservations are a must. Ask about their cheese truck (see **The Cheese Truck,** p. 253).

Dog Watch Cafe, Dodson Boatyard, 194 Water St., Stonington; (860) 415-4510; dogwatchcafe.com; $$. The deck view of sunsets is nonpareil and the seafood, for a place whose deck overlooks the water, is not bad either. Signature dishes are the dogwiches (sandwiches), ahi tuna tempura with three sauces, and whole belly clams. Also tempting are the lobster rolls, southwestern chicken egg rolls, Watch Hill oysters, and fried calamari salad.

Feast Gourmet Market, 159 Main St., Deep River; (860) 526-4056; $. Nibbling here can mean robust and unusual sandwiches on good bread, with natural and/or organic ingredients from neighboring farms and vendors. It might also mean hot pasta lunches made daily or anytime snacks of sandwiches and fresh pastries. Keep in mind there's also gourmet takeout and catering available.

Green Well Organic Tea & Coffee, 44 Crown St., New Haven; (203) 773-0590; greenwellnewhaven.com; $. Green walls (surprise!) with arty pictures surround this modest-size, all-green interior. Here you'll find lots of tea (not all green) and coffee, of course; artisanal sandwiches; hummus plates; quiches with kale chips; organic fruit juices; smoothies; trail mix snacks; and all kinds of muffins, proscuitto and cheese scones, biscotti, banana bread, and other baked goods. Opened in 2012, this little shop has already attracted a loyal following for breakfast, nibbles, snacks, and lunches.

Ibiza Tapas and Wine Bar, 1832 Dixwell Ave., Hamden; (203) 909-6512; ibizatapaswinebar.com; $. When I first mentioned going to a tapas bar some years ago, people thought I was saying "topless." That just shows how far we have come gastronomically. Ignacio Blanco may have started the current craze for tapas when he first brought genuine Spanish food to Connecticut, with restaurants in Norwalk (Meson Galicia) and New Haven (**Ibiza,** p. 312), and most recently (2009) this tapas bar in Hamden. Tapas have really caught on big time as more and more people are enjoying small plates or nibbles. This bar features many of my favorites: melt-in-the-mouth codfish croquettes, Bomba rice with chicken and chorizo, oxtail gnocchi, and fresh sardines lightly fried. Ignacio also offers some terrific Spanish wines, all very well priced.

Kitchen Little, Mystic River Marina, 36 Quarry Rd., Mystic; (860) 536-2122; kitchenlittle.org; $. Breakfast outdoors on a deck patio right on a lazy river, what could be nicer in warm weather? This handy spot is cozy indoors the rest of the year. Owner Flo Klewin has been dishing up goodies three times a day—breakfast, lunch, and dinner—since 1983. That's a pretty good record. I favor breakfast here, especially the eggs Benedict and Portuguese fisherman's omelet, but the seafood is fresh, from local waters, and lobster bisque and Rhode Island chowder are menu standards. Beer and wine are available.

Kitchen Zinc Artisan Pizza and Bar, Temple Plaza Courtyard, 966 Chapel St., (behind Zinc), New Haven; (203) 772-3002; kitchen zinc.com; $. Denise Appel, chef-owner of Kitchen Zinc, knows a good thing when she does it, and some time ago she added this annex, which is just around the corner from her original restaurant, **Zinc** (p. 325). Kitchen Zinc displays the same panache of its older sister but is more casual and modest. In short, it's a good pre- or post-theater stop for a quick bite, snack, or pizza.

Lobster Landing, 152 Commerce St., Clinton; (860) 669-2005; $$. Located next to a marina, what could be more appropriate for a lobster shack? This one, resting on pilings directly over the waters of Long Island Sound, with its sign nailed to a post, dates back 100 years and has been knocked down twice by hurricanes and rebuilt. For fans, it's worth it. The lobster is caught daily and served in rolls dressed with butter and lemon. Service is snappy and seating—for 60—is outdoors, shaded by awnings. Open from the last week in Apr through Dec. Call ahead to be sure it's open.

Pasta Cosi, 1018 Main St., Branford; (203) 483-9397; pastacosi .com; $. Plain and simple decor, delicious pasta. That pretty well sums up this small luncheonette-like place. Go with the pastas, all made in-house, Tuscan-influenced style, all with natural house-made sauces, all served in steroid-muscular portions. Owner Billy DiLegge's sauces are marketed elsewhere, though you can buy them here as well (see **Pasta Cosi** on p. 260). I'm partial to the *fusilli Gorgonzola di marino* (with chicken breast, toasted pine nuts, spinach, herbs, and cheese). The house cappuccino is great, too. Closed Mon.

The Place Restaurant, 901 Boston Post Rd. (US 1), Guilford; (203) 453-9276; theplaceguilford.com; $$. What makes this unassuming spot (holding sway since 1971) different from your usual clam shack, where the standard MO is fried everything, is that the Place cooks with hardwood, on a 24-foot grill, giving all the briny items a pleasing smoky quality. Fire-roasted clams, bluefish, catfish, shrimp, salmon, and lobster are among many delights, as well as landlubber dishes like grilled chicken and rib eye steak. Corn on the cob is the only side on the menu but feel free to bring your own salads, chips, and wine or beer. All the cooking is done outdoors, back in an oak tree–shaded parking area. The adjacent seating consists of cut tree stumps, so if it rains, you are out of luck. Cash only. Open from late Apr to mid- or late Oct, depending on the weather.

Pot au Pho, 77 Whitney Ave., New Haven; (203) 776-2248; $. If you say the name really fast, you'll catch the pun (pot au feu). Actually, this minuscule storefront cafe is not French, it's Vietnamese, the real deal, with authentic soups (like pho with beef, rice and noodles, or tamarind soup), noodle dishes, and salads like *goi ngo sen* (lotus stem with tofu or shrimp and pork). Many dishes are vegetarian; all of them let diverse flavors sing out. And the prices are outlandishly cheap.

Prime Time Cafe, 1 West Broad St., Pawcatuck; (860) 599-3840; ptcafe.com; $. "Downtown dining on the river" is this friendly cafe's motto, and it fits. The dining room is cozy, the food is tasty, and the price is right—low. Some of the dishes might be salmon and mussels Valencia, pine nut–encrusted salmon, crab-stuffed flounder with hazelnut cream sauce, pastas, and even vegetarian dishes. Open for lunch and dinner, but check the hours. The lounge stays open a tad longer.

RJ Cafe & Bistro, 768 Boston Post Rd., Madison; (203) 318-8008; rjjulia.com; $. Bookstore cafes are often utilitarian places for a quick bite while shopping. That is not the case at RJ Cafe, where tasty meals are the norm. Tucked in the rear of the state's most famous independent bookstore, RJ Julia, the cafe offers daily specials in soups, sandwiches (like the gooey and yummy grilled cheddar, fig, and arugula), paninis, quiches, salads, and entrees. La Rosticceria in Guilford supplies desserts—cookies, Irish-baked scones, biscotti, and cupcakes.

Savvy Tea Gourmet, Station Square, 28 Durham Rd., Madison; (203) 318-8666; savvyteagourmet.com; $. For Sunday brunch or regular lunch, this eat-plus-shop emphasizes tea. It features 250 loose teas, and sells teapots and other tea equipment as well as tea wholesale. The shop, which offers free Wi-Fi, has soups, artisan cheeses (from cows, goats, and sheep), and bakery treats. Thurs and Fri are Bistro Nights with a moderate prix-fixe menu for three courses. Closed Mon and Tues.

Somewhere in Time, 3175 Gold Star Hwy. East, Mystic; (860) 536-1985; somewhereintimecafe.com; $. Breakfast joints abound, but it's nice to find a comfy one like this little frame house. For one thing, it serves breakfast all day—and it's as ample or light as you want it. Some of the best comfort foods are the pancakes, omelets, and French toast. You might go for the Hocus Poaches (eggs of course), *huevos rancheros,* breakfast burritos, or Garden Scramble.

Sundial Gardens, 59 Hidden Lake Rd., Higganum; (860) 345-4290; sundialgardens.com. You want tea and company? You'll find it on a back road in Higganum. Sundial Gardens, a teatime treasure, is worth the hunt. Proprietor Ragna Tischler Goddard is both a tea and a garden expert, and a visit here allows you to enjoy her expertise. Her tea knowledge is extraordinary. Tea events are held once a month. For a small registration fee, Ragna offers a tasting of three teas; a dessert made by Ragna's husband, Tom (a skilled pastry chef); a brief lecture on tea; and a demonstration of tea implements. Many teas are for sale at the tea shop and via the online catalog, along with Ragna's herbal tisanes, small handmade Yixing teapots from China, and tea accessories. There's a tiny fee to visit the three formal architectural gardens (knot, 18th century, and topiary). Check the website or call to make a tea date reservation. During the Christmas season, the shop also has delicious food imports for sale—German stollen, *lebkuchen,* and marzipan and French preserves.

Turkish Kebab House, 1157 Campbell Ave., West Haven; (203) 933-0002; $. This is the third and most unassuming of the Turkish restaurants in the New Haven area. Like **Saray Turkish Restaurant** (p. 322), but unrelated to it, the Kebab House is also on Campbell Avenue and also BYO. As the name suggests, you'll find an array of sizzling hot kebabs here, *pirzola* (lamb chops), *doner kebab, adana kebab,* and chicken *kofte kebab,* along with an informal atmosphere and friendly service.

Learn to Cook

The Viking Center at HADCO, formerly Delia's Culinary Forum, 4 Laser Ln., Wallingford; (203) 303-2000, ext. 376; vikingcenter .com. Every Mon in spring and fall, Chef Cristiana Bryant hosts food demonstration classes that usually feature well-known Connecticut restaurant chefs. Held in a first-rate 21st-century facility, these seminars are typically attended by 20 people, though Cristiana offers personal hands-on classes for smaller groups and private one-on-one lessons as well. It's best to call ahead or check the website for the schedule.

Learn about Wine

Mt. Carmel Wine & Spirits Co., 2977 Whitney Ave., Hamden; (203) 281-0800; mtcarmelwine.com. Every year since 2002, this splendid shop has been voted Connecticut's Best Retail Wine Shop by *Connecticut* magazine for the range of its selections from all over the world. Mt. Carmel has had plenty of time to get its act together. When Prohibition ended in 1934, Sydney Levine devoted a corner of his family's general store to wine and spirits, which eventually took over the entire store. Descendants Ben and Bob Feinn now run the store, which is a source for rare wines, specialty wines, and value wines (those representing the best value for their price), taste tested and often imported exclusively and directly from small wineries in France and elsewhere. Hard-to-find older vintages are a specialty—notably Bordeaux, red and white Burgundies, Rhônes, and Ports. In addition to a great depth of French wines, the store offers wines from other parts of the world. Mt. Carmel's website is a helpful source for upcoming wine events—tastings and dinners—in the area. It also lists the store's weekly wine specials, with frank appraisals of specific wines. Closed Sun.

Landmark Eateries

Alforno Trattoria, 1654 Post Rd., Old Saybrook; (860) 399-4166; alforno.net; $-$$. While thin-crusted pizza is a specialty at this comfortably casual place, with its dominantly vibrant mural, the pastas are even better. Small plate versions make this a wonderful place for nibbles and/or a full meal. Bob Zemmel has been running this low-key favorite for over 20 years and clearly knows what he's doing—as does his wife and co-owner, Linda Giuca, formerly the food editor at the *Hartford Courant*. Some of the best pastas are the spaghetti with white clam sauce, tagliatelle Bolognese, four-cheese ravioli, pappardelle in wild boar sauce, and cannelloni Florentine. Desserts are mostly classically Italian: tiramisu, cannoli filled with sweet ricotta, and a molten chocolate cake. There are two dining rooms, but the second, smaller room is open only in summer and on weekends. See Linda's recipe for **Spaghetti with Clams** on p. 404.

Almost Everybody's Favorite Lobster Shack

Abbott's Lobster in the Rough, 117 Pearl St., Noank; (860) 536-7719; abbotts-lobster.com; $. This place flies below the radar screen, but for more than 30 years, multitudes have braved the hairpin-twisting, convoluted, and scary shore route to find this tucked-away gem. Fortunately, the road is well signposted. Once you have arrived at this unpresumptuous place, by a picture-pretty marina at Noank, facing Fishers Island Sound, the drill is simple. You order at the counter, wait briefly, then take your booty to a picnic table inside the "shack" or outside on the deck or grassy lawn. Accoutrements are basic plastic and paper, but a head-on view of the boats and water is so peaceful you might feel you are at the upper reaches of Maine. Though Abbott's has other choices, including a respectable clam chowder, Bay of Fundy steamers, and oysters on the half shell, the magnet is

Bentara, 76 Orange St., New Haven; (203) 562-2511; bentara .com; $$. Bentara ("King's highest servant" in Malay) opened in 1995 in East Haven, moved to New Haven in 1997, and has been there ever since, ensconced in this spacious restored building. With its shadow puppets, baskets, bamboo screen, and ceramic pots, the decor reminds me of many happy years spent in Asia—and so does the food, which reflects Malaysia's polyglot heritage, a mixture of Chinese, Indonesian, Indian, and Thai influences. Everything here is lobster. I prefer the lobster roll, a toasted, buttery bun piled high with luscious, tender, pure lobster meat, but lobster mavens with bigger appetites crave the whole crustacean—up to 10 pounders—steamed and served with drawn butter, coleslaw, and potato chips. Abbott's claims a "more humane" approach to preparing its lobsters: in a cooker in which the lobster is steamed above the boiling water, not in it. Tell that to the lobster. You can also order take-out lobster bakes in a canister (with live lobsters, steamers, mussels, corn on the cob, white and sweet potatoes, all nestled in damp seaweed), all ready to pop on the stove, outdoor grill, or campfire. Just remember: no fried foods here. Open daily from early May through Labor Day, thereafter on 3-day weekends (Friy to Sun) through Columbus Day. *A reminder:* It's BYOB and cash only.

aromatic and tasty (and well described on the menu) and complements the cosmopolitan wine list. I am partial to the coconut curry mussels, *satay, rojak* (salad with pineapple cubes, shrimp paste, and peanut sauce), *popia* (spring rolls), *kicapgoreng* (sweet and salty chicken with vegetables), *nasi goreng,* and *ikan percik* (grilled marinated salmon with coconut turmeric lime sauce), among many delights. The original Bentara, by the way, is in Malaysia, operated by the chef's mother.

Bistro Mediterranean and Tapas Bar, 383 Main St., East Haven; (203) 467-2500 or (203) 467-4300; bistromediterraneanandtapasbar.com; $–$$. Call them tapas, small plates, or appetizers, at this newish (2011) enterprise of the Garreno brothers, Leonardo (the chef) and Gabriel (front-of-house manager), they rule the roost here. True, you can have a regular meal, and it will be really, really good, but the tapas are so diverse and so delicious that a bunch of them makes a very rewarding lunch or dinner all by themselves. Spanish *piquillo* peppers stuffed with lamb, mashed potato and salted cod croquettes, and sautéed artichoke hearts are among those I remember fondly. The salads are zesty too, as are such entrees as the grilled salmon *a la plancha,* duck breast with sweet potato puree, and sea scallops in a lobster-Champagne sauce, to cite just a few. As you'd expect at a Spanish restaurant, the Spanish wines are fine choices, too. Reservations are strongly advised.

The Blue Oar, 16 Snyder Rd. (off Rte. 154), Haddam; (860) 345-2994; $$. This is a genuine sleeper. In fact, it sleeps most of the year, as it is open only from mid-May (Mother's Day) through mid-Oct (Columbus Day). That's because the cafe, the inspiration of owners Jody and Jim Reilly (who also own **Simon's Marketplace,** p. 273, in Chester), is outdoors at the edge of Midway Marina, which hugs the Connecticut River. Whether lounging at a vividly painted picnic table under a shade tree or on an open-sided deck, it's a lovely way to laze away a summer day or evening, savoring the Blue Oar's buttery lobster rolls, steamers, or even a grilled seafood dinner. This is no-frills eating at its most pastoral—simplest dishes are best here (and less pricey)—with BYO and plastic utensils the rule. Best dishes are salads; sandwiches, such as the barbecued beef and burgers; and grilled fish. The casualness may be why locals like CBS's Morley Safer and Chef Jacques Pepin enjoy it, too. No reservations. Cash only.

Boom, 63 Pilots Point Dr., Westbrook; (860) 399-2322; boomrestaurant.net; $$. The bad news about Boom is that the mother ship in Stonington is gone. The good news is that this Boom is thriving. There are many good things to eat at Boom—duck quesadilla, ginger-marinated pork chops, and sweet potato and walnut ravioli, for instance. But no meal is complete without a side of the signature razor-thin red onion rings, which are as crunchy and heavenly as ever. In warm weather you can dine outside and watch the yachts moored in Pilots Point Marina, where there are 1,000 slips. The marina is closed in Jan and Feb—and so is Boom.

Bravo Bravo Restaurant, 20 East Main St., Mystic; (860) 536-3228; bravobravoct.com; $$. Small, smart, and stylish, Bravo Bravo is a surprise to find in a tourist center like Mystic, where faster food is the norm. Owner Carol Kanabis's Italian-accented menu more than lives up to the urbane interior of white walls, mirrors, oak floors, and well-napped tables. The pasta dishes are most inspired, especially chicken-and-lobster ravioli (if it is on the menu when you visit), black-pepper fettuccine tossed with grilled scallops and sun-dried tomatoes in a Gorgonzola Alfredo sauce, and Cajun barbecue shrimp over polenta. I am always partial to a succulent *osso buco,* and Bravo Bravo makes a fine one. Located in the Whaler Inn, the restaurant has an entrance directly on the street. Closed Mon. You'll find the same ownership and efficiency at **Azu,** 32 West Main St., Mystic (860-536-6336), and at **Olio** (p. 319).

Cafe Routier, 1353 Boston Post Rd., Westbrook; (860) 399-8700; caferoutier.com; $–$$. When this French-style cafe first moved from Old Saybrook to Westbrook, some of the French village flavor went missing. It's back now, and dishes like pan-roasted ginger-chamomile monkfish, braised boneless short ribs, and "camp-style" grilled trout are pleasures to behold—and devour. A different region of the world is featured and changes every 2 months. At the bar you'll find small plates and tapas, light meals in themselves. A 40-seat lounge adjoins the bar and serves small plates after 10 p.m. Fri and Sat. Dinner only.

Claire's Corner Copia, 1000 Chapel St., New Haven; (203) 562-3888; clairescornercopia.com; $. Claire Criscuolo, chef, owner, and resident expert on vegetarian cooking, holds sway over this longtime mainstay in downtown New Haven. It opened in 1975 and loyal patrons regard the pudding-plain place almost like a private club. Claire herself is a registered nurse and knows whereof she cooks. Her vegetarian, vegan, organic, gluten-free, and kosher offerings, available all day long, are both imaginative and nutritious. In warm weather there's outdoor seating facing both Chapel and College

Streets. Next door at 1006 Chapel is Claire's second restaurant, **Basta Trattoria** (203-772-1715), drawing on Claire's Italian family traditions and recipes. It offers sustainable, organic, wild, natural food and line-caught fish and seafood but is not vegetarian. Open daily, but check as hours differ on different days. See Chef Claire Criscuolo's recipe for **Chef Claire's Lentil Soup** on p. 391.

Flanders Fish Market & Restaurant, 22 Chesterfield Rd. (Rte. 161), East Lyme; (860) 739-8866 or (800) 242-6055 (Connecticut); flandersfish.com; $$. What started as a modest fish market in 1983, when Paul and Donna Formica began selling her clear clam chowder at the fish counter, expanded little by little to a restaurant with 150 seats. On entering this modern building, which is highlighted by wraparound glass-windowed dining areas and a wooden deck with tables and sun umbrellas, you pass by the market's refrigerated display cases, often filled with the freshest of fresh cod, catfish, salmon, sea bass, fresh shad and shad roe (in season), and dozens of other deep-water denizens. I especially enjoy the clam fritters, oyster stew, whole clam bellies, charbroiled Stonington sea scallops, Gorgonzola shrimp, and velvety lobster bisque, a signature dish. As if they weren't busy enough, Flanders also caters kids' parties and old-fashioned New England clambakes, and ships any size lobster anywhere in the country by next-day air. On Sun there's a sumptuous seafood buffet.

Gelston House, 8 Main St., East Haddam; (860) 873-1411; gelston house.com; $$. This handsome Italianate Victorian building, a companion in period and architectural style to its immediate neighbor, the Goodspeed Opera House (same mid-19th-century era) next door, has had more ups and downs than a skyscraper elevator. Closed periodically, Gelston House is, happily, open again, serving meals in its dramatic 125-seat, slightly formal dining room with a sweeping overview of the Connecticut River below. More informal dinner menus are offered in the casual **Tavern Room** and on the patio. The menu is straightforward American, with lots of salads, burgers, and sandwiches available at lunch. Steak, seafood, and pasta are the main focus at dinner, along with a raw bar. Closed on Mon after Labor Day through the winter.

Geronimo Tequila Bar and Southwest Grill, 271 Crown St., New Haven; (203) 777-7700; geronimobarandgrill.com; $$. As the name—and the buffalo skulls and strings of dried chilis on the walls—might suggest, the 85-seat Geronimo specializes in the foods and drinks of Santa Fe and the Southwest. That means Mexican, Apache, Navajo, and Anglo American—with a contemporary twist. The twist translates into smoked bison brisket tamales; grilled mahimahi taco with mango *pico de gallo;* pork *relleno,* chorizo, and fig Navajo fry bread; chicken quesadillas; chicken breast mole; tuna tartare tacos; and pork *pibil.* It also means 300 tequilas available, which may have cornered the tequila market in the entire state of Connecticut. But there's more than just tequila (and mescals and margaritas) here. A large patio, seating 50, for nice weather dining and imbibing, adds to a really rocking scene.

G-Zen, 2 East Main St., Branford; (203) 208-0443; g-zen.com; $. Mark Shadle, who used to co-own **It's Only Natural** (p. 233) in Middletown, has moved on. He and his wife, Ami, now own and operate G-Zen, also a vegetarian restaurant, combining fresh local organic ingredients with a farm-to-table philosophy. Among their offerings are gluten-free pizza, Thimble Island crab cakes, Rock the Casbah Morrocan stew, sweet potato and Mayan sun enchiladas, sweet potato fries, carrot cake, chocolate-hazlenut cake, and even a fruity sangria, all served in zen-like surroundings that have the feel of a Japanese inn.

Ibiza, 39 High St., New Haven; (203) 865-1933; ibizanewhaven .com; $$$. Ibiza, named for one of Spain's Balearic Islands, began life as Pika Tapas, a tapas bar. It is now a full-fledged, first-rate restaurant, unquestionably one of the best Spanish ones in the country. As a lifetime Hispanophile, I pinch myself that we Nutmeggers are so lucky. Whether it's *calamares a la plancha,* braised oxtail with wild mushrooms, *bacalao confit, arroz de setas,* braised boneless short ribs, half a dozen other specialties, or the prix-fixe tasting menu, I'm confident you will enjoy Ibiza. And for tapas lovers, some 17 inspired ones await you at the bar. *Paella* for two (four different types) is available only Tues evening. Closed Sun. Co-owner Ignacio Blanco has another place, **Ibiza Tapas and Wine Bar** (p. 296), in Hamden.

Istanbul Cafe, 245 Crown St., New Haven; (203) 787-3881; istan bulcafect.com; $-$$. This touch of Turkey was the first Turkish restaurant in New Haven, from 1998 onward—and remains, after 15 years, one of the best. While Turkish cuisine is underrepresented throughout Connecticut, there are now, at last count, five Turkish restaurants in the entire state. A pity, too, given the cuisine's hearty, creative, and well-seasoned repertoire. Amid Turkish kilims and other Anatolian artifacts on the walls, you'll enjoy many authentic specialties, including such delights as *iman bayildi* (stuffed baby eggplant), *ispanak ezme* (pureed spinach with yogurt), *patlican musakka, yaprak doner kebab,* and *istim kebab* (broiled lamb shank). Handily located on the walking-to-the-theater route between the

THE ODDS ARE IN YOUR FAVOR AT THESE CASINO BETS

The Mohegan Sun Casino in Uncasville offers many fine dining establishments, including the first-rate Michael Jordan Steak House, Bobby Flay's Bar Americain, and the two excellent restaurants below, both established by acclaimed Boston chefs.

Jasper White's Summer Shack, Mohegan Sun Casino, 1 Mohegan Sun Blvd., Uncasville; (860) 862-9500; mohegansun.com; $$. In a setting that is relatively casual, the seafood is superior, whether you head for the oyster bar or the restaurant proper. Among Chef White's winning bets: New England dishes, such as chowders, Jason's garlicky clams casino, roasted lobster, and skillet-fried chicken, and Native American–derived cuisine, most evident in the corn and crab fritters, wild rice salad, and wood-grilled venison skewers with dried cranberry compote. Reservations recommended.

Todd English's Tuscany, Mohegan Sun Casino, 1 Mohegan Sun Blvd., Uncasville; (888) 226-7711; mohegansun.com; $$$. In a faux-rustic setting, deafened by the roar of man-made waterfalls, labeled "Taughannock waterfalls", this Tuscan restaurant in the heart of casino-land is a welcome and surprising reminder of Italy's Tuscan region. The lighting isn't quite dim enough to eclipse such starters as brick-oven oysters, spicy fried calamari with Calabrese peppers, rabbit gnocchi, or baked crespelle, all delicious. Entrees of note include chicken Calabrese, wood-grilled Kurabuto pork shank, crispy-skin salmon, and veal pappardelle. Desserts are all superb, whether pecan pie crème brûlée, fallen chocolate cake, honey almond *panna cotta*, ricotta pie, chocolate bread pudding, or 2-inch-high lemon meringue tart. The menu changes often, but there's always something exciting to bet on. At lunch there's a generous Tuscan Table buffet that's both a real pleasure and a bargain.

Shubert and Yale Repertory Theaters, it is a natural meal stop on the way to either one.

LaBelle Aurore, 75 Pennsylvania Ave., Niantic; (860) 739-6767; labelleaurorebistro.com; $$. If the name of this locally sourced, 44-seat bistro sounds familiar, it is. It is the name of the Paris bistro in the movie *Casablanca* where Rick and Ilsa meet for the last time before they both wash up in Morocco. This Niantic version is more down-to-earth, literally so, as it draws on ingredients grown by 15 area farms for its mostly organic farm-to-table cuisine and changes its menu monthly. Wally Bruckner is the chef and a co-owner with his wife, Dawn. Some of the dishes you might encounter are chicken potpie, venison chop, rainbow trout, tilapia Provençal, Terra Firma Farm–pulled barbecue pork, 4 Mile River Farm hanger steak, Stonington sea scallops, or shrimp-black-bean-cilantro ravioli. Brunch might produce cruciferous omelets and pancakes. LaBelle Aurore also stocks regional boutique beers and ales and interesting wines. A gift shop, called the Farmacy (farm-acy, hee-hee-hee), offers sweets, snacks, and food gifts. Closed Tues.

Le Petit Cafe, 225 Montowese St., Branford; (203) 483-9791; lepetitcafe.net; $$. Hong Kong–born chef-owner Roy Ip seemingly works miracles in miniature storefront quarters, across from the Branford Green. He consistently offers a well-priced, four-course, prix-fixe dinner nightly Wed through Sun. Chef Ip is a master of classic French cuisine, seasoned with an occasional Asian or Caribbean flourish. The menu changes weekly and might include lamb and pork pâté, warm duck leg confit, *cassoulet,* roasted Hawaiian ahi tuna with curried sesame crust, baked miso-glazed Chilean sea bass, or New York steak *au poivre.* Le Petit Cafe is a pleasant dining experience. Dinner only; on weekends there are two seatings, at 6 and 8:30 p.m. Closed Mon and Tues.

Noah's Restaurant, 113 Water St., Stonington; (860) 535-3925; noahsfinefood.com; $–$$. In a plain-frame building on the corner of Church and Water Streets, the 75-seat Noah's has been a mainstay of this charming seaside town for decades. Locals love the generous Sunday brunch, which features such dishes as Portuguese sausage and eggs, eggs Benedict, and all kinds of pancakes. Even weekday breakfasts are special, with Irish oatmeal (often polka dotted with bananas, walnuts, or raisins); house-made granola, yogurt, muffins, and scones; and a different type of pancake daily (blueberry is always on the menu). Most everything at Noah's is made from scratch, which may be why this unassuming place has earned such a loyal following and expanded into a second storefront space. At lunch or dinner you might encounter steamers or mussels (flavorful and briny), sautéed Stonington sea scallops, many lightly prepared fish dishes, and desserts with a mom-made flair (like blueberry crumble or blueberry bread pudding in season). A display case lets you ponder dessert while enjoying the first part of your meal. Closed Mon, except for Memorial Day and Labor Day.

Inn Places to Be

The days of "quaint"—relish trays and cottage cheese—at Connecticut country inns are long past. Now some of the loveliest modern food is served at inns whose decor may be at least a century older. The following four places, clustered together near the Connecticut River, are known even more for their food than their comfortable surroundings.

The Bee & Thistle Inn & Spa, 100 Lyme St., Old Lyme; (860) 434-1667; beeandthistleinn.com; $$$. A favorite romantic getaway, this nine-guest-room inn on 5 acres, with its Americana decor, is as charming as its creative, modern, American food is delicious. The dining room has been renovated by owners Linnea and David Rufo as the Chestnut Grille with prix-fixe menus. Offerings include house-cured gravlox, pan-seared diver scallops, and beef tenderloin with wild mushroom risotto. From early Oct through Mar, on Thurs, Fri, and Sat afternoons, from noon to 3 p.m., it's teatime, when an elaborate English-style tea is served. Reservations suggested. Closed for meals Sun and Mon.

Copper Beech Inn, 46 Main St., Ivoryton; (860) 599-6674; copperbeechinn.com; $$$. Easily spotted by the gorgeous giant copper beech tree in its front yard, this impeccably maintained inn, owned by Ian and Barbara Phillips, has 22 exquisitely furnished rooms and suites (four in the main house, the rest in two other houses on the property). In two dining rooms elegant French food with a modern American accent is served—the likes of poached lobster, Atlantic cod, veal, and lamb dishes. The menu changes seasonally. Be sure to check out the excellent wine list.

Griswold Inn, Main Street, Essex; (860) 767-1776; griswoldinn.com; $$. When it comes to food, the "Gris," as this historic 18th-century inn is known, is famous for its Hunt Breakfast, probably the best-known Sunday brunch in the state. It supposedly started when the British commandered the inn during the War of 1812. The prix-fixe Hunt Breakfast provides approximately 10 main dishes. "Givens" are fruit-wood smoked bacon, sausages, scrambled eggs, five salads, fresh fruits, and an array of fresh-baked breads, coffee cakes, and desserts. There is an omelet station and a waffle station with fresh strawberries and chocolate sauce. You must reserve ahead, as the inn is a mob scene every Sun. The inn's dining areas consist of five rooms: the Covered Bridge Room, the wood-paneled Library with a fireplace, the musket-laden Gun Room, the Ward Room, and the Essex Room. Lunch and dinner are served daily, and there's always a lively scene each evening in the Tavern, a cozy room with a bar menu and live music every night.

Old Lyme Inn, 85 Lyme St., Old Lyme; (860) 434-2600 or (800) 434-5352; oldlymeinn.com; $$$. Inside the handsome 1856 house are three dining areas (main dining room; casual taproom with fire-place and century-old, long oak bar; and patio). There have been many changes at this stalwart old inn after a full year of renovations by Ken and Chris Kitchings, the new owners. Right now the range is in the experienced hands of Chef Dennis Young, formerly at Todd English's Tuscany in the Mohegan Sun Casino. The taproom is open daily (except Mon) year-round, with a seasonal American menu for lunch and dinner, both casual and formal. Stonington sea scallops with saffron risotto; veal with pappardelle noodles; skewered shrimp and linguica sausage; and desserts, such as lemon pie, cheesecake, and warm flourless chocolate cake, are among the many treats.

THREE ON THE ROAD, THE POST ROAD, THAT IS

When summer comes and the livin' is lazy, Nutmeggers head to the shore and the no-frills clam shacks that line US 1 for a seasonal clam out on fried clams, scallops, and clam chowder. Here are three favorites. Two are year-round eateries, but the Clam Castle is only open Apr through Oct, depending on the weather at each end.

Johnny Ad's, 910 Boston Post Rd., Old Saybrook; (860) 388-4032; johnnyads.com; $. Comfort is not an operative word here. Your mission is to eat clam chowder and clams, sweet, fresh, delicious ones, ever-so-lightly coated and seasoned, served with fresh-made coleslaw. The sea scallops are almost as tasty and just as lightly breaded. By the way, it may be heresy to say so about a clam shack, but the hot dogs are good too.

The Clam Castle, 1324 Boston Post Rd., Madison; (203) 245-4911; $. In addition to light, sweet-tasting fried clams, cod, sea scallops,

Octagon, Mystic Marriott Hotel, 625 North Rd., Groton; (860) 326-0360; octagonsteakhouse.com; $$$. The two dining rooms here are so striking in their theatricality (wood, marble, high ceilings, floor-to-ceiling windows, provocative mural at one end) it takes awhile to concentrate on the food, primarily steak and more steak, even grilled *churrasco* steak, with very high-quality beef. Some very fresh seafood goes along for the ride—dishes like garlic-steamed mussels, shrimp lobster rolls, and soft-shell crabs, this modest little place boasts a delicious fish chowder, just the way I like it: creamy with chunks of fish, bacon, and potatoes (maybe a tad too many of the latter). I also like the light naturalness of the batter used to coat the deep-fried oysters, clams, and other sea critters. You can eat indoors, outdoors at a picnic table, or ferry your sea booty home. Credit cards accepted for orders of $10 or more. Closed Mon through Wed.

Lenny and Joe's Fish Tale, 1301 Boston Post Rd., Madison; (203) 245-7289; ljfishtale.com; $. As clam shacks go, this is a McMansion, with additional colonies in Westbrook and Westerly, Rhode Island. Not that Lenny and Joe's is fancy, but it is now a substantial building with an enclosed porch and full-service seafood restaurant (BYO)—a contrast to its humble beginnings in 1979 as a real shack. The fried clams and scallops, hot buttered lobster roll, and broiled catfish are still magnets, and all are delicious. If you're very hungry, try the generous Fish Tale platter. There's also a kiddie menu.There's a second L & J's in Westbrook, at 86 Boston Post Rd. (860-669-0767). Still a third L&J's is in New Haven at 501 Long Wharf Drive (203-691-6619).

escabeche, sesame-seared tuna, grilled swordfish in pomegranate beurre blanc, or Stonington scallops au poivre. Breakfast daily (because it's part of a hotel); otherwise dinner only. The Lounge at Octagon is open from 11 a.m. onward, with a lighter menu.

Olio, 33 King's Hwy., Groton; (860) 445-6546; olioct.com; $$. Olio specializes in eclectic American fare, with elements of Italy, Mexico,

Asia, and Cajun country. *Smart* is the operative word, both in Olio's simple good looks and medium-size menu with a number of tempting lunch and dinner choices. I like especially the Cajun barbecued shrimp with grilled polenta (an appetizer), cheese tortellini with tomato vodka sauce, and the grilled pizzas (most notably with the grilled portobello, scallops, and Gorgonzola toppings). No wonder Olio is good—the ownership's the same as **Bravo Bravo Restaurant** (p. 307) in Mystic.

Pacifico, 220 College St., New Haven; (203) 772-4002; pacifico restaurants.com; $$$. When Rafael Palomino decided to venture north from his two Port Chester, New York, restaurants, his first stop was New Haven. Loosely following a Pacific theme gives him leeway to include many Asian- and Latin American–accented dishes on his eclectic, Nuevo Latino menu. This leads to such smoothly rendered dishes as tilapia on a crab-filled tortilla in a tomatillo sauce, Asian-style shrimp dumplings, *empanadas,* seafood paella, seared sea scallops and shrimp in a chipotle-honey Chardonnay sauce, and pan-seared tilapia with a yucca crust. A late-night menu (available Fri and Sat) features a dozen tapas, a few *bocadillos* (bite-size sandwiches), and desserts, such as chocolate cake and velvety *dulce de leche* cheesecake—an excuse to morph into a night owl. The color-happy decor is as lively as the mostly youngish clientele.

Restaurant L&E, 59 Main St., Chester; (860) 526-5301; restau rantfrench75bar.com; $$$. What was for 30 years Restaurant du Village is now Restaurant L&E, named after the current owners, Linda and Everett Reid, who have given the familiar place a face-lift. They have removed the lace curtains, added many antiques, and developed a snappy new **French 75 Bar,** which doubles as the restaurant's entrance and where small plates are the mode. In the main, somewhat formal tin-ceilinged dining room you may dine on truffled sweetbreads, roast loin of venison, smoked eel, crispy Long Island Sound squid, or cumin-crusted loin lamb chops, among many creative options. Desserts, such as a gingerbread ice-cream sandwich and chocolate *pot de crème,* are also tasty. Dinner only. On Fri and Sat evenings a second dining room upstairs is open with a separate menu.

River Tavern, 23 Main St., Chester; (860) 526-9417; rivertavern chester.net; $$$. It is a surprise to find two charming restaurants in such a small town as Chester. (See **Restaurant L&E** above.) River Tavern, Chef-Owner Jonathan Rapp's well-kept establishment, uses limited space to make a very strong culinary statement with globally conscious food, made with mostly local ingredients. Add a well-chosen wine list and compelling artworks by Sol Lewitt. A short eclectic menu, threaded with a touch of Asia, Europe, and South America, might include Thai noodle salad, Lapsong Souchong–brined duck breast or pan-roasted flounder with chicken-of-the-woods mushrooms, house-smoked salmon, and, in season, oven-roasted shad. There are lovely desserts, too, like bittersweet chocolate soufflé, warm date pudding, and almond *dacquoise*. Whatever you choose, the food is usually exemplary. Mon and Tues are half-price wine nights, and Wed is half-price cocktails. At Sun family meals, there's a special low-priced children's menu. Reservations are recommended.

Saigon City, 1315 Boston Post Rd., Old Saybrook; (860) 388-6888; saigoncityoldsaybrook.com; $. Once upon a time this Vietnamese-Thai waystation was in downtown New Haven. It is now comfortably rooted in two dining rooms of an old, renovated, 18th-century clapboard house in Old Saybrook. There aren't many Vietnamese restaurants left in Connecticut (a short-lived fad that seems to have passed), but Bernadette and Vu Nguyen of Saigon City provide an authentic taste of subtle Vietnamese cooking, with a touch of Thailand tossed in to spice things up a bit and a few French dessert accents. Red curry pork, Saigon spicy chicken, shrimp or beef curry, Thai spring rolls, "shaking tofu," and Thai chicken wings are among many dishes you might encounter on the menu. Dinner only; closed Mon.

Saray Turkish Restaurant, 770 Campbell Ave., West Haven; (203) 937-0707; saraykebab.com; $$. As far as I know, there are just five Turkish restaurants in all of Connecticut and three are in the New Haven area (the others are in Waterbury and Bridgeport). This one, in West Haven, offers a good sampling of a tantalizing cuisine, served in a pleasant carpeted dining room surrounded by walls hung with Turkish kilims. The focus here is on a wide array of entree kebabs, unusual salads, and tempting appetizers,

> "Why does man kill? He kills for food. And not only food: frequently there must be a beverage."
>
> —Woody Allen

such as *muhammara, haydari, mevsim,* and *gavurdagi* salads and cumin-flecked hummus. The mixed grill platter is a good way to get acquainted with Turkish cuisine. Even the desserts are worthy, especially the baklava, *kazandibi,* and *kadayif.* Just remember, it's BYO. On Fri and Sat there is usually live music.

Swagat, 215 Boston Post Rd., West Haven; (203) 931-0108; swagat ct.com; $. It is always good news to learn of a restaurant that serves really good food at frugal prices. Swagat is such a place, a little jewel to be visited, revisited, and treasured—if you enjoy Indian food. The specialties in this minuscule storefront are mostly from South India, with a smattering from the north. Chef-Owner John Nanneti hails from Calcutta, but his cooking skills travel the subcontinent. While he serves such South Indian specialties as *masala dosa, idli, upma,* and lamb Madras, I like some of his traditional dishes as well, such as lamb *saag* and *rogan josh.* The prices will astonish you. BYO. Closed Sun.

Thali Regional Cuisine of India, 4 Orange St., New Haven; (203) 777-1177; thali.com; $$. Thali is a mini-empire, this being the third (and some say best) of four Indian restaurants with the same name and owner, Prasad Chirnomula, a gifted chef himself. Softly lit, with space between tables, this Thali features creative gems like *jeera alu* (cumin potatoes), Goan mussels, prawn *gassi,* *Andhra* chicken, *ghosht banjara* (spicy goat), *Marathi ghosht* (lamb stew), fish *tikka,* and a host of delicious breads. Other **Thalis** are at 87 Main St., **New Canaan,**(203-972-8332); 296 Ethan Allen Hwy. (Rte. 7), **Ridgefield** (203-894-1080)—with a fabulous Sun buffet—and **Thali Too,** 65 Broadway, New Haven (203-776-1600), featuring vegetarian Indian specialties with a special *lassi* bar and patio.

Union League Cafe, 1032 Chapel St., New Haven; (203) 562-4299; unionleaguecafe.com; $$$. This cafe, with one of the handsomest public dining rooms in New Haven, is located in one of the city's most historic structures, the Sherman Building, a brownstone erected in 1860 on the site of Roger Sherman's home. Sherman was New Haven's first mayor and the only man to sign all three founding documents of the fledgling US. Stately and neoclassic, with pink-granite columns, wide windows overlooking Chapel Street, and a welcoming fireplace, the dining room makes a worthy stage for the polished, contemporary French-brasserie cooking of Chef-Owner Jean Pierre Vuillermet. The food follows the seasons. If on the menu, his *moules marinières* and *confit de canard aux cepes* are mouthwatering ways to begin a meal, perhaps followed by wild striped bass or poached duck breast with parsnip puree. Other super choices are wild mushroom ravioli with chestnut fricassee, or seared New England cod. House-made ice creams or luscious pastries might complete a meal to be cherished and remembered. Mon through Fri between 5 and 6 p.m. there's a special two-course prix-fixe menu that makes dining early a savvy thing to do. *Note:* There is also a less-elaborate, less-pricey Club Room bistro menu available on weeknights. Reservations recommended. Closed Sun.

Zinc, 964 Chapel St., New Haven; (203) 624-0507; zincfood.com; $$. Not only is Zinc sophisticated in its minimalist good looks (love that long zinc bar!) and modern American menu, but the food is also executed with great panache. Chef-Owner Denise Appel calls Zinc's food "market inspired and globally infused," and indeed many of the best dishes have foreign accents, mostly Asian or Italian. Some of the dishes I'm addicted to are steamed pork and ginger dumplings, Korean barbecue smoked duck, grilled tamari-cured tuna, and desserts, such as star anise *crème brûlée* and goat's milk cheesecake. The artisanal cheese plate is a beauty, too, with local and regional cheeses. Closed Sun. **Kitchen Zinc Artisan Pizza and Bar** (p. 297) is Zinc's cheaper and more casual offspring around the corner.

Brewpubs & Craft Breweries

Beer'd Brewing Company, 22 Bayview Ave., Unit 15, Stonington; (860) 857-1014; beerdbrewing.com. The beer child of Aaren Simoncini, Beer'd Brewing received its state license approval in September 2012 and has beer available now. Currently a nanobrewery with a production of just three barrels (93 gallons) per batch, Beer'd Brewing's principal product is Whisker'd Wit, a Belgian-style wheat. "Due to our small production size, you can expect several experimental brews a year and different takes on classic styles on a regular basis," Aaren says, "Our aim is to reincarnate the days gone by when beer was produced by someone on your block rather than a multinational corporation."

Bru Rm at BAR, 254 Crown St., New Haven; (203) 495-8924; barnightclub.com. You don't have to be an Eli to enjoy the funky atmosphere of this multiplex, a couple of blocks from Yale University. The starting pint of this favorite watering hole for Yalies (and other thirsty folks) centers on attractions like Toasted Blonde, Damn Good Stout, a pleasingly bitter Pale Ale, and an Amber Ale that has overtones of caramel malts (which goes down well with

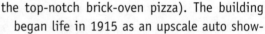

the top-notch brick-oven pizza). The building began life in 1915 as an upscale auto showroom and later was empty for years. In 1991 BAR, a handsome discotheque, opened here. Five years later, Bru Rm ("brew room") was added, as the city's first—and only—brewpub. Currently dinners, lunches, and great pizzas are served daily. And at BARtropolis music rolls on daily; each Sunday brings live music from one or more modern bands. Call for schedule and events.

The Cask Republic, 179 Crown St., New Haven; (475) 238-8335; thecaskrepublic.com. Although not a brewpub, this tavern takes its beer seriously. So seriously it maintains 58 rotating taps, with an additional 80-plus bottled brews—many of them vintage aged. Countries represented include the US, the UK, Belgium, Germany, Italy, Switzerland, and Japan, with almost as many different kinds of glassware to complement the suds. Cask Republic is affiliated with the Ginger Man chain of upscale beer pubs.

Cottrell Brewing Company, 100 Mechanic St., Pawkatuck; (860) 599-8213; cottrellbrewing.com. In 1996 Charles Cottrell Buffum established a microbrewery in a 19th-century printing press factory that once belonged to his great-great-grandfather. The next year the spigots began flowing with Old Yankee Ale, a medium-bodied American Amber that became an instant hit with residents along the Connecticut–Rhode Island state line. Then came Mystic Bridge IPA. You might call the brews a two-state phenomenon as the water used in the brewing process is Westerly White Rock artisan well water, which gives a clear, crisp taste to the product. Tours are available by appointment.

Mikro Craft Beer Bar and Bistro, 3000 Whitney Ave., Hamden; (203) 553-7676; mikrobeerbar.com; $. What lurks behind run-of-the-mill gauzy curtains in an ordinary nine-store strip mall? A jumpin' 44-seat bar that is one of Connecticut's liveliest after-work hangouts. A long, oak-surfaced counter is equipped with 18 spigots, the better to serve a rotating selection of craft brewery beers, from

Altbiers to Porters and Stouts, many from New England states, such as Maine's Allagash Victoria and Vermont's Long Trail Double IPA. There are also many bottled beers, 19 from elsewhere in the US; 15 Belgian ales, including Chimay Grande Reserve; and some from England and Germany. Added to the wide range of good brews is pub grub with a creative flair, whose menu suggestions match dishes to certain brews. You might encounter such items as local *burrata,* an artisanal cheeseboard, pork belly wraps, a Cubano sandwich stuffed with ham and pork belly tidbits, and whole wheat flatbread spread with duck confit and smoky blue cheese—items you won't find at your usual neighborhood bar.

New England Brewing Company, 7 Selden St., Woodbridge; (203) 387-2222; newenglandbrewing.com. **Rob** Leonard, a well-respected brewmaster in the trade, runs the show at this craft brewery, which moved to Woodbridge from Norwalk in 2001. The year-round products are a widely praised Atlantic Amber, Sea Hag IPA, and Elm City Lager. Other specialty brews are made from time to time throughout the year. Open for tours Mon through Sat, but call ahead for hours.

SBC in Branford, Hamden, and Milford. See **SBC Downtown Restaurant Brewery** p. 106.

Thimble Island Brewing Company, 53 East Industrial Rd., Branford; (203) 433-1890; thimbleislandbrewery.com. **This** is very much a homegrown operation, with local lads Justin Gargano, Mike

Fawcett, and Dave Morgan making and selling their beer in their spare time. The hope is that if their flagship product, an amber-colored American Ale, grows in popularity, they will be able to give up their day jobs and ramp Thimble Island's 8-barrel batch up to 5,000 barrels a year and expand the distribution beyond the Branford–New Haven area. Plans also call for the eventual release of a Pilsner and Porter.

Wine Trail

Six of the wineries in southeast coastal Connecticut are on the Connecticut Wine Trail. Visit ctwine.com for a trail map and more information about the wineries. And don't forget your winery passport!

Chamard Vineyards, 115 Cow Hill Rd., Clinton; (860) 664-0299; chamard.com. This vineyard was installed on 5 acres by William Chaney and family in 1984, on a grand hilltop overlooking Long Island Sound. Rich, stony soil, plus vines and a maritime microclimate, along with Chardonnay, Cabernet Sauvignon, and Pinot Noir grapes, were the bases for the wines. Over time Chamard varieties have won many medals in wine competitions. There are eight wines: two Chardonnays, Pinot Grigio, Riesling, Merlot, Cabernet Franc, Cabernet Sauvignon, and Rosé. Some current wines are Bah Hum Bug Merlot, Stone Cold White Riesling, Silent Night Chardonnay, and Fa La La Chardonnay. Bonnie and Jonathan Rothberg are the current owners of the Chamard Vineyards, which has grown to 20 acres and

> "During one of our trips through Afghanistan, we lost our cork-screw. We had to live on food and water for several days."
> —W. C. Fields in *My Little Chickadee*

includes an impressive chateau. There is also a stand-alone tasting house equipped with a small shop and an attractive lounge that boasts a stone fireplace, soaring cathedral ceiling, and exposed wood beams. Tastings and tours are available from Tues through Sun year-round. There's a small fee and you may keep your wine glass. Fri and Sat evenings from July to Sept, there is free live music.

Gouveia Vineyards, 1339 Whirlwind Hill Rd., Wallingford; (203) 265-5526; gouveiavineyards.com. This stone and wood winery, overlooking woodlands, a small lake, and rows of vines, is run by Joe and Lucy Gouveia. They're serious about wine, as was their family, which cultivated grapes here on 32 acres, and, many years ago, back in Portugal. Joe and Lucy now work many grape strains yearly, whose varieties include Pinot Noir, Merlot, Vignoles, and others. The results? Eleven award-winning wines. Stone House in both reds and whites, and two types of Chardonnay, in separate classic blends and vintage aged. Others now on the list are a deep purple Merlot, a Cayuga white, a fruity Seyval Blanc, and a Cabernet Franc, Whirlwind Rosé vinifera hybrid. Visiting tasters have a grand time here, picnicking at lakeside, on the terrace of the stone tasting house, inside on a couch by the fire, or at window tables overlooking fields of grapevines. There are even free snacks—cheese, dips, and salsa—for nibbling with your wine sips. The tasting room is open Thurs through Sun; on Sat there is entertainment from 4 to 7 p.m. Cellar tours are offered Sat and Sun. Call for details.

Jonathan Edwards Winery, 74 Chester Maine Rd., North Stonington; (860) 535-2626; jedwardswinery.com. It may seem ironic to be on a beautiful North Stonington hilltop sipping wines made from Napa Valley grapes, imported from California. But it's not unusual for Connecticut vintners to get their stock elsewhere. In this case, Jonathan Edwards selects, handpicks, and contracts for grapes, sending them refrigerated to his vintage (circa 1800) dairy barn. Here the grapes are crushed, blended, barrel aged, and bottled, making his Merlot, Syrah, Cabernet Sauvignon, Chardonnay, and Zinfandel wine authentic Connecticut products. At the same time, the family is developing Stonington Estate Wines, an entirely Connecticut-grown group of wines, with 20 acres under cultivation, using Riesling, Gewürztraminer, and other grapes. Tastings require prior reservations. If the tasting room is not too crowded, you might snare a table and enjoy a snack of sandwich wraps, olives, and **Cato Corner Farm** (p. 341) artisanal cheeses, available for sale to eat along with your wine samplings.

Maugle Sierra Vineyards, 825 Colonel Hwy., Ledyard; (860) 464-2987; mauglesierravineyards.com. One of the newer vineyards in the area, Maugle Sierra produces three delicious dessert wines, known for their creamy-smooth fruit flavors: Qué Sera, Sirah; Aura (a late harvest Vidal Blanc); and Espíritu de St. Croix, a Ledyard estate grown. Among Maugle Sierra's other wines are Ledyard Sunset White, 1740 Ledyard Rosé (from St. Croix grapes), Rendezvous (a blend of Riesling, Seval, and Chardonnay), Ledyard Sunset Red, and 1740 Ledyard House Red (estate-grown St. Croix with Cabernet Franc). The large, high-ceiling tasting room with fireplace is open Fri and Sat.

Paradise Hills Vineyard, 15 Windswept Hill Rd., Wallingford; (203) 284-0123; paradisehillsvineyard.com. The Ruggiero family opened this vineyard in 2011, but they have been growing grapes for 16 years—Cayuga, Chardonnay, Chambourcin, and Vidal Blanc grapes. They used to sell them to **Jerram Winery** (p. 168) in New Hartford, but always yearned for their own winery. Now they have it—on 65 acres. The idea was a brotherly dream—that of Albert and Richard Ruggiero. Richard and his wife, Brenda, passed the dream on to their daughters, Natalie and Margaret, and it is Margaret who has been the guiding force in making the dream come true. Their wines have geothermal equipment in a new tasting area, built to resemble a Tuscan farmhouse, with slate floor, vaulted ceiling, and glistening copper-topped bar. There is room for 16 to 20 people, and there is additional space outdoors. The wines available for tasting are Washington Trail White (a blend of Chardonnay and Seyval Blanc), Vino Blanco del Paradiso (Cayuga grapes and Trebbibiano from Italy), Washington Trail Red (a blend of Cabernet

Sauvignon, Merlot, and Chambourcin) and Cayuga, a nondry white. The tasting room is open year-round, Thurs through Sun.

Saltwater Farm Vineyard, 349 Elm St., Stonington; (860) 415-9072; saltwaterfarmvineyard.com. The converted airport hanger located near a former landing strip looks more like a Quonset hut than a winery chateau. Step inside, though, and you'll find the old hanger has been beautifully retrofitted with a new granite fireplace, cherry wood stairs, mezzanine tasting area, and big picture windows that oversee the vineyard and all the way into Watch Hill, Rhode Island. This winery, new in 2010, makes six wines from grapes grown onsite: a puckery Sauvignon Blanc; Cabernet Rosé; a tank-aged Chardonnay; Cabernet Franc, with fruity whispers of clove; a Pinot Noir; and a smooth Merlot. The vineyard property is surrounded by a tidal inlet and salt marsh, flooded with bird life, inspiring vintner Michael Connery (who calls himself a "recovering lawyer") to place a great egret on his wine labels. Fifteen of Saltwater Farm's 108 acres are cultivated with vines, growing four grape varieties. In October 2012 the vineyard's dry white Chardonnay 2010 won first place, and its 2008 Estate Cabernet Franc won third place in its category in a *Connecticut* magazine tasting contest of Connecticut wines. The winery is open for tastings Wed through Sun.

Stonington Vineyards, 523 Taugwonk Rd., Stonington; (800) 421-9463 or (860) 535-1222; stoningtonvineyards.com. In 1987 Nick and Happy Smith bought southern-sloping Stonington uplands for their 12-acre vineyard. Finding elements recalling Bordeaux, they focused on European-style wines and over the years have won awards for them using Chardonnay, Riesling, Cabernet Franc, Fumé Vidal Blanc, and other French-type grapes. In a *Connecticut* magazine tasting contest of Connecticut wines, the vineyard won a first for its red Stonington 2008 Cabernet Franc. Stonington is best known for its barrel-fermented Chardonnays and proprietory blends (Seaport White and Triad Rosé). You can learn about these wines on a short winemaking tour. Otherwise, enjoy the tasting room daily from May 1st through Nov. The winery hosts a number of events, including Barrel Tasting in mid-May, a Summer Cellar-bration in mid-July, and a festival of picking grapes/watching the crush (call for the date). Events include live music, food from local restaurants, and plenty of wine.

Northeast Connecticut

Connecticut is a state with scores of small towns, small enough to have just a single zip code for the entire town. This is most evident in the northeast area, sometimes called "the quiet corner." "Peaceful" or "tranquil" would be just as appropriate, for this is a terrain of rolling hills, woodlands, marshes, ponds, brooks, small streams, and clusters of state forests and state parks, such as Mashamoquet Brook State Park near Pomfret. It is also a land of dairy farms; pasturelands; an abundance of apple, peach, and pear orchards, and fields; and fields of strawberries and blueberries.

Such expansive farmland is punctuated by hamlets and villages whose historic names can be found on a map of the world: Lebanon, Hebron, Lisbon, Coventry, Canterbury. Yet each of these towns is quintessentially New England. Many have deep roots in American history, like Coventry, where American Revolutionary War hero Nathan Hale was born and where you can still visit his family

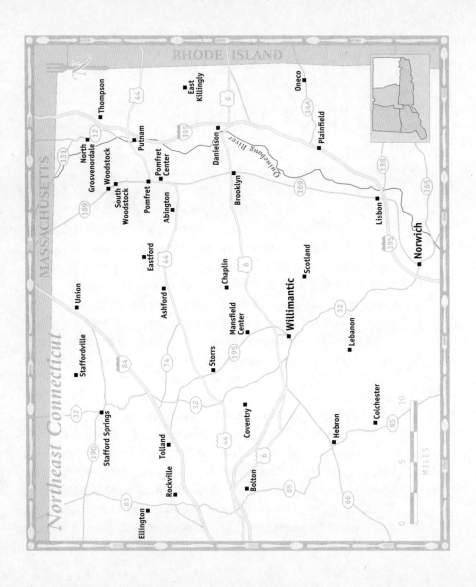

farmhouse. Norwich, on the Thames River (pronounced as spelled, not "Tems," as the British say it), is the birthplace of Benedict Arnold. Norwich was also home to Colonel Christopher Leffingwell, a supplier for Washington's Continental army; his historic home is open for viewing. The town's current claim to fame is a spa-and-inn complex, considered one of the most elegant spas in the state.

In Lebanon, with its town-long Green, George Washington stabled his horse during the American Revolution. The Wadsworth stable is still there and still viewable. The state's only colonial governor, Jonathan Trumbull, lived in this town; his house, too, is open to visitors. Peaceful Canterbury has the restored home of Prudence Crandall, an intrepid Quaker who ran the first school for African-American girls in pre–Civil War America.

Quiet does not mean somnolent, as the presence here of so many farmers, dairymen, and food entrepreneurs attests. There is even a distillery in the area, dedicated to making eau-de-vie. The University of Connecticut in the bucolic hills around Storrs began life as an agricultural land-grant college; it is now a prestigious university with two famous basketball teams (male and female), but the rich homemade ice cream sold at the university's dairy bar is almost as popular in the region as the Huskies' mascot.

Brooklyn is a pastoral New England village, whose environs now encompass vineyards, a bison farm where American buffalo roam free, maple sugar houses, scores of orchards, a church with Tiffany stained-glass windows, and a unique restaurant in the middle of a working farm. On the Green in Woodstock is one of the most unusual historic houses in the state—the vibrant-pink Roseland Cottage, a rare example of Gothic Revival inside and out. Its many celebrated 19th-century visitors included four US presidents. Food lovers in Woodstock may be almost as delighted by one of the area's largest apple orchards and farm store across the Green. Pomfret, another pastoral villagescape, is home to a well-known prep school and also to a lively cafe that is a social center for the entire area. Nearby Putnam, named for American Revolutionary War hero Israel Putnam, is a classic example of the Connecticut enterprising spirit. When its large, textile-manufacturing companies moved out of state, Putnam didn't passively fall into decay. First it reinvented itself as a major antiques center of southern New England. When eBay undermined the antiques market, Putnam began to reinvent itself yet again—this time as a restaurant town, on a scale befitting its small size, fairly bustling with renewed Yankee spunk. In Willimantic, what was once the largest thread mill in the US has been converted into a museum of the textile industry; of even greater interest to beer drinkers is the way the town's old post office has been recycled into a lively brewery, brewpub, and cafe.

"Quiet" in this area is no synonym for "boring," as the following pages will reveal.

Beltane Farm, 59 Taylor Bridge Rd., Lebanon; (860) 887-4709; beltanefarm.com. Paul Trubey, a former social worker in hospice care, was always interested in farming. As a kid he wanted to have a goat as a pet. Now he has 115 of them. They are Oberhasli (Swiss dairy goats), Saanen, and La Manchas (a small-eared California breed, a cross between Swiss and Spanish goats), all known for the creamy quality of their milk. He raises them on 8 acres, feeding them local hay and grass, with no prophylactic antibiotics or animal rennet. The results produce a rich, silky-smooth chèvre, which Trubey, in partnership with Oak Leaf Dairy, forms into 4-ounce logs and rolls in various herbs. Other Beltane Farm cheeses are Danse de la Lune; Harvest Moon (a hard, nutty, Spanish-style cheese); Beltane's Vesters (soft French style); and a sharp feta aged in brine; plus several cheese spreads, such as pumpkin chèvre and chocolate chèvre. Trubey also makes a Greek-style yogurt. Most Trubey cheeses are sold on his website and at 12 farmers' markets in season—with Highland Park Markets, Whole Foods in Hartford and Glastonbury, and **Priam Vineyards** (p. 382), among other outlets. You can taste the cheeses at the farm on Sun in the spring and fall and meet the goats and Nester, the farm donkey. Check the website for tasting dates and for other stores that sell the cheeses.

Birch Hills Farm, 236 Bebbington Rd., Ashford; (860) 429-8665. What does a UPS driver do after he retires? If he is Peter Piecyk, he

 buys a 6-acre farm, grows fields of berries, and starts making and selling fruit jams and jellies from his just-picked fruits. The jams come in raspberry peach, blueberry, peach, and strawberry peach. The fruit flavors are intense and are bottled in 8- and 12-ounce jars. Peter also makes and sells maple syrup at craft fairs and farmers' markets.

Brown Cow Cafe, Ekonk Hill Turkey Farm, 227 Ekonk Hill Rd., Sterling; (860) 564-0248; ekonkhillturkeyfarm.com. You've heard of twofers, well, this is a ninefer or multinumberer. While this cafe/ farm shop sells many locally made or grown products—honey, maple syrup, cheeses, grass-fed beef, farm-raised pork—its main claims to local fame are its frozen turkey pies (from the farm's own free-range turkeys) and its ice cream. The ice cream, from Blossom's milk (Ekonk Hill's Jersey cow), is served in milk shakes, sodas, floats, specialty sundaes, Brown Cow floats (with root beer), and atop house-made blueberry pie. Then there's the Hot Gobbler Sundae—no, it's not cold, it's a hot dish of mashed potatoes, topped with a turkey slice, gravy, and stuffing, a tasty cold-weather treat. Closed on Thanksgiving, Christmas, and New Year's.

Bush Meadow Farm, 738 Buckley Hwy. (Rte. 190), Union; (860) 684-3089; bushmeadowfarm.com. Nancy and Barry Kapplan's 37-acre dairy farm began life in 1997 as a forestry farm. By 2004 it had expanded to livestock, a dairy farm with goats, not cows. Today there are 50 Nubian dairy goats. The Kapplans raise these frisky creatures for their milk and feta and blue cheese. The farm is licensed by the state and FDA-inspected to process and sell fresh, bottled goat's milk, two kinds of goat cheeses, and farm-smoked pork and beef, which include smoky pepper-cured pastrami, ham, three kinds of bacon, sausage, and beef jerky. Charcuterie and custom meat orders are taken by request. At the Kapplan store/cafe they also sell free-range eggs and farm-made breads and rolls. For more information about the cafe, see **Bush Meadow Farm** on p. 367.

Cato Corner Farm, 178 Cato Corner Rd., Colchester; (860) 537-3884; catocornerfarm.com. Elizabeth MacAlister and her son, Mark Gilman, produce remarkable and quite different artisanal cheeses from the raw milk of their herd of 45 Jerseys. Half of their 75-acre farm is pastureland, which allows the cows an open range on which to roam. That the cows' meat is untainted by hormones, herbicides, subtherapeutic antibiotics, or chemical fertilizers may explain in part why Cato Corner's cheeses are so delicious and distinctive. The operation is also fastidious. In 1997 Elizabeth built an underground cave so that her raw milk cheeses could age properly at a temperature of 50°F to 55°F. Elizabeth and Mark support other area producers, by, for example, rubbing their Drunk Monk in a brown ale from the **Willimantic Brewing Co. and Main Street Cafe** (p. 379), washing their Drunken Hooligan in a **Priam Vineyards'** (p. 382) red wine, and giving their Desparado a similar treatment with fermented pear mash and Pear William eau-de-vie from **Westford Hill Distillers** (p. 350). Cato Corner's top seller is the creamy, trappist-style Bridgid's Abbey, based on a Belgian monastery recipe. Another big hit is Bloomsday, named after Leopold Bloom in James Joyce's *Ulysses,* possibly the only cheese named after such an august literary work. Cato's Hooligan, a soft, brine-washed Muenster type, copped a gold medal award in a competition held in 2006 at the Gallo Family Vineyards, where Cato Corner Farm also won the Never Stop Growing award as a family-owned producer. Other Cato Corner cheeses include Black Ledge Blue, a good-selling blue cheese; Gouda-style Dutch Farmstead; Jeremy River Cheddar, aged 8 months or so in the English style; Vivace Bambino, sweet like a young provolone; and Womanchego, nutty and sharp, based on the Spanish Manchego. They now make 22 different cheeses, three of which took awards from the American Cheese Society in 2010 and 2011. Shameless punsters, they have given some of their cheeses names like Myfawny (like a Glouchester/Cheshire) and Dairyere (Gruyère-style). The cheeses are sold (with tastings) at their farm shop, which is open Sat and Sun year-round. They are also available at farmers' markets in the area, gourmet shops, groceries, restaurants (**Max Downtown** and all its sister locations, p. 231, for example), and wineries (**Priam Vineyards,** p. 382, in Colchester) throughout Connecticut, New York, the mid-Atlantic area, and as far west as Ohio, Illinois, and California. Phone and e-mail orders are shipped via UPS with one- or two-day delivery.

Colchester Bakery, 96 Lebanon Ave., Colchester; (860) 537-2415; colchesterbakery.com. Some of the area's best Jewish rye bread, Russian pumpernickel, challah, Vienna bread, rye, and *babka*, all low in fat and without preservatives, are created every day within the confines of a large building up a nondescript side street. This houses Colchester Bakery and has since 1947. Arrive there early, and you'll find the display cases in the front overflowing with fresh fruit pies, coffee cakes, turnovers, biscotti, crispy elephant ears, assorted Danish and other pastries, black and whites, almond "horseshoes" and éclairs, lemon popovers, French butter cookies, biscotti and phyllo dough "pretzels" (in chocolate, raspberry, and cinnamon), as well as yogurt and cheeses from local farms. There is a self-serve coffee bar along one side of the large shop, convenient for a drink along with a Danish.

Creamery Brook Bison, 19 Purvis Rd., Brooklyn; (860) 779-0837; creamerybrookbison.net. You may not think of Connecticut as the home where the buffalo roam, but Deborah and Austin Tanner have been raising bison (American buffalo) on their 100-acre farm since 1990. So if you happen to be driving by and see 80 or 100 bison grazing in a meadow, you are not hallucinating. Deborah praises bison as "the original health food" because the red meat is all natural and low fat, with fewer calories and less cholesterol than most cuts of beef, chicken, and turkey. The animals are fed only corn and grass, no growth hormones or antibiotics. The Tanners sell their meat (processed for them in Groton, Massachusetts) directly from the store on their farm. Frozen steaks, chuck, ground meat and patties, sausage, short ribs, Texas ribs, shanks and boneless ribs, and steaks are all available. Cookouts and wagon tours to see the free-roaming bison are conducted Sat from July through Oct.

The Farmer's Cow, 49 Chappell Rd., Lebanon; (860) 642-4600 or (866) 355-2697; thefarmerscow.com. A group of six family-owned dairy farms in the northeast part of Connecticut joined forces in 2004 to produce and sell farm-fresh milk, free of artificial growth hormones, from their large herds of (mostly) Holstein cows. Using state-of-the-art milking machines and other equipment, the six are called the Farmer's Cow. They are Cushman Farms in North Franklin, Fairvue Farms in Woodstock, **Fort Hill Farms** (p. 361) in Thompson, Graywall Farms in Lebanon, Hytone Farm in Coventry, and Mapleleaf Farm in Hebron. Their milk is sold at markets all over the state, including Highland Park Markets, Stop & Shop, and Big Y, as well as at **Bishop's Orchards Farm Market and Winery** (p. 280) in Guilford. Together they milk some 2,300 cows and manage 6,000 acres. They recently added Farmer's Cow ice cream in 11 flavors to their repertoire, as well as eggs, half-and-half, and apple cider.

Fish Family Farm Creamery & Dairy, 20 Dimock Ln., Bolton; (860) 646-9745; fishfamilyfarm.com. Driving up to the dairy store at this beautiful 211-acre farm, you are likely to see Jersey cows grazing idyllically in the meadows. In 1981 Don and Sharon Fish bought what was then a beef cattle farm and turned it into a dairy farm with a 50-cow herd of registered Jerseys. They built a bottling plant, and they now process, pasteurize, homogenize, and bottle their own milk in old-fashioned glass bottles, which they sell in their store and also to **Munson's Chocolates** (p. 348) in Bolton, which uses the cream in candy making. Don Fish jokes that "our milk has been in outer space, because our astronauts made a gift of Munson's Chocolates to the Russian astronauts on the space station." Inside the spotless little store is a freezer, where premium-quality Fish Family Farm Creamery Ice Cream is sold by the quart. There are 10 rich flavors: vanilla, maple walnut, coffee, peanut butter chip, cherry vanilla, chocolate chip, Heath bar and chocolate, mint Oreo, black raspberry, and vanilla fudge. Through a plexiglass window you can watch the processing. Ice-cream cones are served in summer, when high school students work the scoops. Sales the rest of the year, including for such items as jams, jellies, fresh eggs, farm-fresh milk, butter, farmer's cheese, heavy cream, and chocolate milk, are on the honor system. There are no organized tours of the farm, but visitors may wander around on their own and watch the 3:30 p.m. milking if they wish. Closed Sun. Cash only.

Frank's Marinara Sauce, 26 Hawks Landing, Hebron; (860) 228-0745. Frank Parseliti has a track record in the marinara-sauce business. He developed his first commercial marinara in 1993 from a recipe his father created after opening Frank's restaurant in Hartford in 1944. For decades Frank's was the hangout of Hartford politicos. In 1995 the restaurant closed, and Frank Jr. began expanding his sauce line. Now there are five sauces: marinara, basil and roasted garlic, vodka, fra diavolo, and New York-style Sicilian gravy, plus Frank's Bloody Mary Mix. Several factors make his chunky, textured sauces so fresh tasting: all-natural ingredients, gluten free, no added sugars, and the use of whole peeled tomatoes and only extra-virgin olive oil. Four of the sauces are vegan (not the vodka). The sauces are distributed to 800 stores throughout Connecticut and in 12 states. In this area, you will find them at Stop & Shop, all Highland Park Markets, and many upscale groceries.

Hosmer Mountain Beverages, 217 Mountain St., Willimantic; (860) 423-1555; hosmersoda.com. There aren't many independent soft-drink manufacturers left in Connecticut, but Hosmer is one. This survivor opened in 1912 and is still going strong. In addition to most of the usual flavors, Hosmer's newest product is Red Lightning, an energy antioxidant drink with pomegranate juice, grape skin, and ginger beer. Hosmer also takes custom orders. Closed Sun. Another outlet, the **Hosmer Mountain Soda Shack,** 15 Spencer St., Manchester (860-643-6923), also sells Hosmer beverages, but has no tours.

La Brioche French Bakery, 36 Ward St., Rockville; (860) 896-0750. Don't judge *this* book by its plain-looking cover, that is, its shop. The well-worn linoleum floors and pine wainscoting are legacies of a previous tenant. This bakery is authentically French. Its owner, Colette Berube, is an experienced baker and what emerges from her ovens is nothing short of magical: puff pastry apricot frangipane, *palmiers,* cheese stars, chocolate and vanilla éclairs, flaky croissants from plain to almond, chocolate, and raspberry. Then there are the breads: baguettes, round *boules,* sourdough, multigrain, pumpernickel, alpines, and brioches. The secret ingredient in all these pastry gems is butter. Butter, butter, and more butter. Only the cookies are not baked in-house, so plan to concentrate on all the other wonders. Special orders for breads, cakes, and pastries are cheerfully accommodated. Closed Mon and Tues. Cash or check only.

Meadow Stone Farm, 199 Hartford Rd., Brooklyn; (860) 617-2982; meadowstonefarm.com. Goats, about 30 of them—Golden Guernsey and Saanen Swiss dairy goats—dominate on the 8-acre farm of Annemarie Prause and Kristopher Noiseux. These animals supply the raw goat's milk the couple sells in their farm shop (by appointment only) and that is used to produce pasturized cheeses like Caprino Romano, Elsa's fresh goat's milk chèvre, farmstead aged and goat soaps, shampoos, crèmes, and butters. Milk from Jersey cows also goes into other farm cheeses—Abbey, Hot Chili

"A gourmet is just a glutton with brains."

—Philip W. Haberman

Moo Mama, White Knight (Camembert), Blue Knight (a blue), Bliss (standard brie), and others. Eggs and berries in season are also sold in the farm shop. Closed Feb and Mar.

Munson's Chocolates, 174 Hop River Rd. (Rte. 6), Bolton; (860) 649-4332 or (888) 686-7667; munsonschocolates.com. When Ben and Josephine Munson opened their first candy store in 1946 in Manchester, they called it the Dandy Candy Company. Ben mixed up batches of creams and caramels and hand-dipped them in chocolate; Josephine assembled and packaged them for sale. Their young business was dandy indeed and is now the largest retail chocolate manufacturer in Connecticut, run by the second and third generations of Munsons. The company employs 130 in nine stores (Farmington, Foxwoods Mashantucket, Glastonbury, Olde Mystic Village, Newington, Orange, South Windsor, West Hartford, and West Simsbury) plus the main store. Bestsellers are almond butter crunch, pecan caramel patties (turtles), and chocolate nut bark, followed by chocolate-layered truffles and chocolate cordial cherries. There are also candy bars, four flavors of fudge, peanut brittle, boxed fruit slices, and chocolate-covered pretzel rods, with new products being taste tested at the Bolton shop from time to time. Myriad assortments are sold via mail order, on the website, and in the Munson shops. If it can be found in chocolate, Munson's probably makes it.

The Purple Pear by Tina, Wilmington; (860) 933-1033; the purplepearbytina.com. Tina Fearnley makes fabulous dessert toppings. Her butter almond cream won Product of the Year at the 2010 and 2011 Connecticut Specialty Food Association show. Tina's five other toppings are hot fudge cream, chocolate peanut butter hot fudge, French caramel cream, French caramel pecan cream, and fresh summer berries (a mix of blueberries, blackberries, strawberries, raspberries, lemons, and rhubarbs), most of which have won prizes in the same specialty food shows in different categories. The toppings are perfect on ice cream and cheesecake, and also on French toast, waffles, and baked brie. They come in nine-ounce jars with the Purple Pear label and are available at Whole Foods, **Rein's Delicatessen** (p. 189) in Vernon, **Fromage Fine Foods and Coffees** (p. 268) in Old Saybrook, **Fish Family Farm Creamery & Dairy** (p. 344) in Bolton, among other outlets, and also on the website. See Tina's recipe for **Fresh Summer Berry Balsamic Dressing with Chicken** on p. 400.

University of Connecticut Dairy Bar, 3636 Horsebarn Rd. Extension (off Rte. 195, Storrs), Storrs/Mansfield; (860) 486-2634; dairybar.uconn.edu. Devotees consider this the best ice cream in this part of Connecticut, which may be why the plain-as-vanilla store draws more than 200,000 visitors a year and has been a UConn icon for generations. Fans praise the ice cream's creaminess, due in large measure to its 14 percent butterfat content. And also for the fact that it is made right on the premises every day from the university's own cows. The Dairy Bar makes a total of 28 flavors, of which

24 are available at any one time. The most famous is Jonathan Supreme (vanilla swirled with peanut butter and chocolate-covered peanuts), named for UConn's mascot. Also popular are Husky Tracks (vanilla, fudge swirls, and peanut butter cups), black raspberry, coffee espresso crunch, chocolate peanut butter swirl, and the seasonal pumpkin and peppermint stick. Another favorite flavor is Chocolate Cow Pie (chocolate with marshmollow swirl and Oreo pieces—tastier than its, ugh-oh, name).

We-Li-Kit Farm Ice Cream Stand, 728 Hampton Rd. (Rte. 97), Abington; (860) 974-1095; welikit.com. Just opposite the milking center, on a farm of 120 acres with 60 Holstein cows, is this ice-cream stand, a scoop shop that offers remarkably rich farmstead ice cream. Whimsical names don't detract from the ice cream's popularity—names like Ape's Delight (banana with chocolate chips and walnuts), Guernsey Cookie (coffee with Oreos), Holstein (chocolate studded with white chocolate chips and almonds), and, most popular of all, despite the name, Road Kill (vanilla with cherry swirl, white chocolate chips, and walnuts). There are 25 flavors, about 17 available on any given day. Strawberry rhubarb and Guernsey Cookie are two of the new flavors. Maple products are another attraction, as are the wagon-driven hay and sleigh rides, but ice cream is the magnet for miles around. The stand is open daily from early Apr to the end of Oct.

Westford Hill Distillers, 196 Chatey Rd., Ashford; (860) 429-0464; westfordhill.com. Margaret Chatey and her husband, Louis, have gone in for "artisan distilling" on the 200-acre hilltop farm that the family has worked since 1919. They have installed a state-of-the-art distillery in their huge New England barn and produce various types of eau-de-vie—the clear, fruit-flavored brandy that is a popular tradition in Europe. They recently added a vodka called Rime to their repertoire. "We were licensed in 1998," says Margaret, who runs the project from mashing to marketing, "and sold our first fruit spirits in 1999." The line of eaux-de-vie includes cherry (kirsch), raspberry (framboise), strawberry (fraise), and pear (Pear William), which won a gold medal in two recent competitions, plus a 12-year aged apple brandy and an elegant *poire prisonnière* (pear in a heart-shaped bottle), which won a Best of Show in package design at another. How do Bartlett pears get into the bottles? Simple, they grow there. The bottles are placed around baby pears at **Holmberg Orchards** (p. 282) in Gales Ferry, allowing the pears to mature within the bottles. Those glass containers are then scrubbed with water and filled with Westford Hill's Pear William eau-de-vie, corked, and finished. All the regular eaux-de-vie come in beautiful elongated bottles with the appropriate fruit depicted on the label. All Westford products are available in liquor stores and in many restaurants throughout the state—for example, **Zinc** (p. 325) in New Haven, **Metro Bis** (p. 202) in Simsbury, **85 Main** (p. 372) in Putnam, and the **Whelk** (p. 103) and **Dressing Room** (p. 82) in Westport. Distillery visits are possible if you call ahead. See Margaret's recipe for **Double Chocolate Raspberry Biscotti** on p. 412.

Martha's Herbary, 589 Pomfret St. (junction of Rte. 44, Rte. 97, and Rte. 169), Pomfret; (860) 928-0009; marthasherbary.com. This unusual shop, owned by Michelle King, is located directly across the road from the **Vanilla Bean Cafe** (p. 370). Martha's carries unusual types of fresh basil, tarragon, sorrel, and other herbs and herb books, along with rare teas and such nonedibles as clothes, scarves, jewelry, hats, potpourris, and other gift items. And when you are finished browsing, feel free to wander the herb gardens and sunken garden, where there is a pond with a waterfall and a bird-house fence. Closed Mon.

Mrs. Bridges' Pantry, 292 Rte. 169, South Woodstock; (860) 963-7040; mrsbridgespantry.com. Proprietors Pamela Spaeth and Susan Swenson guard the British pedigree of this charming little shop and tearoom. British imports range from Walker's shortbreads, Cadbury chocolate fruit and nut bars, Fry's chocolate, preserves, and jams to 200 varieties of teas (Jackson's of Picadilly, Yorkshire, London Herb & Spice, Metropolitan, and Ahmad, among others). A freezer contains English bangers (made by an English butcher in California), sausage rolls, Cornish pasties, meat pies, steak and kidney pies, blood sausages, soups, and sauces. There are English teapots, accessories, knitting and crochet supplies, and gift items, such as Bromley scents and creams, for sale as well. Closed Tues. For more information about the tearoom, see **Mrs. Bridges' Pantry** on p. 369.

Willimantic Food Co-op, 91 Valley St., Willimantic; (860) 456-3611; willimanticfood.coop. This lively food co-op (whose motto is "member owned and operated") has been functioning since 1984, benefiting members and nonmembers alike. For an annual fee, members get discounts on the voluminous numbers of food products for sale; nonmembers pay a bit more. The co-op's emphasis is on locally grown, organic, and natural foods, which come in all shapes and sizes—fruits, vegetables, cow and goat's milk, meats, regional artisanal cheeses, honey, maple syrup, bakery breads and pastries, gluten-free foods, Fair Trade teas and coffees, plus health and beauty products.

Farmers' Markets

For up-to-the-minute information about dates and times, call the Connecticut Department of Agriculture at (860) 713-2503, visit its website at state.ct.us/doag, or e-mail ctdeptag@po.state.ct.us.

Ashford Farmers' Market, Pompey Hollow Park, across from Town Hall, Ashford. Sun from 10 a.m. to 1 p.m., mid-July through Oct.

Bozrah Farmers' Market, Maple Farm Park, 45 Bozrah St., Bozrah. Fri from 3:30 to 7 p.m., early July through early Oct.

Brooklyn Farmers' Market, Ocean State job lot parking lot, 560–574 Providence Rd. (Rte. 6), Brooklyn. Wed from 4 to 6 p.m., June through Oct.

Canterbury Farmers' Market, Josie's General Store, 189 Butts Bridge Rd., Canterbury. Last Sat of every month from 9 a.m. to 2 p.m., late May through Oct.

Colchester Farmers' Market, St. Joseph Polish Society, 395 South Main St., Colchester. Sun from 9 a.m. to noon, early June through Oct.

Colchester Priam Vineyards Farmers' Market, Shailor Rd. (Rte. 2), exit 16, Colchester. Sun from noon to 3 p.m., early July through early Oct.

Coventry Farmers' Market, Nathan Hale Homestead, 2299 South St., Coventry. Sun from 11 a.m. to 2 p.m., early June through Oct. **Winter market:** Coventry High School, Coventry. Sun from 11 a.m. to 2 p.m., mid-Nov through late Feb.

Danielson Farmers' Market, Killingly Memorial Library, 25 Wescott Rd., Danielson. Sat from 9 a.m. to noon, early June through Oct.

Ellington Farmers' Market, Arbor Park, Town Center, 35 Main St., Ellington. Sat from 9 a.m. to noon, early May through Oct.

Franklin Farmers' Market, Cedar Hill Market Place, 828 Rte. 32, Franklin. Fri from 3 to 7 p.m., June through first week of Nov.

Hebron Farmers' Market, Hebron Elementary School (Rte. 85), Hebron. Sat 9 a.m. to noon, mid-June through mid-Oct.

Hebron Farmers' Market II, Church of Hope of Hebron, 1 Main St., Hebron. Sat from 9 a.m. to 12:30 p.m., mid-June through early Oct.

Lebanon Farmers' Market, Town Hall Green, Lebanon. Sat from 9 a.m. to noon, early June through mid-Oct.

Lisbon Farmers' Market, Lisbon Meadows Park, Rte. 169, Lisbon. Thurs from 3:30 to 6:30 p.m., late June through Oct.

Norwich Downtown Farmers' Market, Howard Brown Park (Rte. 2), Norwich. Wed from 10 a.m. to 2 p.m., early June through Oct.

Norwich–Greenville Section Farmers' Market, Sixth Street between Central Avenue and Prospect Street, Norwich. Sat from 9 a.m. to 1 p.m., end of June through Oct.

Norwich Uncas on Thames Farmers' Market, Uncas on Thames, 401 W. Thomas St. (Rte. 32), Campbell Bldg, Norwich. Mon and Fri from 10 a.m. to 1 p.m., early July through Oct.

Plainfield Farmers' Market, St. John's School parking lot, 482 Norwich Rd. (Rte. 12), Plainfield. Tues from 4 to 6 p.m., mid-June through Oct.

Putnam Farmers' Market, Dunkin' Donuts parkling lot, 325 Woodstock Ave., Putnam. Mon and Thurs from 3:30 to 6 p.m., early May through Oct.

Putnam Farmers' Market II, 18 Kennedy Dr. and Bridge Street, Putnam. Mon and Thurs from 4:30 to 6 p.m., early June through Oct.

Scotland Farmers' Market, Scotland Green (junction of Rte. 14 and Rte. 97), Scotland. Wed from 3 to 6 p.m., late May through Oct.

Somers Farmers' Market, corner of Main and Battle Streets, Somers. Sat from 10 a.m. to 2 p.m., mid-June through early Oct.

Stafford Springs Farmers' Market, Mocko's Lot (junction of Rte. 32 and Rte. 190), Stafford Springs. Mon and Thurs from 10 a.m. to 1 p.m., early July through late Oct.

Storrs Farmers' Market, Mansfield Town Hall parking lot (Rte. 195), Storrs. Sat from 3 to 6 p.m., May through mid-Nov.

Storrs Winter Farmers' Market, Mansfield Community Center, 10 South Eaglesville Rd., Storrs. Second and fourth Sat of every month from 3 to 5 p.m., Dec through Apr.

Tolland Farmers' Market, Tolland Green, Tolland. Sat from 9 a.m. to noon, first week in May through mid-Nov.

Waterford Farmers' Market, 15 Rope Ferry Rd., Waterford. Sat from 9 a.m. to noon, late June through Oct.

Westbrook Farmers' Market, Tanger Outlet Center, 314 Flat Rock Place, Westbrook. Thurs from 11 a.m. to 3 p.m., June through Oct.

Willimantic Farmers' Market, corner of Union and Jackson Streets, under the pavilion, near the Frog Bridge, Willimantic. Sat from 8 a.m. to noon, early June through first week of Nov.

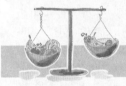

Farm Stands

Apple Barn, 494 Rte. 169, Woodstock; (860) 928-2225; wood stockorchardsllc.com. Woodstock Orchards' neat farm store is on a road that shoots off from the Green in the center of Woodstock. That's where you'll find the fresh vegetables, blueberries, peaches, pears, and 25 types of apples (Ida Red, Red Delicious, Russet, Empire, McIntosh, and Cortland among them) that Harold and Doug Bishop; Donna Young; and Donna's son, Eric, grow on their 65-acre spread. The Apple Barn also retails preserves, corn relish, pickled mushrooms, Dragon's Blood Elixir hot sauce, pickled garlic buds, and other foods with the Woodstock Orchards label, as well as the farm's own sweet cider, locally made honey and maple syrup, fresh-ground peanut butter, fresh mums, and gourmet foods. Fresh-pressed apple cider is available from early Sept through May 1. They are especially proud of their Crisp-Aire apples, which are stored in a climate-controlled "vault," with the atmosphere lowered to less than 5 percent oxygen. This allows the fruit to retain its crispy-fresh texture even after several months. You may also pick your own blueberries and apples in season (for apples Labor Day until mid-Oct). Open Aug through May daily. Call ahead for the picking schedule.

Bats of Bedlam Maple Syrup, 101 Bedlam Rd., on Rte. 198, Chaplin; (860) 455-9200; bob_dubos@charter.net. It's not bats but maple syrup that Pat and Bob Dubos have focused on for more than 30 years on their Bedlam farm. Starting with 10 acres of "sugar bush"—dedicated maple trees—they harvest buckets of top-quality maple sap, which they then boil down into syrup and sugar for waffles, pancakes, and other tasties. As for the bats, don't worry. There's nothing batty about this operation. Their first-of-the-year run of syrup and sugar usually begins in late Feb and continues into Mar. The name refers to Bob's previous profession as vertebrate zoologist and curator of the research collection, which includes bats, at the University of Connecticut. If you miss the tap/sap process, you can buy the Dubos' maple products at the sugarhouse or their own house throughout the year—such treats as maple syrup, sugared nuts, maple cream, maple brittle, maple candy, maple sugar–coated nuts, maple vinegar, maple syrup, maple butter, and maple pancake mix (but call ahead first). Some of their products are also available at the **Willimantic Food Co-op,** p. 353.

Blackmer Farm, 441 Quinebaug Rd., North Grosvenordale; (860) 923-2710; rblackmer@charter.net. With 10 greenhouses, 40 cows, 40 acres of sweet corn, a roster of fresh vegetables, and a farm stand on their family farm, Myrtie and Randy Blackmer really have their hands full. Since this isn't a pick-your-own place, it's a good thing they can rely on the help of sons Tod and Mark and their nieces, too, at harvest time, when the stand is stocked with fresh-picked-daily cucumbers, egg-plants, broccoli, peppers, summer squashes, melons, pumpkins, sweet corn, and tomatoes, as well as plants and flowers. The Blackmer farm stand is open daily from May through Oct. Take Rte. 12 north, then left on Rte. 131 north.

Buell's Orchard, 108 Crystal Pond Rd., Eastford; (860) 974-1150; buellsorchard.com. Henry Buell bought 120 acres here in 1889 and planted Rhode Island Greening apples. His great-grandchildren, Jonathan and Jeffrey Sandness, have not just followed his lead, growing 20 types of apples (Macouns are their bestseller; Cameo and Honey Crisp are their newest), but they've also diversified. Now Buell's also grows peaches, pears, strawberries, cantaloupes, tomatoes, peppers, yellow and green squashes, eggplants, pumpkins, and 2 acres of blueberries. All are available as pick your own, except the pears, which are sold (with the other produce) at the farm store on the property. Also for sale are jams, jellies, local honey, cider donuts, and, in fall, chrysanthemums. An additional treat is watching the candied apple–processing machine churn through some 750,000

If you covet a farm-raised turkey, especially at Thanksgiving, let's talk turkey now about where to find one. Here are three growers in the northeast corner of the state that can fill your request. But order well in advance or you'll discover the birds have flown the coop.

Abbott Spring Farm, 293 Brayman Hollow Rd., Pomfret Center; (860) 974-1268 or (860) 974-2484.

Red & White Orchard, 335 Lebanon Rd. (Rte. 87), Franklin; (860) 642-6791.

Sweet Farm, 330 Canterbury Rd. (Rte. 169), Brooklyn; (860) 779-0212.

apples every autumn. From late Aug to Halloween, 45 to 50 apples a minute enter the processor as naked, unadorned fruit, emerging seconds later rolled in cinnamon-flavored caramel with coconut topping, taffy covered with Heath bar chunks, embedded all over with sprinkles, or covered in peanuts. It is a fascinating transformation to witness. The store (off Rte. 198 via Westford Road) is open early June until Christmas. Closed Sun. The website tells you exactly when each crop is ready to pick, for example, strawberries in June, blueberries in mid-July, peaches in Aug, and apples by type (Gala from Labor Day to late Sept, Ida Red from early to late Oct, and so on).

Chase Road Growers, 174 Chase Rd., Thompson; (860) 923-9926; chaserdgrowers@aol.com. Jayne and Warren Reynolds have a nursery that specializes in flowers until fall, but it is in their big red barn that you will find fresh vegetables in season. Expect sweet corn, tomatoes, peppers, cucumbers, and other vegetables as they ripen, with pumpkins and gourds available later on, into late October. They open the first week of May and stay open until the greenhouses are empty. Sweet corn is usually sold from late July. There are also Christmas trees and wreaths available later. Call ahead to confirm hours and available crops.

Fort Hill Farms, 260 Quaddick Rd., Thompson; (860) 923-3439; thefarmerscow.com. What was once an Indian fortress has been—for the past century—a bustling, modern dairy farm. In addition to the 400 Holstein cows that Kristin and Peter Orr raise on their 1,000-acre property, they also cultivate 2 acres of organic blueberries, which are pickable from early July to late Aug. The Orrs have also planted a labyrinth with edible organic, pick-your-own lavender, which you may wander through from early June through early Oct. There are also 66 display gardens, bursting with flowers in summer, and an unusually large nursery of 2,000 varieties of ornamental perennials. Flowers are for sale from May through Nov. In the fall there's a corn maze, hay-rides, hiking trails, and farm tours. The creamery sells Farmer's Cow ice cream year-round. See Kristin's recipe for **Lavender Blueberry Banana Bread** on p. 414.

Lapsley Orchard, 403 Orchard Hill Rd. (Rte. 169), Pomfret Center; (860) 928-9186. John Wolchesky has been tilling his 200-acre farm for more than 20 years and can provide you with a wide variety of fruit and vegetables. He has 28 types of apples, for instance, ranging from the popular McIntosh and Macouns to the newer Honey Crisp and Braeburns. The prize is the century-old apple tree that still produces Gravensteins. Visitors are welcome to tackle the pick-your-own apples as soon as the earliest ones ripen—the Jerseymacs usually are first in early Aug—continuing into Oct. John also has blueberries, 16 varieties of peaches, 12 of pears, and nectarines. His 20 acres of vegetables include sweet corn, tomatoes, and pumpkins, as well as fresh flowers for cutting from mid-July onward. In addition to all the produce, John's farm stand carries jams, jellies, sweet cider, fresh eggs, and eight or more kinds of fresh herbs. Free horse-drawn hayrides are available on Sun in Sept and Oct. Open daily, July through Dec.

Norman's Sugarhouse, 387 County Rd., Woodstock; (860) 974-1235; r.norman@snet.net. For more than 3 decades, Richard and Avis Norman have been putting 1,200 taps into the sugar maples on their 50 acres—an annual ritual of converting the sweet sap into delectable edibles. Their results can be seen, sampled, and carried home from their sugarhouse, in the form of maple syrup, granulated maple sugar, maple cream, maple jelly, and candies. Call ahead if you want to witness "the boil," which transforms maple sap into syrup; it goes on from Presidents' Day in Feb for 6 or 8 weeks. Visitors are welcome at other times of the year, but always call ahead.

Palazzi Orchard, 1393 North Rd., East Killingly; (860) 774-4363. This orchard, owned by Mark and Jean Palazzi, may be best known for its 20 varieties of pick-your-own apples, but it also yields peaches in Aug and, later, pumpkins and winter squashes. The Palazzis offer hayride tours on weekends at harvest time. Beyond the mouthwatering produce, you'll savor the four-state views from the hilltop; nearby is a Revolutionary War cemetery with the old Charter Oak tree. Open daily, Aug through Dec. Check them out on Facebook.

River's Edge Sugar House, 326 Mansfield Rd. (Rte. 89), Ashford; (860) 429-1510; riversedgesugarhouse.com. Driving up a long dirt road (1.5 miles south of Rte. 44), you will know you have arrived at River's Edge when you see the horses in the field next to a log house and, in the parking area, a neat wooden building that is both a shop and a processing plant. Proprietors Bill and Amy Proulx make maple syrup there, a process you may watch in Feb and Mar. In addition to maple syrup, year-round Proulx products include honey, maple syrup, maple candy, maple jelly, and maple creams. Visitors are welcome most Sat and Sun. (Call ahead about tours for schools and families.) Cash only.

Wayne's Organic Garden, 1080 Plainfield Pike (Rte. 14A), Oneco; (860) 564-7987; waynesorganicgarden.com. Wayne Hansen is best known for his unusual certified organic vegetables, 30 different kinds. Fingerling-size purple Peruvian potatoes (try saying it fast), pink-outside/yellow-inside Laratte potatoes, Walla Walla onions (similar to Vidalias), Italian cipollini, Borretana onions, celeriac, and radicchio are among the specialties Wayne grows and sells at the **Willimantic Food Co-op** (p. 353) and farmers' markets in Putnam, Old Saybrook, Danielson, and Coventry. From mid-May through early June, Wayne's heirloom tomatoes, garlic, and greenhouse vegetable plants are for sale at his Plainfield Pike farm. Call for days and times.

Winterbrook Farm, 116 Beffa Rd., Staffordville; (860) 684-2124; info at winterbrookfarm@cox.net. Winterbrook's big red barn and farmhouse have been on this spot on Beffa Road since the 1700s. Owners Kirby and Laura Judd haven't been raising Dorset sheep for quite that long, but their tradition of supplying Easter lambs to churches in the area and others who savor lamb does stretch back several years. Order your own Easter or freezer lamb in early March to have it available for delivery the week before Easter. The Judds also make maple syrup in their sugarhouse (after Mar), grow rhubarb in spring, and cultivate pick-your-own blueberries (July through Sept), all without herbicides or pesticides. Open mid-July through Sept, but best to call ahead for specific days, hours, and crop availability.

Wright's Orchards & Dried Flower Farm, 271 South River Rd., Tolland; (860) 872-1665; wrightsorchard.com. If you like to pick your own, you will love the dwarf and semi-dwarf apple trees, some 250 of them, that Todd and Joyclyn Wright grow here, making picking easier. Also ripe for the picking are blueberries, raspberries, peaches, and (later) pumpkins. The Wrights, who have farmed along the Willimantic River since 1981, also raise tomatoes, cucumbers, squashes, and other vegetables. Flower fanciers will appreciate how unusual and beautiful the Wrights' dried flowers look as they cure in the 1840 barn, now a gift shop. The Wright farm stand, with its wide array of fruits, vegetables, flowers, fresh cider, preserves, and pies, is open from Aug until Christmas. Closed Wed.

Food Happenings

March

Annual Hebron Maple Festival, Hebron; (860) 228-1110; (860) 228-0246 or (860) 649-0841; hebronmaplefest.com. This festival is held the second or third weekend in Mar. Maple products are the order of the day, with self-guided tours of three Hebron sugar-houses: Wenzel, Woody Acres, and Winding Brook.

May

Shuck-Off Annual Oyster Festival, Rotary Park, Putnam. For information about this popular local May event, check out 85main .com/OysterFest.php or call the folks at 85 Main (860-928-1660), who are always participants. There's live music, competitions, and lots and lots of fresh seafood.

September

Woodstock Fair, Woodstock Fairgrounds (Rte. 169 and Rte. 171), South Woodstock; (860) 928-3246; woodstockfair.com. This old-fashioned country fair has been an annual event since 1860 that takes place on Labor Day weekend, from Fri through Mon. There's food galore, plus livestock exhibits, pie-eating contests, and all the timeless activities you'd expect at an old-timey fair.

Taste of the Valley, Golden Lamb Buttery, 299 Wolf Den Rd., (Rte. 169), Brooklyn. This celebratory event occurs at the end of Sept on the rolling grounds of the popular Golden Lamb Buttery restaurant. It's a one-day happening with 35 towns in this part of Connecticut participating. Enjoy the pleasures in this part of the state: the foods, crafts, and food products. Area chefs show their goodies and a great time is had by all.

October

The Downtown Country Fair, Willimantic Food Co-op parking lot, 91 Valley St., Willimantic; (860) 456-3611; willimanticfood .coop. This celebration of local businesses is held the first Sun of Oct. Local restaurants, farmers, craftspeople, and musicians hold a daylong fiesta that attracts locals and visitors alike. Call to confirm the date and hours.

Buell's Orchard Annual Fall Festival, 108 Crystal Pond Rd., Eastford; (860) 974-1150; buellsorchard.com. Ever since 1978 this annual harvest event has been held Sat and Mon—but not the Sun sandwiched in between—on Columbus Day weekend. Hot dogs, chicken barbecue, burgers, desserts, and other foods are available for sale; cider and doughnuts are free. There are seven hayrides through the orchards to the pumpkin patch, which is open for pick-your-own pumpkins, and you can watch the candied apple–processing machine, adding to a very rewarding day-at-the-farm experience for one and all. There's live music, too.

Nibbles

Bidwell Tavern & Cafe, 1260 Main St., Coventry; (860) 742-6978; bidwelltavern.com; $–$$. Call them nibbles, snacks, or starters, but by all means try the buffalo wings at Bidwell. These aren't plain old deep-fried chicken wings with the usual blue cheese dip. The dips here come in 25 different flavors, or as the tavern claims, "hot, mild and complicated." Examples include sesame garlic pepper, Mexican spice, teriyaki sesame, hickory horseradish, sweet and sour, Cajun spice, honey barbecue Cajun, lemon pepper, and even some with dry rubs. Combine the wings with a Woodchuck Amber Cider or a hefty beer, from a choice of 24 on draft—such as Bidwells Old Abernathy—and a number in bottles as well—and you've got the makings of a great snack time.

Bush Meadow Farm, 738 Buckley Hwy. (Rte. 190), Union; (860) 684-3039; bushmeadowfarm.com; $. Nancy and Barry Kapplan have carried the farm-to-table locavore concept to an extreme. Almost everything they serve in their small, 18-seat cafe at breakfast and lunch (and in their attached shop) is made and processed on their farm. The popular pepper-cured pastrami sandwiches (the meat sliced and heated to order), free-range eggs, breads, rolls, muffins, French toast, the maple syrup poured over the pancakes, the various goat cheeses (from feta to seasoned blue), the goat's milk, even the house ketchup—the whole gazoo, all are made on their family farm. Both the cafe and shop are open Sat and Sun.

The Farmer's Cow Calfé and Creamery, Staples Plaza, 86 Storrs Rd., (across from the Eastbrook Mall), Mansfield; (860) 642-4600; thefarmerscowcalfe.com; $. Even if you groan at the pun in this cafe's name, you'll love the ice cream. The Farmer's Cow is a mini-conglomerate of six farms in this corner of the state that pool their resources. They have come up with their own ice cream (try the Red White and Moo Summer Berry, made with fresh raspberries and blueberries) and sell it to area stores. They also have their very own cafe, 'scuse me, calfé. In addition to the rich and creamy ice cream, shakes, and sundaes, it serves breakfast and Up Early coffee, which you can enjoy indoors or in the outdoor courtyard.

Heritage Trail Cafe at The Winery, 291 North Burnham Hwy. (scenic Rte. 169), Lisbon; (860) 376-0659; heritagetrail.com; $$. When Laurie and Harry Schwartz bought the Heritage Trail Winery in 1996, one of their first moves was to add a cafe, which seats 55 indoors and 48 outside. Laurie is the vintner, Harry the chef. He serves a number of agreeable dishes, such as starters like seafood chowder, pan-seared Bomster scallops, apricot-sesame chicken, and smoked mozzarella caprice. All of these are enhanced by the house wines. Closed Mon. It is advisable to call ahead.

Mrs. Bridges' Pantry, 292 Rte. 169, South Woodstock; (860) 963-7040; mrsbridgespantry.com; $. This pleasant merry-olde-England shop doubles as a tearoom and is a good place for lunch. The lunch side of the L-shaped shop has 10 tables, seating 30, plus 5 tables outside in front. Lunch options include house-made soups, Cornish pasties, ploughman's lunch, quiches, shepherd's pie, sandwiches, vegetable curries, and authentic English pork pies. Afternoon tea, a real delight, consists of crumpets, scones, clotted cream, locally made pastries, Eccles cake, tea sandwiches, and house-made strawberry jam (from the owners' own berry patch). The tearoom is closed on Tues.

Roseland Cottage, 556 Rte. 169, Woodstock; (860) 928-4074; historicnewengland.org; $. This "cottage" is a rare example of a Victorian Gothic Revival house (built for Woodstock native Henry Bowen) with a beautiful old-fashioned garden. Usually twice a year, late summer and early Sept, a prix-fixe Victorian dessert tea (with scones, several desserts, fruit, and tea) is served in the carriage barn. Included in the price is a tour of the house, which is packed with history. Bowen was the publisher of an abolitionist newspaper and entertained four US presidents at his pink house. For information and reservations for the tea or for group tours, call or check the website.

The Vanilla Bean Cafe, 450 Deerfield Rd. (intersection of Rte. 169, Rte. 44, and Rte. 97), Pomfret; (860) 928-1562; thevanilla beancafe.com; $. Inside a big, restored, 19th-century barn at a crossroads in the middle of nowhere is "the" gathering place—attracting Pomfret School students, faculty, and locals from miles around. The draw is fresh-tasting, home-cooked comfort food—muffins; soups (don't miss the New England clam chowder); chili; burgers of all types, including vegetarian; other veggie specialties; and luscious pies and cakes—as well as good wine and beer lists and a laid-back atmosphere. Breakfast, lunch, and live entertainment on weekends (running the gamut from folk-music concerts, bluegrass, and poetry readings to jam sessions and open-mike nights) are also part of the mix. "The Bean" (as everyone calls it), which siblings Barry, Brian, and Eileen Jessurun opened in 1989, had just 16 seats at first; it is now an ever-expanding northeastern Connecticut institution. From two dining rooms, the action—from Apr through Nov—spills out to the tree-shaded brick patio. According to Brian, they use local products as much as possible and local produce exclusively during the growing season. "Our burgers are made from local free-range, grass-fed New Boston Beef," he says. He is proud of their many house-made soups and gluten-free offerings, such as English muffins; cookies; brownies made from black beans, Ghirardelli chocolate, and espresso; and also their popular chili ("we sell 8 tons of it a year").

Learn to Cook

Dalice Elizabeth, 6 Amos Rd., Preston; (860) 889-WINE (9463); daliceelizabeth.com. Mary-Lee Dalice Wilcox offers 3-hour Italian cooking classes for a minimum of six per class at this farm winery.

Martha's Herbary, 589 Pomfret St. (junction of Rte. 44, Rte. 97, and Rte. 169), Pomfret; (860) 928-0009; marthasherbary.com. Cooking classes are held in winter, spring, and fall. If you call and leave your e-mail address, information about the classes will be sent to you. Past classes have included soups with herbs, gifts using lavender, pie making, appetizers, and gluten-free cooking.

Learn about Wine

Dalice Elizabeth, 6 Amos Rd., Preston; (860) 889-WINE (9463); daliceelizabeth.com. John Wilcox conducts wine seminars at his farm winery. Call for dates and times and to make arrangements in advance.

Landmark Eateries

Altnaveigh Inn & Restaurant, 957 Storrs Rd. (Rte. 195), Storrs; (860) 429-4490; altnaveighinn.com; $$$. A restored 1740 house, the white clapboard Altnaveigh Inn, with three dining rooms (two of them warmed in winter by fireplaces), has been a waystation for generations of hungry UConn students and their parents. The cooking is continental, but with such starters as clams casino, Maryland crab cakes, lobster bisque, and scallops wrapped in bacon more consistent than the entrees, I'd suggest making a meal of appetizers. (That will save your wallet too, as entrees are on the pricey side.) In warm weather you can dine outside on a pleasant patio. There are five guest rooms, so staying overnight is definitely an option, one that is more appealing since new owners Gail and Doug Parks completed extensive renovations to the inn. Closed Sun and Mon.

85 Main, 85 Main St., Putnam; (860) 928-1660; 85main.com; $$. When well-traveled professional chef James Martin bought the Vine Bistro in 2005 with his partners, Barry and Brian Jessurun of the **Vanilla Bean Cafe** (p. 370) in Pomfret, the first thing he did was change the name to 85 Main. The second was to change the decor (now with earth tones and sleeker sophistication than before) and enlarge the interior (making room for a new bar and a raw bar). Then came the menu changes to modern American fusion, with emphasis on shellfish. His raw bar is a rarity in this part of the state and now he has a full sushi menu as well. James's dining patio jumps with activity in warm weather. Look for such dishes as mussel fritters (battered in Newcastle Brown Ale), lobster risotto, shrimp pappardelle, and maple-glazed New Bedford sea scallops. Of course, not everything at 85 Main is of the briny shell variety. Aside from wild Alaskan salmon, there are grilled house-cut Angus rib eye, orange and coriander half-chicken, and barbecue platter (with North Carolina pulled pork and pork ribs, corn bread, and seared greens), among several zesty entrees. The small wine list emphasizes Californian, Italian, and South American choices; note also the presence of several palate-satisfying craft-brewed beers and ales. Closed Thanksgiving, Christmas Eve and Day, July 4th, and Labor Day.

The Fireside Tavern at Sharpe Hill Vineyards, 108 Wade Rd., Pomfret; (860) 974-3549; sharpehill.com; $$. Lunch or dinner in the Fireside Tavern evokes the past in looks and spirit, though the food—prepared on a wood-burning stove by Catherine Vollweiler, the vineyard's co-owner—is deliciously modern. The ancient-looking barn-red building dates back only to 1998, but it exemplifies Catherine's eye for American antiques and details. The cozy tavern, up a winding wooden stairway, has a double fireplace in the center of the room, ladder-back chairs, and charming murals. It seats a mere 40

The Golden Lamb Buttery, 299 Wolf Den Rd. (Rte. 169), Brooklyn; (860) 774-4423; thegoldenlamb.com; $$. This one-of-a-kind restaurant, unique in Connecticut and maybe anywhere, is ensconced in a big, rambling barn on a working farm of 1,000 acres. It has been a restaurant since 1963, with the same family management (the late Jimmie and Bob Booth started it and ran it for decades) at the same locale. The Golden Lamb is now in the capable hands of the Booths' granddaughter, Katie Bogert. Visitors will find things much the same as when the Booths were alive. The prix-fixe dinner begins with drinks and a hayride (to live guitar accompaniment) through freshly mowed fields, past sheep, cows, horses, and donkeys, grazing on the hillsides. Then guests drift into the converted barn, with its high ceilings, barn-siding walls, fireplace, and hayloft. Festooned with garden flowers,

people. A single large dining table is on the ground floor near the bar for those who can't handle the stairs. A mere bunny hop from the vineyards is the spacious outdoor terrace, with four weeping cherry trees in the center, where meals are served in warm weather. Though the menu changes often, you will always find grilled dishes, such as wood-fired lamb chops with rosemary potatoes, swordfish grilled with rosemary and Vidalia onions, or wood-smoked Jamaican chicken marinated in a fiery jerk sauce. Look for an exceptionally attractive cheese platter, consisting of English, French, and other European cheeses. Served at their full ripeness, the cheeses make the dining room decor is best described as sophisticated country casual. There is a choice of soup, maybe chilled borscht or vegetable peasant, followed by a choice of four entrees, which might include chateaubriand, rack of lamb, or roast duckling, accompanied by six or seven fresh garden vegetables, always prepared in interesting ways (for example, lemony artichokes au gratin, fresh peas tossed with mint, and orange-glazed carrots with roasted fennel). During dinner, a guitarist strolls through the rooms, singing folk songs. Good food, a genuinely friendly staff, and the appealing farm-like surroundings make an evening here a rare and memorable experience. The Golden Lamb is a destination in itself, one that I never tire of revisiting. Dinner reservations are essential. The schedule is limited to lunch Tues through Sat, prix-fixe dinner Fri and Sat only, early Apr through New Year's Eve.

a fine accompaniment to the vineyard wines. Lunch and dinner are on a limited schedule: Fri, Sat, and Sun by reservation only. It is prudent to plan 3 weeks or more ahead; Fireside Tavern is *that* busy. Fri evenings Jan through Mar, New England lobsters are broiled on a wood-burning grill, and weekends throughout winter offer special theme nights.

The Inn at Woodstock Hill, 94 Plaine Hill Rd., Woodstock; (860) 928-0528; woodstockhill.com; $$. There aren't many Connecticut inns as entwined with the town history as this imposing white clapboard house. It was built in 1816 by William Bowen, a descendant of one of the 13 so-designated "Goers," who founded the town in 1686. William was the grandfather of Henry Bowen, whose pink Victorian Gothic house, Roseland Cottage, is Woodstock's leading landmark. The inn, with 18 guest rooms (plus 3 in a guest cottage), serves meals (including Sunday brunch) in several bright and pleasant dining rooms. As you feast upon rack of lamb Dijon or grilled filet mignon with Madagascar green peppercorn sauce, you may learn that most of the nearby hills and meadows still belong to the Bowen family. The inn itself, now owned by Richard Naumann, was in the Bowen family until 1981. That's continuity for you! Closed for lunch Mon through Wed.

Mahzu Japanese Restaurant, 624 West Main St., Norwich; (860) 889-8288; mahzusushinorwichct.com; $–$$. Sushi bars are usually expensive, but Mahzu is an exception. Prices are reasonable for really, really, fresh fish. And although the restaurant itself is small, it has a real Japanese air, with Japanese sushi chefs in attendance and the wall adornments reminiscent of a sushi bar in the home country. The simplest dishes may be best—like the tuna roll, dragon roll, and sushi-sashimi combination—but the chefs have a flair for creative arrangements, as in special rolls like the elaborate Godzilla (salmon, eel, striped bass, and fluke), Sumo (yellowtail, eel, tuna flakes, and avocado), and Holmdel (spicy tuna, eel, and avocado). Many choices, many pleasures. Reserve ahead.

Main Street Cafe, 967 Main St., Willimantic; (860) 423-6777; willibrew.com; $. Partnered with the **Willimantic Brewing Co.** (p. 379), this pleasant cafe occupies the former workroom of an old 1909 U.S. Post Office building, vacant for almost 30 years when Cindy and David Wollner took it over. As you enjoy a bowl of baked onion-ale soup, casual flatbread pizza, quesadillas, chicken sliders, a sandwich, or a full-fledged dinner, note all the post office memorabilia, along with a monumental 12-by-17-foot mural by Gordan Mac-Donald, which depicts Main Street in the 1920s. Note also that most dishes on the eclectic American menu are named after northeastern Connecticut towns, so it is possible to order by zip code, as in "I'll have an 06268" (Gurleyville garlic-walnut chicken) or "give me an 06043" (Bolton beer-battered fish-and-chips). Closed Mon for lunch.

The Spa at Norwich Inn, Rte. 32, Norwich; (860) 425-3630; thespaatnorwichinn.com; $$$. In 1983 Edward J. Safdie, owner of the Sonoma Mission Inn & Spa in Sonoma, California, converted a rustic old inn in Norwich into an upscale spa and inn, with handsome public areas, rooms, villas, and grounds. The Mashantucket Pequot Tribal Nation now owns the property, but little has changed. Kensington's is the main dining room, with graceful chandeliers, carpeting, and well-spaced tables. The food is modern American, with attention paid to healthful eating. They aren't kidding about the spa: The amounts of calories, fat, protein, and carbohydrates are listed under each dish on the menu so that you may choose accordingly (or not). It is difficult to avoid the temptation of amaretto shrimp in almond emulsion, lobster Bolognese, Tuscan-spiced duck breast, or *osso buco*—diet be darned! If you are on hand for lunch in temperate weather, the deck, shaded by huge trees, is a wonderfully relaxed place to eat. For a quicker, lighter meal, try Ascot's, a knotty-pine-paneled pub with a fireplace, whose tasty items include New England clam chowder, smoked wraps, and burgers. There is also casual dining poolside. Reservations are suggested for dinner.

Trattoria da Lepri, 89 West Rd., Ellington; (860) 875-1111; trattoriadalepri.com; $$. This pleasant Italian trattoria, seating 50, with a big blackboard displaying the daily menu, is situated in a strip mall. Frank Lepri, chef and co-owner (with his wife, Debbie), was the chef at the former Pastis, a French brasserie in Hartford. Thus the trattoria is a twofer, with a few French classics like escargot and beef *bourguignonne* on the menu, along with many Italian traditionals and originals, like *rigatoni Bolognese,* pork *saltimbocca* with aged provolone polenta, three-cheese tortellini with sage sausage, shrimp and *sambuca* (a Lepri original), house-made pappardelle with braised beef in a truffled brown sauce, and balsamic braised short rib ravioli. Closed Sun and Mon. Frank and Debbie have recently opened **Lepri's Grill at** 167 Tolland Stage Rd., Tolland (860-875-4444). It is often quite good, but sometimes uneven, whereas Trattoria da Lepri is almost always on target.

Traveler Restaurant: The Food & Book People, 1257 Buckley Hwy., off Rte. 84 (exit 74), Union; (860) 684-4920; $. When you reach the Connecticut-Massachusetts line, you'll see a sign that states, "Food and Books," outside a simple frame building. It marks one of the most unusual eateries in the state—a restaurant and bookstore combined. The plain, knotty-pine-walled dining room and glassed-in porch are awash in books—in bookcases, on ledges, and on counters, in fact, everywhere you turn. The books are secondhand, but the food is fresh at breakfast, lunch, and dinner. With every order of food, customers can help themselves to three free books. Art and Karen Murdock, the owners, claim they give away 100,000 books a year, many of which they acquire through library sales. The food is hearty, generous, modestly priced, and appetizing, though in no way fancy. There is a 10 percent senior discount on Tuesday. Thursday through Saturday pizzas and grinders are added to the menu. I particularly like the fried clam strips, whole belly clams, and packed lobster roll on the lunch menu. After choosing your free books, you might wander down a short flight of stairs to browse in Traveler's bona fide secondhand-book store (interesting tomes, but no freebies there!).

Brewpubs & Craft Breweries

Willimantic Brewing Co. and Main Street Cafe, 967 Main St., Willimantic; (860) 423-6777; willibrew.com; $$. The beers at this brewery/cafe are in the town's oldest post office (a stately granite and sandstone building, vintage 1909). They range from the light palate of Certified Gold to P.S. Pale Bock's multinational blend of malts. Brewer and co-owner David Wollner crafts these and more (including many, many seasonals) on the premises, and from the aging tanks they move directly to the taps of the 60-foot mahogany bar that dominates the former post-office customer lobby. Over 12 brews are produced each month; on any given day there are 20 brews on tap, some from other craft brewers. David's seasonal suds include Rail Mail Rye, an unfiltered rye pale ale, and AmBerlicious, an American blend with calomel. Then there is Hop Addiction, an unfiltered IPA, made with European Munich, Vienna rye, and pale malts. It is fun to explore all the postal memorabilia while sipping the house brews. David advises the first-timer to begin with a sampler of five or six tastes. The old post office's sorting room is separated by a glass partition from the dining room over which David's wife, Cindy, has presided since the Main Street Cafe opened in 1991. Not coincidentally, the cafe offers various beer dinner events each week and special events almost nightly.

Wine Trail

Five of the wineries in northeast Connecticut are on the Connecticut Wine Trail. Visit ctwine.com for a map and more information. And remember, if you get a wine passport (available free at any winery on the trail), you can have it stamped at each winery you visit, then turn it in and possibly win a prize.

Cassidy Hill Vineyard, 454 Cassidy Hill Rd., Coventry; (860) 896-9144 or (860) 498-1126; cassidyhillvineyard.com. This relatively new winery is already producing seven wines. Among them are Jets Red (a blend of Merlot, Siray, and Malbec), Pinot Grigio, Riesling, Summer Breeze (a sweetish wine made with Cayuga white grapes), and Late Harvest Vidal Blanc (with Vidal grapes). Tastings are held Fri through Sun.

Dalice Elizabeth, 6 Amos Rd., Preston; (860) 889-WINE (9463); daliceelizabeth.com. In a lovely setting on the Amos River, John and Mary-Lee Dalice Wilcox, the proprietors of this small farm winery, produce—with the assistance of their grandson, Blaze Faillaci—a variety of wines, using blends of various grapes, Syrah, Cabernet Franc, Cabernet Sauvignon, Chardonnay, Old Vine Zinfandel, Sangiovese, Pinot Grigio, and Merlot. Tastings, with wine, cheeses, olives, and bruschetta, are held Thurs through Sun in season. But it is essential to reserve ahead. The vineyard also holds wine dinners, featuring nine wines.

Heritage Trail Vineyards and Cafe, 291 North Burnham Hwy., Lisbon; (860) 376-0659; heritagetrail.com. Harry and Laurie Schwartz own this property, which has 8 acres of grapes, and have expanded it from a winery to a winery-plus-cafe and gelateria. The main building is an 18th-century (1785) Cape Cod house, where the

> "A man is a fool if he drinks before he reaches the age of fifty and a fool if he doesn't afterward."   —Frank Lloyd Wright

Schwartzes live. To the right of it in the rear of the driveway is the barn with the cafe (**Heritage Trail Cafe at The Winery**, p. 368) and wine-tasting room. Beyond that is the barn with renovated winemaking equipment. The vineyard plantings include Chardonnay, Cabernet Franc, Merlot, and hybrids Cayuga white and Vignoles grapes. Quinebaug White, Rochambeau Red (introduced in 2007), Sweet Reserve (which does double duty as an aperitif), Shetucket Red, and the newest label, Winthrop White, are among Heritage Trail's seven wines. Closed Mon.

Priam Vineyards, 11 Shailor Hill Rd., Colchester; (860) 267-8520; priamvineyards.com. This winery was started in 1998, when Gloria Priam and her husband, Gary Crump, bought 27 acres of hillside, which they have since augmented with another 13 acres. Gloria's grandfather and father were in the wine trade in Budapest in the 1890s, later in the US, so she simply followed family tradition when she and Gary planted Seyval, Chardonnay, Cayuga, and other grapes and turned their property into a vineyard. In 2001 their Salmon River White won the gold in an international competition, and in 2003 they struck gold again with their Riesling and silver with their Salmon River Red. Their wine list now includes 6 reds and 10 whites; they include the crisp Barrel Select Chardonnay, Westchester Red,

Blackledge White, a Rosé and Gewürztraminer. In 2012 their Late Harvest Riesling won a first in the dessert wine category in a tasting by *Connecticut* magazine oenophiles. Priam now boasts two tasting counters (with local cheeses for sale also), Fri night concerts from July through Sept, and self-guided tours of the vineyard. The latter is accentuated by 35-mile views from the hilltop. The vineyard is open Mar through Dec, Fri to Sun and holidays.

Sharpe Hill Vineyards, 108 Wade Rd., Pomfret; (860) 974-3549; sharpehill.com. The curving drive from Rte. 97 to Sharpe Hill Vineyards is 1.5 miles under a canopy of trees, suggesting a property far more ancient than a winery that has only been active since 1992. Young though Sharpe Hill Vineyards may be, its poetically named Ballet of Angels white wine (the state's most popular Connecticut-produced wine), late-harvest Vignoles, and three separate Chardonnays have earned gold medals in international competitions. (That Chardonnay and a late-harvest Vignoles have earned high praise from *Wine Spectator* magazine, too.) The Cuvee Ammi Phillips Chardonnay alone has won six medals. One of the newer wines is Angelica Rosé, which won a first in a 2012 *Connecticut* magazine tasting. Its Dry Summer Rosé won a second in the same tasting. The 100-acre property is no less poetic than the names of some of its products, with vineyards, gardens, and barn-red buildings scattered across the grounds. The rolling hills rise 700 feet above the countryside, and on a clear day you can see forever . . . well, at least into Massachusetts and Rhode Island. Owners Steven and Catherine Vollweiler have handsomely furnished their tasting room

> "I like to keep a bottle of stimulant handy in case I see a snake—
> which I also keep handy."   —W. C. Fields

(where you may sample the range, including wines made with the vineyard's Cabernet Franc, St. Croix, and Carmine grapes) in 18th-century style, with many handcrafted objects. It is open Fri through Sun, year-round. There is also a restaurant onsite (**The Fireside Tavern at Sharpe Hill Vineyards,** p. 373). Sharpe Hill delivers to 400 package stores and restaurants in New England.

Taylor Brooke Winery, 848 Rte. 171, Woodstock; (860) 974-1263; taylorbrookewinery.com. Owners Linda and Dick Augur produce several dry wines and fruit-infused Rieslings, made from their own grapes and fruit juices, including whites, such as Green Apple Riesling, Summer Peach, Traminette, Winter Pomegranate, Woodstock Hill, and reds, such as Roseland, St. Croix, and Woodstock Valley. Then there are their dessert wines: Late Harvest Riesling and the popular Chocolate Essence and Raspberry Rendezvous. Visitors may taste two wines for free; there is a small fee for eight tastings, and a larger, but still modest fee for tasting all the wines. You might have a tasting accompanied by cheeses from **Beltane Farm** (p. 339) and then browse the winery gift shop for Connecticut-made foods and take a self-guided vineyard tour during regular business hours. Tastings are Fri through Sun.

Recipes

Appetizers

Crab Fondue (Bill Taibe of the Whelk and Le Farm), 388

Crispy Lobster Potato Roll (Susan Goodman of Susan Goodman Catering), 389

Soups

Puree of Chestnut Soup (Carole Peck of Carole Peck's Good News Cafe), 390

Chef Claire's Lentil Soup (Claire Criscuolo of Claire's Corner Copia), 391

Salads

Cilantro Couscous Salad (Kathleen Jonah Lenane of Bear Pond Farm), 393

Mango Shrimp Salad (Toby Fossland of the Hopkins Inn), 394

Vegan Kale Salad (James O'Shea of West Street Grill), 395

Main Dishes

Adrienne's Lobster and Filet Mignon Wrapped in Phyllo (Adrienne Sussman of Adrienne), 397

Baked Layered Moroccan Eggplant and Beef Ragu (Riad Aamar of Oliva), 398

Fresh Summer Berry Balsamic Dressing with Chicken (Tina Fearnley of the Purple Pear by Tina, 400

Slow Baked Halibut, Stuffed Artichokes, Barigoule Broth, and Truffle Butter (by Leonardo Marino of Napa & Co.), 401

Spaghetti with Clams (Linda Giuca of Alforno Trattoria), 404

Sides

Asparagi alla Parmigiana (Sally Maraventano of Cucina Casalinga), 405

Ina's Cannelini Beans and Escarole (Ina Bomze of Fabled Foods), 406

Jean-Louis's Famous Potato au Gratin (Jean-Louis Gerin), 407

Metro Bis's Brussels Sprouts, Bacon, and Honey (Chris Prosperi of Metro Bis), 409

Desserts

Chaiwalla's Strawberry-Rhubarb Cobbler (Mary O'Reilly of Chaiwalla), 410

Debra Ponzek's Madeleines (Debra Ponzek of Aux Délices), 411

Double Chocolate Raspberry Biscotti (Margaret Chatey of Westford Hill Distillers), 412

Lavender Blueberry Banana Bread (Kristin Orr of Fort Hill Farms), 414

Sweet Maria's Chunkey Monkey Cake (Maria Bruscino Sanchez of Sweet Maria's), 415

Honey Figs with Goat Cheese and Pecans (Marina Marchese of Red Bee Honey), 417

Crab Fondue

This luscious starter is the creation of Bill Taibe of the Whelk and Le Farm in Westport. It is served as a small plate at the Whelk, but is so rich it could be a light entree. It is delicious when served over soft grits.

Serves 4.

1 cup white verjus
1 cup white wine
½ cup white wine vinegar
1 teaspoon black peppercorns
2 sprigs fresh thyme

1 bay leaf
2 shallots sliced very thin—set aside
½ pound butter

Combine and reduce all ingredients above (except the shallots) in sauce pot.

12 peekytoe crab (picked)
4 ounces fresh sea urchin

Salt to taste
1 tablespoon chives

Heat crab and sea urchin slowly in butter sauce. Add salt to taste and chives.

Shallots
Cornstarch

Salt and pepper

Toss sliced shallots with cornstarch. Fry shallots in canola oil at 300°F until light brown. Season with salt and pepper to taste.

Wasabi tobiko

Finish with wasabi tobiko.

Grits

4 cups whole milk	2 ounces butter
1 cup Anson Mills grits	Salt and pepper

Boil milk. Whisk in grits to bloom. Cook slowly, stirring often. Finish with butter. Season with salt and pepper to taste

Courtesy of Bill Taibe of the Whelk and Le Farm, Westport, CT (pp. 103, 102)

Crispy Lobster Potato Roll

As a caterer, Susan Goodman is popular in the New Canaan area, and she is generous about sharing some of her favorite appetizers.

Serves 6.

6 small potatoes—red bliss, Peruvian purple, Idaho, or small russets	½ cup cooked lobster meat, diced and tossed with butter
¼ cup of melted butter	¼ cup of fresh-snipped chives
¼ cup canola oil	

Preheat oven to 400°F.

Slice the potatoes ¼-inch thick and place them on a parchment-lined baking sheet.

Mix the melted butter and oil togther; set aside.

Bake the potatoes for 10 minutes, then brush with the butter-oil mixture and bake an additional 20 minutes, until brown and crispy.

Top with small teaspoon of lobster meat and garnish with chives. Serve hot.

Courtesy of Susan Goodman of Susan Goodman Catering, New Canaan, CT (p. 71)

Soups

Puree of Chestnut Soup

This is a luscious Carole Peck recipe, easy to make and good for company or on a cold night.

Makes 1 gallon or 16 cups.

- 8 ounces butter
- 1 pound shallots, peeled and diced
- 1 tablespoon ground cinnamon
- 2 teaspoons ground allspice
- ½ teaspoon honey
- 1 cup brandy
- 1 #202 can chestnut paste or 5 pounds fresh chestnuts, roasted, shelled, and peeled
- 3 quarts chicken stock
- Salt to taste
- 3 cups heavy cream
- 2 tablespoons sherry vinegar
- 1 teaspoon chopped fresh chives

Melt the butter in a 1½- or 2-gallon pot. Add the shallots and sweat over medium heat until transparent.

Add the cinnamon, allspice, and honey. Cook about 1 minute to bloom the spices. Add the brandy and flame to burn off alcohol.

Add the paste or chestnuts. Stir and cook approximately 3 minutes.

Pour in the chicken stock and blend well. Bring to a boil, stirring occasionally, and season with salt to taste.

Cook 30 minutes on a low boil; stir. Whisk in all the heavy cream except ¼ cup and bring back to a boil. Reduce heat and cook 10 minutes more.

Add sherry vinegar and cook 10 minutes more. Puree with an immersion blender and you are ready to serve.

Garnish with a dollop of whipped cream (made from the ¼-cup heavy cream) and chives.

Courtesy of Carole Peck of Carole Peck's Good News Cafe Woodbury, CT (p. 155)

Chef Claire's Lentil Soup

This hearty soup is served at Claire's Corner Copia with the kitchen's own bread, a combination of wheat and white dough that is made fresh daily.

Serves 8.

- 4 quarts water
- 12 ounces organic lentils, picked over for stones
- 1 bay leaf
- 5 tablespoons extra-virgin olive oil

4 large cloves garlic, finely chopped

1 medium yellow onion, finely chopped

8 ribs organic celery, cut into ½-inch slices, including leaves

6 medium organic carrots, cut into ½-inch-thick slices

1 large bulb fennel, cut into bite-size pieces

1 (6-ounce) can organic tomato paste

¼ cup finely chopped organic Italian flat-leaf parsley

Sea salt and pepper to taste

10-ounce container organic baby spinach

2 cups tubetti pasta, cooked according to package directions

Place the water, lentils, and bay leaf in a large pot. Cover and bring to a boil over high heat. Lower the heat to medium.

Add the oil, garlic, onion, celery, carrots, fennel, tomato paste, parsley, salt, and pepper. Stir well to mix.

Cover and cook at a medium-high boil (the soup will return to a boil after about 5 minutes), stirring occasionally, for about 1 hour, or until the lentils and celery are tender.

Add the spinach. Stir well to mix. Cover and continue cooking, stirring occasionally, for 5 minutes, or until the spinach is tender.

Stir in the cooked pasta. Taste for seasonings.

Courtesy of Claire Criscuolo of Claire's Corner Copia, New Haven, CT (p. 308)

Cilantro Couscous Salad

Kathleen Jonah Lenane, a partner at Bear Pond Farm, offered this simple-to-make recipe that really gives a welcome zap to couscous. This dish also makes a good accompaniment to a grilled meat or chicken entree and may be served warm, chilled, or at room temperature.

Serves 2.

1 cup couscous
1½ cups fresh zucchini squash, cut into ½-inch cubes
1½ cups fresh or frozen corn kernels
3–4 tablespoons Bear Pond Farm Rich Cilantro pesto

(or any pesto of your choice)
2 chopped scallions
Salt and pepper to taste

Cook couscous, following package directions.

Meanwhile, steam the zucchini and corn kernels until cooked through; drain and set aside. When couscous is cooked through, remove to a serving dish and fluff with a fork.

Thoroughly mix the pesto into the warm couscous. Add the vegetables and scallions. Salt and pepper to taste.

Courtesy of Kathleen Jonah Lenane of Bear Pond Farm, Glastonbury, CT (p. 176)

Mango Shrimp Salad

Toby Fossland of the Hopkins Inn volunteered this recipe for a delicious, different, and refreshing salad.

Serves 2 as an appetizer; adjust quantity for a light lunch entree or add mesclun greens, mâche, or Boston lettuce for more substance.

1 large mango, peeled, sliced
thin in hemispheres

1 large ripe tomato, sliced
slightly thicker in
hemispheres

8 large shrimp, peeled, cooked,
and butterflied

2 teaspoons raspberry
vinaigrette

2 leaves fresh basil, cut
chiffonade

12 fresh raspberries

Alternate mango and tomato hemispheres in a circular pattern. Stand butterflied shrimp up, tails together in center of plate.

Drizzle with raspberry vinaigrette and garnish with basil and raspberries.

Raspberry Vinaigrette

Raspberry vinegar
Olive oil

Sugar
Salt and pepper

Mix vinegar and olive oil in a 1:3 or 1:4 ratio. Add sugar to taste to reduce acidity, then add salt and pepper to taste.

Dressing can be made in small quantities for immediate use or may be stored in larger quantities in the refrigerator indefinitely.

Courtesy of Toby Fossland of the Hopkins Inn, New Preston, CT (p. 158)

Vegan Kale Salad

In describing his kale salad, James O'Shea of West Street Grill says, "Kale salad's high nutrient content makes it a delicious and important addition to the vegan diet. Originating centuries ago in Europe, this member of the cabbage family provides an exceptional and varied amount of vitamins and nutrients, such as beta carotene, vitamin D, vitamin K, and vitamin C. A unique substitution for plain lettuce, kale will surprise any consumer with delicious texture and flavor in its raw state."

Serves 4.

Salad

- 2 bunches (4-5 cups) of organic Lacinato/Tuscan kale, in chiffonade
- 2 tablespoons of dried, tart, sour cherries
- 1 cup organic-only (never use commercial grown to avoid chemical usage) celery, tough fibers and strings removed and thinly sliced
- ½ cup sprouted walnuts (available at Whole Foods), bashed in a plastic bag with a rolling pin

- 8 Medjool dates, 4 pitted and diced and 4 quartered
- 1 Granny Smith apple, cored and julienne
- 1 Hass avocado, cut in half, pit and skin removed. Place each half face down and slice paper thin
- 1 teaspoon dulse flakes (Maine Sea Coast vegetables, a member of the seaweed family; sea salt substitute)

Dressing

2 tablespoons apple cider vinegar, unfiltered

1 tablespoon lemon juice

1 teaspoon organic pale agave
nectar

3 tablespoons + 1 teaspoon
extra-virgin olive oil

Freshly ground Montauk white
pepper, to taste

*In a bowl, whisk all dressing ingredients, except the dulse flakes, until combined.
Set aside.*

*Toss all salad ingredients, except the apple, avocado, and quartered dates, in a
large bowl. Pour the dressing over the salad and mix really well.*

*Allow the salad to sit 2 to 3 minutes to maximize full flavor potential. Divide
the salad equally onto four plates and dress each portion with the apple, avocado,
and dates. Sprinkle dulse flakes over each salad.*

Optional: Top with grilled citrus-marinated tofu slices for added protein.

Courtesy of James O'Shea of West Street Grill, Litchfield, CT (p. 162)

Adrienne's Lobster and Filet Mignon Wrapped in Phyllo

When I asked Adrienne Sussman of Adrienne in New Milford for a recipe to include in this book, she generously obliged with not one but two, both so compelling I couldn't choose between them—so I included both.

Serves 8.

1 package phyllo dough, thawed	(recipe follows)
1 pound butter, melted	2 blocks Boursin cheese,
16 ounces lobster meat, prefer-	quartered
ably knuckle and claw	½ pound asparagus, steamed
8 4-ounce filet mignon, seared	

Preheat oven to 375°F.

Lay out one sheet of phyllo and brush with melted butter. Place 2 ounces lobster meat, one filet mignon, and one quarter of cheese in the center of the sheet and fold over sides to create a package.

Place package on cookie tray lined with parchment paper.

Repeat with remaining sheets of phyllo.

Bake until the dough browns, about 15 to 20 minutes and serve with steamed asparagus. Asparagus can be steamed for 5-7 minutes while lobster is finishing. Serve asparagus separately or, if you prefer, decoratively arranged on the same platter.

Seared Filets

8 4-ounce filet mignon

Salt and pepper to taste

2 tablespoons olive oil

2 tablespoons salted butter

Season the filet mignon with the salt and pepper on all sides.

In a large saute pan, add the oil and butter and place over medium-high heat. When the butter browns, add the filets (do not crowd the pan, because the meat won't brown) and cook until a deep brown on all sides. This should be done on as high a heat as possible so you brown the outside of the meat quickly and you don't cook them too much.

When the filets are seared, place on a tray and refrigerate until cool.

Courtesy of Adrienne Sussman of Adrienne, New Milford, CT (p. 154)

Baked Layered Moroccan Eggplant and Beef Ragu

According to Riad Aamar, chef-owner of Oliva in New Preston, this aromatic dish is a favorite with Oliva "regulars." And no wonder!

Serves 4–6.

3 large eggplants, peeled and sliced into ½-inch pieces

½ cup extra-virgin olive oil,

plus oil for brushing on eggplants

Salt and pepper

1 cup chopped onion
1 cup chopped celery
1 cup chopped carrot
1 teaspoon whole cloves
2 pounds lean ground beef (may substitute ground lamb or diced chicken breast)
3 cups tomato sauce
Dash of crushed red pepper
½ cup chopped parsley
½ cup chopped fresh mint, plus 3 extra sprigs for garnish
2 tablespoons chopped fresh cilantro
½ teaspoon ground ginger
1 teaspoon ground cumin
¼ teaspoon ground cinnamon
¼ teaspoon ground nutmeg
1 tablespoon mustard seeds
½ cup shredded mozzarella, or other cheese
¼ cup toasted pine nuts
3–6 basil leaves for garnish

Arrange sliced eggplants on a baking sheet and brush with olive oil. Roast until brown on both sides. Season with salt and pepper.

In sauté pan, heat olive oil and sauté onion, celery, and carrot until brown. Add cloves, cook for 1 minute, then discard cloves. Add meat and brown for at least 5 minutes. Add tomato sauce, a dash of crushed red pepper, and salt and pepper to taste. Add parsley, mint, cilantro, and the rest of the spices and cook over low heat for at least 30 minutes.

Preheat oven to 400°F. In a baking dish, spread a thin layer of sauce on the bottom and top with layers of the roasted eggplants, overlapping each slice. Pour half of remaining sauce over the eggplants and then cover with half of cheese. Top with another layer of sliced eggplants, the remaining sauce and cheese, and bake in oven until brown.

Cool for at least 20 minutes; serve warm, garnished with mint sprigs, pine nuts, and basil. Serve with mashed potatoes, vegetables, soft polenta, couscous, or rice.

Courtesy of Riad Aamar of Oliva, New Preston, CT (p. 160)

Fresh Summer Berry Balsamic Dressing with Chicken

Tina Fearnley makes a number of scrumptious toppings—for desserts and for main dishes. This recipe works well with poultry, and you can also use it as a topping for cheesecake or ice cream!

Serves 4.

1 (7.5 ounce) jar of Fresh Summer Berry topping
1 tablespoon Dijon mustard
Pinch of kosher salt
¼ teaspoon granulated garlic
¼ cup aged balsamic vinegar

¾ cup extra-virgin olive oil
6 cups field green lettuce
4 small roasted chicken breasts, heated or room temperature, as you prefer

Whisk together the topping, mustard, salt, garlic, and vinegar. Slowly add the olive oil and continue whisking until well blended.

Place lettuce on a platter. Top with the chickens.

Drizzle dressing over the chicken and serve.

Courtesy of Tina Fearnley of the Purple Pear by Tina, Wilmington, CT (p. 349)

Slow Baked Halibut, Stuffed Artichokes, Barigoule Broth, and Truffle Butter

This lovely entree, provided by Mary Schaffer of Napa & Co., was created by the restaurant's executive chef, Leonardo Marino.

Serves 4.

Halibut

4 (5-ounce) pieces of fresh halibut, skin off
Olive oil
Salt and pepper
1 teaspoon thinly sliced chives, for garnish

Barigoule Broth

12 medium artichokes
6 whole lemons, juiced
2 carrots, sliced
1 celery stalk, sliced
1 sweet onion, sliced
1 fennel bulb, sliced
8 garlic cloves, sliced
2 parsley sprigs
1 thyme sprig
⅓ cup extra-virgin olive oil
Salt and pepper to taste
2 cups white wine
3 cups light chicken or vegetable stock

Artichoke Stuffing

3 ounces minced shallots
3 ounces diced carrot
3 ounces diced celery
2 tablespoons of olive oil
1 tablespoon minced garlic
Salt and pepper to taste
6 ounces ground panko bread crumbs
1 tablespoon chopped parsley
Olive oil to taste

Truffle Butter

1 can truffle juice	1 tablespoon crème fraîche
4 ounces truffle peelings	½ pound butter

For the Artichoke and Barigoule Broth

Turn the artichokes, removing the outer leaves and woody edges, and place them in lemon water to avoid oxidization.

In a medium-size sauce pot, put shallots, carrots, celery, and all the herbs and sweat lightly in olive oil until the vegetables are tender and have no color. Season the mixture with salt and pepper to taste.

Deglaze the vegetable mixture with white wine, allowing the wine to completely cook out. Set aside.

After the wine has evaporated, add artiuchokes and enough chicken or vegetable stock to cover and simmer until the artichokes are tender. Once they are tender, add vegetables and cook 2 to 3 minutes until warm.

Remove the artichokes from the cooking liquid and slice them in half lengthwise. Remove the chokes with a small paring knife and set the cleaned artichokes aside. Strain and reserve the broth.

For the Artichoke Stuffing

Add cooked vegetables (not artichokes) to the bread crumbs and the parsley and mix. Adjust the seasoning by adding more salt and pepper to taste and add some olive oil if the mixture is too dry.

Stuff the heart of the artichokes that were sliced lengthwise with the bread-crumb mixture and set aside.

For the Truffle Butter

In a small sauce pan reduce the truffle juice with the truffle peelings by half.

Add 1 tablespoon of crème fraîche and stir.

Slowly whisk in the room temperature butter until it becomes an emulsion and coats the back of a spoon.

Add garlic and hold the truffle butter aside in a warm area.

For the Assembly

Preheat the oven to 350°F.

Season the halibut with salt and pepper, and coat with olive oil on both sides.

Place the halibut on a baking tray and bake 6 to 8 minutes until it reaches an internal temperature of 110°F.

Place the stuffed artichokes on a separate baking tray and place in the oven with the fish until the stuffing is golden brown.

Gently reheat the truffle butter sauce and the barigoule broth separately.

Place the halibut in the center of a warm plate and then place three of the artichokes around it in a tripod formation. Gently pour in the barigoule broth, being careful not to compromise the quality of the stuffed artichokes by pouring too much broth. Gauge it to cover lightly but not overwhelm. Coat the halibut with the truffle butter and garnish with sliced chives.

Courtesy of Mary Schaffer of Napa & Co., Stamford, CT (pp. 72, 90)

Spaghetti with Clams

Linda Giuca, co-owner of Alforno Trattoria in Old Saybrook, shared this recipe. Says Linda, "It's our most popular entrée." You'll know why when you make it.

Serves 4.

48 littleneck clams
4 quarts cold water
2 tablespoons kosher salt
1 pound spaghetti (preferably DeCecco)
½ cup extra-virgin olive oil
4 large garlic cloves, chopped
Hot red pepper flakes (optional)

¼ cup white wine
1 tablespoon chopped fresh Italian parsley
¼ cup extra-virgin olive oil
Kosher salt and freshly ground pepper to taste
4 tablespoons extra-virgin olive oil for drizzling

Put clams in a large strainer and run under cold water for a few minutes. If clams are especially sandy, use a kitchen brush to clean the outside of the shells. Rinse again and drain.

Fill a large pot with the water and bring to a boil over high heat. Add the kosher salt and the spaghetti, return the water to a boil and cook, stirring occasionally, until spaghetti is al dente.

While the spaghetti is cooking, bring ½ cup olive oil to barely smoking in a high-sided sauté pan over medium heat.

Add garlic and red pepper and cook for a few seconds, until garlic becomes fragrant but not browned.

Add white wine and clams. Turn heat to high, cover, and cook, shaking the pan, until all of the clams have opened, about 5 minutes. Discard any clams that didn't open.

When the clams have opened and the spaghetti is al dente, strain the spaghetti and add to the clams. Add the parsley and stir.

Remove pan from heat and stir in ¼ cup olive oil. Divide among four soup bowls.

Drizzle each portion with a tablespoon of olive oil. Serve immediately.

Courtesy of Linda Giuca of Alforno Trattoria, Old Saybrook, CT (p. 303)

Sides

Asparagi alla Parmigiana

Chef-Instructor Sally Maraventano of the Cucina Casalinga cooking school has an enthusiasm for Italian food that is infectious. This recipe, from her cookbook, Festa del Giardino, epitomizes, to me, Sally's zest for fresh, wholesome, natural ingredients. All that and it's a cinch to make, pretty to serve, and delicious to eat.

Serves 6.

2 pounds fresh asparagus spears, bottoms snapped off, spears scraped with a vegetable peeler, and rinsed well

6 tablespoons butter
½ cup freshly grated Parmesan cheese or more to taste
Fresh grated nutmeg

Preheat oven to 400°F.

Cook the asparagus using an asparagus cooker or a large skillet:

Asparagus cooker: Fill the cooker half full with lightly salted water and bring to a boil. Stand the asparagus spears upright in the pot, with spear tips up. Bring back to a boil, cover, and lower heat to a simmer. Cook until just fork tender, about 8 minutes.

Large skillet: Place the asparagus in a skillet and cook at low-to-medium heat covered for about 8 minutes.

Melt 3 tablespoons of butter in a baking dish and place the asparagus lengthwise in the dish. Dot with the remaining butter and sprinkle with Parmesan and nutmeg.

Bake for 7 minutes or until the top forms a light golden crust. Serve immediately.

Courtesy of Sally Maraventano of Cucina Casalinga, Wilton, CT (p. 70)

Ina's Cannelini Beans and Escarole

This recipe from Fabled Foods's Ina Bomze can be served as part of a vegetarian meal or as accompaniment to veal, beef, or another meat entree. As Ina says, "Mangia!"

Serves 4.

1¼ cups dried cannelini beans
2 tablespoons olive oil
¼ teaspoon red pepper flakes

2 heads escarole, washed and torn into pieces like a salad
6 garlic cloves, minced

1 large can plum tomatoes (San Marzano preferred), torn by hand into bite-size pieces

Rind of Parmigiano Reggiano, cut into small pieces
2 tablespoons balsamic vinegar

Soak beans for 8 hours (or overnight). Drain.

Cook beans in a large pot with a generous amount of water covering them. Bring to a boil. Lower to a simmer for about an hour or hour and a half, depending on beans. Check beans for consistency after about an hour.

When beans are done, drain, reserving some of the liquid.

In a very large pot, heat oil, then add red pepper flakes. Add escarole with water clinging to the leaves. Then add garlic. Toss with tongs to coat everything. Add beans and gently toss to mix.

Add the tomatoes, Parmigiano Reggiano, a little bit of the reserved liquid from the beans, and the balsamic vinegar. Continue simmering the mixture over a low flame for 10 to 15 minutes.

Transfer to a serving dish and serve.

Courtesy of Ina Bomze of Fabled Foods, Deep River, CT (p. 255)

Jean-Louis's Famous Potato au Gratin

The secret of this simple dish of Jean-Louis Gerin formerly of the now-closed Restaurant Jean-Louis in Greenwich, is in the cream/milk mix. He prefers it creamy, whereas many chefs are satisfied with a 50/50 ratio. He also uses the natural starch of the potato with no extra additives. In Jean-Louis's words, "There is a famous Riviera restaurant that recommends blanching the potato in milk, throwing the milk away, then adding powdered starch to the cream . . . oh la la! I have also heard some horror stories about egg in the gratin. . . . Note that some recipes are just better when they have had time to rest. Potato au gratin is one of them! If you can, cook your gratin a day in advance. The next day, add a half-cup cream or so to the gratin, then reheat it slowly in a 275°–300° oven until the cream starts to boil."

Serves 10.

1 tablespoon minced garlic	**2½ teaspoons salt**
3¼ pounds baking potatoes, peeled and rinsed	**1¼ teaspoons freshly ground white pepper**
3½ cups heavy cream	**Dash nutmeg**
1 cup whole milk	**½–1 cup heavy cream, for reheating**

Preheat oven to 350°F. Spread the minced garlic over the bottom of a large gratin or 3-quart baking pan. Cut potatoes into slices between ⅛- and ¼-inch thick. Do NOT rinse these slices; it is their natural starch that will thicken the gratin. Spread the potato slices on top of the garlic in the baking pan.

Heat cream and milk together in a medium pot until boiling. Add salt, white pepper, and nutmeg. Pour the hot cream and milk mixture over the potato slices in the pan. Stir slices so that they are all just about submerged. Place pan in the oven and bake until potatoes are tender and the top is well browned, about 1½ hours. Let rest at least 3 hours, or overnight if desired.

When ready to serve, add ½–1 cup cream and reheat in the oven (275°F–300°F) until the cream starts to boil.

Courtesy of Jean-Louis Gerin of Restaurant Jean-Louis, Greenwich, CT (now closed)

Metro Bis's Brussels Sprouts, Bacon, and Honey

Chris Prosperi of Metro Bis loves Brussels sprouts—the little cabbagey "heads" growing on stalks with many others—which is one reason he always looks forward to the fall harvest. "If picked in early fall, before the frost," he says, "these members of the cabbage family have a bitter, nutty taste. Harvested after a couple of chilly nights, the sprouts actually sweeten with the freeze." Chris developed this recipe at the Litchfield Farmers' Market, using early-harvest sprouts, which he sweetens with local honey. As the fall season progresses, the sprouts are less bitter and therefore less honey is needed.

Makes about 1 quart.

1 tablespoon oil	½ cup water
1 cup diced onion	1 tablespoon rubbed sage
¾ cup minced carrot	2 teaspoons curry powder
1 teaspoon kosher salt	3 tablespoons honey
5 strips of bacon, chopped	1 tablespoon red wine vinegar
1 pound Brussels sprouts, sliced	

Heat the oil over medium-high heat in a heavy bottomed pan, then add the onion.

Cook for 1 minute or until lightly caramelized, then stir in the carrot and salt. Add the bacon and cook for 2 to 3 minutes.

Mix in the Brussels sprouts. Cook for an additional minute and then add the water.

Lower the heat to medium and cook for 8 to 10 minutes or until the sprouts are soft. Be careful not to let the pan become dry. Add water 2 tablespoons at a time as needed until sprouts are done.

Stir in the sage and curry powder, then cook for 30 seconds.

Remove from the heat, then add the honey and vinegar. Taste and adjust the seasoning with more salt and more honey if necessary.

Courtesy of Chris Prosperi of Metro Bis, Simsbury, CT (p. 202)

Desserts

Chaiwalla's Strawberry-Rhubarb Cobbler

Mary O'Reilly, whose Chaiwalla tearoom is known locally for its scrumptious desserts, says this recipe is one of Chaiwalla's most popular and also the easiest to make. Other fresh fruits can be used instead of strawberries and rhubarb.

Serves 6.

Enough fresh strawberries and chopped rhubarbs to fill a 9-inch pie tin

1 tablespoon plus 1 cup sugar
1 cup flour
1 stick butter

Preheat oven to 350°F.

Mix together berries, rhubarbs, and 1 tablespoon sugar and pour evenly into a pie tin.

Combine remaining sugar and flour. Cream butter. Add the sugar and flour mixture to the butter. Mix well.

Pour the sugar-flour-butter mixture evenly over the fruit.

Bake 45 minutes or until crunchy on top.

Courtesy of Mary O'Reilly of Chaiwalla, Salisbury, CT (p. 147)

Debra Ponzek's Madeleines

Debra Ponzek, whose four gourmet take-out shops and one cafe now grace the Fairfield County landscape, happily shares her recipe for madeleines.

Makes 3 dozen.

Vegetable spray
1 cup sugar
8 ounces butter, melted
1 cup flour

1 teaspoon baking powder
1 teaspoon vanilla
4 large eggs

Spray two madeleine pans with vegetable spray and set aside.

Preheat the oven to 350°F.

Combine the sugar and melted butter and stir. Stir in the flour. Add the baking powder and the vanilla, stirring to combine. Add the eggs, one at a time.

Chill the batter for 1 to 2 hours.

Pour the batter into the madeleine molds, filling each halfway.

Bake for approximately 15 minutes, or until just firm to the touch. Cool and pop them out of the molds.

They will keep in an airtight container for at least 3 days.

Courtesy of Debra Ponzek of Aux Délices, Stamford, CT (pp. 29, 69)

Double Chocolate Raspberry Biscotti

This recipe was provided by Margaret Chatey, proprietor of Westford Hill Distillers.

Makes 3 dozen.

Cookie

½ cup butter, room temperature

¾ cup sugar

2 eggs

2 tablespoons Westford Hill Distillers' framboise eau-de-vie

2¼ cups all-purpose flour

1¾ teaspoons baking powder

⅓ cup unsweetened cocoa

¼ teaspoon salt

⅔ cup chocolate chips (for more intense raspberry flavor, use ⅓ cup raspberry flavored chips and ⅓ cup chocolate chips)

⅔ cup coarsely chopped walnuts, lightly toasted

Glaze

1½ cups confections' sugar
1 tablespoon cocoa powder

3 teaspoons Westford Hill Distillers' framboise eau-de-vie

Combine glaze ingredients and cook in small saucepan over low heat until well mixed. Set aside until needed.

Heat oven to 325°F.

In a mixing bowl cream butter and sugar until light and fluffy. Beat in eggs and the framboise eau-de-vie.

In another bowl combine the flour, baking powder, cocoa, and salt. Add to the creamed mixture until blended.

Fold in chips and nuts. Divide dough in half. (If dough is too sticky to handle, add a bit more flour.)

On a greased and floured cookie sheet or a cookie sheet lined with parchment paper, pat out into two logs about ½-inch high, 1½-inches wide, and 14 inches long, spacing at least 2 inches apart.

Bake in the middle of the oven for 25 minutes or until lightly browned. Let cool about 5 minutes. With a serrated knife slice diagonally at a 45-degree angle, about ½-inch thick.

Separate the slices upright on the baking sheet, add glaze evenly with a pastry brush, then rest for 10 more minutes to dry slightly and let cool on a rack.

Courtesy of Margaret Chatey of Westford Hill Distillers, Ashford, CT (p. 350)

Lavender Blueberry Banana Bread

Kristin Orr, of Quintessential Gardens at Fort Hill Farms in Thompson, grows edible organic lavender and shares this unusual recipe. She calls it "a good dessert for foodies."

Makes one small loaf—serves 4-to-6 at teatime.

1 stick butter	½ teaspoon salt
⅔ cup sugar	1 cup whole wheat flour
2 eggs	3 bananas, mashed
1 cup all-purpose flour	1¼ cup organic blueberries
1 tablespoon finely ground organic lavender buds	½ cup walnuts, chopped
1 teaspoon baking soda	1 teaspoon vanilla extract

Preheat the oven to 350°F.

Grease a 9 x 5-inch loaf pan. Combine butter and sugar. Beat with electric mixer until fluffy. Add eggs, beat well.

Sift all-purpose flour, lavender, baking soda, and salt into another bowl. Stir in whole wheat flour. Beat into the butter mixture.

Fold in bananas, blueberries, walnuts, and vanilla.

Pour into pan. Bake 55 minutes. Cool in pan 10 minutes.

Remove from pan and cool on rack.

Courtesy of Kristin Orr of Fort Hill Farms, Thompson, CT (p. 361)

Sweet Maria's Chunkey Monkey Cake

This delicious, moist banana nut cake is filled with chocolate chunks and frosted with cream cheese icing. Maria Bruscino Sanchez calls it "perfect for dads or grads!"

Makes one 9-inch layer cake, about 12 to 15 servings.

¼ pound unsalted butter,
   softened

1 cup sugar

½ cup brown sugar

1 teaspoon vanilla extract

3 eggs

2 cups cake flour

1 teaspoon baking powder

1 teaspoon baking soda

½ teaspoon salt

2 cups mashed bananas (2–3
   bananas)

¾ cup sour cream

1 cup large walnut pieces

Preheat oven to 350°F. Grease and flour or line two 9-inch cake pans with parchment paper. Set aside.

In an electric mixer, cream butter and both sugars until light. Add vanilla. Add eggs, one at a time, beating well after adding each one.

In a medium bowl, combine flour, baking powder, baking soda, and salt. In a small bowl, combine bananas and sour cream. Pour each of these mixtures alternately into the butter mixture. Begin and end with the flour mixture. Mix just until blended. Stir in walnuts.

Pour batter evenly into prepared pans. Bake 20 to 25 minutes or until a tester inserted into the center of the cake comes out with a fine crumb. Remove pans from the oven and place on wire cooling racks. Cool cakes in pan for 10 to 15 minutes. Carefully remove cakes from the pans and continue to cool on wire racks. Remove and discard parchment. Cool cakes completely before frosting.

Sweet Maria's Cream Cheese Frosting

¼ pound unsalted butter,
  softened
16 ounces cream cheese,
  softened

6 cups confectioners' sugar

In an electric mixer, cream butter and cream cheese on medium speed for 3 to 4 minutes, or until fluffy. On low speed, gradually add confectioners' sugar until blended and smooth. Beat on high speed 3 to 4 minutes. Use immediately or store refrigerated in an airtight container. Let refrigerated frosting come to room temperature and briefly rewhip before using.

Assembly

22 (9-inch) banana nut cake
  layers
cream cheese frosting

2 cups chocolate chips or
  coarsely chopped chocolate
  pieces
2 cups chopped walnuts

Level off tops of cake layers. Place one layer, cut side up, on a cake plate or a doily-covered cake circle. Spread a layer of frosting on the cake layer. Sprinkle with chocolate chunks. Place the other cake layer, cut side down, onto bottom layer. Using a metal spatula, frost the outside of the cake with remaining frosting.

Adhere walnuts to the sides of the cake. Garnish top of cake, as desired, with chocolate chunks.

Refrigerate about a half hour to let cake set before serving. Store remaining cake in the refrigerator, but let pieces come to room temperature before serving.

Courtesy of Maria Bruscino Sanchez of Sweet Maria's, Waterbury, CT (pp. 122, 153)

Honey Figs with Goat Cheese and Pecans

Marina Marchese, whose Red Bee Honey is sold at farmers' markets and online, is sharing this simple but oh-so-satisfying hive-to-table dessert.

Serves 6.

1 cup chopped pecans
Coarse salt and freshly ground
   pepper
6-ounce log of goat cheese

12 fresh figs (calimyrna or
   black mission), halved
¾ cup of Red Bee Honey

Place the chopped pecans in a shallow dish and season with salt and pepper.

Roll the log of goat cheese evenly in the pecans.

Refrigerate the log until it is firm. Then cut it into rounds, enough for 6 portions.

Divide the figs evenly and place portions on dessert plates. Top the figs with a round of pecan-crusted cheese.

Dizzle 2 tablespoons of honey over each serving. Serve immediately.

Courtesy of Marina Marchese of Red Bee Honey, Weston, CT (p. 24)

Appendix A: Specialty Foods & Produce

The following businesses, farms, and shops are especially known for these items that they produce or grow.

Almonds
Dr. Lankin's Specialty Foods (Groton), 268

Apples & Cider
Apple Barn (Woodstock), 357
Averill Farm (Washington), 136
Beardsley's Cider Mill & Orchard (Shelton), 45
Belltown Hill Orchards (South Glastonbury), 198
Bishop's Orchards Farm Market and Winery (Guilford), 280
Blue Jay Orchards (Bethel), 46

Buell's Orchard (Eastford), 359
Clark Farms at Bushy Hill Orchard & Cider Mill (Granby), 199
Deercrest Farm (Glastonbury), 200
Dondero Orchard Farm Stand & Bakery (South Glastonbury), 200
Drazen Orchards (Cheshire), 201
Easy Pickin's Orchard (Enfield), 201
Ellsworth Hill Orchard & Berry Farm (Sharon), 137
Farmer's Cow, The (Lebanon), 344
Gotta's Farm and Cider Mill (Portland), 204

Hickory Hill Orchards
(Cheshire), 204
High Hill Orchard (Meriden), 204
Holmberg Orchards (Gales
Ferry), 282
Karabin Farms (Southington), 205
Lapsley Orchard (Pomfret
Center), 362
Lyman Orchards (Middlefield), 206
March Farm (Bethlehem), 140
Palazzi Orchard (East
Killington), 363
Roberts Orchard (Bristol), 141
Rogers Orchards
(Southington), 207
Rose's Berry Farm (South
Glastonbury), 209, 222
Scott's Orchard & Nursery
(Glastonbury), 209
Silverman's Farm (Easton), 49
Starberry Farm (Washington
Depot), 142
Tonn's Orchard (Terryville), 144
Woodland Farm (South Glaston-
bury), 211
Wright's Orchards & Dried Flower
Farm (Tolland), 364

Beef and Pork Products
Brown Cow Cafe (Sterling), 340
Bush Meadow Farm (Union),
340, 367
Cato Corner Farm (Colchester), 341
DiBacco Food Imports
(Hartford), 184
Dutch Epicure Shop, The
(Litchfield), 125
Eagle Wood Farm and Retail Store
(Barkhamsted), 137
Fairfield Meat Emporium
(Fairfield), 31
Four Mile River Farm & Greenhouse
(Old Lyme), 281
La Molisana Italian Sausage
(Waterbury), 129
Noack's Meat Products (South
Meriden), 179
Stone Gardens Farm (Shelton), 50
Stone Wall Dairy Farm (Cornwall
Bridge), 143
Tulmeadow Farm Store (West
Simsbury), 210

Breads & Bakery Goods
Avventura (Waterbury), 124

Bantam Bread Company (Bantam), 117

Beldotti Bakeries (Stamford), 14

Belltown Hill Orchards (South Glastonbury), 198

Billy's Bakery (Fairfield), 14

Bishop's Orchards Farm Market and Winery (Guilford), 280

Chabaso Bakery (New Haven), 251

Colchester Bakery (Colchester), 343

Collinsville Baking Company (Pine Meadow), 117

DiBacco Food Imports (Hartford), 184

Drawing Room, The (Cos Cob), 59

Everybody's Market (Cheshire), 185

Fabled Foods (Deep River), 255

Flour Garden Bakery (Woodbury), 126

4 & Twenty Blackbirds Bakeshop (Guilford), 256

Freund's Farm Market and Bakery (East Canaan), 138

Harpo's Bakery (South Glaston-bury), 219

Holbrook Farm (Bethel), 47

Isabelle et Vincent (Fairfield), 64

Judies European Bakery and Cafe (New Haven), 258

La Brioche French Bakery (Rockville), 346

La Sorpresa (Norwalk), 21

Libby's Italian Pastry Shop (New Haven), 258

Lombardi's Bakery (Torrington), 120

Michele's Pies (Norwalk, Westport), 22

Mozzicato De Pasquale Bakery & Pastry Shop (Hartford), 188

Nine Main Bakery & Deli (New Preston), 131

Nothin' But Premium Foods (Westport), 24

Olive Market, The (Georgetown), 36

Plasko's Farm (Trumbull), 48

Scotts Jamaican Bakery (Hartford), 223

Silverman's Farm (Easton), 49

SoNo Baking Company & Cafe, The (South Norwalk), 66

Wave Hill Bread & Cafe (Norwalk), 28, 68

Whistle Stop Muffin Company (Ridgefield), 69

Buffalo Meats

Creamery Brook Bison
   (Brooklyn), 343

**Cakes, Pies, Pastries &
Desserts**

Aux Délices (Darien, Greenwich,
   Stamford, Westport), 29, 69
Avventura (Waterbury), 124
Bantam Bread Company
   (Bantam), 117
Belltown Hill Orchards (South
   Glastonbury), 198
Bishop's Orchards Farm Market and
   Winery (Guilford), 280
Blue Jay Orchards (Bethel), 46
Chimirri's Italian Pastry Shoppe
   (Wethersfield), 177
Clark Farms at Bushy Hill Orchard
   & Cider Mill (Granby), 199
Colchester Bakery (Colchester), 343
Cupcake Truck, The (varies), 253
Dagmar's Desserts (Old
   Saybrook), 254
Dondero Orchard Farm Stand
   & Bakery (South
   Glastonbury), 200

Dutch Epicure Shop, The
   (Litchfield), 125
Everybody's Market (Cheshire), 185
Flour Garden Bakery
   (Woodbury), 126
4 & Twenty Blackbirds Bakeshop
   (Guilford), 256
Freund's Farm Market and Bakery
   (East Canaan), 138
Gotta's Farm and Cider Mill
   (Portland), 204
Harpo's Bakery (South
   Glastonbury), 219
Holbrook Farm (Bethel), 47
Isabelle et Vincent (Fairfield), 64
La Palette Bakery Cafe Gallery
   (Watertown), 119, 149
Libby's Italian Pastry Shop (New
   Haven), 258
Lombardi's Bakery (Torrington), 120
Lyman Orchards (Middlefield), 206
March Farm (Bethlehem), 140
Matthews 1812 House (Cornwall
   Bridge), 120
Michele's Pies (Norwalk), 22
Modern Pastry Shop
   (Hartford), 186

Mozzicato De Pasquale Bakery &
    Pastry Shop (Hartford), 188
Mystic Market East (Mystic), 271
Mystic Market West (Mystic), 271
Nine Main Bakery & Deli (New
    Preston), 131
Plasko's Farm (Trumbull), 48
Roberts Orchard (Bristol), 141
Rogers Orchards
    (Southington), 207
Rose's Berry Farm (South
    Glastonbury), 209, 222
Savor Fine Foods (Waterbury), 121
Scotts Jamaican Bakery
    (Hartford), 223
Sweet Harmony Cafe & Bakery
    (Middletown), 225
Sweet Maria's (Waterbury),
    122, 153
Versailles Bistro and Patisserie
    (Greenwich), 65
Whistle Stop Muffin Company
    (Ridgefield), 69

Candied Apples
Belltown Hill Orchards (South
    Glastonbury), 198

Buell's Orchard (Eastford), 359
Dondero Orchard Farm Stand
    & Bakery (South
    Glastonbury), 200

Cheeses & Dairy Products
Beltane Farm (Lebanon), 339
Bon Appetit (Hamden), 266
Brie & Bleu (New London), 294
Bush Meadow Farm (Union),
    340, 367
Caseus Fromagerie & Bistro (New
    Haven), 295
Cato Corner Farm (Colchester), 341
Cheese Truck, The (New
    Haven), 253
Darien Cheese & Fine Foods
    (Darien), 30
Delicacy Market (West
    Hartford), 187
Dutch Epicure Shop, The
    (Litchfield), 125
Fairfield Cheese Company
    (Fairfield), 31
Fratelli Market (Stamford), 34
Fromage Fine Foods and Coffees
    (Old Saybrook), 268

Kaas & Co. (South Norwalk), 34

Liuzzi Gourmet Food Market (North Haven), 270

March Farm (Bethlehem), 140

Meadow Stone Farm (Brooklyn), 347

Monastic Art Shop, The (Bethlehem), 130

Mozzicato De Pasquale Bakery & Pastry Shop (Hartford), 188

Mystic Market East (Mystic), 271

Mystic Market West (Mystic), 271

Nodine's Smokehouse (Goshen), 120

No. 109 Cheese & Wine (Ridgefield), 35

Pantry, The (Washington Depot), 132

Romeo and Cesare's Gourmet (New Haven), 272

Rustling Wind Creamery (Falls Village), 142

Sankow's Beaver Brook Farm (Lyme), 261

Star Fish Market (Guilford), 273

Wild Raspberry, The (Cromwell), 190

Willimantic Food Co-op (Willimantic), 353

Chocolates & Other Candies

Bridgewater Chocolate (Brookfield), 15

Cocoa Michelle (Westport), 59

Deborah Ann's Sweet Shoppe (Ridgefield), 16

Divine Treasures Belgian Chocolates (Manchester), 184

Fascia's Chocolates (Waterbury), 118

Given Fine Chocolates & Indulgences (Madison), 269

Hauser Chocolatier (Bethel), 19

Kent Coffee & Chocolate Company, The (Kent), 128

Knipschildt Chocolatier (Norwalk), 20

Litchfield Candy Company, The (Litchfield), 129

Little Chocolate Company, The (Greenwich), 22

Munson's Chocolates (Bolton), 348

Nothin' But Premium Foods (Westport), 24

Sweet Cioccolata (Wallingford), 274
Sweet Pierre's Boutique du Choco-
   lat (Ridgefield, Wilton), 40
Thompson Brands (Meriden), 179
Tschudin Chocolates & Confections
   (Middletown), 180

Chutneys, Relishes, Salsas &
Sauces
Baltyk Deli (Stratford), 30
Bear Pond Farm (Glastonbury), 176
Frank's Marinara Sauce
   (Hebron), 345
Freund's Farm Market and Bakery
   (East Canaan), 138
Giff's Original (Cheshire), 178
Gracious Gourmet, The
   (Bridgewater), 119
Newman's Own (Westport), 23
Nip 'N Tang (West Hartford), 178
Olé Molé (Stamford), 62
Oriental Food Market (Norwalk), 37
Palmieri Food Products Inc.
   (New Haven), 259
Pasta Cosi (Branford), 260, 298
Silverman's Farm (Easton), 49
Steve's Market (Norwalk), 40

Sweet Sunshine Gourmet
   Conveniences (Litchfield), 123
Waldingfield Farm (Washington
   Depot), 123
White Oaks Farm & Table
   (Westport), 28

Coffees
Arcadia Cafe (Old Greenwich), 56
Ashlawn Farm (Lyme), 264
Daybreak Coffee Roasters
   (Glastonbury), 183, 219
Fromage Fine Foods and Coffees
   (Old Saybrook), 268
Kent Coffee & Chocolate Company,
   The (Kent), 128
Omar Coffee Company
   (Newington), 189
Simon's Marketplace (Chester), 273
Spic and Span Market
   (Southport), 33
Zumbach's Gourmet Coffee (New
   Canaan), 41

Eggs & Poultry Products
Bush Meadow Farm (Union),
   340, 367

Dondero Orchard Farm Stand
& Bakery (South
Glastonbury), 200
Flamig Farm (West Simsbury), 203
Four Mile River Farm & Greenhouse
(Old Lyme), 281
Holbrook Farm (Bethel), 47
Karabin Farms (Southington), 205
Meadow Stone Farm (Brooklyn), 347
Medlyn's Farm Market
(Branford), 285
Ogre Farm/George Hall Farm
(Simsbury), 206
Shortt's Farm & Garden Center
(Sandy Hook), 49
Stone Wall Dairy Farm (Cornwall
Bridge), 143
Walking Wood (Woodbridge), 263
Windy Hill Farm (Goshen), 144

Fish, Fresh
Atlantic Seafood (Old
Saybrook), 265
Flanders Fish Market & Restaurant
(East Lyme), 309
Gulf Shrimp Seafood Company
(Plantsville), 185

New Wave Seafood (Stamford), 35
Star Fish Market (Guilford), 273

Goat Products
Beltane Farm (Lebanon), 339
Bush Meadow Farm (Union),
340, 367
Eagle Wood Farm and Retail Store
(Barkhamsted), 137
Meadow Stone Farm
(Brooklyn), 347
Rustling Wind Creamery (Falls
Village), 142
Willimantic Food Co-op
(Willimantic), 353

Herbs & Spices
Dutch Epicure Shop, The (Litch-
field), 125
Gilbertie's Herb Farm and Gardens
(Westport), 47
Kaas & Co. (South Noerwalk), 34
Martha's Herbary (Pomfret),
352, 371
Passiflora Tea Room, Cafe and
Herbal Shoppe (New
Hartford), 150

Penzey's Spices (Norwalk), 37
Sundial Gardens (Higganum), 301

Honey

Clark Farms at Bushy Hill Orchard
& Cider Mill (Granby), 199
Gigi's Native Produce (Enfield), 203
Hunt Hill Farm Trust (New
Milford), 127
Ogre Farm/George Hall Farm
(Simsbury), 206
Red Bee Honey (Weston), 24
River's Edge Sugar House
(Ashford), 363
Rogers Orchards (Southington), 207
Stone Wall Dairy Farm (Cornwall
Bridge), 143

Ice Cream

Brown Cow Cafe (Sterling), 340
Dr. Mike's (Bethel, Monroe), 17
Farmer's Cow Calfé and Creamery,
The (Mansfield), 368
Ferris Acres Creamery
(Newtown), 17
Fish Family Farm Creamery & Dairy
(Bolton), 344
Hallmark Drive-In (Old
Lyme), 257
Il Bacio Ice Cream (Danbury), 20
Mortensen's Ice Cream Shoppe
(Cromwell), 178
Old Lyme Ice Cream Shoppe (Old
Lyme), 259
Panini Cafe (Kent), 150
Rich Farm (Oxford), 25
Shady Glen (Manchester), 224
Tulmeadow Farm Ice Cream Stand
(West Simsbury), 181
University of Connecticut Dairy
Bar (Storrs/Mansfield), 349
Walnut Beach Creamery
(Milford), 26
We-Li-Kit Farm Ice Cream Stand
(Abington), 350
Wentworth Homemade Ice Cream
(Hamden), 264

Italian Ices

Daniella's Gelateria (Greenwich), 18
Gelatissimo (New Canaan), 18
Gelato Guiliana (Wallingford), 257
Libby's Italian Pastry Shop (New
Haven), 258

Volta Gelateria Creperia
(Stamford), 19

Jams & Jellies
Birch Hills Farm (Ashford), 339
Buell's Orchard (Eastford), 359
Freund's Farm Market and Bakery
(East Canaan), 138
Hindinger Farm (Hamden), 282
Kaas & Co. (South Norwalk), 34
March Farm (Bethlehem), 140
Roberts Orchard (Bristol), 141
Rose's Berry Farm (South
Glastonbury), 209, 222
Rustling Wind Creamery (Falls
Village), 142
Shortt's Farm & Garden Center
(Sandy Hook), 49
Silverman's Farm (Easton), 49
Starberry Farm (Washington
Depot), 142
Winding Drive Jams & Jellies
(Woodbury), 124

Lamb Products
Sankow's Beaver Brook Farm
(Lyme), 261

Winterbrook Farm
(Staffordville), 364

**Maple Syrup & Other Maple
Products**
Bats of Bedlam Maple Syrup
(Chaplin), 358
Birch Hills Farm (Ashford), 339
Hunt Hill Farm Trust (New
Milford), 127
Lamothe's Sugar House
(Burlington), 138
McLaughlin Vineyards (Sandy
Hook), 112
Norman's Sugarhouse
(Woodstock), 362
River's Edge Sugar House
(Ashford), 363
Sugar Shack, The (East
Hartland), 210
Sullivan Farm (New Milford), 143
Sweet Wind Farm (East
Hartland), 210
Warrup's Farm (West
Redding), 50
We-Li-Kit Farm Ice Cream Stand
(Abington), 350

Willimantic Food Co-op
(Willimantic), 353
Windy Hill Farm (Goshen), 144
Winterbrook Farm
(Staffordville), 364

Milk

Bush Meadow Farm (Union),
340, 367
Cato Corner Farm (Colchester), 341
The Farmer's Cow (Lebanon), 344
Fish Family Farm Creamery & Dairy
(Bolton), 344
Fort Hill Farms (Thompson), 361
Holbrook Farm (Bethel), 47
Meadow Stone Farm
(Brooklyn), 347
Sankow's Beaver Brook Farm
(Lyme), 261
Stone Wall Dairy Farm (Cornwall
Bridge), 143

Natural Foods

Fairway (Stamford), 33
Nature's Grocer (Vernon), 189
New Morning Natural and Organic
Foods (Woodbury), 130

Trader Joe's (various locations), 38
Urban Oaks Organic Farm (New
Britain), 211
Wayne's Organic Garden
(Coneco), 363
Willimantic Food Co-op
(Willimantic), 353

Pastas

D & D Market (Hartford), 183
DiBacco Food Imports
(Hartford), 184
Fratelli Market (Stamford), 34
Liuzzi Gourmet Food Market (North
Haven), 270
Pasta Cosi (Branford), 260, 298
Star Fish Market (Guilford), 273

Salad Dressings

Bon Appetit (Hamden), 266
Hopkins Inn, The (New
Preston), 158
Metro Bis (Simsbury), 202
Newman's Own (Westport), 23
Olivette (Darien), 36
White Oaks Farm & Table
(Westport), 28

Salt

Hunt Hill Farm Trust (New
Milford), 127

Sausage

Bush Meadow Farm (Union),
340, 367
Delicacy Market (West
Hartford), 187
Eagle Wood Farm and Retail Store
(Barkhamsted), 137
Fairfield Meat Emporium
(Fairfield), 31
Firehouse Deli (Fairfield), 32
Fromage Fine Food and Coffees
(Old Saybrook), 268
Gold's Delicatessen (Westport), 32
La Molisana Italian Sausage
(Waterbury), 129
Liuzzi Gourmet Food Market (North
Haven), 270
Nodine's Smokehouse (Goshen), 120
Oscar's Delicatessen (Westport), 33
Romeo and Cesare's Gourmet (New
Haven), 272
Sankow's Beaver Brook Farm
(Lyme), 261

Spic and Span Market
(Southport), 33

Shellfish

Atlantic Seafood (Old
Saybrook), 265
Briar Patch Enterprises (Milford), 15
Gulf Shrimp Seafood Company
(Plantsville), 185
New Wave Seafood (Stamford), 35
Stonington Seafood Harvesters
(Stonington), 262

Smoked Meats/Game/Fish

Bush Meadow Farm (Union),
340, 367
Delicacy Market (West
Hartford), 187
Fairfield Meat Emporium
(Fairfield), 31
New Wave Seafood (Stamford), 35
Noack's Meat Products
(Meriden), 179
Nodine's Smokehouse
(Goshen), 120
Spic and Span Market
(Southport), 33

Star Fish Market (Guilford), 273

Tulmeadow Farm Store (West
  Simsbury), 210

Syrups and Sweet Sauces

Beardsley's Cider Mill & Orchard
  (Shelton), 45

Birch Hills Farm (Ashford), 339

Knipschildt Chocolatier
  (Norwalk), 20

Purple Pear by Tina, The
  (Wilmington), 349

Teas

A Dong Supermarket (West Hartford), 181

Bon Appetit (Hamden), 266

Celtica (New Haven), 267

Chaiwalla (Salisbury), 147

Delicacy Market (West
  Hartford), 187

Drawing Room, The (Cos
  Cob), 59

Green Well Organic Tea & Coffee
  (New Haven), 296

Harney & Sons Fine Teas
  (Millerton, New York), 126

Hong Kong Grocery (New
  Haven), 270

Lee's Oriental Market (New
  London), 270

Martha's Herbary (Pomfret),
  352, 371

Mrs. Bridges' Pantry (South
  Woodstock), 352, 369

Oriental Food Market
  (Norwalk), 37

Passiflora Tea Room, Cafe and
  Herbal Shoppe (New
  Hartford), 150

Saeed's International Market and
  Café (New London), 272

Simpson & Vail (Brookfield), 39

Sundial Gardens (Higganum), 301

Tofu

Bridge, The (Middletown), 177

Turkeys

Abbott Spring Farm (Pomfret
  Center), 360

Footsteps Farm (Stonington), 260

Golden Acres Farm
  (Harwinton), 140

Gozzi Turkey Farms (Guilford), 260

Kandew Farms (Roxbury), 140

Old Maple Farm (North Stonington), 260

Red & White Orchard (Franklin),
360

Sweet Farm (Brooklyn), 360

Woodbridge Farms (Salem), 260

Appendix B: Food Happenings

January

Taste of Ridgefield (Ridgefield), 51

February

Annual Taste of Stamford (Stamford), 51

March

Annual Hebron Maple Festival (Hebron), 365
Maple Sugaring Demonstrations (Woodbury), 145
Taste of the Nation New Haven (New Haven), 286

May

Dionysos Greek Festival (New Britain), 213
Fairfield County Eats! (Stamford), 52
Shuck-Off Annual Oyster Festival (Putnam), 365

June

Annual Shad Bake (Centerbrooke), 287

Annual Strawberry Festival at Hindinger Farm (Hamden), 287
Branford Festival (Branford), 288
Congregational Church Strawberry Festival (Monroe), 52
Connecticut Chefs Showcase (Hartford), 214
First Congregational Church Strawberry Jazz Festival (Madison), 287
Lyman Orchards Strawberry Festival (Middlefield), 214
North Canton Strawberry Festival (North Canton), 213
Secrets of Great PBS Chefs (Norwalk), 52
South Windsor Strawberry Festival & Craft Fair (South Windsor), 214
Ye Olde-Fashioned Strawberry Festival (Plantsville), 215

July

Clinton Bluefish Festival (Clinton), 288
Lobster Festival & Arts & Crafts Show (Niantic), 288
Market "En Plein Air" (Old Lyme), 289

August

Annual Milford Oyster Festival (Milford), 53
New Haven Food & Wine Festival (New Haven), 289

September

Annual Art of Wine and Food Dinner at the New Britain Museum
    of American Art (New Britain), 216
Annual Norwalk Seaport Association Oyster Festival (Norwalk), 53
Apple Harvest Festival (Southington), 216
Celebration of Connecticut Farms (location varies), 215
Cheshire Fall Festival and Marketplace (Cheshire), 215

Goshen Fair (Goshen), 145

Haddam Neck Fair (Haddam Neck), 290

Harvest Celebration (Warren), 146, 435

Harvest Festival (Litchfield), 146, 436

New Canaan Family Lobsterfest (New Canaan), 54

Nutmegger Cheese & Wine Festival (Shelton), 55

Pig Roast at Miranda Vineyard (Goshen), 145

Taste of the Valley (Brooklyn), 366

Trumbull Arts Festival (Trumbull), 54

Wapping Fair (South Windsor), 215

Woodstock Fair (South Woodstock), 366

October

Annual Apple Festival (Salem), 291

Apple Festival & Craft Fair (Old Saybrook), 290

Apple Harvest (Glastonbury), 217

Buell's Orchard Annual Fall Festival (Eastford), 366

Celebrate Wallingford (Wallingford), 290

Downtown Country Fair (Willimantic), 366

Elm City Legends (New Haven), 291

Greenwich Food + Wine Festival (Greenwich), 55

Harvest Festival at Miranda Vineyard (Goshen), 146, 436

March of Dimes Signature Chefs Auction (Stamford), 56

Signature Chefs Auction (Hartford), 217

December

Gingerbread House Festival (Middlebury), 146

Appendix C: Wine Happenings

February

Olde-Fashioned Winter Celebration, Haight Vineyard, Litchfield; (800) 577-9463. Sample prerelease wines; reservations essential.

March

Barrel Tasting, Haight Vineyard, Litchfield; (800) 577-9463. Early sampling of prerelease wines; reservations essential.

April

Barrel Tasting, Haight Vineyard, Litchfield; (800) 577-9463. Early sampling; reservations essential.

May

Spring Cellar-bration & Barrel Tasting, Stonington Vineyards, Stonington; (800) 421-WINE. Savor last year's harvest, with live music and food from local restaurants.

June

Spring Fest, Jonathan Edwards Winery, North Stonington; (860) 535-0202. Wine, food, and music.

Taste of Litchfield Hills, Haight Vineyard, Litchfield; (800) 577-9463. Cooling off with wine.

July

Summer Jazz series, McLaughlin Vineyards, Sandy Hook; (203) 270-8349. Live music, plus wine, of course.

Summer Cellar-bration Clambake, Stonington Vineyards, Stonington; (800) 421-WINE. Live bands; food from nearby restaurants.

August

Summer Jazz series, McLaughlin Vineyards, Sandy Hook; (203) 270-8349. The music continues (the wine, too).

September

Grape Stomp, DiGrazia Vineyards, Brookfield; (203) 775-1616. You, too, can get blue feet.

Harvest Celebration, Hopkins Vineyard, New Preston; (860) 868-7954. Wine tastings, meet the winemaker, live music, buffet.

Harvest Festival, Haight Vineyard, Litchfield; (800) 577-9463. Live music, artisan crafts, outdoor cafe, pony rides, hayrides, grape-stomping contests.

October

Harvest Fest, Jonathan Edwards Winery, North Stonington; (860) 535-0202. Wine, food, and music.

Harbor Festival, Stonington Vineyards, Stonington; (800) 421-WINE. Picking grapes and see them go through the crush; live bands; food from nearby restaurants.

Connecticut Eateries Index

Abbott's Lobster in the Rough
  (Noank), 304
AD (Westport), 56
Adrienne (New Milford), 154
Alforno Trattoria (Old
  Saybrook), 303
Altnaveigh Inn & Restaurant
  (Storrs), 372
Amerigo Restaurant (Norwalk), 73
Apricots Restaurant & Pub
  (Farmington), 227
Arcadia Cafe (Old Greenwich), 56
Artisan (Southport), 73
Arugula Bistro (West Hartford), 228
Atticus Bookstore Cafe (New
  Haven), 293
Aux Délices (Darien, Riverside,
  Stamford, Westport), 29, 69

Baang Cafe & Bar (Riverside), 74

Bar Bouchon (Madison), 293
Barcelona Restaurant & Wine Bar
  (Fairfield, Greenwich, New
  Haven, South Norwalk,
  Stamford, West Hartford), 229
Bar On20 (Hartford), 218
Bar Rosso (Stamford), 57
Bartleby's Cafe (Mystic), 294
Basso Cafe (Norwalk), 74
Basta Trattoria (New
  Haven), 309
Bee & Thistle Inn & Spa, The
  (Old Lyme), 316
Benlara (New Haven), 304
Bernard's (Ridgefield), 75
Bidwell Tavern & Cafe
  (Coventry), 367
Bistro Latino (Old Greenwich), 75
Bistro Mediterranean and Tapas
  Bar (East Haven), 306

Black-eyed Sally's BBQ & Blues (Hartford), 212
Blue Lemon (Westport), 76
Blue Oar, The (Haddam), 306
Boathouse at Saugatuck, The (Westport), 101
Bobby Q's Barbeque & Grill, (Westport), 76
Bodega Taco Bar (Darien, Fairfield), 57
Bohemian Pizza (Litchfield), 157
Bon Appetit Cafe (Wilton), 266
Boom (Westbrook), 307
Boulevard 18 (New Canaan), 77
Boxcar Cantina (Greenwich), 77
Brasitas (Norwalk, Stamford), 80
Bravo Bravo Restaurant (Mystic), 307
Bricco Trattoria (Glastonbury), 228
Brie & Bleu (New London), 294
Bru Rm at BAR (New Haven), 326
Burger Bar & Bistro (South Norwalk), 58
Bush Meadow Farm (Union), 340, 367

Cafe Flo (Old Lyme), 294

Cafe Lola (Fairfield), 80
Cafe on the Park (New Britain), 226
Cafe Routier (Westbrook), 308
Cambridge House Brew Pub (Granby), 241
Capitol Lunch (New Britain), 218
Carole Peck's Good News Cafe (Woodbury), 155
Caseus Fromagerie & Bistro (New Haven), 295
Cava Wine Bar and Restaurant (New Canaan), 84
Cavey's Restaurant (Manchester), 222
Cedar Street Food Carts (New Haven), 252
Cesco's Trattoria (Darien), 85
Chaiwalla (Salisbury), 147
Cheese Truck, The (New Haven), 253
Chef Luis Restaurant (New Canaan), 80
Chelsea, The (Fairfield), 58
Ching's Table (New Canaan), 110
Chocopologie Cafe (South Norwalk, New Haven, Stamford), 64

City Limits Diner (Stamford), 78

City Steam Brewery Cafe & Restaurant (Hartford), 241

Claire's Corner Copia (New Haven), 308

Clam Castle, The (Madison), 318

Cocoa Michelle (Westport), 59

Community Table (Washington), 156

Cooking Company, The (Haddam, Killingworth), 267

Copper Beech Inn (Ivoryton), 316

Coromandel Cuisine of India (Darien, Orange, Southport, Stamford), 81

Country Bistro (Salisbury), 148

Cracovia (New Britain), 230

Da Pietro (Westport), 85

Daybreak Coffee Roasters (Glastonbury), 183, 219

Doc's Trattoria & Brick Oven Pizza (Kent), 157

Dog Watch Cafe (Stonington), 295

Drawing Room, The (Cos Cob), 59

Dressing Room (Westport), 82

EATS Cafe at the Wadsworth (Hartford), 226

85 Main (Putnam), 372

Eli Cannon's Tap Room (Middletown), 242

Elm (New Canaan), 83

Elm Street Oyster House (Greenwich), 26

Eos Greek Cuisine (Stamford), 83

Fairway Cafe (Stamford), 60

Farmer's Cow Calfé and Creamery, The (Mansfield), 368

Fat Cat Pie Company (Norwalk), 60

Feast Gourmet Market (Deep River), 296

Feng Asian Bistro & Hibachi (Canton), 232

Feng Asian Bistro & Lounge (Hartford), 232

Firebox (Hartford), 232

Firehouse Deli (Fairfield), 32

Fireside Tavern at Sharpe Hill Vineyards (Pomfret), 373

Flanders Fish Market & Restaurant (East Lyme), 309

Frank Pepe Pizzeria Napoletana (Danbury, Fairfield, Manchester, New Haven, Uncasville), 248

Gabriele's Italian Steakhouse (Greenwich), 86
Gelston House (East Haddam), 310
Geronimo Tequila Bar and Southwest Grill (New Haven), 311
Gilson Cafe/Cinema (Winsted), 148
Ginza & Hibachi (Bloomfield, Wethersfield), 232
Golden Lamb Buttery, The (Brooklyn), 374
Gold's Delicatessen (Westport), 32
Grant's Restaurant and Bar (West Hartford), 230
Green Well Organic Tea & Coffee (New Haven), 296
Griswold Inn (Essex), 317
G.W. Tavern (Washington Depot), 156
G-Zen (Branford), 311

Hallmark Drive-In (Old Lyme), 257
Harbor Lights (Norwalk), 27

Harpo's Bakery (South Glastonbury), 219
Harvest Cafe and Bakery (Simsbury), 220
Heritage Trail Cafe at The Winery (Lisbon), 368
Hopkins Inn, The (New Preston), 158

Ibiza (New Haven), 312
Ibiza Tapas and Wine Bar (Hamden), 296
Il Palio (Shelton), 86
Inn at Woodstock Hill, The (Woodstock), 375
Isabelle et Vincent (Fairfield), 64
Istanbul Cafe (New Haven), 312
It's Only Natural (Middletown), 233

Jasper White's Summer Shack (Uncasville), 313
John Bale Book Company Cafe, The (Waterbury), 149
Johnny Ad's (Old Saybrook), 318
John's Cafe (Woodbury), 159
Judies European Bakery and Cafe (New Haven), 258

Kitchen Little (Mystic), 297
Kitchen Zinc Artisan Pizza and Bar
   (New Haven), 297

LaBelle Aurore, (Niantic), 314
Lao Sze Chuan (Milford), 87
La Palette Bakery Cafe Gallery
   (Watertown), 119, 149
La Sorpresa (Norwalk), 21
Le Farm (Westport), 102
Lenny and Joe's Fish Tale (Madison,
   New Haven, Westbrook), 319
Le Petit Cafe (Branford), 314
L'Escale (Greenwich), 94
Little Buddha (Stamford), 88
Little Mark's Big BBQ (Vernon), 234
Little Taste of Texas (South
   Windsor), 234
Little Thai Kitchen (Darien,
   Greenwich), 88
Lobster Landing (Clinton), 298
Lolita Cucina and Tequila Bar
   (Greenwich), 88
Louis' Lunch (New Haven), 284

Mahzu Japanese Restaurant
   (Norwich), 376

Main Street Cafe
   (Willimantic), 377
Main Street Creamery & Cafe (Old
   Wethersfield), 220
Match (South Norwalk), 89
Matsuri (Darien), 89
Max a Mia (Avon), 231
Max Amore (Glastonbury), 231
Max Burger (West Hartford), 231
Max Downtown (Hartford), 231
Max Fish (Glastonbury), 231
Max's Oyster Bar (West
   Hartford), 231
Mayflower Inn, The (Washington
   Depot), 159
Metro Bis (Simsbury), 202
Millwright's Restaurant and
   Tavern, (Simsbury), 235
Miss Thelma's Restaurant
   (Bridgeport), 62
Modern Apizza (New Haven), 249
Monster B's Bar & Grille (Stam-
   ford), 105
Monte Albán (Hartford), 235
Morello Bistro (Greenwich), 89
Mrs. Bridges' Pantry (Woodstock),
   352, 369

Museum Cafe at Mattutuck Museum Arts & History Center, The (Waterbury), 149

Napa & Co. (Stamford), 72, 90
Nat Hayden's Real Pit Barbeque (Windsor), 236
New Canaan Diner, The (New Canaan), 79
Noah's Restaurant (Stonington), 315
Nuage Restaurant and Bar (Cos Cob), 110

Oaxaca Kitchen (New Haven, Westport), 62
Octagon (Groton), 318
Old Lyme Ice Cream Shoppe (Old Lyme), 259
Old Lyme Inn (Old Lyme), 317
Olé Molé (Stamford), 62
Olio (Groton), 319
Oliva (New Preston), 160
Olive Market, The (Georgetown), 36
Ondine (Danbury), 91
O'Rourke's Diner (Middletown), 221
Oscar's Delicatessen (Westport), 33

Pacifico (New Haven), 320
Padre's Mexican Cuisine (Winsted), 150
Panini Cafe (Kent), 150
Pantry, The (Washington Depot), 132
Passiflora Tea Room, Cafe and Herbal Shoppe (New Hartford), 150
Pasta Cosi (Branford), 260, 298
Pastorale Bistro & Bar (Lakeville), 161
Peppercorn's Grill (Hartford), 236
Place Restaurant, The (Guilford), 298
Pond House Cafe (Hartford), 221
Pontos Taverna (Norwalk), 91
Pot au Pho (New Haven), 299
Prime Time Cafe (Pawcatuck), 299

Rathskeller Restaurant and Bar (Southbury), 151
Rawley's (Fairfield), 63
Rebeccas (Greenwich), 92
Rein's Delicatessen (Vernon), 189
Restaurant at Rowayton Seafood, The (Rowayton), 92

Restaurant Bricco (West
    Hartford), 230
Restaurant L&E (Chester), 320
River Tavern (Chester), 321
RJ Cafe & Bistro (Madison), 300
Roger Sherman Inn (New
    Canaan), 93
Roseland Cottage (Woodstock), 369
Rose's Berry Farm (South
    Glastonbury), 209, 222
Rosie (New Canaan), 63

Saigon City (Old Saybrook), 322
Sails American Grill
    (Rowayton), 93
Sal e Pepe (Newtown), 95
Sally's Apizza (New Haven), 248
Salute (Hartford), 237
Sarah's Wine Bar (Ridgefield), 75
Saray Turkish Restaurant (West
    Haven), 322
Savvy Tea Gourmet (Madison), 300
SBC Downtown Restaurant Brewery
    (Branford, Hamden, Milford,
    Stamford), 106
Schoolhouse at Cannondale, The
    (Wilton) 95

Scotts Jamaican Bakery
    (Hartford), 223
Shady Glen (Manchester), 224
Shish Kebab House of Afghanistan
    (West Hartford), 237
Silvermine Market, The (New
    Canaan), 66
Smokin' With Chris
    (Southington), 224
Somewhere in Time (Mystic), 300
SoNo Baking Company & Cafe, The
    (South Norwalk), 66
Southport Brewing Co.
    (Southport), 107
Spa at Norwich Inn, The
    (Norwich), 377
Splash (Westport), 96
Spot, The (New Haven), 249
Spotted Horse Tavern
    (Westport), 96
Stand Cafe and Juice Bar, The
    (Norwalk), 67
Stanziato's Wood Fired Pizza
    (Danbury), 60
Strada 18 (South Norwalk), 97
Stretch's Pizza (Newington), 224
Sundial Gardens (Higganum), 301

Sun Splash Jamaican Restaurant (Hartford), 225

Super Duper Weenie (Fairfield), 67

Swagat (West Haven), 323

Sweet Harmony Cafe & Bakery (Middletown), 225

Taco Loco Restaurant (Bridgeport), 67

Tarry Lodge Enoteca Pizzeria (Westport), 61

Tengda Asian Bistro (Darien, Greenwich, Westport, Milford), 111

Ten Twenty Post (Darien), 98

Terrain Garden Cafe (Westport), 98

Thali Regional Cuisine of India (New Canaan, New Haven, Ridgefield), 323

Thali Too (New Haven), 324

Thomas Henkelmann at Homestead Inn (Greenwich), 99

Tigin Irish Pub (Stamford), 107

Tinto Bar Tapas (Norwalk), 100

Todd English's Tuscany (Uncasville), 313

Trattoria da Lepri (Ellington), 378

Traveler Restaurant (Union), 379

Treva (West Hartford), 238

Trumbull Kitchen (Hartford), 238

Tullycross Tavern & Microbrewery (Manchester), 244

Turkish Kebab House (West Haven), 301

Tuscany (Bridgeport), 100

Union League Cafe (New Haven), 324

Utsav Indian Cuisine (Vernon), 239

Valencia Luncheria (Norwalk), 68

Vanilla Bean Cafe, The (Pomfret), 370

Versailles Bistro and Patisserie (Greenwich), 65

Watch Factory Restaurant, The (Cheshire), 239

Wave Hill Bread & Cafe (Norwalk), 28, 68

West Street Grill (Litchfield), 162

Whelk, The (Westport), 103

Whistle Stop Muffin Company (Ridgefield), 69

White's Diner (Bridgeport), 79
Willimantic Brewing Co. and Main
    Street Cafe (Willimantic), 379
Winvian (Morris), 163
Wood Creek Bar and Grill
    (Norfolk), 152

Wood's Pit BBQ & Mexican Cafe
    (Bantam), 163
Woodward House, The
    (Bethlehem), 164

ZaZa (Stamford), 102
Zinc (New Haven), 325

General Index

Abbott's Lobster in the Rough, 304

Abbott Spring Farm, 360

AD, 56

A Dong Supermarket, 181

Adrienne, 154, 397

Alforno Trattoria, 303, 404

Altnaveigh Inn & Restaurant, 372

Amerigo Restaurant, 73

Annual Apple Festival, 291

Annual Art of Wine and Food
   Dinner at the New Britain
   Museum of American Art, 216

Annual Hebron Maple Festival, 365

Annual Milford Oyster Festival, 53

Annual Norwalk Seaport Association Oyster Festival, 53

Annual Shad Bake, 287

Annual Strawberry Festival at
   Hindinger Farm, 287

Annual Taste of Stamford, 51

Apple Barn, 357

Apple Festival & Craft Fair, 290

Apple Harvest, 217

Apple Harvest Festival, 216

Apricots Restaurant & Pub, 227

Arcadia Cafe, 56

Arisco Farms, 197

Artisan, 73

Artisan Food Store, 124

Arugula Bistro, 228

Ashford Farmers' Market, 353

Ashlawn Farm, 264

Atlantic Seafood, 265

Atticus Bookstore Cafe, 293

Aux Délices, 29, 69, 411

Averill Farm, 136

Avery's Beverages, 176

Avon Farmers' Market, 191

Avon Meat House Farmers'
   Market, 191

Avventura, 124

Baang Cafe & Bar, 74

Back East Brewing, 240

Backstage, 165

Baltyk Deli, The, 30

Bantam Bread Company, 117
Bantam Farmers' Market, 133
Bar Americain, 313
Bar Bouchon, 293
Barcelona Fairfield, 229
Barcelona Greenwich, 229
Barcelona New Haven, 229
Barcelona Restaurant & Wine
    Bar, 229
Barcelona SoNo, 229
Barcelona Stamford, 229
Bar On20, 218
Barrel Tasting, 435
Bar Rosso, 57
Bartleby's Cafe, 294
Basso Cafe, 74
Bats of Bedlam Maple Syrup, 358
Beardsley's Cider Mill &
    Orchard, 45
Bear Pond Farm, 176, 393
Beer'd Brewing Company, 325
Bee & Thistle Inn & Spa, The, 316
Beldotti Bakeries, 14
Belltown Hill Orchards, 198
Beltane Farm, 339
Bentara, 304
Berlin Farmers' Market, 191

Bernard's, 75
Bethany Farmers' Market, 191
Bethel Farmers' Market, 41
Bidwell Tavern & Cafe, 367
Big Green Truck Pizza, The, 252
Billy's Bakery, 14
Birch Hills Farm, 339
Bishop's Orchards Farm Market and
    Winery, 280
Bistro Latino, 75
Bistro Mediterranean and Tapas
    Bar, 306
Black-eyed Sally's BBQ & Blues,
    212
Blackmer Farm, 359
Bloomfield Farmers' Market, 191
Blue Jay Orchards, 46
Blue Lemon, 76
Blue Oar, The, 306
Boathouse at Saugatuck, The, 101
Bobby Q's Barbeque & Grill, 76
Bodega Taco Bar, 57
Bohemian Pizza, 157
Bon Appetit, 266
Bon Appetit Cafe, 58
Boom, 307
Botticello Farms, 198

Boulevard 18, 77
Boxcar Cantina, 77
Bozrah Farmers' Market, 353
Branford Farmers' Market, 275
Branford Festival, 288
Brasitas, 80
Bravo Bravo Restaurant, 307
Brewhouse, The, 104
Briar Patch Enterprises, 15
Bricco Trattoria, 228
Bridgeport Farmers' Market, 41
Bridge, The, 177
Bridgewater Chocolate, 15
Brie & Bleu, 294
Bristol Farmers' Market, 133
Brooklyn Farmers' Market, 353
Brown Cow Cafe, 340
Bru Rm at BAR, 326
Buell's Orchard, 359
Buell's Orchard Annual Fall
    Festival, 366
Burger Bar & Bistro, 58
Burlington Farmers' Market, 133
Bush Meadow Farm, 340, 367

Cafe Flo, 294
Cafe Lola, 80

Cafe on the Park, 226
Cafe Routier, 308
Cambridge House Brew Pub, 241
Canterbury Farmers' Market, 354
Capitol Lunch, 218
Carole Peck, Cooking Classes and
    Provence Culinary Tours, 152
Carole Peck's Good News Cafe, 155
Caseus Fromagerie & Bistro,
    266, 295
casinos, 313
Cask Republic, The, 327
Cassidy Hill Vineyard, 381
Cato Corner Farm, 341
Cavalry Brewing, 104
Cava Wine Bar and Restaurant, 84
Cavey's Restaurant, 222
Cedar Street Food Carts, 252
Celebrate Wallingford, 290
Celebration of Connecticut
    Farms, 215
Celtica, 267
Cesco's Trattoria, 85
Chabaso Bakery, 251
Chaiwalla, 147, 410
Chamard Vineyards, 329
Chase Road Growers, 361

Cheese Truck, The, 253
Chef Luis Restaurant, 80
Chelsea, The, 58
Cheshire Fall Festival and
    Marketplace, 215
Chester Village Farmers' Market, 275
Chimirri's Italian Pastry
    Shoppe, 177
Ching's Table, 110
Chocopologie Cafe, 64
City Limits Diner, 78
City Steam Brewery Cafe & Restau-
    rant, 241
Claire's Corner Copia, 308, 391
Clam Castle, The, 318
clams, 292
Clark Farms at Bushy Hill Orchard
    & Cider Mill, 199
Clinton Bluefish Festival, 288
Clinton–Chamard Vineyards
    Farmers' Market, 275
Clinton Farmers' Market, 275
Cocoa Michelle, 59
Colchester Bakery, 343
Colchester Farmers' Market, 354
Colchester Priam Vineyards
    Farmers' Market, 354

Collinsville Baking Company, 117
Collinsville Farmers' Market, 191
Community Table, 156
Congregational Church Strawberry
    Festival, 52
Connecticut Chefs Showcase, 214
Connecticut Creative Store, 182
Connecticut Valley Winery, 166
Cooking Company, The, 267
Cooking with Adrienne, 152
Copper Beech Inn, 316
Cornwall Farmers' Market, 134
Coromandel Cuisine of India, 81
Cosmos International, 187
Cottrell Brewing Company, 327
Country Bistro, 148
Coventry Farmers' Market, 354
Cracovia, 230
Creamery Brook Bison, 343
Cromwell Farmers' Market, 191
Crown Market, The, 182
Cucina Casalinga, 70, 405
Cupcake Truck, The, 253

Dagmar's Desserts, 254
Dalice Elizabeth, 371, 381
Danbury Farmers' Market, 42

Daniella's Gelateria, 18
Danielson Farmers' Market, 354
Da Pietro, 85
Darien Cheese & Fine Foods, 30
Darien Farmers' Market, 42
Daybreak Coffee Roasters, 183, 219
D & D Market, 183
Deborah Ann's Sweet Shoppe, 16
Deep River Farmers' Market, 275
Deercrest Farm, 200
Delicacy Market, 187
delis, 32
DiBacco Food Imports, 184
DiGrazia Vineyards, 109
diners, 78
Dionysos Greek Festival, 213
Divine Treasures Belgian
    Chocolates, 184
Doc's Trattoria & Brick Oven
    Pizza, 157
Dog Watch Cafe, 295
Dondero Orchard Farm Stand &
    Bakery, 200
Downtown Country Fair, 366
Drawing Room, The, 59
Drazen Orchards, 201
Dressing Room, 82

Dr. Lankin's Specialty Foods, 268
Dr. Mike's, 17
Durham Farmers' Market, 192
Dutch Epicure Shop, The, 125

Eagle Wood Farm and Retail
    Store, 137
East Granby Farmers' Market, 192
East Haddam Farmers' Market, 275
East Hartford Farmers' Market, 192
East Haven Farmers' Market, 275
East Lyme Farmers' Market, 276
Easton Farmers' Market, 42
East Windsor Farmers' Market, 192
Easy Pickin's Orchard, 201
EATS Cafe at the Wadsworth, 226
eggs, 309
85 Main, 372
Eli Cannon's Tap Room, 242
Ellington Farmers' Market, 192, 354
Ellsworth Hill Orchard & Berry
    Farm, 137
Elm, 83
Elm City Legends, 291
Elm Street Oyster House, 26
Enfield Farmers' Market, 192
Eos Greek Cuisine, 83

Essex Farmers' Market, 276
Everybody's Market, 185

Fabled Foods, 255, 406
Fairfield Cheese Company, 31
Fairfield County Eats!, 52
Fairfield–Greenfield Hills Farmers'
    Market, 42
Fairfield Meat Emporium, 31
Fairway, 33
Fairway Cafe, 60
Farmer's Cow Calfé and Creamery,
    The, 368
Farmer's Cow, The, 344
Farmington Hill–Stead Museum
    Farmers' Market, 192
Fascia's Chocolates, 118
Fat Cat Pie Company, 60
Feast Gourmet Market, 296
Feng Asian Bistro &
    Hibachi, 232
Feng Asian Bistro & Lounge, 232
Ferris Acres Creamery, 17
Firebox, 232
Firehouse Deli, 32
Fireside Tavern at Sharpe Hill
    Vineyards, The, 373

First Congregational Church Straw-
    berry Jazz Festival, 287
Fish Family Farm Creamery &
    Dairy, 344
Flamig Farm, 203
Flanders Fish Market &
    Restaurant, 309
Flour Garden Bakery, 126
food trucks, 252
Footsteps Farm, LLC, 260
Fort Hill Farms, 361, 414
Four Mile River Farm &
    Greenhouse, 281
4 & Twenty Blackbirds
    Bakeshop, 256
Foxon Park, 256
Franklin Farmers' Market, 354
Frank Pepe Pizzeria
    Napoletana, 248
Frank's Marinara Sauce, 345
Fratelli Market, 34
Freund's Farm Market and
    Bakery, 138
Fromage Fine Foods and
    Coffees, 268
Fusion, 110

Gabriele's Italian Steakhouse, 86

Gelatissimo, 18

gelato, 18

Gelato Giuliana, 257

Gelston House, 310

Georgetown Farmers' Market, 42

Geronimo Tequila Bar and
  Southwest Grill, 311

Giff's Original, 178

Gigi's Native Produce, 203

Gilbertie's Herb Farm and
  Gardens, 47

Gilson Cafe/Cinema, 148

Gingerbread House Festival, 146

Ginza & Hibachi, 232

Given Fine Chocolates &
  Indulgences, 269

Glastonbury-Melzen's Farmers'
  Market, 192

Golden Acres Farm, 140

Golden Lamb Buttery, The, 374

Gold's Delicatessen, 32

Goshen Fair, 145

Gotta's Farm and Cider Mill, 204

Gouveia Vineyards, 330

Gozzi Turkey Farms, 260

Gracious Gourmet, The, 119

Granby Connecticut Valley Farmers'
  Market, 193

Grant's Restaurant and Bar, 230

Grape Stomp, 436

Green Well Organic Tea &
  Coffee, 296

Greenwich Farmers' Market, 42

Greenwich Food + Wine
  Festival, 55

Griswold Inn, 317

Griswold/Jewett City Farmers'
  Market, 276

Griswold–Pachaug Village Farmers'
  Market, 276

Groton Farmers' Market, 276

Guilford Farmers' Market, 276

Gulf Shrimp Seafood Company, 185

G.W. Tavern, 156

G-Zen, 311

Haddam Neck Fair, 290

Haight-Brown Vineyard, 167

Half Door, The, 243

Half Full Brewery, 105

Hallmark Drive-In, 257

Hamden–Downtown Farmers'
  Market, 276

Hamden–Spring Glen Farmers' Market, 276
Hampton Farmers' Market, 193
Harbor Festival, 437
Harbor Lights, 27
Harney & Sons Fine Teas, 126
Harpo's Bakery, 219
Hartford–Billings Forge Farmers' Market, 193
Hartford Capitol Avenue Farmers' Market, 193
Hartford-Homestead Farmers' Market, 193
Hartford North End Farmers' Market, 193
Hartford Old State House Farmers' Market, 193
Hartford Park Street Farmers' Market, 194
Hartford Regional Market, 194
Hartford West End Farmers' Market, 194
Harvest Cafe and Bakery, 220
Harvest Celebration, 146, 436
Harvest Fest, 437
Harvest Festival, 146, 437

Harvest Festival at Miranda Vineyard, 146
Hauser Chocolatier, 19
Hebron Farmers' Market, 355
Hebron Farmers' Market II, 355
Heritage Trail Cafe at The Winery, 368
Heritage Trail Vineyards and Cafe, 381
Hickory Hill Orchards, 204
Higganum Village Market Farmers' Market, 277
High Hill Orchard, 204
Hindinger Farm, 282
Holbrook Farm, 47
Holmberg Orchards, 282
Hong Kong Grocery, 270
Hopkins Inn, 158, 394
Hopkins Vineyard, 167
Hosmer Mountain Beverages, 346
Hunt Hill Farm Trust, 127

Ibiza, 312
Ibiza Tapas and Wine Bar, 296
Il Bacio Ice Cream, 20
Il Palio, 86
Inn at Woodstock Hill, The, 375

inns, 316
international foods, 187
Isabelle et Vincent, 64
Istanbul Cafe, 312
Italian restaurants, 84
It's Only Natural, 233
Ivoryton Village Alliance Farmers' Market, 277

Jasper White's Summer Shack, 313
J. DeFrancesco & Sons, 283
Jean Jones Cooking Classes, 70
Jerram Winery, 168
John Bale Book Company Cafe, 149
Johnny Ad's, 318
John's Cafe, 159
Jonathan Edwards Winery, 331
Jones Family Farms, 47
Jones Winery, 109
Judies European Bakery and Cafe, 258

Kaas & Co., 34
Kandew Farms, 140
Karabin Farms, 205
Kent Coffee & Chocolate Company, The, 128

Kent Farmers' Market, 134
Kent Wine & Spirit, 154
Kitchen Little, 297
Kitchen Zinc Artisan Pizza and Bar, 297
Knipschildt Chocolatier, 20

LaBelle Aurore, 314
La Brioche French Bakery, 346
La Molisana Italian Sausage, 129
Lamothe's Sugar House, 138
Land of Nod Winery, 168
Lao Sze Chuan, 87
La Palette Bakery Cafe Gallery, 119, 149
Lapsley Orchard, 362
La Sorpresa, 21
Lebanon Farmers' Market, 355
Ledyard Farmers' Market, 277
Lee's Oriental Market, 270
Le Farm, 102, 388
Lenny and Joe's Fish Tale, 319
Le Petit Cafe, 314
L'Escale, 94
Libby's Italian Pastry Shop, 258
Lisbon Farmers' Market, 355
Litchfield Candy Company, The, 129

Litchfield Hills Farm-Fresh Farmers'
    Market, 134
Little Chocolate Company, The, 22
Little Mark's Big BBQ, 234
Little Taste of Texas, 234
Little Thai Kitchen, 88
Liuzzi Gourmet Food Market, 270
Lobster Festival & Arts & Crafts
    Show, 288
Lobster Landing, 298
Lolita Cucina and Tequila Bar, 88
Lombardi's Bakery, 120
Louis' Lunch, 284
Lyman Orchards, 206
Lyman Orchards Strawberry
    Festival, 214
Lyme-Ashlawn Farmers'
    Market, 277

Madison Farmers' Market, 277
Madison Rest Area Farmers'
    Market, 277
Mahzu Japanese Restaurant, 376
Main Street Cafe, 377
Main Street Creamery & Cafe, 220
Manchester-CCC Farmers'
    Market, 194

Manchester Community College
    Farmers' Market, 194
Manchester Farmers' Market, 194
Maple Bank Farm, 139
Maple Lane Farm, 285
Maple Sugaring
    Demonstrations, 145
Maple View Farm, 140
March Farm, 140
March of Dimes Signature Chefs
    Auction, 56
Market "En Plein Air", 289
Marlborough Farmers' Market, 194
Martha's Herbary, 352, 371
Match, 89
Matsuri, 89
Matthews 1812 House, 120
Maugle Sierra Vineyards, 331
Max a Mia, 231
Max Amore, 231
Max Burger, 231
Max Downtown, 231
Max Fish, 231
Max's Oyster Bar, 231
Max's Tavern, 231
Mayflower Inn, The, 159
McLaughlin Vineyards, 112

Meadow Stone Farm, 347

Medlyn's Farm Market, 285

Meriden Farmers' Market, 195

Metro Bis, 202, 409

Michael Jordan Steak House, 313

Michele's Pies, 22

Middlebury Farmers' Market, 134

Middletown Farmers' Market, 195

Middletown II Farmers' Market
North End, 195

Middletown Wesleyan indoor
market, 195

Mikro Craft Beer Bar and
Bistro, 327

Milford Downtown Farmers'
Market, 42

Milford-Village of Devon Farmers'
Market, 43

Milford Woodmont Farmers'
Market, 43

Millwright's Restaurant and
Tavern, 235

Miranda Vineyard, 169

Miss Thelma's Restaurant, 62

Modern Apizza, 249

Modern Pastry Shop, 186

Monastic Art Shop, The, 130

Monroe Farmers' Market, 43

Monster B's Bar & Grille, 105

Monte Albán, 235

Morello Bistro, 89

Morris Farmers' Market, 134

Mortensen's Ice Cream
Shoppe, 178

Mountview Plaza Wines and
Liquors, 72

Mozzicato De Pasquale Bakery &
Pastry Shop, 188

Mrs. Bridges' Pantry, 352, 369

Mt. Carmel Wine & Spirits Co., 302

Munson's Chocolates, 348

Museum Cafe at Mattutuck Museum
Arts & History Center, 149

museums, 226

Mystic/Denison Farmers'
Market, 277

Mystic Farmers' Market, 277

Mystic Market East, 271

Mystic Market West, 271

Napa & Co., 72, 90, 401

Nat Hayden's Real Pit
Barbeque, 236

Nature's Grocer, 189

Naugatuck Farmers' Market, 43
New Britain Farmers' Market, 195
New Britain/Urban Oaks Farmers'
    Market, 195
New Canaan Diner, The, 79
New Canaan Family Lobsterfest, 54
New Canaan Farmers' Market, 43
New England Brewing Company,
    106, 328
New Hartford Farmers' Market, 134
New Haven Cityseed Downtown
    Farmers' Market, 278
New Haven Cityseed Edgewood
    Park Farmers' Market, 278
New Haven Cityseed Wooster
    Square Farmers' Market, 278
New Haven Fair Haven Farmers'
    Market, 278
New Haven Food & Wine
    Festival, 289
New Haven State Street Farmers'
    Market, 278
New Haven/The Hill Farmers'
    Market, 278
Newington Farmers' Market, 195
New London-Fiddleheads Food
    Coop Farmers' Market, 278

New London Field of Greens
    Farmers' Market, 279
Newman's Own, 23
New Milford Farmers' Market, 134
New Morning Natural and Organic
    Foods, 130
Newtown–Fairfield Hills Farmers'
    Market, 43
New Wave Seafood, 35
Niantic Farmers' Market, 279
Nine Main Bakery & Deli, 131
Nip 'N Tang, 178
No. 109 Cheese & Wine, 35
Noack's Meat Products, Inc., 179
Noah's Restaurant, 315
Nodine's Smokehouse, 120
Norfolk Farmers' Market, 134
Norman's Sugarhouse, 362
North Canton Strawberry
    Festival, 213
North Guilford–Dudley Farmers'
    Market, 279
Northwinds Vineyard, 169
Norwalk Health Department
    Farmers' Market, 43
Norwalk-Rainbow Plaza Farmers'
    Market, 44

Norwalk-Ryan Park Farmers' Market, 44
Norwich Downtown Farmers' Market, 355
Norwich–Greenville Section Farmers' Market, 355
Norwich Uncas on Thames Farmers' Market, 355
Nothin' But Premium Foods, 24
Nuage Restaurant and Bar, 110
Nutmegger Cheese & Wine Festival, 55

Oaxaca Kitchen, 62
Octagon, 318
Ogre Farm/George Hall Farm, 206
Olde Burnside Brewing Company, 243
Olde-Fashioned Winter Celebration, 435
Old Greenwich Farmers' Market, 44
Old Lyme Ice Cream Shoppe, 259
Old Lyme Inn, 317
Old Maple Farm, 260
Old Saybrook Farmers' Market, 279
Olé Molé, 62
Olio, 319

Oliva, 160, 398
Olive Market, The, 36
Olivette, 36
Omar Coffee Company, 189
Ondine, 91
Orange Farmers' Market, 279
Oriental Food Market, 37
O'Rourke's Diner, 221
Oscar's Delicatessen, 33
oysters, 26

Pacifico, 320
Padre's Mexican Cuisine, 150
Palazzi Orchard, 363
Palmieri Food Products, Inc., 259
Panini Cafe, 150
Pantry, The, 132
Paradise Hills Vineyard, 332
Passiflora Tea Room, Cafe and Herbal Shoppe, 150
Pasta Cosi, 260, 298
Pastorale Bistro & Bar, 161
Pawcatuck Farmers' Market, 279
Penzey's Spices, 37
Peppercorn's Grill, 236
Pickin' Patch, The, 207
Pig Roast at Miranda Vineyard, 145

pizza, 60, 157, 248
Place Restaurant, The, 298
Plainfield Farmers' Market, 355
Plainville Farmers' Market, 195
Plasko's Farm, 48
Pond House Cafe, 221
Pontos Taverna, 91
Pot au Pho, 299
Priam Vineyards, 382
Prime Time Cafe, 299
Purple Pear by Tina, The, 349, 400
Putnam Farmers' Market, 356
Putnam Farmers' Market II, 356

Rathskeller Restaurant and Bar, 151
Rawley's, 63
R + D Chocolates, 24
Rebecca's, 92
Red Bee Honey, 24, 417
Red Fence Farm, 309
Red & White Orchard, 360
Rein's Delicatessen, 189
Relic Brewing Company, 243
Restaurant at Rowayton Seafood,
   The, 92
Restaurant Bricco, 230
Restaurant L&E, 320

Rich Farm, 25
River House Tavern, 101
River's Edge Sugar House, 363
River Tavern, 321
Riverton Farmers' Market, 135
RJ Cafe & Bistro, 300
Roberts Orchard, 141
Rocky Hill Farmers' Market, 196
Roger Sherman Inn, 93
Rogers Orchards–Home Farm, 207
Rogers Orchards–Sunnymount
   Farm, 208
Romeo and Cesare's Gourmet, 272
Ronnie Fein School of Creative
   Cooking, 71
Rosedale Farms and Vineyards, 245
Roseland Cottage, 369
Rose's Berry Farm, 209, 222
Rose's Berry Farm at Wickham
   Hill, 209
Rosie, 63
Rowayton Farmers' Market, 44
Rustling Wind Creamery, 142

Saeed's International Market and
   Cafe, 272
Saigon City, 322

Sails American Grill, 93
Sal e Pepe, 95
Sally's Apizza, 248
Saltwater Farm Vineyard, 333
Salute, 237
Sandy Hook Organic Farmers'
  Market, 44
Sankow's Beaver Brook
  Farm, 261
Saray Turkish Restaurant, 322
Saugatuck River views, 101
Savor Fine Foods, 121
Savvy Tea Gourmet, 300
SBC, 328
SBC Downtown Restaurant
  Brewery, 106
Schoolhouse at Cannondale,
  The, 95
Scotland Farmers' Market, 356
Scotts Jamaican Bakery, 223
Scott's Orchard & Nursery, 209
Scott's Yankee Farmer, 285
Secrets of Great PBS Chefs, 52
Seymour Farmers' Market, 44
Shady Glen, 224
Sharpe Hill Vineyards, 383
Shelton Farmers' Market, 44

Shish Kebab House of
  Afghanistan, 237
Shortt's Farm & Garden
  Center, 49
Shuck-Off Annual Oyster
  Festival, 365
Signature Chefs Auction, 217
Silo Cooking School at Hunt Hill
  Farm, The, 153
Silverman's Farm, 49
Silvermine Market, 66
Simon's Marketplace, 273
Simpson & Vail, 39
Simsbury–Community Farm
  Farmers' Market, 196
Simsbury Farmers' Market, 196
Smith's Acres, 286
Smithy, The, 133
Smokin' With Chris, 224
Somers Farmers' Market, 356
Somewhere in Time, 300
SoNo Baking Company & Cafe, 66
SoNo Marketplace, 39
Southbury Farmers' Market, 135
Southington-Plantsville Farmers'
  Market, 196
Southport Brewing Co., 107

South Windsor Farmers'
   Market, 196
South Windsor Strawberry Festival
   & Craft Fair, 214
Spa at Norwich Inn, The, 377
Spic and Span Market, 33
Spiritus Wines, 227
Splash, 96
Spotted Horse Tavern, 96
Spot, The, 249
Spring Cellar-bration & Barrel
   Tasting, 435
Spring Fest, 436
Stafford Springs Farmers'
   Market, 356
Stamford Farmers' Market, 44
Stamford-High Ridge Farmers'
   Market, 45
Stand Cafe and Juice Bar, The, 67
Stanziato's Wood Fired Pizza, 60
Starberry Farm, 142
Star Fish Market, 273
Steve's Market, 40
Sticky-Nuts, 25
Stone Gardens Farm, 50
Stone Wall Dairy Farm, 143
Stonington Farmers' Market, 279

Stonington Seafood
   Harvesters, 262
Stonington Vineyards, 333
Storrs Farmers' Market, 356
Storrs Winter Farmers' Market, 356
Strada 18, 97
Stratford Farmers' Market, 45
Stretch's Pizza, 224
Suffield Farmers' Market, 196
Sugar Shack at Sweet Wind Farm,
   The, 210
Sullivan Farm, 143
Summer Cellar-bration
   Clambake, 436
Summer Jazz series, 436
Sundial Gardens, 301
Sunset Meadows Vineyards, 169
Sun Splash Jamaican
   Restaurant, 225
Super Duper Weenie, 67
Susan Goodman Catering,
   71, 389
Swagat, 323
Sweet Cioccolata, 274
Sweet Farm, 360
Sweet Harmony Cafe &
   Bakery, 225

Sweet Maria's, 122, 153, 415
Sweet Pierre's Boutique du
    Chocolat, 40
sweets, 64
Sweet Sunshine Gourmet
    Conveniences, 123

Taco Loco Restaurant, 67
Taibe, Bill, 102
Tarry Lodge Enoteca Pizzeria, 61
Taste of Ridgefield, 51
Taste of the Nation New
    Haven, 286
Taste of the Valley, 366
Taylor Brooke Winery, 384
Tengda, 111
Tengda Asian Bistro, 111
Tengda Asian Bistro and
    Hibachi, 111
Ten Twenty Post, 98
Terrain Garden Cafe, 98
Thali Regional Cuisine of
    India, 323
Thimble Island Brewing
    Company, 328
Thomas Henkelmann at
    Homestead Inn, 99

Thomas Hooker Brewing
    Company, 244
Thomaston Farmers' Market, 135
Thompson Brands, 179
Tigin Irish Pub, 107
Tinto Bar Tapas, 100
Todd English's Tuscany, 313
Tolland Farmers' Market, 356
Tonn's Orchard, 144
Torrington Farmers' Market, 135
Trader Joe's, 38
Trattoria da Lepri, 378
Traveler Restaurant: The Food &
    Book People, 379
Treat Farm, 50
Treva, 238
Trumbull Arts Festival, 54
Trumbull Farmers' Market, 45
Trumbull Kitchen, 238
Tschudin Chocolates &
    Confections, 180
Tullycross Tavern &
    Microbrewery, 244
Tulmeadow Farm Ice Cream
    Stand, 181
Tulmeadow Farm Store, 210
turkeys, 140, 260, 360

Turkish Kebab House, 301
Tuscany, 100
Two Roads Brewing Company, 108
Two Steps Downtown Grille, 71

Union League Cafe, 324
University of Connecticut Dairy
   Bar, 349
Urban Oaks Organic Farm, 211
Utsav Indian Cuisine, 239

Valencia Luncheria, 68
Vanilla Bean Cafe, The, 370
Versailles Bistro and Patisserie, 65
Viking Center at HADCO, 302
Volta Gelateria Creperia, 19

Waldingfield Farm, 123
Walker Road Vineyards, 170
Walking Wood, 263
Wallingford Gardeners'
   Market, 279
Walnut Beach Creamery, 26
Wapping Fair, 215
Warrup's Farm, 50
Watch Factory Restaurant,
   The, 239

Waterbury-Mall Farmers'
   Market II, 135
Waterbury on the Green Farmers'
   Market, 135
Waterbury–South End Farmers'
   Market, 135
Waterford Farmers' Market, 357
Watertown Farmers' Market, 136
water views, 94
Wave Hill Bread & Cafe, 28, 68
Wayne's Organic Garden, 363
We-Li-Kit Farm Ice Cream
   Stand, 350
Wentworth Homemade Ice
   Cream, 264
Westbrook Farmers' Market, 357
Westford Hill Distillers, 350, 412
West Hartford Farmers' Market, 196
West Hartford Whole Foods
   Farmers' Market, 197
West Haven Farmers' Market, 280
Weston Farmers' Market, 45
Westport Farmers' Market, 45
West Street Grill, 162, 395
West Suffield Farmers' Market, 197
Wethersfield Farmers' Market, 197
Whelk, The, 103, 388

Whistle Stop Muffin Company, 69
White Gate Farm, 309
White Horse Pub, 165
White Oaks Farm & Table, 28
White's Diner, 79
White Silo Farm and Winery, 170
Wild Raspberry, The, 190
Willimantic Brewing Co. and Main
   Street Cafe, 379
Willimantic Farmers' Market, 357
Willimantic Food Co-op, 353
Wilson/Windsor Farmers'
   Market, 197
Winding Drive Jams & Jellies, 124
Windsor Farmers' Market, 197
Windy Hill Farm, 144
Winsted Farmers' Market, 136
Winterbrook Farm, 364

Winvian, 163
Woodbridge Farms, 260
Woodbury Farmers' Market, 136
Wood Creek Bar and Grill, 152
Woodland Farm, 211
Wood's Pit BBQ & Mexican
   Cafe, 163
Woodstock Fair, 366
Woodward House, The, 164
Wright's Orchards & Dried Flower
   Farm, 364

Ye Olde-Fashioned Strawberry
   Festival, 215

ZaZa, 102
Zinc, 325
Zumbach's Gourmet Coffee, 41

Regional Travel at Its Best

Secrets of Living the Good Life—For Free!

THE CHEAP BASTARD'S GUIDE TO
Washington, D.C.

100 BEST
Resorts of the Caribbean

OFF THE BEATEN PATH®
WASHINGTON
A GUIDE TO UNIQUE PLACES

The Luxury Guide to
Walt Disney World® Resort
Revised Edition
How to Get the Most Out of the
Best Disney Has to Offer

shifra stein's
day trips®
from kansas city
fifteenth edition

NINTH EDITION
JOHN HOWELL S III
CHOOSE COSTA RICA
FOR RETIREMENT

fun with the family Texas
hundreds of ideas for day trips with the kids

Tampa

SCENIC DRIVING
COLORADO
STEWART M. GREEN